Fundamentals of Economics

William Boyes

Arizona State University

Michael Melvin

Arizona State University

HOUGHTON MIFFLIN COMPANY　Boston　New York

To our families

W. B.   M. M.

Editor-in-Chief: Bonnie Binkert
Assistant Editors: Adrienne Vincent and Bernadette Walsh
Project Editor: Elizabeth Gale Napolitano
Senior Production/Design Coordinator: Carol Merrigan
Senior Manufacturing Coordinator: Marie Barnes
Marketing Manager: Juli Bliss

Cover Design: Cathy Hawkes/Cat and Mouse Design
Cover Illustration: Deborah Melmon

Printed in the U.S.A.

Library of Congress Catalog Card Number: 98-71994

ISBN: 0-395-90339-4

3   4   5   6   7   8   9   VH   02   01   00

Brief Contents

Contents

Preface

As the text's engaging cover illustrates, economics is an adventure—an exploration of the economic concepts and issues that confront us in the news and in our daily lives. We invite you to travel with us in exploring the economic landscape of the world around you. Whether your major is business, psychology, English, education, engineering, or whether you're going on in economics, you will be faced with economic choices and issues. You will be asked to consider fundamental questions such as

- What are the benefits of trade? (Chapter 1)
- What causes price to change? (Chapter 2)
- Do rent controls and minimum wages benefit me? (Chapter 3)
- Why have health care costs risen so much? (Chapter 3)
- How do firms create profits? (Chapter 6)
- How is poverty measured? (Chapter 8)
- How does the international sector affect the economy? (Chapter 9)
- How is money traded internationally? (Chapter 10)
- What is inflation? (Chapter 11)
- What are the effects of budget deficits? (Chapter 13)
- How do banks "create" money? (Chapter 14)
- How is monetary policy set? (Chapter 15)
- Why do countries restrict international trade? (Chapter 17)

To help you understand these and other issues, we've tried to boil down economics to its fundamentals—the basic core concepts. Rather than focusing on formal economic theories, we have chosen to emphasize relevant applications and policy issues, the same issues you read about in today's newspapers.

OUR GOALS IN WRITING THE TEXT

This book is intended for a one-term course in economics, a course that covers the fundamentals of micro- and macroeconomics. The text was written with several objectives in mind. First, one of our goals is to demonstrate the value of economic analysis in explaining daily events. We also want to show how economic analysis can help us understand why individuals, business firms, and even governments behave as they do. To accomplish this, we relate each concept to the individual. For example, we show what diminishing marginal returns means to you and how money supply growth affects your paycheck. We

believe that using real-world examples as illustrations of economic concepts is a more effective learning approach than relying on examples of hypothetical products, firms, and people.

Second, we want to present the world as a global economic environment and to present the tools you need to understand and live in this environment. While other texts ignore or isolate international coverage, we fully integrate a global perspective within our discussion of the traditional, fundamentals of economics. Topics such as the Asian monetary crisis of 1998, the rising value of the dollar, the effect of an exchange rate on firms, prices, and employees, are all discussed within the context of economic analysis.

A third, overarching goal is to engage students with concepts that are currently meaningful. We want our readers to learn the fundamentals and to develop an economic way of thinking about issues that confront them. We strive to present only the essential topics rather than force readers to delve into abstract topics so they become lost in the "forest" and lose sight of the "trees."

A Focus on Fundamental Questions

Earlier, we introduced some of the fundamental questions considered in the text. These and other questions provide the organizing framework for the text and its accompanying ancillary package. *Fundamental Questions*, in fact, open and organize each chapter, highlighting the critical issues. Students should preview the chapters with these questions in mind, reading actively for understanding and retention. *Fundamental Questions* also frame the chapter summaries, thereby serving as a valuable review device. Finally, *Fundamental Questions* are used as the integrating framework for the text and the entire ancillary package. For example, brief paragraph answers to each of the questions are found in the *Study Guide*.

An Integration of International Issues

As previously noted, the text incorporates a global perspective. In addition to the full international chapter—Chapter 17, *Issues in International Trade and Finance*—every chapter incorporates global examples to provide a more realistic picture of the economy. Topics include

- The effects of exchange rates on the demand and supply of individual markets (Chapter 2)
- The issue of price discrimination on an international basis (Chapter 4)
- Comparative analysis of fiscal policies in different countries (Chapter 13)

- "Global money" and international reserve currencies, as well as the prohibition of interest in Islamic banks (Chapter 14)
- Foreign exchange market intervention as part of the central bank policy (Chapter 15)
- Business cycles and economic growth issues as important macroeconomic policy issues (Chapter 16)

A Real-World Framework

We have developed a real-world framework that shows how markets work, focusing on competition and the behavior of firms. Instead of becoming bogged down in a theoretical discussion of each market structure model, students learn how businesses behave, compete, create profit, and attempt to sustain profits over time. They learn what business competition means and how it affects their daily lives.

To further connect the text to the real world, we incorporate "Economic Insight" boxes that focus on the policies of today's leaders and the business decisions of real companies and governments from around the world. The goal is to help students think critically about news stories and to respond to them with greater insight. Some examples are

- *Economic Insight: The Disappearing Bikes* (The Yellow Bike Program in Portland, Oregon)
- *Economic Insight: The American Girls Phenomenon* (An historical doll collection from the Pleasant Company, an example of the market process)
- *Economic Insight: Does the Minimum Wage Really Cause Unemployment Among Teens?*
- *Economic Insight: The Taxpayer's Federal Government Credit Card Statement*

Proven, Pedagogical Features

The text incorporates a number of pedagogical features that proved to be successful in our best-selling principles of economics text. This series of built-in learning aids makes teaching easier by enhancing student learning.

In-text Referencing System. Sections are numbered for easy reference and to reinforce hierarchies of ideas. The numbering system serves as an outline of the chapter, allowing instructors flexibility in assigning reading, and making review easy for students. A section numbering system is used throughout the ancillary package; the *Test Bank, Study Guide,* Web site, and *Instructor's Resource Manual* are organized according to the same system.

Fundamental Questions. These questions provide an organizing framework for the text and ancillary package.

Recaps. Briefly listing the main points covered, a Recap appears at the end of each major section. Students are able to quickly review what they have just read before going on to the next section.

Summary. The Summary at the end of each chapter is organized according to the list of *Fundamental Questions* and includes a brief synopsis of the discussion that helps students answer those questions. Students may refer back to the full text discussion.

Key Terms. A list of important terms is provided at the end of each chapter.

Exercises. Several exercises are included at the end of each chapter, providing excellent self-checks for students and homework options for instructors.

Internet Exercises. Appearing at the end of each chapter, these exercises connect students to the real world through the World Wide Web. Students are instructed to go to the Boyes/Melvin Web site and click on the appropriate chapter exercises. The exercises will link students to real data in, for example, the *Economic Report of the President,* the annual report for the Coca-Cola Company, the home page for the Sierra Club, and the World Trade Organization. Additional Web-based assignments and resources are also available on the Boyes/Melvin Web site for both instructors and students.

A Pedagogically Sound Art Program

Economics can be intimidating, which is why we've incorporated a number of pedagogical devices to help students read and interpret graphs. Annotations on the art point out areas of particular concern or importance. For example, students can see at a glance what parts of the graph illustrate a shortage or a surplus, a change in consumption, or consumer surplus.

Tables that provide data from which graphs are plotted are paired with their graphs. A good example is Figure 6 in Chapter 2. There, color is used to show correlations between the art and the table, and captions clearly explain what is shown in the figure, linking them to the text discussion.

A Complete Teaching and Learning System

Our ancillary package provides the breadth and depth of support needed by both instructors and students. To foster the development of consistent teaching and study strategies, the ancillaries follow the same pedagogical format as the text, incorporating the *Fundamental Questions* and in-text referencing system throughout.

Instructor's Resource Manual by Ali Kutan, Southern Illinois University, Edwardsville, follows the *Fundamental Questions* framework. It contains a Lecture Outline with teaching strategies, Opportunities for Discussion, answers to end-of-chapter questions, and answers to homework questions in the *Study Guide.* Each chapter also includes an Active-Learning Exercise that instructors can assign as homework or conduct in class.

Test Bank and *Computerized Test Bank,* developed by the text authors, include over 1,700 questions with a mix of difficulty levels. There are multiple-choice, true/false, and essay questions, including approximately 10 questions per chapter paralleling those in the *Study Guide*. All are linked to the in-text referencing system so instructors can conveniently test down to the paragraph level.

Study Guide by Janet Dimmen and James Clark, Wichita State University, provides brief answers to the *Fundamental Questions*, Quick Check Quizzes, Practice Questions and Problems, *Thinking About and Applying* sections, and Sample Tests that include several questions that are the same or similar to those in the *Test Bank*.

Web Sites for Instructor and Student (located at http://www.hmco.com/college) provide an extended learning environment and a rich store of teaching resources. For the instructor, we offer economic and teaching resource links, teaching tips, and Web-based assignment material. Students can also access the site and click on Web-based assignments linked to the text, in addition to other Web exercises, key economic links for every chapter, on-line tests, plus access to the *Economist's Guide to the Internet*.

ACKNOWLEDGMENTS

We are grateful to our friends and colleagues who have so generously given their time, creativity, and insight to help us create this text. In particular, we would like to thank Andrea Worrell, ITT Educational Services, Inc. for inspiring us to write the text with students like hers in mind. We also valued the constructive comments we received from Denise L. Stanley, University of Tennessee; Roger F. Riefler, University of Nebraska; and Arthur J. Janssen, Emporia State University. We'd also like to thank Ali Kutan for his work on the *Instructor's Resource Manual;* Melissa Hardison and Eugenio Suarez who worked with us in developing the *Test Bank;* and Janet Dimmen and Jim Clark for developing a strong *Study Guide*.

Finally, we want to thank the staff at Houghton Mifflin Company for their support and publishing expertise: specifically, Bonnie Binkert, Adrienne Vincent, Bernadette Walsh, Liz Napolitano, Carol Merrigan, Joanne Cavanaugh, and our freelance development editor, Joanne Dorff.

W. B.   M. M.

I

The Price System

1

Economics and the World Around You

Preview

Two women duked it out. Two men crashed their cars. One woman wrote a letter to her grandmother and read 150 pages in a paperback while sitting for 3 and a half hours. Why? Cheap gas. To announce the grand opening of Circle K's first new stores in five years, the company sold gasoline between 10 A.M. and noon on a Saturday for the price of $.49 per gallon. Whitney Hamilton got in line at 6:30 A.M. "I was in line before there was a line. I've never seen gas prices this low. I don't think I'll ever see them this low again." Vera Lugan drove the 15 or so miles from her home, arriving at 8 A.M. Seven cars were ahead of her. "I was already on empty, so I put in $1.00 and drove over," Lujan said. A 15-gallon limit on the fill-ups was enforced. "I think I burned more gas than I'm going to get," Ben Valdez said as he approached the pumps after waiting 90 minutes. A fistfight broke out when one woman tried to cut in front of another. John Fecther came for the gas but saw the long lines and tried to make a U-turn away from the area. He was hit by another vehicle. "I was going to get the heck out of here," he said as he filled out a police report. "People are crazy. You're only going to save a little."

The people in this story decided to purchase 15 gallons of gas at the very low price of $.49 per gallon. In so doing they had to wait in line more than an hour and in some cases travel several miles to the store. At a price of $1.20 per gallon, the $.49 per gallon saved about $10. But don't forget the time and the gas burned in waiting. These are costs as well. Nevertheless, comparing the costs to the savings, many people decided it was worthwhile to make the trip, wait in line, and purchase the gas.

Choices like these are made all the time. To some of us, the decision to purchase the gas might seem silly. To others, it is very reasonable. But for all of us, the process of deciding whether to purchase the gas or not is basically the same. We compare the costs of the decision to the benefits.

We all have to make choices all the time. Why? Because we don't have everything we want and we can't get everything we want. Since you are reading this text you are most likely taking some type of post–high school economics class. Are you at the same time working 40 hours a week, playing tennis or golf, cycling, surfing, watching a movie, reading a novel, and socializing with friends? Probably not. You simply don't have time to do it all. You have to select some of these activities and forgo others. This is what economics is about—trying to understand why people do what they do.

To study economics is to seek answers: why people choose to devote a considerable amount of time to purchase cheap gasoline; why economies go through cycles, at times expanding and creating new jobs or dipping into recessions; why some people lose jobs to join the ranks of the unemployed while others who are unemployed find new jobs; why some people live on welfare; why some nations are richer than others; why the illegal drug trade is so difficult to stop; why health care is so expensive; or, in general, why the world is what it is.

People have unlimited wants—they always want more goods and services than they have or can purchase with their incomes. Whether they are wealthy or poor, what they have is never enough. Since people do not have everything they want, they must use their limited time and income to select those things they want most and forgo the rest. The choices they make and the manner in which the choices are made explain much of why the real world is what it is. ∎

1. THE DEFINITION OF ECONOMICS

Why are diamonds so expensive while water and air—necessities of life—are nearly free? The reason is that diamonds are relatively more scarce, that is, relative to the available quantities, more diamonds are wanted than water or air. Actually, air is not always cheap or free. In Mexico City, air, at least breathable air, is far from free. One of the most successful new business ventures in Mexico City is providing clean, breathable air. In this city of 19 million people and 3 million cars, dust, lead, and chemicals make the air unsafe to breathe more than 300 days a year. Private companies are now operating oxygen booths in local parks and malls. Breathable air, which costs more than $1.60 per minute, has become a popular product.

Why is breathable air in Mexico City rather expensive while in Douglas, Arizona it is free? The same reason diamonds are relatively more expensive than water or air. Breathable air in Mexico City is more scarce than it is in Douglas, Arizona. Diamonds are more scarce than water and air, in general.

1.a. Scarcity

■ **scarcity:**
occurs when the quantity people want is greater than the quantity available

■ **free good:**
a good for which there is no scarcity

■ **economic bad:**
any item for which people pay to have less

■ **resources:**
inputs used to create goods and services

■ **land:**
the general category of resources encompassing all natural resources, land, and water

■ **labor:**
the general category of resources encompassing all human activity related to the productive process

■ **capital:**
the equipment, machines, and buildings used to produce goods and services

■ **financial capital:**
the stocks and bonds used to purchase capital

Scarcity refers to the idea that there is not enough of something to satisfy everyone who would like that something. If there is enough of an item to satisfy wants, even at a zero price, the item is said to be a **free good.** If people would pay to have less of an item, that item is called an **economic bad.** Examples include pollution, garbage, and disease.

Some goods are used to produce other goods. For instance, to make chocolate chip cookies we need flour, sugar, chocolate chips, butter, our own labor, and an oven. To distinguish between the ingredients of a good and the good itself, we call the ingredients **resources.** (Resources are also called factors of production and inputs; the terms are interchangeable.) The ingredients of the cookies are the resources, and the cookies are the goods.

As illustrated in Figure 1(a), economists have classified resources into three general categories: land, labor, and capital.

1. **Land** includes all natural resources, such as minerals, timber, and water, as well as the land itself.
2. **Labor** refers to the physical and intellectual services of people and includes the training, education, and abilities of the individuals in a society.
3. **Capital** refers to products such as machinery and buildings that are used to produce other goods and services. You will often hear the term *capital* used to describe the financial backing for some project to finance some business. Economists refer to funds used to purchase capital as **financial capital.**

People obtain income by selling their resources or the use of their resources, as illustrated in Figure 1(b). Economists define payment to the owners of land as rent, payment to people who provide labor services as wages, and payment to owners of capital as interest.

Figures 1(a) and 1(b) are linked because the income that resource owners acquire from selling the use of their resources provides them the ability to buy goods and services. And producers use the money received from selling their goods to pay for the resource services. In Figure 1(c), the flows of money are indicated along the outside arrows, and the flows of goods or resource services are indicated along the inside arrows. The resource services flow from resource owners to producers of goods in return for income; the flows of goods go from the producers of the goods to resource owners in return for the money payment for these goods.

1.b. Opportunity Costs

Scarcity of resources (and thus income) means that choices have to be made. A choice is simply a comparison of alternatives. For instance if you were

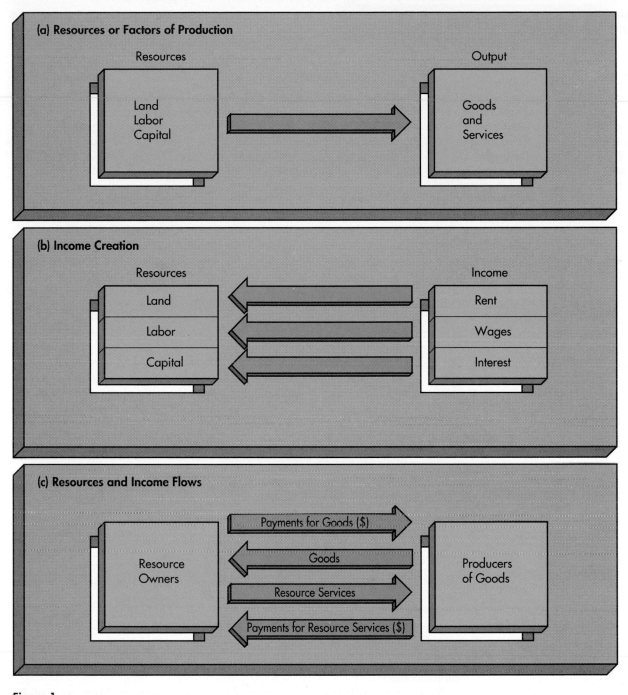

Figure 1
Flow of Resources and Income
Three types of resources are used to produce goods and services: land, labor, and capital. See 1(a). The owners of resources are provided income for selling their services. Landowners are paid rent, laborers receive wages, and capital receives interest. See 1(b). Figure 1(c) links Figures 1(a) and 1(b). People use their resources to acquire income with which they purchase the goods they want. Producers use the money received from selling the goods to pay for the use of the resources in making goods. Resources and income flow between certain firms and certain resource owners as people allocate their scarce resources to best satisfy their wants.

Diamonds and Water

For over two hundred years economists have grappled with the problem of why diamonds are so expensive and water so inexpensive when water is so much more useful and necessary. The answer is that relative to the available quantities, more diamonds are wanted than water. Interestingly though, diamonds are not all that scarce. The amount of diamonds available for sales has been tightly and carefully controlled. For about 100 years there has been only one source for diamonds, DeBeers, the South African company, which sells its own diamonds and those from other sources through a single agency, the Central Selling Organization.

The Central Selling Organization, has operated what it calls a single channel marketing system on behalf of the world's big producers, such as Botswana, Namibia, and Russia, and for De Beers' own mines in South Africa. The Selling Organization manages the stock of diamonds so that prices remain high. During bad times, the organization stockpiles diamonds, storing them until times improve. Then, during good times, the organization releases diamonds to the market in a carefully controlled stream.

Many people argue that De Beers is a monopolist—the only seller—and should, therefore, not be allowed to remain in business. In the United States, monopolies are illegal unless specifically created by government. In most developed countries, monopolies are either illegal or seriously frowned on. De Beers is very careful not to have any assets in the United States because of the fear that the United States' laws against monopolies would affect its operations. Other countries, like Britain, have decided that a monopoly in diamonds doesn't matter. Diamonds aren't used for anything, so who cares if there is a monopoly.

Although diamonds are not particularly useful, they have always fascinated people. Part of the fascination is how they reflect light, and part of the fascination is the symbol of wealth, success, and love. An American advertising agency invented the slogan "A Diamond is For Ever" for De Beers as long ago as 1948. De Beers spends about $200 million a year promoting diamonds as love tokens. Japanese couples once sipped cups of tea when they became engaged to be married. De Beers persuaded many of them to give diamond engagement rings instead. Japan is now the second largest market for diamonds, after the United States.

It may be time for a change, however, as two big newcomers begin to mine diamonds in Canada's Northwest Territories. Broken Hill Proprietary is Australia's biggest company, and Rio Tinto is the world's biggest mining group. They are breaking ground for major mining operations and plan to sell outside of the Central Selling Organization.

---

deciding whether to buy a new car, what would your alternatives be? They would be other makes of automobiles, trucks, even bicycles. They also would be virtually anything else on which the money could be spent. When you choose one thing, the benefits you might get from other things are forgone. Economists refer to the forgone benefits of the next best alternative as **opportunity costs**—the highest-valued alternative that must be forgone when a choice is made.

■ **opportunity costs:**
the highest valued alternative that must be forgone when a choice is made

Opportunity costs are part of every decision and activity. Your opportunity costs of reading this book are whatever else you could be doing—perhaps watching TV, talking with friends, working, or listening to music.

1.b.1. The Opportunity Cost of Going to School

Suppose you decided to attend a school where the tuition and other expenses add up to $4,290 per year. Are these your total costs? If you answer yes, you are ignoring opportunity costs. If instead of going to school you would have chosen to work full time, then the benefits of full-time employment are your opportunity costs. If you could have obtained a position with an annual income of $20,800, the actual cost of school is the $4,290 of direct expenses plus the $20,800 of forgone salary, or $25,090.

Each term you must decide whether to register for school or not. You could work full time and not attend school, attend school and not work, or work part time and attend school. The time you devote to school will decrease as

Having only a few minutes before his economics class begins, and having to reach the building located on the lower peninsula, this student grabs his hang glider and prepares to jump off the cliff. He knows that instead of attending class, he might continue hang gliding, hike in the Guatemalan mountains, or sail in the beautiful waters. However, he has compared benefits and costs of attending class versus not attending; he decided to attend class.

■ tradeoffs:
what must be given up to acquire something else

you devote more time to work. You trade off hours spent at work for hours spent in school. If you went to school full time, you might earn the highest grades. As you work more hours, you gain additional income but might earn lower grades. If this situation occurs, we say that you trade off grades and income.

Societies, like individuals, face scarcities and must make choices, that is, have **tradeoffs.** Because resources are scarce, a nation cannot produce as much of everything as it wants. When it produces more health care, it must forgo the production of education, automobiles, or military hardware. When it devotes more of its resources to the military, fewer resources are available to devote to healthcare, education, or consumer goods.

RECAP

1. Scarcity exists when people want more of an item than exists at a zero price.

2. Goods are produced with resources (also called factors of production and inputs). Economists have classified resources into three categories: land, labor, and capital.

3. Choices have to be made because of scarcity. People cannot have or do everything they desire all the time. Economics is the study of how people choose to use their scarce resources in an attempt to satisfy their wants.

4. Opportunity costs are the benefits that are forgone due to a choice. When you choose one thing you must give up—forgo—others.

5. Opportunity cost is an individual concept but can be used to demonstrate scarcity and choice for a society as a whole.

2. SPECIALIZATION AND EXCHANGE

Are you good with computers or reading or writing? Are you a good golfer or tennis player? Can you fix electrical or plumbing problems or work on large

TABLE 1
Production Possibilities

100 Percent of Effort Devoted To:	Output Per Day	
	Maria	*Able*
Math Problems	10	10
Pages of an Economics Paper	10	5

appliances? Even if you are good at all these things, do you do them all? Michael Jordan is an incredible athlete, a fantastic basketball player, a AAA-level baseball player, a very good golfer, and is probably good at other endeavors. He chose to play basketball. Why? Because he is better at basketball than he is at other things; he would have to forgo or give up too much trying to be a professional golfer or baseball player. Martha Stewart has developed an amazing business. She seems to be into everything—gardening, decorating, cooking, designing, and so on. While she has superb ideas and is very creative, she chooses to have others manage her business and invest her money. Why? Because she is relatively better at presenting the gardening, cooking, and decorating ideas than she is in the day-to-day management of her business. She would have to forgo or give up too much if she focused her attention on managing the business and investing her money. Neither these two superstars nor any of us can do everything. Even if Martha Stewart is a great business manager, she is relatively better as a television and magazine personality. She can't do everything. Even if Michael Jordan is an incredible athlete he is relatively better at basketball. He can't do everything. Similarly, we can't do everything. We have scarce resources, including limited time, and must choose to do what we do relatively best.

2.a. Trade

At any moment in time individuals are endowed with certain resources and abilities. People can choose to be self-sufficient—using and consuming their resources and output themselves—or they can choose to exchange goods and services with others. By trading, they get more than they can by being self-sufficient.

Consider a very simple example. Suppose two people, Maria and Able, have resources and abilities to produce the combinations of two goods, math problems and pages of an economics paper, shown in Table 1. If Maria devotes all of her time and energy to pages of an economics paper, she would be able to write 10 pages of an economics paper a day. If she devotes all of her resources to math problems, she could complete 10 math problems a day. Able, on the other hand could write 5 pages of an economics paper if he devoted his entire time to the paper or he could complete 10 math problems a day if he concentrated on the math.

2.b. Comparative Advantage

Notice the costs of these activities to the two people. If Maria focuses on the economics paper, she writes 10 pages but she gives up completing the 10 math problems. Her opportunity cost of producing 10 pages of an economics paper is, therefore, 10 math problems. Able's opportunity cost of producing 5 pages of an economics paper is 10 math problems. Thus, while Able's opportunity cost of producing 1 page of an economics paper is 2 math problems, Maria's opportunity cost of 1 page of an economics paper is 1 math problem.

Maria is more efficient at writing the economics paper. We say that Maria

The fruit of the prickly pear cactus is popular in salads and drinks. Recently, the extract from the cactus leaves has been found to relieve some of the symptoms of diabetes. Physicians in Mexico and Japan prescribe the extract as a substitute for insulin in some cases and as an enhancement to insulin in others. Though the prickly pear cactus grows in the southwestern United States as well, the harvesting of the cacti occurs mainly in Mexico because most of the prickly pear cactus forests are in Mexico, and the labor-intensive harvesting process is less costly in Mexico than it would be in the United States. Mexico has a comparative advantage in the harvesting of the cacti.

■ **comparative advantage:**
the ability to produce a good or service at a lower opportunity cost than someone else

has a **comparative advantage** in writing the paper. Able, then, has a comparative advantage in math problems—he gives up 1/2 page of an economics paper for each math problem he completes while Maria gives up 1 page of the paper for each math problem.

Maria and Able could each produce both the paper and the math problems, or one could write the papers and the other do the math problems. If each specializes where each has a comparative advantage—Maria produces the economics paper and Able completes the math problems—they can then trade to get what they want. Suppose Able wanted 5 pages of an economics paper. Maria might be willing to write 5 pages for Able, but only if she could get no less than 1 completed math problem in exchange for each page she writes. Since Able is willing to give any amount up to 2 completed math problems for each page of an economics paper, a trade could be arranged.

2.c. Gains from Trade

Suppose Able agrees to do 8 math problems for Maria if she will write 5 pages of an economics paper for him. Then Maria ends up with 8 completed math problems and has a 5-page economics paper for herself, while Able gets 2 completed math problems and a 5-page economics paper. Maria by herself could have completed only 5 math problems and written 5 pages of an economics paper, so she gains 3 math problems with the trade. Able by himself could have written only 5 pages of an economics paper. He would not have completed any math problems, so he gains 2 completed math problems with the trade.

■ **gains from trade:**
the additional amount traders get relative to what they could produce without trade

Both parties have gained from the trade. The amount each party gets beyond what each alone could have produced is called the **gains from trade.**

This simple example illustrates how the real world works. People focus on what they do best and then trade with others. You cook and your roommate cleans; you work on computers and let someone else fix your car; you purchase groceries letting someone else grow the food.

We have to decide how to use our own scarce resources. We must choose where to devote our energies. Few of us are jacks-of-all-trades. Nations, similarly, have limited amounts of resources and must choose where to devote those resources.

Our objective as individuals and as citizens of a nation is to get the most at the least cost. We can do this by specializing in those activities that require us to give up the smallest amount of other things, in other words, where we have a comparative advantage. A plumber does plumbing and leaves teaching to the teachers. The teacher teaches and leaves electrical work to the electrician. Grenada specializes in spice production and leaves manufacturing to the United States. But if we specialize, how do we get the other things we want? The answer is that we trade.

RECAP

1. Exchange occurs because all parties believe the exchange can be beneficial.
2. Opportunity cost is the amount of one good or service that must be given up to obtain one additional unit of another good or service.
3. The rule of specialization is: the individual (firm, region, or nation) will specialize in the production of the good or service that has the lowest opportunity cost.
4. Specialization and trade enable individuals, firms, and nations to get more than they could without specialization and trade.
5. By specializing in an activity one does relatively better than other activities, one can trade with others and gain more than if one carried out all activities oneself. These are referred to as gains from trade.

3. INTERNATIONAL TRADE

Trade occurs because it makes people better off. Trade among nations (or international trade) occurs because it makes the citizens of those nations better off than they would be if they could consume only domestically produced products.

Trade between the United States and the Asian nations has been growing for several years even though some of the Asian nations attempt to restrict the sale of foreign goods in their country or to otherwise limit trade. In the photo on the left, it is clear that Coca Cola has been able to enter the Korean market, dominating its soft drink industry. The United States has been relatively open to foreign goods. Although threatening trade sanctions against Japan or China at times, citizens of the United States clamor for goods made in other nations. In the photo on the right, seamstresses in Korea prepare clothes for major distributors in the United States.

3.a. Trade Patterns

Table 2 shows patterns of trade between two large groups of countries: the industrial countries and the developing countries. The industrial countries include all of Western Europe, Japan, Australia, New Zealand, Canada, and the United States. The developing countries are, essentially, the rest of the world. The table shows the dollar values and percentages of total trade between these groups of countries. The vertical column at the left lists the origin of exports (sales), and the horizontal row at the top lists the destination of imports (purchases).

As Table 2 shows, trade between industrial countries accounts for the bulk of international trade—$2.4 trillion in value and 47 percent of world trade. Exports from industrial countries to developing countries represent 19 percent of total world trade. Exports from developing countries to industrial countries account for 19 percent of total trade, while exports from the developing countries to other developing countries currently represent 15 percent of international trade.

More United States' products are sold to Canada than any other country—about 22 percent of all of U.S. exports. The U.S. purchases more from Japan than it does any other country; about 21 percent of all U.S. purchases from other countries are from Japan. The biggest trading partners with the United States are Canada, Japan, Mexico, the United Kingdom, and Germany.

3.b. Barter and Money

By specializing in activities in which opportunity costs are lowest and then trading, each trader (country, individual) will end up with more than if each tried to produce everything. Specialization and trade enable nations to acquire combinations of goods that are greater than what their own resource capabilities would allow, just like specialization and trade enable people to acquire combinations of goods that are greater than what they alone could produce. Even though one person, one firm, or one nation is limited to the combinations of goods it can produce using its own resources, through specialization and trade more goods can be acquired. This is why people, firms, and nations trade.

Traders are simply buyers and sellers. When you go to the store to purchase groceries, you are trading money for groceries. When you purchase your textbooks, you are trading money for textbooks. The McDonald's employee acts as a middleman for the firm and trades the hamburger, fries, and shake for money. The employee is trading his or her time for money.

TABLE 2
The Direction of Trade
(in billions of dollars and percentages of world trade)

	Destination	
	Industrial Countries	*Developing Countries*
Origin		
Industrial Countries	$2,435 47%	$1,011 19%
Developing Countries	$961 19%	$770 15%

Source: International Monetary Fund, *Direction of Trade Statistics,* Annual Edition, 1997

barter:
trade without the use of money

In some cases, people trade goods for goods or services for services and no money changes hands. These cases are referred to as **barter** trades. In most instances, barter is too complicated to serve as a means of trade. Let's say you needed a textbook. In a barter world, you would have to find someone with the textbook who also wanted something you had. If you did not have what he wanted, then you would have to find another person who wanted what you had and had what the textbook owner wanted. Then you would have to make two trades to get the textbook. This type of world would get very complicated quickly. This is why money has arisen in virtually every society from the beginning of time. There are reports of rocks and shells being used for money in primitive societies, and gold and silver have been used in modern times. Today, most monies are printed and/or coined out of inexpensive materials.

Each nation has its own money or currency. Table 3 lists the currency name and symbol for several countries.

exchange rate:
the price at which one currency is exchanged for another

Since each nation has its own currency, currencies have to be exchanged in order for nations to trade. The price at which currencies are exchanged is called an **exchange rate.** For instance, the exchange rates existing on January 23, 1998, between the U.S. dollar and a few currencies are listed in Table 4. According to the data, the Australian dollar was worth a little less than $.67; the British pound was worth a little less than $1.63; and so on. Exchange rates are reported daily in most newspapers.

TABLE 3
International Currency Symbols, Selected Countries

Country	Currency Name	Currency Symbol
Australia	Dollar	A$
Austria	Schilling	Sch
Belgium	Franc	BF
Canada	Dollar	C$
China	Yuan	Y
Denmark	Krone	DKr
Finland	Markka	FM
France	Franc	FF
Germany	Deutsche mark	DM
Greece	Drachma	Dr
India	Rupee	Rs
Iran	Rial	Rl
Italy	Lira	Lit
Japan	Yen	¥
Kuwait	Dinar	KD
Mexico	Peso	Ps
Netherlands	Guilder	Fl
Norway	Krone	NKr
Russia	Ruble	Rub
Saudi Arabia	Riyal	SR
Singapore	Dollar	S$
South Africa	Rand	R
Spain	Peseta	Pts
Sweden	Krona	SKr
Switzerland	Franc	SF
United Kingdom	Pound	£
United States	Dollar	$
Venezuela	Bolivar	B

TABLE 4
**Exchange Rate Between the U.S. Dollar and Selected Currencies,
January 23, 1998**

Country	U.S. $ Equivalent
Australia (dollar)	.6678
Belgium (franc)	.02630
Britain (pound)	1.6270
Canada (dollar)	.6935
Germany (mark)	.5438
Japan (yen)	.00778

If in January 1998 a U.S. buyer wanted to purchase a pair of Doc Marten shoes priced at £80 from a British seller, the buyer would have had to first exchange enough dollars to get £80. Since one pound was worth 1.627 dollars, it would take $1.627 \times 80 = \$130.16$ dollars. For another example, suppose you were asked by an international agency to do some work for them. The agency agreed to pay you 20,000 BF (Belgian francs). How much would that be in dollars? In January 1998, the U.S. dollar equivalent of the BF was .0263. So, 20,000BF $\times$ \$/BF.0263 = \$526. As we shall learn later, exchange rate changes have important implications for international trade.

RECAP

1. Trade is typically carried out using money; however, some trades are goods for goods or services for services. These are called barter trades.
2. International trade requires that the currencies of the trading nations be converted from one to another. The price at which the currencies are exchanged is the exchange rate.
3. What is traded, that is, the pattern of trade, depends on comparative advantage and on consumer preferences.

SUMMARY

▣▣ What is economics?

1. The objective of economics is to understand why the real world is what it is.
2. The resources that go into the production of goods are land, labor, and capital.
3. Economics is the study of how people choose to allocate scarce resources to satisfy their unlimited wants.

▣▣ What are the principles of economics?

4. Scarcity is universal; it applies to anything people would like more of than is available at a zero price. Because of scarcity, choices must be made.

▣▣ What are opportunity costs?

5. Opportunity costs are the forgone opportunities of the next best alternative. Choice means both gaining something and giving up something. When you choose one option, you forego all others. The benefits of the next best alternative are the opportunity costs of your choice.

▣▣ How are specialization and opportunity costs related?

6. Comparative advantage is when one person (one firm, one nation) can perform an activity or produce a good with fewer opportunity costs than someone else.

7. Comparative advantage accounts for specialization. We specialize in the activities in which we have the lowest opportunity costs, that is, in which we have a comparative advantage.

8. Specialization and trade enable those involved to acquire more than they could by not specializing and engaging in trade. The additional amount acquired from trade is called the gains from trade.

9. Trade can be made using barter—trading goods for goods or services for services—or using money.

10. If international trade occurs and the countries have different monies, or currencies, then the currencies have to be convertible. The rate at which currencies are convertible is called the exchange rate.

KEY TERMS

scarcity

free good

economic bad

resources

land

labor

capital

financial capital

opportunity costs

tradeoffs

comparative advantage

gains from trade

barter

exchange rate

EXERCISES

1. Which of the following are economic goods? Explain why each is or is not an economic good.
   a. Steaks
   b. Houses
   c. Cars
   d. Garbage
   e. T-shirts

2. It is well documented in scientific research that smoking is harmful to our health. Smokers have higher incidences of coronary disease, cancer, and other catastrophic illnesses. Knowing this, about 30 percent of young people begin smoking and about 25 percent of the U.S. population smokes. Are the people who choose to smoke irrational? What do you think of the argument that we should ban smoking in order to protect these people from themselves?

3. Use economics to explain why diamonds are more expensive than water, when water is necessary for survival and diamonds are not.

4. Use economics to explain why people leave tips in the following two cases: (a) at a restaurant they visit often; (b) at a restaurant they visit only once.

5. Use economics to explain why people contribute to charities.

6. In presidential campaigns, candidates always seem to make more promises than they can fulfill. In their first campaign, President Clinton and Vice President Gore promised more and better health care, a better environment, only minor reductions in defense, better education, and better roads, bridges, sewer systems, and water systems, and so on. Accepting the promises as facts, what economic concept were the critics claiming that Clinton and Gore ignored?

7. Perhaps you've heard of the old saying "There is no such thing as a free lunch." What does it mean? If someone invites you to a lunch and offers to pay for it, is it free to you?

8. During China's Cultural Revolution in the late 1960s and early 1970s, many people with a

high school or college education were forced to move to farms and work in the fields. Some were common laborers for eight or more years. What does this policy say about specialization? Would you predict that the policy would lead to an increase in output?

9. Use Table 4 to calculate the U.S. dollar price of:

A shirt manufactured in Belgium and selling there for 5,000BF.

A boomerang selling in Australia for 40A$.

A box of tea selling in Britain for 5£.

A car selling in Japan for 50,000¥.

 **INTERNET EXERCISE**

This chapter focuses on specialization and trade. Use the Internet to examine international trade across countries. Go to the Boyes/Melvin *Fundamentals of Economics* Web site at http://www.hmco.com/college/ and click on the Internet Exercise link for Chapter 1. Now answer the questions found on the Boyes/Melvin Web site.

1

Working with Graphs

1. READING AND CONSTRUCTING GRAPHS

It is important to understand how the axes (the horizontal and vertical lines) are used and what they measure. Let's begin with the horizontal axis, the line running across the page in a horizontal direction. Notice in Figure 1(a) that the line is divided into equal segments. Each point on the line represents a quantity, or the value of the variables being measured. For example, each segment could represent 10 years or 10,000 pounds of diamonds or some other value. Whatever is measured, the value increases from left to right, beginning with negative values, going on to zero, which is called the origin, and then moving on to positive numbers.

A number line in the vertical direction can be constructed as well, also shown in Figure 1(a). Zero is the origin, and the numbers increase from bottom to top. Like the horizontal axis, the vertical axis is divided into equal segments; the distance between 0 and 10 is the same as the distance between 0 and −10, between 10 and 20, and so on.

Figure 1
The Axes, the Coordinate System, and the Positive Quadrant
Figure 1(a) shows the vertical and horizontal axes. The horizontal axis has an origin, measured as zero, in the middle. Negative numbers are to the left of zero, positive numbers to the right. The vertical axis also has an origin in the middle. Positive numbers are above the origin, negative numbers below. The horizontal and vertical axes together show the entire coordinate system. Positive numbers are in quadrant I, negative numbers in quadrant III, and combinations of negative and positive numbers in quadrants II and IV.

Figure 1(b) shows only the positive quadrant. Because most economic data are positive, often only the upper right quadrant, the positive quadrant, of the coordinate system is used.

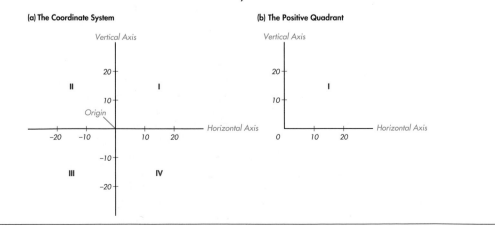

(a) The Coordinate System

(b) The Positive Quadrant

Putting the horizontal and vertical lines together lets us express relationships between two variables graphically. The axes cross, or intersect, at their origins, as shown in Figure 1(a). From the common origin, movements to the right and up, in the area—called a quadrant—marked I, are combinations of positive numbers; movements to the left and down, in quadrant III, are combinations of negative numbers; movements to the right and down, in quadrant IV, are negative values on the vertical axis and positive values on the horizontal axis; and movements to the left and up, in quadrant II, are positive values on the vertical axis and negative values on the horizontal axis.

Economic data are typically positive numbers: the unemployment rate, the inflation rate, the price of something, the quantity of something produced or sold, and so on. Because economic data are usually positive numbers, the only part of the coordinate system that usually comes into play in economics is the upper right portion, quadrant I. That is why economists may simply sketch a vertical line down to the origin and then extend a horizontal line out to the right, as shown in Figure 1(b). When data are negative, the other quadrants of the coordinate system may be used.

1.a. Constructing a Graph from a Table

■ **production possibilities curve:**
shows the maximum output that can be produced using resources fully and efficiently

Now that you are familiar with the axes, that is, the coordinate system, you are ready to construct a graph using the data in the table in Figure 2. The graph we'll plot is called the **production possibilities curve (PPC).** It shows the maximum output that can be produced with a limited quantity and quality of resources. In this case we are considering the production of two types of goods—defense goods and nondefense goods. Units of defense goods and services are measured on the vertical axis, and units of nondefense goods and services are measured on the horizontal axis.

If all resources are allocated to producing defense goods and services, then 200 million units can be produced, but the production of nondefense goods and services will cease. The combination of 200 million units of defense goods and services and 0 units of nondefense goods and services is point A_1, a point on the vertical axis. At 175 million units of defense goods and services, 75 million units of nondefense goods and services can be produced (point B_1). Point C_1 represents 125 million units of nondefense goods and services and 130 million units of defense goods. Point D_1 represents 150 million units of nondefense goods and services and 70 million units of defense goods and services. Point E_1, a point on the horizontal axis, shows the combination of no production of defense goods and services and total production of nondefense goods and services.

The PPC is a picture of the tradeoffs facing society. A production possibilities curve shows that more of one type of good can be produced only by reducing the quantity of other types of goods that are produced; it shows that a society has scarce resources.

1.a.1. Interpreting Graphs: Points Inside the Production Possibilities Curve
Suppose a nation produces 130 million units of defense goods and services and 25 million units of nondefense goods and services. That combination, point F_1 in Figure 2, lies inside the production possibilities curve. A point lying inside the production possibilities curve indicates that resources are not being fully or efficiently used. If the existing work force is employed only 20 hours per week, it is not being fully used. If two workers are used when one would be sufficient—say, two people in each Domino's Pizza delivery car—then resources are not being used efficiently. If there are resources available for use, society can move from point F_1 to a point on the PPC, such as point C_1. The move would gain 100 million units of nondefense goods and services with no loss of defense goods and services.

Combination	Defense Goods and Services (millions of units)	Nondefense Goods and Services (millions of units)
A_1	200	0
B_1	175	75
C_1	130	125
D_1	70	150
E_1	0	160
F_1	130	25
G_1	200	75

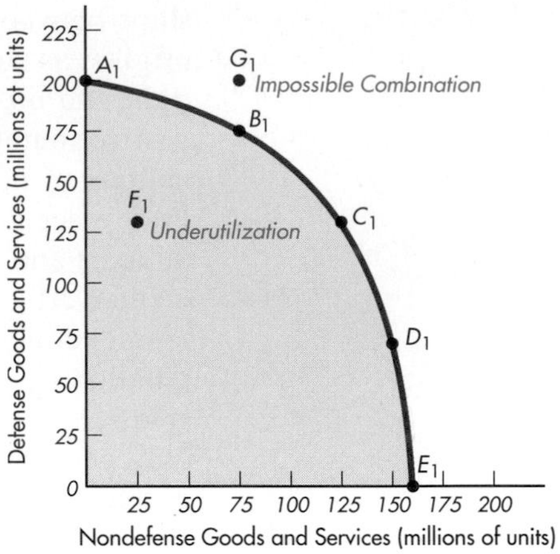

Figure 2
The Production Possibilities Curve
With a limited amount of resources, only certain combinations of defense and nondefense goods and services can be produced. The maximum amounts that can be produced, given various tradeoffs, are represented by points A_1 through E_1. Point F_1 lies inside the curve and represents the underutilization of resources. More of one type of good and less of another could be produced, or more of both types could be produced. Point G_1 represents an impossible combination. There are insufficient resources to produce quantities lying beyond the curve.

1.a.2. Interpreting Graphs: Points Outside the Production Possibilities Curve

Point G_1 in Figure 2 represents the production of 200 million units of defense goods and services and 75 units of nondefense goods and services. Point G_1, however, represents the use of more resources than are available—it lies outside the production possibilities curve. Unless more resources can be obtained and/or the quality of resources improved so that the nation can produce more with the same quantity of resources, there is no way the society can currently produce 200 million units of defense goods and 75 million units of nondefense goods.

1.b. Shifts of Curves

Graphs can be used to illustrate the effects of a change in a variable not explicitly shown on the graph. For instance, if a nation obtains more resources, points outside its current production possibilities curve become attainable. Suppose a country discovers new sources of oil within its borders and is able to greatly increase its production of oil. Greater oil supplies would enable the country to increase production of all types of goods and services.

Figure 3 shows the production possibilities curve before (PPC_1) and after (PPC_2) the discovery of oil. PPC_1 is based on the data given in Figure 2. PPC_2 is based on the data given in Figure 3 (see table), which shows the increase in production of goods and services that results from the increase in oil supplies. The first combination of goods and services on PPC_2, point A_2, is 220 million units of defense goods and 0 units of nondefense goods. The second point, B_2, is a combination of 200 million units of defense goods and 75 million units of nondefense goods. C_2 through F_2 are the combinations shown in the table of Figure 3. Connecting these points yields the bowed-out curve, PPC_2. Because of the availability of new supplies of oil, the nation is able to increase production of all goods, as shown by the shift from PPC_1 to PPC_2. A comparison of the two curves shows that more goods and services for both defense and nondefense are possible along PPC_2 than along PPC_1.

Combination	Defense Goods and Services (millions of units)	Nondefense Goods and Services (millions of units)
A_2	220	0
B_2	200	75
C_2	175	125
D_2	130	150
E_2	70	160
F_2	200	165

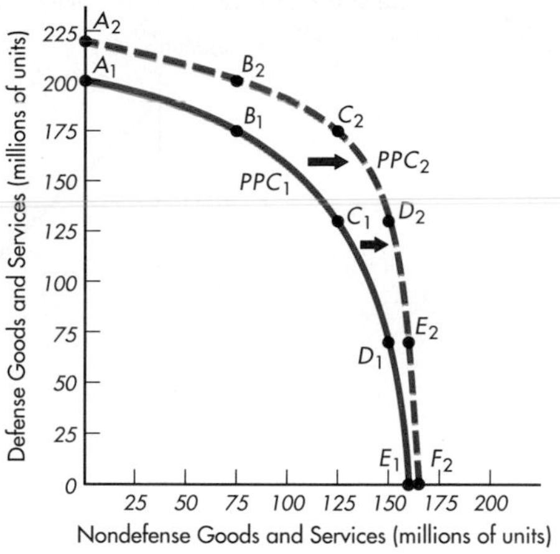

Figure 3
A Shift of the Production Possibilities Curve
Whenever everything else is not constant, the curve shifts. In this case, an increase in the quantity of a resource enables the society to produce more of both types of goods. The curve shifts out, away from the origin.

The outward shift of the PPC can be the result of an increase in the quantity of resources, but it also can occur because the quality of resources improves. For instance, a technological breakthrough could conceivably improve the way that communication occurs, thereby requiring fewer people and machines and less time to produce the same quantity and quality of goods. The work force could become more literate, thereby requiring less time to produce the same quantity and quality of goods. Each of these quality improvements in resources could lead to an outward shift of the PPC.

Curves shift when things that affect the relationship between the variables measured on the graphs change. The PPC measures combinations of two different types of products that a country could produce. When technology improves, then the combinations of the two goods that could be produced changes, and the PPC shifts.

1.c. Application: Gains from Trade

Let's use the trading problem between Maria and Able discussed in the chapter to illustrate the use of the PPC graph. Review Table 1: Production Possibilities, on page 8.

Figure 4 shows Maria's and Able's production possibilities curves based on the information given in the table. The output per day has been plotted for each. Maria's PPC is given in the graph on the left. It indicates that she can produce 10 pages of an economics paper and no math problems, 10 units of math problems but no pages of an economics paper, or any combination lying along the line. Able, similarly, can produce those combinations shown along the line in the figure on the right. Maria can produce only those combinations along her production possibilities line or combinations inside the line. Able can also produce only those combinations along or inside his production possibilities line. The production possibility curves in this example are actually straight lines. For our purposes, the difference between a straight line PPC and a bowed PPC does not matter. Both shapes illustrate the idea that the combina-

Figure 4
Gains from Trade

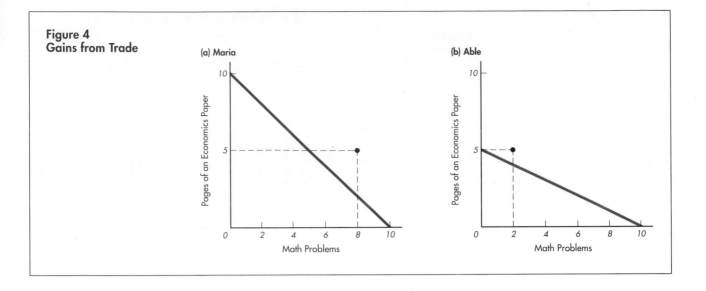

tions along the PPC are the maximum a person or a nation can produce given current limited resources.

Maria and Able could each produce both the paper and the math problems, or one could write the papers and the other do the math problems. Remember, if each specializes where each has a comparative advantage (Maria produces the economics paper and Able completes the math problems), they can then trade to get what they want. Suppose Able wanted 5 pages of an economics paper. Maria might be willing to write 5 pages for Able, but only if she could get no less than 1 completed math problem in exchange for each page she writes. Since Able is willing to give any amount up to 2 completed math problems for each page of an economics paper, a trade could be arranged.

Suppose Able agrees to do 8 math problems for Maria if she will write 5 pages of an economics paper for him. Then Maria ends up with 8 completed math problems and has a 5-page economics paper for herself, while Able gets 2 completed math problems and a 5-page economics paper. Maria by herself could have completed only 5 math problems and written 5 pages of an economics paper, so she gains 3 math problems with the trade. Able by himself could have written only 5 pages of an economics paper. He would not have completed any math problems, so he gains 2 completed math problems with the trade. Gains from trade are shown by the combinations of pages of an economics paper and math problems that lie beyond the production possibility lines.

SUMMARY

1. Most economic data are positive numbers, so often only the upper right quadrant of the coordinate system is used in economics.

2. The production possibilities curve shows the maximum amount that a nation can produce at any given time given the quantity of resources and the use of those resources.

3. A curve on a graph shifts—changes position—when something other than the two variables measured on the axes affects the relationship between the two variables.

KEY TERMS

production possibilities curve (PPC)

EXERCISES

1. Plot the data listed in the table below.
   a. Measure price along the vertical axis and quantity along the horizontal axis and plot the first two columns.
   b. Show what quantity is sold when the price is $550.
   c. Directly below the graph in part a, plot the data in columns 2 and 3. In this graph, measure quantity on the horizontal axis and total revenue on the vertical axis.
   d. What is total revenue when the price is $550? Will total revenue increase or decrease when the price is lowered?

Price	Quantity Sold	Total Revenue
$1,000	200	200,000
900	400	360,000
800	600	480,000
700	800	560,000
600	1,000	600,000
500	1,200	600,000
400	1,400	560,000
300	1,600	480,000
200	1,800	360,000
100	2,000	200,000

2. Listed below are the production possibility curves for two countries producing health care and food. If they devote all resources to health care, Haiti can care for 1,000 people a month while Cuba can care for 500. If they split their resources 50-50, Haiti can care for 500 people and produce 7 tons of food while Cuba can care for 250 and produce 3 tons of food. Putting all resources into food, Haiti can produce 10 tons while Cuba can produce 7.

Percent of Effort Devoted to Health Care:

Percent of Effort Devoted to Health Care:	Haiti health care	food	Cuba health care	food
100	1,000	0	500	0
50	500	7	250	3
0	0	10	0	7

   a. Plot their production possibility curves.
   b. Can you see any possible gains from trade that might occur?
   c. What would Haiti specialize in? What would Cuba specialize in?

3. Plot the PPC given by the following data.

Combination	Health Care	All Other Goods
A	0	100
B	25	90
C	50	70
D	75	40
E	100	0

   a. Calculate the opportunity cost of each combination compared to the combination before. Compare A to B, B to C, C to D, and D to E.
   b. What is the opportunity cost of combination C?
   c. Suppose a second nation has the following PPC. Plot the PPC and then determine which nation has the comparative advantage in which activity. Show whether the two nations can gain from specialization and trade.

Combination	Health Care	All Other Goods
A	0	50
B	20	40
C	40	25
D	60	5
E	65	0

2

Markets and the Market Process

*Preview*

P eople (and firms and nations) can get more if they specialize in certain activities and then trade with one another to acquire the goods and services they desire. But how are the specialized producers to get together or to know who specializes in what? We could allow the government to decide, or we could rely on first-come, first-served, or even simply luck. Typically it is the market mechanism—buyers and sellers interacting via prices—we rely on to ensure that gains from trade occur. To see why, consider the following situation and then carry out the exercise. ■

I. At a sightseeing point, reachable only after a strenuous hike, a firm has established a stand where bottled water is sold. The water, carried in by the employees of the firm, is sold to thirsty hikers in six-ounce bottles. The price is $1 per bottle. Typically only 100 bottles of the water are sold each day. On a particularly hot day, 200 hikers want to buy at least one bottle of water. Indicate what you think of each of the following means of distributing the water to the hikers by responding to each allocation approach with one of the following five responses:

a. Completely fair

b. Acceptable

c. Unfair

d. Very unfair

e. Totally unfair

1. Increasing the price until the quantity of water bottles hikers are willing and able to purchase exactly equals the number of water bottles available for sale.

2. Selling the water for $1 per bottle on a first-come, first-served basis.

3. Having the local authority (government) buy the water for $1 per bottle and distribute it according to its own judgment.

4. Selling the water at $1 per bottle following a random selection procedure or lottery.

The following is a similar situation but involving a different product.

II. A physician has been providing medical services at a fee of $100 per patient and typically sees 30 patients per day. One day the flu bug has been so vicious that the number of patients attempting to visit the physician exceeds 60. Indicate what you think of each of the following means of distributing the physician's services to the sick patients by responding with one of the following five answers:

a. Completely fair

b. Acceptable

c. Unfair

d. Very unfair

e. Totally unfair

1. Raising the price until the number of patients the doctor sees is exactly equal to those patients willing and able to pay the doctor's fee.

2. Selling the services at $100 per patient on a first-come, first-served basis.

3. The local authority (government) pays the physician $100 per patient and chooses who is to receive the services according to its own judgment.

4. Selling the physician's services for $100 per patient following a random selection procedure or lottery.

The fundamental economic problem is scarcity—that is, not enough to satisfy everyone. When a good or resource is scarce, there is a cost to acquiring it. The cost may be the price of the good or resource if the price is used as the allocating mechanism. The cost may be the time devoted to acquiring the good or resource when the price is not used as the allocation mechanism. In this case, people are spending hours in line just so they can obtain a couple of gallons of drinking water.

1. ALLOCATION MECHANISMS

How did you respond to the alternative choices? Did you notice that in fact each allocation mechanism is unfair in the sense that someone gets the good or service and someone doesn't? With the market system, it is those without income or wealth who must do without. Under the first-come, first-served system, it is those who arrive later who do without. Under the government scheme, it is those not in favor or those that do not match up with the government's rules who do without. And, with a random procedure, it is those who do not have the lucky ticket or correct number who are left out.

Since each allocation mechanism is in a sense unfair, how do we decide which to use? One way might be the incentives each creates. Suppose, just as a thought experiment, that everything—and we mean everything—in a society were allocated using a single allocation mechanism.

With the first-come, first-served allocation scheme, the incentive is to be first. You would have no reason to improve the quality of your products or to increase the value of your resources. Your only incentive would be to be first. Supply would not increase. Why would anyone produce when all everyone wants is to be first? As a result, growth and standards of living would not rise. A society based on first-come, first-served would die a quick death.

A government scheme provides an incentive either to be a member of government and thus help determine the allocation rules or to perform according to government dictates. There are no incentives to improve production and efficiency or quantities supplied and, therefore, no reason for the economy to grow. We've seen how this system fared with the collapse of the Soviet Union.

The random allocation provides no incentives at all—simply hope that manna from heaven will fall on you.

With the market system, the incentive is to acquire purchasing ability (to obtain income and wealth). This means you must provide goods that have high value to others or resources that have high value to producers. For example, you can enhance your worth as an employee by acquiring education or training, which increases the value of the resources you own.

The market system also provides incentives for quantities of scarce goods to increase. In the case of the water stand in the first scenario, if the price of the water increases and the owner of the water stand is earning significant profits, others may carry or truck water to the top of the hill and sell it to thirsty hikers, and the amount of water available thus increases. In the case of the doctor in the second scenario, other doctors may think that opening an office near the first might be a way to earn more, and the amount of physician services available increases. Since the market system creates the incentive for the amount supplied to increase, economies grow and expand and standards of living improve. The market system also ensures that resources are allocated to where they are most highly valued. If the price of an item rises, consumers may switch over to another item or another good or service that can serve about the same purpose. When consumers switch, production of the alternative good rises and thus resources used in its production must increase as well. The resources then flow from the now lower-valued use to the new higher-valued use.

1.a. Efficiency

■ **efficiency:**
the measure of how well an allocation system satisfies peoples' wants and needs

Economists evaluate the outcome of an economic system in terms of **efficiency.** Efficiency is a measure of how well a system satisfies people's wants and needs. An efficient economic system exists when resources are allocated such that no one can be made better off without harming someone else. In contrast, an inefficient allocation is wasteful; better use of the available resources would make some people better off without harming anyone else.

A system of markets and prices is generally the most efficient means of coordinating and organizing activities. Why? Because it takes fewer resources to work than any other system. Individuals offer to sell goods and services at various prices and other individuals offer to buy goods and services at various prices. Without having anyone coordinating the buyers and sellers, the market determines a price for each traded good at which the quantities that people are willing and able to sell are equal to the quantities that people are willing and able to buy. This price informs buyers and sellers what they must give up to acquire a unit of the good (that is, their opportunity costs) and thereby lets them know whether their activities have value and in which activities they should specialize.

Day in and day out, without any conscious central direction, the market system induces people to employ their talents and resources in the most effective manner. People do not have to be fooled, cajoled, or forced to do their parts in a well-functioning market system but instead pursue their own objectives as they see fit. Workers, attempting to maximize their own individual happiness and well-being, select the training, careers, and jobs where their talents and energy are most valuable. Producers, pursuing only private profits, develop the goods and services on which consumers put the highest value and produce these goods and services at the lowest possible costs. Owners of resources, seeking only to increase their own wealth, deploy these assets in socially desirable ways.

1.b. Alternatives to Market Allocation

The price or market system is the predominant allocation mechanism in most industrial societies today because it is generally the most efficient. Yet, not all exchanges take place through the market system. Many medical services are provided on a first-come, first-served basis. Classes in schools are often allocated on a first-come, first-served basis. The use of highways or roadways is typically first-come, first-served. Governments allocate many goods: airline routes, radio and television broadcast bands, land use (zoning), rights-of-way at intersections, and many others. Even luck—random allocation—plays a part in the allocation of some items such as concert tickets, lottery winnings, and other contest prizes. If the market system is such an efficient mechanism, why is it not universally relied on? One reason is that for some products people do not like the outcome of the market system. Another reason is that the market system is inefficient in some cases.

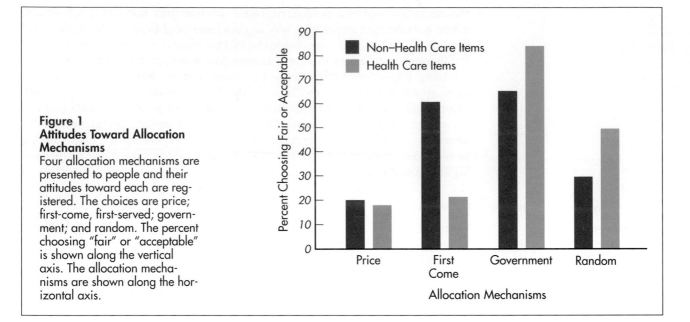

Figure 1
Attitudes Toward Allocation Mechanisms
Four allocation mechanisms are presented to people and their attitudes toward each are registered. The choices are price; first-come, first-served; government; and random. The percent choosing "fair" or "acceptable" is shown along the vertical axis. The allocation mechanisms are shown along the horizontal axis.

1.b.1. Disagreement with the Market Outcome

The response of several hundred people to an expanded version of the questionnaire above points out how people especially prefer something other than the market system for health care. In Figure 1, allocation mechanisms are shown along the horizontal axes and the percentage of people choosing either a or b in the questionnaire (completely fair or acceptable) is shown along the vertical axes. Figure 1 shows non-health-related goods and services and health-related goods and services.

Comparing non-health care items to health care items, you can see that people feel much less comfortable with the market system for allocating medical goods and services than for other types of goods and services. People tend to favor a government allocation scheme for medical goods and services. Looking at Figure 1, you can also see that many people simply do not like the outcome of the market system for any good or service. Only 20 percent think the market system is fair or acceptable. When people do not like the outcome, they may expend resources to attempt to implement some other allocation mechanism. They lobby the government or attempt to convince voters that some other scheme would be preferable. Thus, in many cases we see allocation mechanisms other than price just because people do not like the outcome of the market system.

1.b.2. Inefficiency

Another reason the market system may not be used is that it is not efficient in certain circumstances. Two reasons for inefficiency are imperfect information and benefits and costs not accounted for by the market.

A market price is only as good an indicator as the information that exists in the market, and people might not be perfectly informed, nor will everyone have the same information. When market information is not perfect, least-cost combinations of resources may not be used, or resources may not be used where they have the highest value. Often, in such cases, people have argued for the government to step in with rules and regulations concerning the amount of information that must be provided. The government requires, for example, that specific information be provided on the labels of food products, that warning labels be placed on cigarettes and alcohol products, and that statements about the condition of a used car be made available to the buyer.

The market system works efficiently only if the market price reflects the full costs and benefits of producing and consuming a particular good or service. Recall that people make decisions on the basis of their opportunity costs, and the market price is a measure of what must be forgone to acquire some good or service. If the market price does not reflect the full costs, then decisions cannot reflect opportunity costs. More resources may go into an activity than if the external cost was accounted for. For instance, more styrofoam cups are produced and sold than if McDonald's and its customers had to pay the additional cost of discarding the cups; when you drive, you don't pay for all of the pollution created by your car; and when homeowners allow their properties to be come run-down, they reduce the value of neighboring properties, but they don't pay for the loss of value. Again, government is often called upon to intervene in the market to resolve such problems.

RECAP

1. Allocation mechanisms are the means used to distribute scarce goods and resources. Common allocation mechanisms are first-come, first-served, government, random, or the market system.

2. The outcome of an exchange system is evaluated on the basis of efficiency. An efficient allocation of resources is one in which resources are allocated so that no one can be made better off without harming someone else.

3. The price or market system is relied on for most exchanges because it is the most efficient. It creates incentives that lead to growth and improvements in standards of living.

4. Some of the outcomes of a market exchange are not favorable to specific individuals or groups. As a result, they try to change the outcome, to use another exchange mechanism.

5. The market system does not result in economic efficiency when there is imperfect information or when the costs or benefits of the transaction are borne by parties not directly involved in the transaction. The government is often called upon to resolve these market system inefficiencies.

2. HOW MARKETS FUNCTION

We have discussed the market and the market system but have not defined what a market is or how markets work. Let's turn to that now. A market was once an event that occurred in a particular location at a particular time. Consumers would go there to meet suppliers and compare goods and prices. People no longer have to walk between market stalls appraising one supplier's price and quality against another's. A market may be confined to one location, as in the case of a supermarket, but it may encompass a city, a state, a country, or the entire world. The market for agricultural products, for instance, is international, but the market for labor services is mostly local or national.

2.a. The Market Process

When the Mazda Miata was introduced in the United States in 1990, the little sports roadster was an especially desired product in southern California. As shown in Figure 2, the suggested retail price was $13,996, the price at which it was selling in Detroit. In Los Angeles, the purchase price was nearly $25,000.

Several entrepreneurs recognized the profit potential in the $10,000 price differential and sent hundreds of students to Detroit to pick up Miatas and drive them back to L.A. Within a reasonably short time, the price differential between Detroit and L.A. was reduced. The increased sales in Detroit drove the price there up while the increased number of Miatas being sold in Los Angeles reduced the price there. The price differential continued to decline until it was less than the cost of shipping the cars from Detroit to Los Angeles.

The process of buying and selling an identical product at different prices is referred to as **arbitrage.** Arbitrage is the simple process of buying a product in a market where the price is low and selling the same product in a market where the price is high to profit from the price differential.

Suppose a consumer electronics firm is inefficient, its employees surly, and its products not displayed well. To attempt to earn a profit, the firm charges more than the efficiently run firm down the street. Where do customers go? Obviously, they seek out the best deal and go to the efficient firm. The more efficient store has to get more supplies, hire more employees, acquire more space, etc. The inefficient store lays off employees and sells used equipment and supplies. In short, the resources flow from where they are not as highly valued to where they are more highly valued.

> The market process tends to ensure that the products consumers want are provided at the lowest possible price, that resources are used where they are most highly valued, and that inefficient firms and inefficiency in general do not last.

Why does the market process work? For a very simple reason. People are looking for the best deal—the highest quality products at the lowest prices.

■ **arbitrage:**
buying a product at a low price and selling the same product at a high price to make a profit

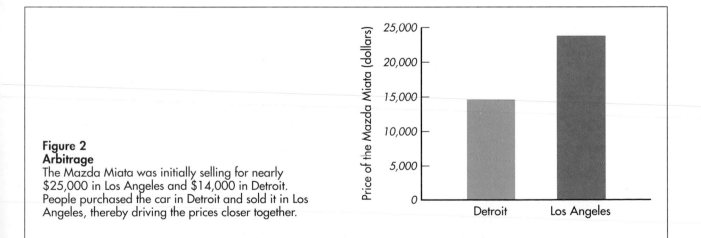

Figure 2
Arbitrage
The Mazda Miata was initially selling for nearly $25,000 in Los Angeles and $14,000 in Detroit. People purchased the car in Detroit and sold it in Los Angeles, thereby driving the prices closer together.

So when an opportunity for a "best deal" arises, people respond to it by purchasing where the price is low and/or selling where the price is high. And as long as people can buy and sell at will, the market process works.

A market consists of demand and supply and buyers and sellers. In the rest of this chapter we will look at the market process in more detail by examining demand, then supply, and then putting the two together.

RECAP

1. A market need not be a specific location. A market exists when buyers and sellers interact to buy and sell a specific product.
2. The market process refers to the buying and selling of a good and the resulting allocation of resources to their highest valued uses.

3. DEMAND

■ **demand:**
the amount of a product that people are willing and able to purchase at every possible price

The demand for a good or service captures the behavior of the buyers of that good or service. **Demand** is a relationship between the price of the good or service and the quantity of that good or service people are willing and able to buy. That relationship is such a strong one that it is referred to as a law—the law of demand.

3.a. The Law of Demand

■ **law of demand:**
inverse relationship between price and quantity demanded

The **law of demand states** that:

1. the quantity of a well-defined good or service that
2. people are willing and able to purchase
3. during a particular period of time
4. decreases as the price of that good or service rises and increases as the price falls
5. everything else held constant.

The first phrase ensures that we are referring to the same item, that we are not mixing different goods. A Rolex watch is different from a Timex watch; Polo brand golf shirts are different goods than generic brand golf shirts; Mercedes-Benz automobiles are different goods than Yugo automobiles.

The second phrase indicates that people must not only want to purchase some good, they must be able to purchase that good in order for their wants to be counted as part of demand. For example, Sue would love to buy a membership to the Paradise Valley Country Club, but because the membership costs $55,000, she is not able to purchase the membership. Though willing, she is not able. At a price of $5,000, however, she is willing and able to purchase the membership.

The third phrase points out that the demand for any good is defined for a specific period of time. Without reference to a time period, a demand relationship would not make any sense. For instance, the statement that "at a price of $3 per Happy Meal, 13 million Happy Meals are demanded" provides no useful information. Are the 13 million meals sold in one week or one year? Think of demand as a rate of purchase at each possible price over a period of time—2 per month, 1 per day, and so on.

The fourth phrase points out that price and quantity demanded move in opposite directions; that is, as the price rises, the quantity demanded falls, and as the price falls, the quantity demanded rises.

The final phrase, everything else held constant, ensures that things or events that affect demand other than price do not change. The demand for a good or service depends on the price of that good or service but also depends on income, tastes, prices of related goods and services, expectations, and the number of buyers. If any one of these changes, demand changes.

3.b. The Demand Schedule

■ **demand schedule:**
a table listing the quantity demanded at each price

A **demand schedule** is a table or list of the prices and the corresponding quantities demanded of a particular good or service. The table in Figure 3 is a demand schedule for video rentals (movies). It shows the number of videos that a consumer named Bob would be willing and able to rent at each price during the year, everything else held constant. As the rental price of the videos gets higher relative to the prices of other goods, Bob would be willing and able to rent fewer videos.

At the high price of $5 per video, Bob indicates that he will rent only 10 videos during the year. At a price of $4 per video, Bob tells us that he will rent 20 videos during the year. As the price drops from $5 to $4 to $3 to $2 and to $1, Bob is willing and able to rent more videos. At a price of $1, Bob would rent 50 videos during the year, nearly 1 per week.

3.c. The Demand Curve

■ **demand curve:**
a graph showing the law of demand

A **demand curve** is a graph of the demand schedule. The demand curve shown in Figure 3 is plotted from the information given in the demand schedule. Price is measured on the vertical axis, quantity per unit of time on the horizontal axis. Point *A* in Figure 3 corresponds to combination *A* in the table: a price of $5 and 10 videos demanded. Similarly, points *B*, *C*, *D*, and *E* in Figure 3 represent the corresponding combinations in the table. The line connecting these points is Bob's demand curve for videos.

Figure 3
Bob's Demand Schedule and Demand Curve for Videos
The number of videos that Bob is willing and able to rent at each price during the year is listed in the table, or demand schedule. The demand curve is derived from the combinations given in the demand schedule. The price-quantity combination of $5 per video and 10 videos is point A. The combination of $4 per video and 20 videos is point B. Each combination is plotted, and the points are connected to form the demand curve.

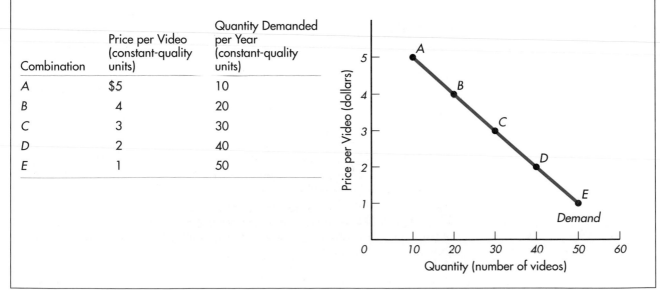

Combination	Price per Video (constant-quality units)	Quantity Demanded per Year (constant-quality units)
A	$5	10
B	4	20
C	3	30
D	2	40
E	1	50

3.d. From Individual Demand Curves to a Market Curve

■ market demand:
the sum of individual demands

Unless Bob is the only renter of the videos, his demand curve is not the total, or market demand, curve. **Market demand** is the sum of all individual demands. To derive the market demand curve, then, the individual demand curves of all consumers in the market must be added together. The table in Figure 4 lists the demand schedules of three individuals, Bob, Helen, and Art. Because in this example the market consists only of Bob, Helen, and Art, their individual demands are added together to derive the market demand. The market demand is the last column of the table.

Bob's, Helen's, and Art's demand schedules are plotted as individual demand curves in Figure 4(a). In Figure 4(b) their individual demand curves have been added together to obtain the market demand curve. (Notice that we add in a horizontal direction—that is, we add quantities at each price, not the prices at each quantity.) At a price of $5, we add the quantity Bob would buy, 10, to the quantity Helen would buy, 5, to the quantity Art would buy, 15, to get the market demand of 30. At a price of $4, we add the quantities each of the consumers is willing and able to buy to get the total quantity demanded of 48. At all prices, then, we add the quantities demanded by each individual consumer to get the total, or market quantity, demanded.

3.e. Changes in Demand and Changes in Quantity Demanded

■ quantity demanded:
the amount of a product that people are willing and able to purchase at a specific price

Economists distinguish between the terms *demand* and *quantity demanded.* When they refer to the *quantity demanded* they are talking about the amount of a product that people are willing and able to purchase *at a specific price.* When they refer to demand, they are talking about the amount that people would be willing and able to purchase *at every possible price.* Thus, the statement that "the demand for U.S. white wine rose after a 300 percent tariff was applied to French white wine" means that at each price for U.S. white wine, more people were willing and able to purchase U.S. white wine. And the statement that "the quantity demanded of white wine fell as the price of white wine rose" means that people were willing and able to purchase less white wine because the price of the wine rose.

When the price of a good or service is the only factor that changes, the quantity demanded changes but the demand curve does not. Instead, as the price of the video rentals is decreased (increased), everything else held constant, the quantity that people are willing and able to purchase increases (decreases). This change is merely a movement from one point on the demand curve to another point on the same demand curve, not a shift of the demand curve.

■ determinants of demand:
things that influence demand other than the price

The demand curve shifts when any one of the **determinants of demand** changes: income, tastes, prices of related goods, expectations, or the number of buyers. Let's consider how each of these determinants of demand affects the demand curve.

Income The demand for any good or service depends on income. The higher someone's income is, the more goods and services that person can purchase at any given price.

Tastes The demand for any good or service depends on individuals' tastes and preferences, and tastes can change. When they do change, demand changes. For decades, the destination of choice for college students in the East and Midwest during spring break was Fort Lauderdale, Florida. In the early 1990s, many students decided that Mexico offered a more exciting destination than Fort Lauderdale. Regardless of the prices of the Fort Lauderdale and Mexican vacations, tastes changed so that more students went to Mexico.

Prices of Related Goods and Services Goods and services may be related in two ways. If buyers can use either of two or more goods for the same

Figure 4
The Market Demand Schedule and Curve for Videos

The market is defined as consisting of three individuals: Bob, Helen, and Art. Their demand schedules are listed in the table and plotted as the individual demand curves shown in Figure 4(a). By adding the quantities that each demands at every price, we obtain the market demand curve shown in Figure 4(b). At a price of $1 we add Bob's quantity demanded of 50 to Helen's quantity demanded of 25 to Art's quantity demanded of 27 to obtain the market quantity demanded of 102. At a price of $2 we add Bob's 40 to Helen's 20 to Art's 24 to obtain the market quantity demanded of 84. To obtain the market demand curve, for every price we sum the quantities demanded by each market participant.

Price per Video	Quantities Demanded per Year by						
	Bob		Helen		Art		Market Demand
$5	10	+	5	+	15	=	30
4	20		10		18		48
3	30		15		21		66
2	40		20		24		84
1	50		25		27		102

(a) Individual Demand Curves

(b) Market Demand Curve

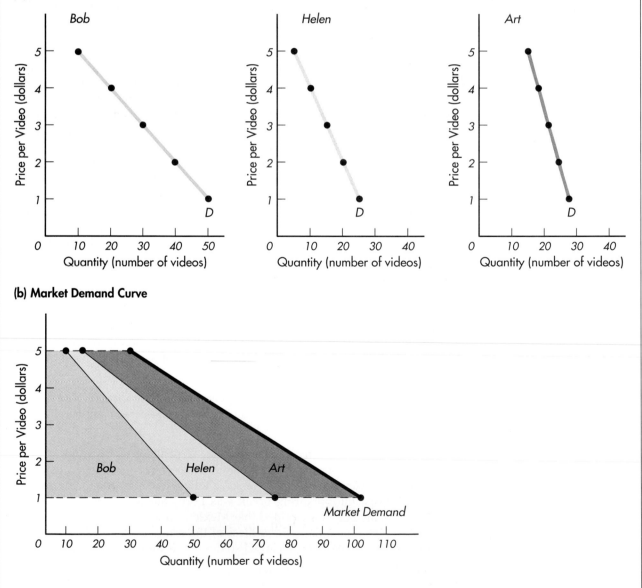

substitute goods:
items that can be used in place of each other; as the price of one rises, demand for the other falls

complementary goods:
items that are used together; as the price of one rises, demand for the other falls

purpose, then these are called **substitute goods.** Substitute goods can be used for each other, so that as the price of one rises, the demand for the other rises. Bread and crackers, BMWs and Acuras, video rentals and theater movies, universities and community colleges, Coca Cola and Pepsi are, more or less, pairs of substitutes.

If two or more goods or services are used together so that as the price of one rises, demand for the other falls, they are called **complementary goods.** Bread and margarine, beer and peanuts, cameras and film, shoes and socks, CDs and CD players, video rentals and VCRs are examples of pairs of complementary goods.

Expectations   Expectations about future events can have an effect on demand today. People make purchases today because they expect their income level to be a certain amount in the future, or they expect prices to be different in the future.

Number of Buyers   Market demand consists of the sum of the demands of all individuals. The more individuals there are with income to spend, the greater the market demand is likely to be. For example, the populations of Florida and Arizona are much larger during the winter than they are during the summer. The demand for any particular good or service in Arizona and Florida rises (the demand curve shifts to the right) during the winter and falls (the demand curve shifts to the left) during the summer.

3.f. International Effects

The law of demand says the amount of a good or service that people are willing and able to purchase during a particular period of time falls as the price rises and rises as the price falls. It does not indicate whether those people are residents of the United States or some other country. The demand for a product that is available to residents of other countries as well as to residents of the United States will consist of the sum of the demands by U.S. and foreign residents. However, because nations use different monies or currencies, the demand will be affected by the rate at which the different currencies are exchanged.

If the exchange rate changes, then the foreign price of a good produced in the United States will change. To illustrate this, let's consider an example using Levi's blue jeans sold to both U.S. and Japanese customers. The Japanese currency is the yen (¥). In January of 1996, it took 120 yen to purchase one dollar. Suppose that a pair of Levi's blue jeans is priced at $20 in the United States. That dollar price in terms of yen is ¥2,400. ¥2,400 = $20 × 120¥/$. In 1998 the exchange rate was ¥123 per dollar. The U.S. price of the blue jeans remained at $20, while in Japan, the yen value of the blue jeans rose to $20 × ¥123/$ = ¥2,460. Since the blue jeans were more expensive in Japan because of the exchange rate change, fewer Japanese consumers purchased U.S. blue jeans. Even though the U.S. price of blue jeans had not changed, the demand for U.S. blue jeans fell.

RECAP

1.   According to the law of demand, as the price of any good or service rises (falls), the quantity demanded of that good or service falls (rises) during a specific period of time, everything else held constant.

2.   A demand schedule is a listing of the quantity demanded at each price.

3.   The demand curve is a downward-sloping line plotted using the values of the demand schedule.

4.   Market demand is the sum of all individual demands.

5. Demand changes when one of the determinants of demand changes. A demand change is a shift of the demand curve.

6. The quantity demanded changes when the price of the good or service changes. This is a change from one point on the demand curve to another point on the same demand curve.

7. The determinants of demand are income, tastes, prices of related goods and services, expectations, and number of buyers.

8. The exchange rate also is a determinant of demand when a good is sold in both the United States and other countries.

4. SUPPLY

supply:
the quantities suppliers are willing and able to supply at each price

The supply of a good or service captures the behavior of the producers and sellers of that good or service. **Supply** is a relationship between the price of the good or service and the quantity of that good or service people or firms are willing and able to supply. That relationship is such a strong one that it is referred to as a law—the law of supply.

4.a. The Law of Supply

law of supply:
as the prices rises, the quantity supplied rises and vice versa

Like the law of demand, the **law of supply** also consists of five phrases:

1. the quantity of a well-defined good or service that

2. producers are willing and able to offer for sale

3. during a particular period of time

4. increases as the price of the good or service increases and decreases as the price decreases

5. everything else held constant.

The first phrase is the same as the first phrase in the law of demand. The second phrase indicates that producers must not only want to offer the product for sale but must be able to offer the product. The third phrase points out that the quantities producers will offer for sale depend on the period of time being considered. The fourth phrase points out that more will be supplied at higher than at lower prices. The final phrase ensures that the determinants of supply do not change. The **determinants of supply** are those factors that influence the willingness and ability of producers to offer their goods and services for sale—the prices of resources used to produce the product, technology and productivity, expectations of producers, the number of producers in the market, and the prices of related goods and services. If any one of these should change, supply changes.

determinants of supply:
those factors that affect supply other than price

4.b. The Supply Schedule and Supply Curve

supply schedule:
a list of prices and quantities supplied

A **supply schedule** is a table or list of the prices and the corresponding quantities supplied of a good or service. The table in Figure 5 presents MGA's supply schedule of videos. The schedule lists the quantities that MGA is willing and able to supply at each price, everything else held constant. As the price increases, MGA is willing and able to offer more videos for rent.

supply curve:
a plot of the supply schedule

A **supply curve** is a graph of the supply schedule. Figure 5 shows MGA's supply curve of videos. The price and quantity combinations given in the supply schedule correspond to the points on the curve. For instance, combination A in the table corresponds to point A on the curve; combination B in the table corresponds to point B on the curve, and so on for each price-quantity combination.

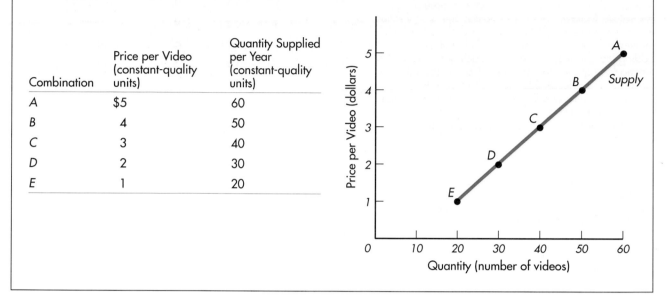

Figure 5
MGA's Supply Schedule and Supply Curve for Videos
The quantity that MGA is willing and able to offer for sale at each price is listed in the supply schedule and shown on the supply curve. At point A, the price is $5 per video and the quantity supplied is 60 videos. The combination of $4 per video and 50 videos is point B. Each price-quantity combination is plotted, and the points are connected to form the supply curve.

Combination	Price per Video (constant-quality units)	Quantity Supplied per Year (constant-quality units)
A	$5	60
B	4	50
C	3	40
D	2	30
E	1	20

4.c. From Individual Supply Curves to the Market Supply

To derive market supply, the quantities that each producer supplies at each price are added together, just as the quantities demanded by each consumer are added together to get market demand. The table in Figure 6 lists the supply schedules of three video rental stores: MGA, Motown, and Blockmaster. For our example, we assume that these three are the only video rental stores. (We are also assuming that the brand names are not associated with quality or any other differences.)

The supply schedule of each producer is plotted in Figure 6(a). Then in Figure 6(b) the individual supply curves have been added together to obtain the market supply curve. At a price of $5, the quantity supplied by MGA is 60, the quantity supplied by Motown is 30, and the quantity supplied by Blockmaster is 12. This means a total quantity supplied in the market of 102. At a price of $4, the quantities supplied are 50 by MGA, 25 by Motown, and 9 by Blockmaster for a total market quantity supplied of 84. The market supply schedule is the last column in the table. The plot of the price and quantity combinations listed in this column is the market supply curve.

4.d. Changes in Supply and Changes in Quantity Supplied

When we draw the supply curve, we allow only the price and quantity supplied of the good or service we are discussing to change. Everything else that might affect supply is assumed not to change. If any of the determinants of supply—the prices of resources used to produce the product, technology and productivity, expectations of producers, the number of producers in the market, and the prices of related goods and services—changes, the supply schedule changes and the supply curve shifts.

Prices of Resources If labor costs—one of the resources used to produce video rentals—rise, higher rental prices will be necessary to induce each store to offer as many videos as it did before the cost of the resource rose. Conversely, if resource prices decline, then supply would increase.

Figure 6
The Market Supply Schedule and Curve for Videos

The market supply is derived by summing the quantities that each producer is willing and able to offer for sale at each price. In this example, there are three producers: MGA, Motown, and Blockmaster. The supply schedules of each are listed in the table and plotted as the individual supply curves shown in Figure 6(a). By adding the quantities supplied at each price, we obtain the market supply curve shown in Figure 6(b). For instance, at a price of $5, MGA offers 60 units, Motown 30 units, and Blockmaster 12 units, for a market supply quantity of 102. The market supply curve reflects the quantities that each producer is able and willing to supply at each price.

Price per Video	Quantities Supplied per Year by			Market Supply
	MGA	Motown	Blockmaster	
$5	60 +	30 +	12 =	102
4	50	25	9	84
3	40	20	6	66
2	30	15	3	48
1	20	10	0	30

(a) Individual Supply Curves

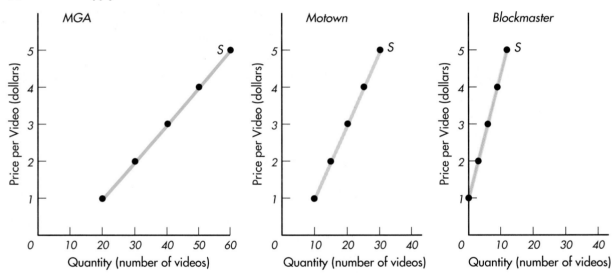

(b) Market Supply Curve

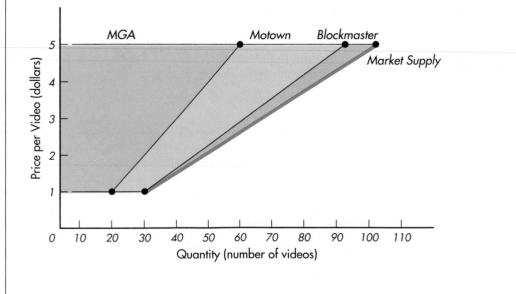

Technology and Productivity If resources are used more efficiently in the production of a good or service, more of that good or service can be supplied for the same cost—supply will rise.

Expectations of Producers Sellers may choose to alter the quantity offered for sale today because of a change in expectations regarding the determinants of supply.

Number of Producers When more producers decide to offer a good or service for sale, the market supply increases.

Prices of Related Goods or Services The opportunity cost of producing and selling any good or service is the forgone opportunity to produce any other good or service. If the price of an alternative good changes, then the opportunity cost of producing a particular good changes. This could cause the supply curve to change.

4.e. International Effects

Many firms purchase supplies from other nations or even locate factories and produce in other nations. Events in other parts of the world can influence their costs and thus the amounts they are willing and able to supply. Nike purchases its shoes from manufacturers in other parts of the world, particularly Asia, and then sells them primarily in the United States. The Malaysian currency, the Ringgit, was worth $.2291 in February 1998. If it cost Nike 261 ringgit to get the shoes manufactured in Malaysia, then that is equivalent to $60 (261 ringgit × .2291$/ringgit). The ringgit was worth $.3511 a year prior, so that the dollar cost of the shoes then was $91 (261 ringgit × .3511$/ringgit). Thus, simply because the exchange rate changed, Nike's costs fell and the quantity of shoes Nike was willing and able to offer for sale at each price rose.

RECAP

1. According to the law of supply, the quantity supplied of any good or service is directly related to the price of the good or service, during a specific period of time, everything else held constant.

2. Market supply is found by adding together the quantities supplied at each price by every producer in the market.

3. Supply changes if prices of relevant resources change, if technology or productivity changes, if producers' expectations change, if the number of producers changes, or if prices of related goods and services change.

4. Changes in supply are reflected in shifts of the supply curve. Changes in the quantity supplied are reflected in movements along the supply curve.

5. EQUILIBRIUM: PUTTING DEMAND AND SUPPLY TOGETHER

■ **equilibrium:**
the price and quantity at which demand equals supply

The demand curve shows the quantity of a good or service that buyers are willing and able to purchase at each price. The supply curve shows the quantity that producers are willing and able to offer for sale at each price. Only where the two curves intersect is the quantity supplied equal to the quantity demanded. This intersection is the point of **equilibrium.**

5.a. Determination of Equilibrium

Figure 7 brings together the market demand and market supply curves for video rentals. The supply and demand schedules are listed in the table and the curves are plotted in the graph in Figure 7. Notice that the curves intersect at only one point, labeled *e*, a price of $3 and a quantity of 66. The intersection point is the equilibrium price, the only price at which the quantity demanded and quantity supplied are the same.

■ **surplus:**
the quantity demanded is less than the quantity supplied

Whenever the price is greater than the equilibrium price, a **surplus** arises. For example, at $4, the quantity of videos demanded is 48 and the quantity supplied is 84. Thus, at $4 per video there is a surplus of 36 videos—that is, 36 videos are not rented. Conversely, whenever the price is below the equilibrium price, the quantity demanded is greater than the quantity supplied and there is a **shortage.** For instance, if the price is $2 per video, consumers will want and be able to pay for more videos than are available. As shown in the table in Figure 7, the quantity demanded at a price of $2 is 84 but the quantity supplied is only 48. There is a shortage of 36 videos at the price of $2.

■ **shortage:**
the quantity demanded is greater than the quantity supplied

Neither a surplus nor a shortage exists for long if the price of the product is free to change. Producers who are stuck with videos sitting on the shelves getting brittle and out of date will lower the price and reduce the quantities they are offering for rent in order to eliminate a surplus. Conversely, producers whose shelves are empty even as consumers demand videos will acquire more videos and raise the rental price to eliminate a shortage. Surpluses lead to decreases in the price and the quantity supplied and increases in the quantity demanded. Shortages lead to increases in the price and the quantity supplied and decreases in the quantity demanded.

5.b. Changes in the Equilibrium Price: Demand Shifts

Once a market is in equilibrium, there is no incentive for producers or consumers to move away from it. An equilibrium price changes only when demand and/or supply changes—that is, when the determinants of demand and/or the determinants of supply change.

Let's consider a change in demand and what it means for the equilibrium price. Suppose that experiments on rats show that watching videos causes brain damage. As a result, a large segment of the human population decides

Figure 7
Equilibrium
Equilibrium is established at the point where the quantity that suppliers are willing and able to offer for sale is the same as the quantity that buyers are willing and able to purchase. Here, equilibrium occurs at the price of $3 per video and the quantity of 66 videos. It is shown as point e at the intersection of the demand and supply curves. At prices above $3, the quantity supplied is greater than the quantity demanded, and the result is a surplus. At prices below $3, the quantity supplied is less than the quantity demanded, and the result is a shortage. The area shaded yellow shows all prices at which there is a surplus—where quantity supplied is greater than the quantity demanded. The surplus is measured in a horizontal direction at each price. The area shaded blue represents all prices at which a shortage exists—where the quantity demanded is greater than the quantity supplied. The shortage is measured in a horizontal direction at each price.

Price per Video	Quantity Demanded per Year	Quantity Supplied per Year	Status
$5	30	102	Surplus of 72
4	48	84	Surplus of 36
3	66	66	Equilibrium
2	84	48	Shortage of 36
1	102	30	Shortage of 72

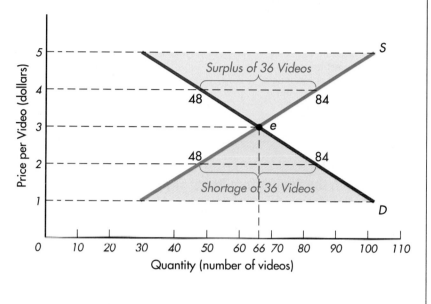

not to rent videos. Stores find that the demand for videos has decreased, as shown in Figure 8 by a leftward shift of the demand curve, from curve D_1 to curve D_2.

Once the demand curve has shifted, the original equilibrium price of $3 per video at point e_1 is no longer equilibrium. At a price of $3, the quantity supplied is still 66, but the quantity demanded has declined to 48 (look at the demand curve D_2 at a price of $3). There is, therefore, a surplus of 18 videos at the price of $3.

With a surplus comes downward pressure on the price. This downward pressure occurs because producers acquire fewer videos to offer for rent and reduce the rental price in an attempt to rent the videos sitting on the shelves. Producers continue reducing the price and the quantity available until consumers rent all copies of the videos that the sellers have available, or until a new equilibrium is established. That new equilibrium occurs at point e_2 with a price of $2.50 and a quantity of 57.

The decrease in demand is represented by the leftward shift of the demand curve. A decrease in demand results in a lower equilibrium price and a lower equilibrium quantity as long as there is no change in supply. Conversely, an increase in demand would be represented as a rightward shift of the demand curve and would result in a higher equilibrium price and a higher equilibrium quantity as long as there is no change in supply.

Figure 8
The Effects of a Shift of the Demand Curve
The initial equilibrium price ($3 per video) and quantity (66 videos) are established at point e_1, where the initial demand and supply curves intersect. A change in the tastes for videos causes demand to decrease, and the demand curve shifts to the left. At $3 per video, the initial quantity supplied, 66 videos, is now greater than the quantity demanded, 48 videos. The surplus of 18 units causes producers to reduce production and lower the price. The market reaches a new equilibrium, at point e_2, $2.50 per video and 57 videos.

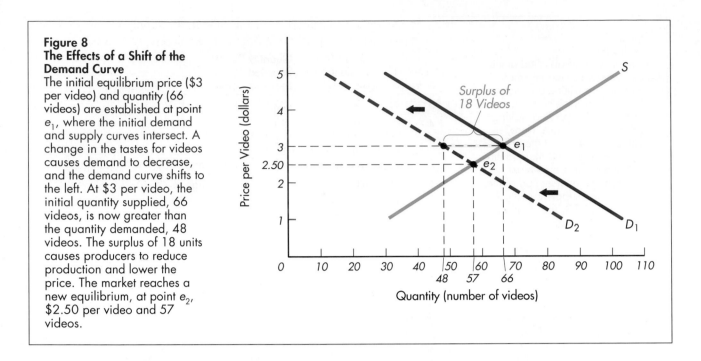

5.c. Changes in the Equilibrium Price: Supply Shifts

The equilibrium price and quantity may be altered by a change in supply as well. For example, petroleum is a key ingredient in videotapes. Suppose the quantity of oil available is reduced by 40 percent, causing the price of oil to rise. Every video manufacturer has to pay more for oil, which means that the rental stores must pay more for each videotape. To purchase the videos and offer them for rent, the rental stores must receive a higher rental price in order to cover their higher costs. This is represented by a leftward shift of the supply curve in Figure 9.

The leftward shift of the supply curve, from curve S_1 to curve S_2, leads to a new equilibrium price and quantity. At the original equilibrium price of $3 at

Figure 9
The Effects of a Shift of the Supply Curve
The initial equilibrium price and quantity are $3 and 66 units, at point e_1. When the price of labor increases, suppliers are willing and able to offer fewer videos for rent at each price. The result is a leftward (upward) shift of the supply curve, from S_1 to S_2. At the old price of $3, the quantity demanded is still 66, but the quantity supplied falls to 48. The shortage is 18 videos. The shortage causes suppliers to acquire more videos to offer for rent and to raise the rental price. The new equilibrium, e_2, the intersection between curves S_2 and D, is $3.50 per video and 57 videos.

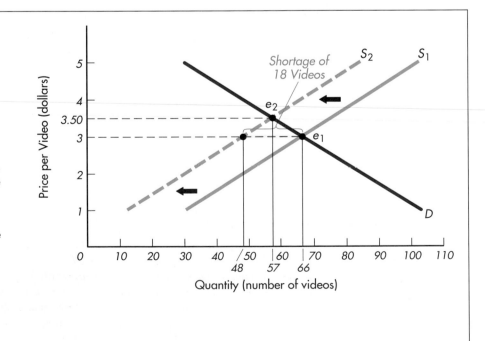

point e_1, 66 videos are supplied. After the shift in the supply curve, 48 videos are offered for rent at a price of $3 apiece, and there is a shortage of 18 videos. The shortage puts upward pressure on price. As the price rises, consumers decrease the quantities that they are willing and able to rent, and sellers increase the quantities that they are willing and able to supply. Eventually, a new equilibrium price and quantity is established at $3.50 and 57 videos at point e_2.

The decrease in supply is represented by the leftward shift of the supply curve. A decrease in supply with no change in demand results in a higher price and a lower quantity. Conversely, an increase in supply would be represented as a rightward shift of the supply curve. An increase in supply with no change in demand would result in a lower price and a higher quantity.

RECAP

1. Equilibrium occurs when quantity demanded and quantity supplied are equal: it is the price-quantity combination where the demand and supply curves intersect.

2. A price that is above the equilibrium price creates a surplus. Producers are willing and able to offer more for sale than buyers are willing and able to purchase.

3. A price that is below the equilibrium price leads to a shortage, because buyers are willing and able to purchase more than producers are willing and able to offer for sale.

4 When demand changes, price and quantity change in the same direction—both rise as demand increases and both fall as demand decreases.

5. When supply changes, price and quantity change but not in the same direction. When supply increases, price falls and quantity rises. When supply decreases, price rises and quantity falls.

SUMMARY

▬ How are goods and services allocated?

1. The allocation of scarce goods, services, and resources can be carried out in any number of ways. The market mechanism is just one possible allocation mechanism.

2. The market mechanism is the most efficient allocation mechanism in most instances.

3. There are cases where the market mechanism is not used because people do not like the result of the market allocation.

4. There are cases where the market mechanism is not used because the market mechanism is not the most efficient.

▬ What is the market process?

5. The market process refers to the interaction between buyers and sellers and how the market goes about allocating scarce resources.

6. Arbitrage is another word for the market process—the idea of seeking the best deal.

Arbitrage means buying at a low price and simultaneously selling at a higher price.

▬ What is demand?

7. Demand is the quantities that buyers are willing and able to buy at alternative prices.

8. The quantity demanded is the amount buyers are willing and able to buy at a specific price.

9. The law of demand states that as the price of a well-defined commodity rises (falls), the quantity demanded during a given period of time will fall (rise), everything else held constant.

10. Demand will change when one of the determinants of demand changes, that is, when income, tastes, prices of related goods and services, expectations, or number of buyers change. In addition, the demand may change when exchange rates change. A demand change is illustrated as a shift of the demand curve.

11. Supply is the quantities that sellers will offer for sale at alternative prices.

12. The quantity supplied is the amount sellers offer for sale at one price.

13. The law of supply states that as the price of a well-defined commodity rises (falls), the quantity supplied during a given period of time will rise (fall), everything else held constant.

14. Supply changes when one of the determinants of supply changes, that is, when prices of resources, technology and productivity, expectations of producers, the number of producers, or the prices of related goods or services change. A supply change is illustrated as a shift of the supply curve.

How is price determined by demand and supply?

15. Equilibrium is the price at which the quantity buyers are willing and able to buy equals the quantity sellers are willing and able to sell.

16. A price that is higher than equilibrium means that buyers are willing and able to buy less than sellers are willing and able to supply. This will force sellers to reduce the price.

17. A price that is lower than equilibrium means that buyers are willing and able to buy more than sellers are willing and able to supply. This will force sellers to raise the price.

What is equilibrium?

18. Together, demand and supply determine the equilibrium price and quantity.

What causes price to change?

19. A price that is above equilibrium creates a surplus, which leads to a lower price. A price that is below equilibrium creates a shortage, which leads to a higher price.

20. A change in demand or a change in supply (a shift of either curve) will cause the equilibrium price and quantity to change.

KEY TERMS

efficiency

arbitrage

demand

law of demand

demand schedule

demand curve

market demand

quantity demanded

determinants of demand

substitute goods

complementary goods

supply

law of supply

determinants of supply

supply schedule

supply curve

equilibrium

surplus

shortage

EXERCISES

1. Illustrate each of the following events using a demand and supply diagram for bananas.

   a. Reports surface that imported bananas are infected with a deadly virus.

   b. Consumers' incomes drop.

   c. The price of bananas rises.

   d. The price of oranges falls.

   e. Consumers expect the price of bananas to decrease in the future.

2. Answer true or false and if the statement is false, change it to make it true. Illustrate your answers on a demand and supply graph.

   a. An increase in demand is represented by a movement up the demand curve.

   b. An increase in supply is represented by a movement up the supply curve.

   c. An increase in demand without any changes in supply will cause the price to rise.

d. An increase in supply without any changes in demand will cause the price to rise.

3. Using the following schedule, define the equilibrium price and quantity. Plot the demand and supply curves and show the equilibrium price and quantity.

PRICE	QUANTITY DEMANDED	QUANTITY SUPPLIED
$ 1	500	100
2	400	120
3	350	150
4	320	200
5	300	300
6	275	410
7	260	500
8	230	650
9	200	800
10	150	975

4. A severe drought in California has resulted in a nearly 30 percent reduction in the quantity of citrus grown and produced in California. Explain what effect this event might have on the Florida citrus market.

5. The prices of the Ralph Lauren "Polo" line of clothing are considerably higher than comparable quality lines. Yet, it sells more than a J.C. Penney brand line of clothing. Does this violate the law of demand?

6. In December, the price of Christmas trees rises and the quantity of trees sold rises. Is this a violation of the law of demand?

7. Evaluate the following statement: "The demand for U.S. oranges has increased because the quantity of U.S. oranges demanded in Japan has risen."

8. In December 1992, the federal government began requiring that all foods display information about fat content and other ingredients on food packages. The displays had to be verified by independent laboratories. The price of an evaluation of a food product could run as much as $20,000. What impact do you think this law had on the market for meat?

9. Draw a downward-sloping demand curve and an upward-sloping supply curve for orange juice. Show what happens in each of the following cases:

   a. A freeze in Florida kills 30 percent of the oranges.

   b. A technological breakthrough has enabled Idaho to grow oranges.

   c. The supply of oranges from Mexico has been banned. The Mexican oranges accounted for about 15 percent of the market.

10. Explain what it means when the supply of television sets rises. Explain what it means when the quantity supplied of television sets rises. Explain how the price of television sets could rise and yet the supply of television sets did not change.

▢ INTERNET EXERCISE

This chapter focuses on demand and supply. Use the Internet to examine the demand for Coca-Cola. Go to the Boyes/Melvin *Fundamentals of Economics* Web site at **http://www.hmco.com/college/** and click on the Internet Exercise link for Chapter 2. Now answer the questions that appear on the Boyes/Melvin Web site.

3

Applications of Demand and Supply

---

1. What is the labor market?

2. Why have health care costs risen so much?

3. What is a price ceiling?

4. What is a price floor?

A recent newspaper article noted that the city commission that oversees the rents at mobile home parks approved a 4 percent rent increase at the Soledad Trailer Lodge, rather than the 13.7 percent hike the manager proposed. The higher increase was rejected because management had failed to take good care of the park, panel member Leslee Bowman said. "It's a slum," she said. "The roads are cracking, the septic tanks are leaking. The wiring appears to be inadequate." The landlord claims that he is losing money and yet continues to maintain facilities as much as he can.

What is the reason the landlord and tenants are fighting? What are their incentives? What do they want? The landlord wants to make money—as much as possible. The renters want quality housing that is cheap—the cheapest possible. It seems there is a conflict. But such conflicts occur all the time in a market system. Customers want quality products at low prices, and suppliers want to make huge profits. When you purchase a book, you want a quality book at a low price. When the book publishers offer their books for sale, they want to get a very high price for the books. You pay what you have to pay to get the book and the publishers sell for the prices that the books will sell at. Buyers and sellers want different things, but the result of their conflicts is a price at which the product sells.

In a market system, the interaction of buyers and sellers determines the price of products being traded. As we noted in the previous chapter, sometimes people don't like the market outcome and seek another way to allocate the same resources. In the landlord/tenant case, the market is not allowed to work. The government controls rents. Why? Because some people did not like the market outcome. What's the result of interfering with the market, that is, switching to the government as the allocator? We'll return to this question later in the chapter. Before we do that we have to understand how markets work. This means examining demand and supply.

In the previous chapter we examined a hypothetical (imaginary) market for video rentals in order to represent what goes on in real markets. We established that the rental price of the video is defined by equilibrium between demand and supply. We found that an equilibrium could be disturbed by a change in demand and/or a change in supply. Let's now look to some real markets and examine how they function. ∎

1. THE MARKET FOR FAST FOODS

Time-starved Americans now spend as much time eating out as they do eating at home. How often do you pick up a quick lunch at a Burger King or Taco Bell? In the 1950s and 1960s, this trend was just beginning. Consumers wanted more restaurants and fast-food outlets. As a result, McDonald's, Wendy's, Big Boy, White Castle, Pizza Hut, Godfather's Pizza, and other fast-food outlets flourished. The trend toward eating away from home reached a fevered pitch in the late 1970s, when the average number of meals per person eaten out (excluding brown-bag lunches and other meals prepared at home but eaten elsewhere) exceeded one per day.

In the 1980s, people wanted the fast food but didn't want to go get it. By emphasizing delivery, Domino's Pizza and a few other fast-food outlets became very successful. In the 1990s, the "takeout taxi" business—where restaurant food is delivered to homes—grew 10 percent per year.

To illustrate how resources get allocated in the market system, let's look at the market for fast foods. Figure 1 shows the market for meals eaten in restaurants. The demand curve, D_1, shows that as the price of a restaurant meal declines, the quantity of meals demanded rises. The supply curve, S,

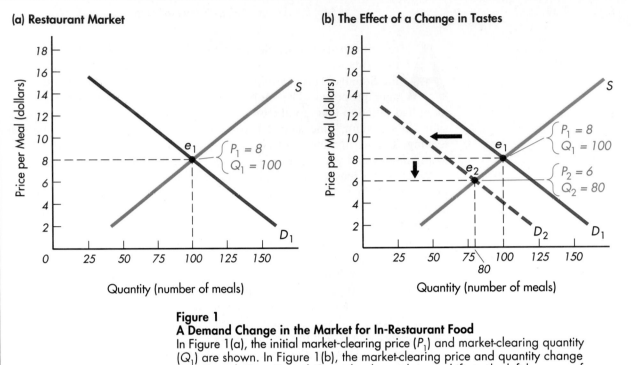

(a) Restaurant Market

(b) The Effect of a Change in Tastes

Figure 1
A Demand Change in the Market for In-Restaurant Food
In Figure 1(a), the initial market-clearing price (P_1) and market-clearing quantity (Q_1) are shown. In Figure 1(b), the market-clearing price and quantity change from P_1 and Q_1 to P_2 and Q_2 as the demand curve shifts to the left because of a change in tastes. The result of decreased demand is a lower price and a lower quantity produced.

shows that restaurants are willing to offer more meals as the price of a meal rises. The demanders are the consumers, the people who want fast food. The suppliers are the firms—Taco Bell, McDonald's, Burger King, and so on. With these demand and supply curves, the equilibrium price (P_1) is $8, and the equilibrium quantity (Q_1) is 100 units (meals) per hour. At this price-quantity combination, the number of meals demanded equals the number of meals sold; equilibrium is reached.

The second part of the figure shows what happens when consumer tastes change; people preferred to have food delivered to their homes rather than eating in a restaurant. This change in tastes caused the demand for in-restaurant meals to decline and is represented by a leftward shift of the demand curve, from D_1 to D_2, in Figure 1(b). The demand curve shifted to the left because fewer in-restaurant meals were demanded at each price. Consumer tastes, not the price of in-restaurant meals, changed first. (Remember: A price change would have led to a change in the quantity demanded and would be represented by a move along demand curve D_1, not a shift of the demand curve.) The shift from D_1 to D_2 created a new equilibrium point. The equilibrium price (P_2) decreased to $6, and the equilibrium quantity (Q_2) decreased to 80 units (meals) per hour.

While the market for in-restaurant meals was changing, so was the market for delivered food. People substituted meals delivered to their homes for meals eaten in restaurants. Figure 2(a) shows the original demand for food delivered to the home. Figure 2(b) shows a rightward shift of the demand curve, from D_1 to D_2, representing increased demand for home delivery. This demand change resulted in a higher market-clearing price for food delivered to the home, from $10 to $12.

The changing profit potential of the two markets induced existing firms to switch from in-restaurant service to home delivery and for new firms to offer delivery from the start. Domino's Pizza, which is a delivery-only firm, grew from a one-store operation to become the second largest pizza chain in the United States, with sales exceeding $2 billion per year. Little Caesar's,

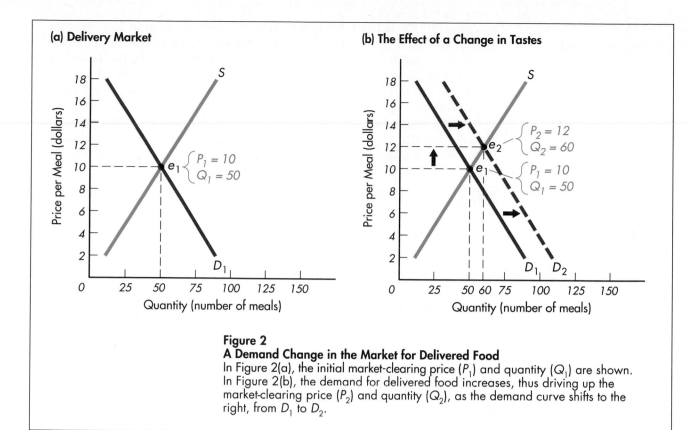

(a) Delivery Market

(b) The Effect of a Change in Tastes

Figure 2
A Demand Change in the Market for Delivered Food
In Figure 2(a), the initial market-clearing price (P_1) and quantity (Q_1) are shown. In Figure 2(b), the demand for delivered food increases, thus driving up the market-clearing price (P_2) and quantity (Q_2), as the demand curve shifts to the right, from D_1 to D_2.

another takeout chain, grew from $63.6 million in sales in 1980 to nearly $1 billion in 1987. Pizza Hut, which at first did not offer home delivery, had to play catch-up; and by 1992, about two-thirds of Pizza Hut's more than 5,000 restaurants were delivering pizza.

As the market-clearing price of in-restaurant fast food fell (from $8 to $6 in Figure 1[b]), the quantity of in-restaurant meals sold also declined (from 100 to 80) because the decreased demand, lower price, and resulting lower profit induced some firms to decrease production. In the delivery business, the opposite occurred. As the market-clearing price rose (from $10 to $12 in Figure 2[b]), the number of meals delivered also rose (from 50 to 60). The increased demand, higher price, and resulting higher profit induced firms to increase production.

Why did the production of delivered foods increase while the production of meals at restaurants decreased? Not because of government decree. Not because of the desires of the business sector, especially the owners of restaurants. The consumer made all this happen. Businesses that failed to respond to consumer desires and failed to provide the desired good at the lowest price failed to survive. Why does the consumer wield such power? The name of the game for business is profit, and the only way business can make a profit is by satisfying consumer wants. In the market system, the consumer, not the politician nor the business firm, ultimately determines what is to be produced. A firm that produces something that no consumers want will not remain in business very long. Consumer sovereignty—the authority of consumers to determine what is produced through their purchases of goods and services—dictates what goods and services will be produced.

After demand shifted to home-delivered food, the resources that had been used in the restaurants were available for use elsewhere. A few former waiters, waitresses, and cooks were able to get jobs in the delivery firms, and other employees got jobs at department stores, local pubs, and hotels. Some of the equipment used in eat-in restaurants—ovens, pots, and pans—was purchased by the delivery firms and some was sold as scrap or sold to other restaurants. Even ingredients that previously would have gone to the eat-in restaurants were bought by the delivery firms. In other words, the resources moved from an activity where their value was relatively low to an activity where they were more highly valued. No one commanded the resources to move. They moved because they could earn more in some other activity.

Markets allocate scarce goods and resources. Markets exist not only for products but also for the services of people—this is also called *labor*. (Recall that *labor* is defined in Chapter 2.) Let's turn now to the market for labor.

RECAP

1. The market price is the equilibrium price, established where demand and supply are equal.
2. If demand and/or supply changes, then the equilibrium price and the quantity purchased will change.
3. When demand changes, the price changes, the quantity produced and purchased changes, and thus the resources that are used to produce and sell the product changes.

2. THE LABOR MARKET

Older workers tend to earn higher wages than younger workers; males earn more than females; whites earn more than blacks and Hispanics; and union-ized workers earn more than nonunionized workers. Why? The answer is given in the labor market. The labor market consists of the demand for and the supply of labor.

Labor demand depends on the value of workers to the firm. How many work-ers does a firm hire? Those that bring in at least as much revenue for the firm as they cost the firm in wages and salaries would be valuable to the firm; they would be hired. The higher the price of labor (the more it costs the firm), the less labor that the firm will demand. Thus, the labor demand curve slopes down.

The labor supply comes from households. People decide whether to work and how many hours to work at each possible wage. The higher the hourly wage, the more hours that people are willing and able to work, at least up to a point. In addition, some people who would not be willing to work at a low wage may decide to enter the labor force if the wage gets high enough. This means that the labor supply curve slopes up.

The labor demand and labor supply curves are shown in Figure 3. The inter-section of the labor demand and labor supply curves determines the equilibrium wage (W_e) and the quantity of hours people work at this equilibrium wage (Q_e).

The labor market pictured in Figure 3 suggests that as long as workers are the same and jobs are the same, there will be one equilibrium wage. In fact, workers are not the same, jobs are not the same, and wages are definitely not the same. College-educated people earn more than people with only a high school education, and people with a high school education earn more than those with only a grammar school education. Riskier jobs pay more than less risky jobs. There is, in reality, a labor market for each type of worker and each type of job.

Some jobs are quite unpleasant because they are located in undesirable locations or are dangerous or unhealthy. How does a firm get someone to take a dangerous or unhealthy job? People choose to work in unpleasant occupa-tions because they earn more money. Workers mine coal, clean sewers, and weld steel beams fifty stories off the ground because, compared to alternative jobs for which they could qualify, these jobs pay well.

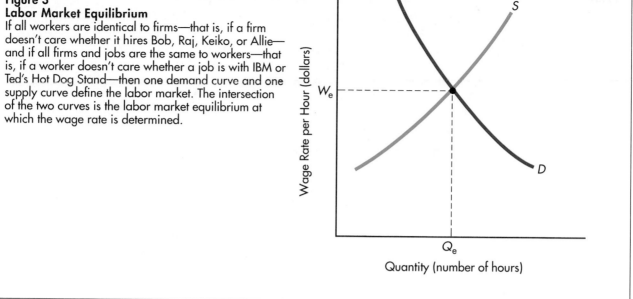

Figure 3
Labor Market Equilibrium
If all workers are identical to firms—that is, if a firm doesn't care whether it hires Bob, Raj, Keiko, or Allie—and if all firms and jobs are the same to workers—that is, if a worker doesn't care whether a job is with IBM or Ted's Hot Dog Stand—then one demand curve and one supply curve define the labor market. The intersection of the two curves is the labor market equilibrium at which the wage rate is determined.

In Figure 4, two labor markets are represented: one for a risky occupation and one for a less risky occupation. At each wage rate, fewer people are willing and able to work in the risky occupation than in the less risky occupation. Thus, if the demand curves were identical, the supply curve of the risky occupation would be above (to the left of) the supply curve of the less risky occupation. Fewer people are willing to take the riskier job than the less risky job if the riskier job pays the same as the less risky job. As a result, the equilibrium wage rate in the risky occupation, $60 per hour, is higher than the equilibrium wage rate in the less risky occupation, $35 per hour. The difference between the wage in the risky occupation and the wage in the less risky is an equilibrium differential—the compensation a worker receives for undertaking the greater risk. Unlike the restaurant versus delivered-food case in the fast-food market, this price differential will not attract more workers from the

Some jobs are more dangerous than others. Since fewer people are willing to work in dangerous jobs if they pay the same as less dangerous jobs, it is necessary for employers to pay more for dangerous jobs. To induce people to climb tall buildings to wash windows, to construct skyscrapers, or to paint the Golden Gate Bridge, the pay must be increased. Some employees undertaking risky jobs earn more in two months than they could in a year undertaking a less risky job.

(a) Risky Occupation

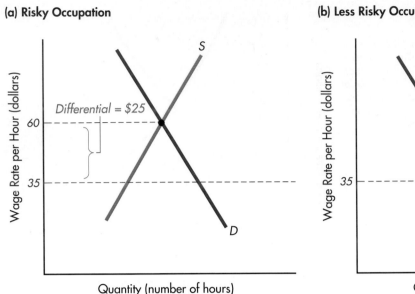

(b) Less Risky Occupation

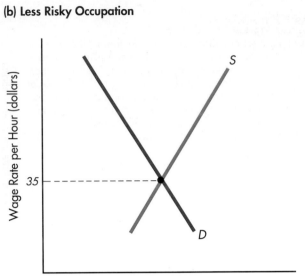

Figure 4
Compensating Wage Differential
Figure 4(a) shows the market for a risky occupation. Figure 4(b) shows the market for a less risky occupation. At each wage rate, fewer people are willing and able to work in the risky occupation than in the less risky occupation. Thus, the supply curve of the risky occupation is higher (supply is less) than the supply curve of the less risky occupation. As a result, the wage in the risky occupation ($60 per hour) is higher than the wage ($35 per hour) in the less risky occupation. The differential ($60 − $35 = $25) is an equilibrium differential—the amount necessary to induce enough people to fill the jobs. If the differential were any higher, more people would flow to the risky occupation, driving wages there down and wages in the less risky occupation up. If the differential were any lower, shortages would prevail in the risky occupation, driving wages there up.

less risky occupation to the risky one. This wage difference is an equilibrium differential—the amount needed to offset the additional risk.

Commercial deep-sea divers are exposed to the dangers of drowning and several physiological disorders as a result of compression and decompression. They choose this job because they earn about 90 percent more than the average high school graduate. Coal miners in West Virginia and in Wales in the United Kingdom are exposed to coal dust, black lung disease, and cave-ins. They choose to work in the mines because the pay is twice what they could earn elsewhere. Wage differentials ensure that deep-sea diving jobs, coal-mining jobs, and other risky occupations are filled.

Any characteristic that distinguishes one job from another may result in a **compensating wage differential**. A job that requires a great deal of travel and time away from home usually pays more than a comparable job without the travel requirements because most people find extensive travel and time away from home to be costly. If people were indifferent to travel, there would be no wage differential.

People differ with respect to their tastes for risky jobs, but they also differ with respect to their training and abilities. These differences influence the level of wages for two reasons: (1) skilled workers are more valuable to most firms than unskilled workers, and (2) the supply of skilled workers is smaller than the supply of unskilled workers because it takes time and money to acquire training and education. These things mean that skilled labor will earn higher wages than less skilled labor. For instance, in Figure 5, the skilled-labor market results in a wage of $35 per hour whereas the unskilled-labor market results in a wage of $8 per hour. The difference exists because the demand for skilled labor relative to the supply of skilled labor is greater than the demand for unskilled labor relative to the supply of unskilled labor.

■ **compensating wage differential**:
wage differences due to different risks or job characteristics

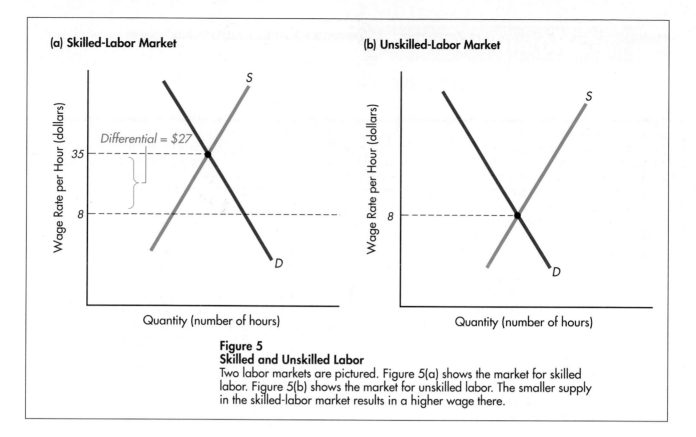

(a) Skilled-Labor Market

Wage Rate per Hour (dollars)

Differential = $27

35

8

S

D

Quantity (number of hours)

(b) Unskilled-Labor Market

Wage Rate per Hour (dollars)

8

S

D

Quantity (number of hours)

Figure 5
Skilled and Unskilled Labor
Two labor markets are pictured. Figure 5(a) shows the market for skilled labor. Figure 5(b) shows the market for unskilled labor. The smaller supply in the skilled-labor market results in a higher wage there.

RECAP

1. The labor market consists of the demand for and supply of labor.
2. The labor supply curve tends to slope up, illustrating the idea that the number of hours people are willing to work rises as the wage rate rises.
3. The labor demand curve tends to slope down, indicating that firms will employ more people or hire people to work more hours as the wage rate declines.
4. The wage rate and the quantities of workers employed are determined by equilibrium between labor demand and labor supply.
5. In reality, there are many different labor markets—markets for skilled versus unskilled labor, markets for dangerous versus nondangerous jobs, and so on.
6. An equilibrium wage differential or compensating wage differential exists when the equilibrium wage in two different labor markets is different.

3. MARKET INTERVENTION: MEDICAL CARE, RENT CONTROLS, AND AGRICULTURAL PRICE SUPPORTS

You now have an idea of how markets work to allocate scarce goods and resources. In fact, you are a participant in many markets every day even though you may not realize it. Every time you purchase something or sell something you are participating in a market. Even choosing to attend school is an activity that is part of a market—the labor market. Understanding how markets work can help us understand why the real world is like it is—help us understand important social issues like poverty, illegal drugs, discrimination, family structures, marriage, dating, divorce, and children. A market allocates

The American Girls Phenomenon

For many years the parents of daughters complained about the dearth of toys available to them. Other than Barbie, what was there? Then came the American Girls, a collection of historical dolls made by Pleasant Company, each with a series of books describing her place in history. Girls love the dolls; nearly 4 million of them were sold in the past 11 years. In addition to the dolls, the Pleasant Company sold clothes, accessories, furniture, craft kits, and even matching clothes in real-girl sizes.

The Pleasant Company dolls were so successful that competitors began to offer their own collections, each with a distinct twist. Like the American Girls, the dolls are sold exclusively by mail order, and each comes with its own predetermined, fantasy history. There's Global Friends, which spins stories about girls from different cultures. Just Pretend, Inc., offers Laurel the Woodfairy with her own trellis and lute and Alissa the Princess with an armoire and a throne. My Twinn dolls are custom made to match photographs of their owners, down to the shape of their eyebrows and placement of freckles. Savannah and her friends from Storybook Heirlooms each have a distinct personality.

Many of these dolls are sized just differently enough that their expensive clothes won't fit on rival collections. The 18-inch American Girls dolls, for example, are too chubby to fit into the clothes made for the more svelte 18-inch Magic Attic Club dolls. The Little Women dolls are 16 inches tall. My Twinn is 23 inches. Global Friends dolls are only 14 inches.

Demand for these dolls seems to have topped out and, as a result, additional companies are not entering the market. Domestic doll sales reached $2.73 billion in 1996, up just slightly from $2.52 billion the year before. American Girls and Mattel, Inc.'s Barbie control more than 40 percent of the U.S. market. Barbie's annual sales of almost $900 million are more than three times larger than those of Pleasant Company's American Girls, which in turn overshadows it competitors.

The doll story illustrates the market process. For years, there was only Barbie—a doll with dimensions that no real person could achieve and which focused on no intellectual aspects. Then an entrepreneur (Pleasant Company) comes up with a new product—American Girls dolls and the whole package of highly readable, fictionalized history books, clothes, and accessories—and is very successful. Other entrepreneurs see the success and want to get in on the good thing. They begin copycat companies, but to be successful they have to be slightly different. In this case, the dolls are different sizes and have different stories than the American Girls. The success of Pleasant Company attracted new resources to the market—new companies. New companies with different approaches continued to enter the doll market until the potential for success looked no better than other industries, and the market topped out.

scarce goods and resources to their highest-valued uses. Markets function to serve the interests of consumers, ensuring that consumers get what they want at the lowest possible prices.

Yet markets are not always allowed to function. Often the government is called on to intervene in the market, perhaps ensuring that the equilibrium price won't be too high or too low. In this section, we'll consider three important areas where government intervention in the market has been pervasive—medical care, rental housing, and agriculture.

3.a. The Market for Medical Care

One of the issues of greatest concern to people in the last five years or so has been the cost of medical care. Since 1990, medical care costs have risen more than 15 percent per year. Let's look at the market for medical care to see if we can understand why the costs have risen so dramatically.

Equilibrium in a market determines the price (P) and the quantity (Q) purchased/sold. Thus, equilibrium also determines total expenditures (price times quantity [$P \times Q$]). Total expenditures on health care have risen tremendously during the past three decades. In the health care market, rising costs or expenditures mean that the demand for medical care has risen relative to supply.

The population of the United States and other industrial nations is aging. The increase in the number of elderly means an increase in the demand for medical care. The question facing many societies, therefore, is how to allocate the scarce resource of medical care to those who need it.

This means either that demand has increased more than supply or that supply has decreased more than demand.

Suppose the initial demand for medical care is D_1, and the supply of medical care is S_1 in Figure 6. The intersection between demand and supply determines the price of medical care, P_1. Total expenditures are just P_1 times Q_1.

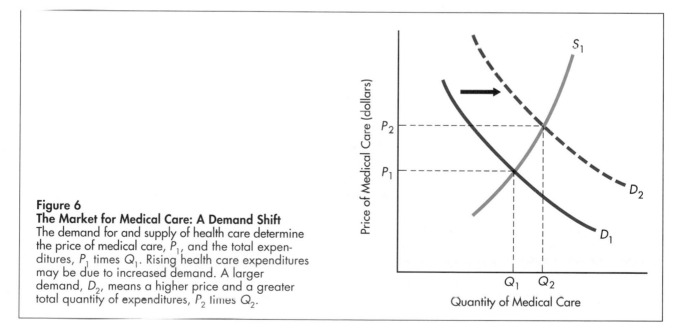

Figure 6
The Market for Medical Care: A Demand Shift
The demand for and supply of health care determine the price of medical care, P_1, and the total expenditures, P_1 times Q_1. Rising health care expenditures may be due to increased demand. A larger demand, D_2, means a higher price and a greater total quantity of expenditures, P_2 times Q_2.

An increase in demand is shown as the outward shift of the demand curve, from D_1 to D_2. This demand increase results in the price of medical care rising from P_1 to P_2. The quantity of medical care purchased and sold also rises, from Q_1 to Q_2. Total expenditures on medical care therefore rise from P_1 times Q_1 to P_2 times Q_2.

Even if the demand curve for medical care was not shifting outward rapidly, the cost of medical care could be forced up by an upward shift of the supply curve, as shown in Figure 7. The supply curve shifts in from S_1 to S_2 resulting in an increase in the equilibrium price to P_2. Notice, however, that the smaller supply need not mean higher total expenditures on medical care because $P_1 \times Q_1$ may be larger than $P_2 \times Q_2$. Since it is rising total expenditures we are trying to understand, we should look to an increase in demand rather than a decrease in supply.

What accounts for the rising demand relative to supply?

3.a.1. Demand Increase   The aging of the population stimulates the demand for health care. The elderly consume four times as much health care per capita as the rest of the population. About 90 percent of the expenditures for nursing home care are for persons sixty-five or over, a group that constitutes only 12 percent of the population. The elderly (sixty-five or older) currently account for 35 percent of hospital expenditures. In contrast, the young, although they constitute 29 percent of the population, consume only 11 percent of hospital care. Per capita spending on personal health care for those eighty-five years of age or over is 2.5 times that for people age sixty-five to sixty-nine years. For hospital care, per capita consumption is twice as great for those age eighty-five or over as for those age sixty-five to sixty-nine; for nursing home care, it is 23 times as great.

For demand to increase, the elderly must be both *willing to buy medical care and able to pay for it.* This is where the government comes in. The gen-

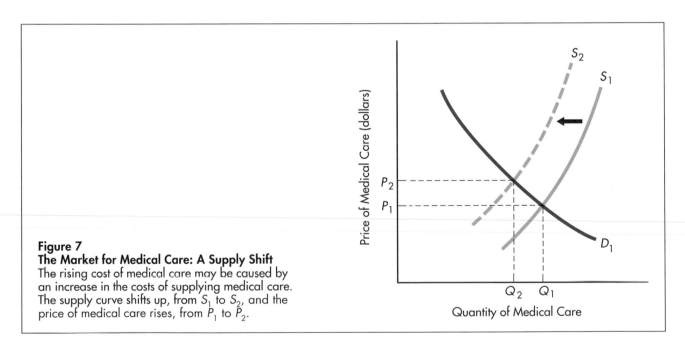

Figure 7
The Market for Medical Care: A Supply Shift
The rising cost of medical care may be caused by an increase in the costs of supplying medical care. The supply curve shifts up, from S_1 to S_2, and the price of medical care rises, from P_1 to P_2.

eral public believes that it has a right to decent medical care and voted for those legislators who would support this belief. The result was Medicare and Medicaid, government programs that purchased medical care for the aged and those unable to afford medical care.

The emergence of Medicare and Medicaid in 1966 gave many elderly the ability to purchase medical care. These government programs pay for medical expenses. The government collects the money with which to pay for the programs using general payroll taxes. This means that many people are able to get medical care without having to pay for it. In any market, if the demanders don't have to pay for the goods and services, they will demand a lot more. This is what has happened in the market for medical care.

The effect of the Medicare and Medicaid programs has been to increase the demand for services. Private sources pay for only about 55 percent of personal health care for the general population, and Medicare and Medicaid pick up most of the remainder. For the elderly, the private share of spending is only 15 percent for hospital care, 36 percent for physicians' services, and 58 percent for nursing home care. Medicaid and Medicare pick up the rest.

3.b. Price Ceilings: The Market for Rental Housing

Equilibrium is established by the interaction of buyers and sellers; the market price and the quantity produced and sold are defined at the point where the demand and supply curves intersect. Looking at last year's sweaters piled up on the sale racks, waiting over an hour for a table at a restaurant, finding that the VCR rental store never has a copy of the movie you want to rent in stock, or hearing that 5 or 6 percent of people willing and able to work are unemployed may make you wonder whether equilibrium is ever established. In fact, it is not uncommon to observe situations where quantities demanded and supplied are not equal. But this observation does not cast doubt on the usefulness of the equilibrium concept. Even if all markets do not reach equilibrium all the time, we can be reasonably assured that market forces are operating so that the market is moving toward an equilibrium. The market forces exist even when the price is not allowed to change.

■ **price ceiling**: price is not allowed to rise above a specific level

A **price ceiling** is the situation where a price is not allowed to rise to its equilibrium level. Los Angeles, San Francisco, and New York are among over 125 U.S. cities that have rent controls. A rent control law places a ceiling on the rents that landlords can charge for apartments. Figure 8 is a demand and supply graph representing the market for apartments in New York. The equilibrium price is $3,000 a month. The government has set a price of $1,500 a month as the maximum that can be charged. The price ceiling is shown by the solid yellow line. At the rent control price of $1,500 per month, 3,000 apartments are available but consumers want 6,000 apartments. There is a shortage of 3,000 apartments.

The shortage means that not everyone willing and able to rent the apartment will be allowed to. Since the price is not allowed to ration the apartments, something else will have to. It may be that those willing and able to stand in line the longest get the apartments. Perhaps bribing an important official might be the way to get an apartment. Perhaps relatives of officials or important citizens will get the apartments. Whenever a price ceiling exists, a shortage results and some rationing device other than price will arise.

Had the government set the rent control price at $4,000 per month, the price ceiling would not have had an effect. Since the equilibrium is $3,000 a month, the price would not have risen to $4,000. Only if the price ceiling is below the equilibrium price will it be an effective price ceiling.

Price ceilings are not uncommon features in the United States or in other economies. China had a severe housing shortage for thirty years because the price of housing was kept below equilibrium. Faced with unhappy citizens and realizing the cause of the shortage, officials began to lift the restrictions

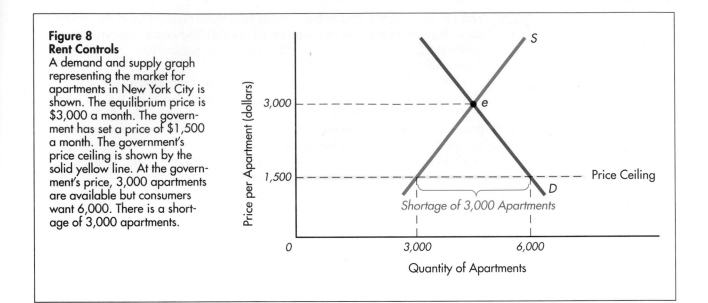

Figure 8
Rent Controls
A demand and supply graph representing the market for apartments in New York City is shown. The equilibrium price is $3,000 a month. The government has set a price of $1,500 a month. The government's price ceiling is shown by the solid yellow line. At the government's price, 3,000 apartments are available but consumers want 6,000. There is a shortage of 3,000 apartments.

on housing prices in 1985. The shortage has diminished. In the former Soviet Union, prices on all goods and services were defined by the government. For most consumer items, the price was set below equilibrium; shortages existed. The long lines of people waiting to purchase food or clothing were the result of the price ceilings on all goods and services. In the United States, price ceilings on all goods and services have been imposed at times. During the First and Second World Wars and during the Nixon administration of the early 1970s, wage and price controls were imposed. These were price ceilings on all goods and services. As a result of the ceilings, people were unable to purchase many of the products they desired. The Organization of Petroleum Exporting Countries (OPEC) restricted the quantity of oil in the early 1970s and drove its price up considerably. The United States government responded by placing a price ceiling on gasoline. The result was long lines at gas stations—shortages of gasoline.

3.c. Price Floors: The Market for Agricultural Products

■ **price floor**:
price is not allowed to fall below a specific level

Price floors are quite common features in economies as well. A **price floor** is the situation where the price is not allowed to decrease below a certain level. Consider Figure 9 representing the market for sugar. The equilibrium price of sugar is $.10 a pound, but because the government has set a price floor of $.20 a pound, as shown by the solid yellow line, the price is not allowed to move to its equilibrium level. A surplus of 250,000 pounds of sugar results from the price floor. Sugar growers produce 1 million pounds of sugar and consumers purchase 750,000 pounds of sugar.

We saw previously that whenever the price is above the equilibrium price, market forces work to decrease the price. The price floor interferes with the functioning of the market; a surplus exists because the government will not allow the price to drop. How does the government ensure that the price floor remains in force? In the case of sugar, the government has to purchase the excess. The government must purchase the surplus so that its price floor of $.20 per pound remains in force.

What would occur if the government had set the price floor at $.09 a pound? Since at $.09 a pound a shortage of sugar would result, the price

Figure 9
A Price Floor
The equilibrium price of sugar is $.10 a pound, but because the government has set a price floor of $.20 a pound, as shown by the solid yellow line, the price is not allowed to move to its equilibrium level. A surplus of 250,000 pounds of sugar results from the price floor. Sugar growers produce 1 million pounds of sugar and consumers purchase 750,000 pounds of sugar.

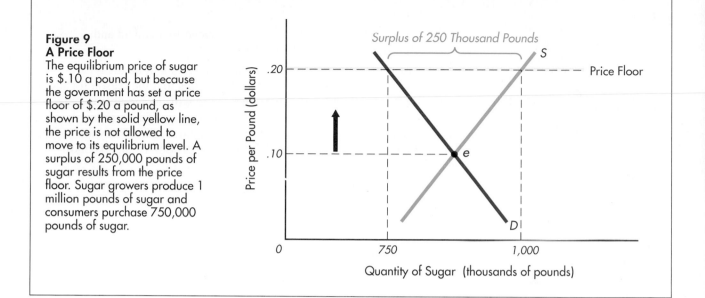

would rise. A price floor only keeps the price from falling, not rising. So the price rises to its equilibrium level of $.10. Only if the price floor is set above the equilibrium price is it an effective price floor.

The agricultural policies of most of the developed nations are founded on price floors the government guarantees that the price of an agricultural product will not fall below some level. Price floors result in surpluses, and this has been the case with many agricultural products. The surpluses in agricultural products in the United States have resulted in cases where dairy farmers dumped milk in the river, where grain was given to other nations at taxpayer expense, and where citrus ranchers picked and then discarded thousands of tons of citrus, all to reduce huge surpluses.

Here we see that a price floor leads to a surplus of blood oranges. The question is how to dispose of the surplus. In many nations the government purchases it. In Sicily, however, the least-cost solution may have been simply to dump the oranges

RECAP

1. Every important event in our life can be described by demand and supply—that is, occurs within a market.

2. One topic of principal interest has been the rising cost of medical care. The analysis of the market for medical care reveals that the reason for the rising costs is a rising demand. More people are willing and able to purchase more medical care than has occurred in the past. They are more willing because they are older and need more medical care. They are more able because government pays for a rising portion of the expenditures.

3. Another pervasive intervention in markets is the price ceiling—the imposition of a limit on how high a price can go. The price ceiling leads to shortages and the use of alternative allocation mechanisms.

4. Price floors are imposed quite often as well. In the agricultural area, it is quite common for the producers to be guaranteed a certain price for their products; the price can not fall below that certain price. Price floors lead to surpluses.

SUMMARY

▪▪ What is the labor market?

1. The labor market consists of the demand for and supply of labor.

2. The wage rate and the quantities of workers employed are determined by equilibrium between labor demand and labor supply.

3. In reality, there are many different labor markets—markets for skilled versus unskilled labor, markets for dangerous versus non-dangerous jobs, and so on.

4. An equilibrium wage differential or compensating wage differential exists when the equilibrium wage in two different labor markets is different.

▪▪ Why have health care costs risen so much?

5. The analysis of the market for medical care reveals that the reason for the rising costs is a rising demand. More people are willing and able to purchase more medical care than has occurred in the past. They are more willing because they are older and need more medical care. They are more able because government pays for a rising portion of the expenditures.

▪▪ What is a price ceiling?

6. A price ceiling is a limit on how high the price can be, which means it is set below the equilibrium price. This creates a shortage.

▪▪ What is a price floor?

7. A price floor is a limit on how low the price can be, which means it is set above the equilibrium price. This creates a surplus.

KEY TERMS

compensating wage differential
price ceiling

price floor

EXERCISES

1. Using the following schedule, define the equilibrium price and quantity. Describe the situation at a price of $10. What will occur? Describe the situation at a price of $2. What will occur?

Price	Quantity Demanded	Quantity Supplied
$ 0	500	100
2	400	120
3	350	150
4	320	200
5	300	300
6	275	410
7	260	500
8	230	650
9	200	800
10	150	975

2. Suppose the government imposed a minimum price of $7 in the schedule of question 1. What would occur? Illustrate.

3. Using the data of question 1, indicate what the price would have to be to represent an effective price ceiling. Point out the surplus or shortage that results. Illustrate a price floor and provide an example of a price floor.

4. A common feature of skiing is waiting in lift lines. Does the existence of lift lines mean that the price is not working to allocate the scarce resource? If so, what should be done about it?

5. Many restaurants don't take reservations. You simply arrive and wait your turn. If you arrive at 7:30 in the evening, you have at least an hour wait. Notwithstanding that fact, a few people arrive, speak quietly with the maitre d', hand him some money, and are promptly seated. At some restaurants that do take reservations, there is a month wait for a Saturday evening, three weeks for a Friday evening, two weeks for Tuesday through Thursday, and virtually no wait for Sunday or Monday evening. How do you explain these events using demand and supply?

6. Give an example of a compensating wage differential in your community. What does it mean?

7. The federal government is trying to change Medicare because it is too expensive. Yet, many senior citizens are upset that the government is trying to change matters. Why would the senior citizens be upset? Using demand and supply, explain what would happen if the government reduced how much it would pay for medical care.

INTERNET EXERCISE

This chapter focuses on labor markets. Use the Internet to explore labor markets in more detail. Go to the Boyes/Melvin _Fundamentals of Economics_ Web site at http://www.hmco.com/college/ and click on the Internet Exercise link for Chapter 3. Now answer the questions that appear on the Boyes/Melvin Web site.

II

Consumers, Firms, and Social Issues

4

The Firm and the Consumer

1. What are total, average, and marginal revenue?

2. Do consumers respond to price changes?

3. What is the relationship between revenue and the price elasticity of demand?

Preview

The owners of a business want that business to make a profit—to sell enough products at a high enough price that the firm can pay its costs and have some money remaining. In the next few chapters we examine how firms attempt to earn profits. We do this in three steps. The first step, taken in this chapter, is to discuss revenue. The second step is to examine costs and the third step is to put revenue and cost together. After all, profit is revenue minus costs. The second and third steps are undertaken in the next chapter. ∎

1. REVENUE

■ **total revenue:**
price times quantity sold

Firms earn revenue by selling goods and services to consumers. **Total revenue** is the price a product sells for multiplied by the number of units of the product that is sold ($P \times Q$). How does a firm know the price to charge and the quantity to produce and/or offer for sale? It must know what the demand for its goods and services is. Demand is a relationship between price and quantity; it tells the firm how much it could sell at each price. Thus, the firm will know what its revenue will be at each price if it knows what the demand for its goods and services is.

1.a. Total, Average, and Marginal Revenue

Let's use the table in Figure 1 to discuss revenue for a bicycle store. Column 1 is the total quantity (Q) of bikes sold. Column 2 is price (P). If the price is $1,700, 1 bike is sold. To sell 2 bikes, the store has to lower the price to $1,600. If the price is $1,500, 3 bikes are sold, and so on.

Total revenue (TR) is found by multiplying the quantity of bikes sold by the price each bike is sold for. If only 1 bike is to be sold, the price is $1,700, and total revenue is $1,700. If 2 bikes are to be sold, the store must lower the price to $1,600 apiece, and total revenue is $3,200. If 3 bikes are to be sold, then the price must be lowered to $1,500 apiece, and total revenue is $4,500.

Columns 4 and 5 present two very useful pieces of information: average and marginal revenue. **Average revenue (AR)** is the per unit revenue, the total revenue divided by the total number of bikes sold. Average revenue is listed in column 4. For the first bike, total revenue is $1,700, and average revenue is $1,700. For 2 bikes, total revenue is $3,200, and average revenue is $1,600. For 3 bikes, total revenue is $4,500, and average revenue is $1,500.

■ **average revenue:**
per unit revenue, total revenue divided by quantity

■ **marginal revenue:**
incremental revenue, change in total revenue divided by change in quantity

Marginal revenue (MR) is the incremental revenue, the additional revenue from selling one more unit of output. Marginal revenue is listed in the fifth column. The marginal revenue of the first bike sold is the *change* in revenue that the firm receives for increasing its sales from 0 to 1 unit. When sold, the first bike brings in $1,700 in revenue, so the marginal revenue is $1,700. The marginal revenue of the second bike sold is the *change* in revenue that the firm receives for increasing its sales from 1 to 2 bikes. The second bike brings in an additional $1,500 in revenue, so the marginal revenue of the second bike is $1,500. The third bike brings in an additional $1,300 in revenue, so the marginal revenue of the third bike is $1,300.

You might have noticed that average revenue is just demand; compare columns 2 and 4 and you'll see that they are the same. So demand provides a great deal of information. It tells us what total revenue is— it is average revenue—and it allows us to calculate the marginal revenue.

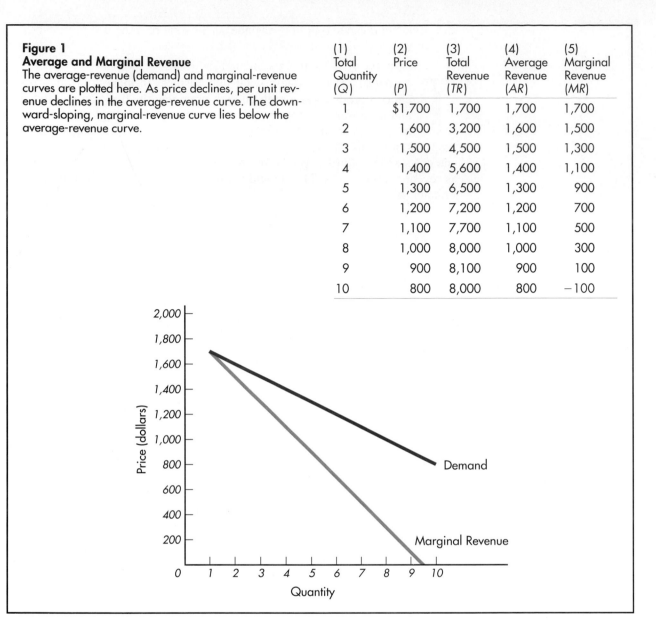

Figure 1
Average and Marginal Revenue
The average-revenue (demand) and marginal-revenue curves are plotted here. As price declines, per unit revenue declines in the average-revenue curve. The downward-sloping, marginal-revenue curve lies below the average-revenue curve.

(1) Total Quantity (Q)	(2) Price (P)	(3) Total Revenue (TR)	(4) Average Revenue (AR)	(5) Marginal Revenue (MR)
1	$1,700	1,700	1,700	1,700
2	1,600	3,200	1,600	1,500
3	1,500	4,500	1,500	1,300
4	1,400	5,600	1,400	1,100
5	1,300	6,500	1,300	900
6	1,200	7,200	1,200	700
7	1,100	7,700	1,100	500
8	1,000	8,000	1,000	300
9	900	8,100	900	100
10	800	8,000	800	−100

You may also have wondered why a firm would care about its average or marginal revenue. Because, as you'll see in the next chapter, average and marginal revenue are very useful managerial tools. They help determine the price to charge and the quantity to offer for sale, which helps determine profit.

The average- and marginal-revenue schedules are plotted in Figure 1. The average-revenue (demand) curve slopes down, indicating that as the price declines, the per unit revenue declines. The marginal-revenue curve also slopes down. It is steeper than the average-revenue curve and lies below it. The marginal-revenue curve is steeper than the average-revenue curve because each additional bike sold brings in less additional revenue than did the previous bike.

RECAP

1. Total revenue is the quantity sold multiplied by the price at which each unit sold.

2. Average revenue (per unit revenue) is the total revenue divided by the number of units sold.

3. Marginal revenue is the incremental revenue, the additional revenue obtained by selling one more unit of output.

4. Average revenue is the same as demand.

2. HOW DOES A FIRM LEARN ABOUT ITS DEMAND?

Demand provides a great deal of information to a business and is something the firm has to know about. There are several ways that a business can learn about the demand for its goods and services. One approach you've probably run across is a survey. Polling organizations are hired by firms to ask consumers questions about demand. You may see the surveys conducted in malls where passers-by are asked a series of questions about a product, or you may get a phone call—usually at dinner time—from a telemarketer.

Another type of survey is called the focus group. A focus group usually consists of several randomly chosen shoppers who are paid to spend a few minutes completing questionnaires or answering questions.

Another approach to obtaining information about demand is to use actual experience. A firm that has been in business for a period of time can use its actual experience to map out its demand—comparing past prices and quantities demanded, levels of income, number of customers, changes in the season, and so on. A new firm might have to rely on the experiences of other firms, using the prices and quantities demanded of a firm with a similar product that has been in business for a period of time. A firm offering a new product might do a test trial, introducing the product in just one city. This allows the firm to learn about the relationship between price and quantity demanded before it introduces the product nationwide.

Many firms have instituted information retrieval or inventory control systems that record demand information on a continuous basis. Wal-Mart was one of the first firms to do this. Its scanning devices at the check-out register are connected to a computer that communicates with another computer at central headquarters. The system keeps track of sales and prices and orders more inventory when necessary.

2.a. Example: Demand for Auto Safety

In the late 1980s, when auto companies were trying to decide whether to introduce air bags, they wondered how the bags would affect demand. GM, for instance, argued that people would not pay more for a car with an air bag. The auto companies turned to consumer surveys to estimate the demand for the safety features. Based on a poll of 200 large fleet buyers, GM found that 33 percent were willing to buy the air bag only if the cost was $50 or less, an additional 28 percent were willing to pay as much as $100, and 19 percent more were willing to pay up to $150. Only 20 percent were willing to pay more than $200 for the air-bag option. As a result, GM offered the air bags on only 20 percent of its models.

Ford, on the other hand, conducted a market experiment by introducing the air bags on one model but not on a similar model to see how consumers would respond. The higher price on the air-bag model did not affect sales as much as the GM survey indicated. As a result, Ford introduced the air bags on more models than GM did.

2.b. Example: Demand for Oranges

Researchers from the University of Florida examined the competition between California and Florida Valencia oranges. The researchers convinced nine supermarkets in Grand Rapids, Michigan to vary the prices charged for Florida and California Valencia oranges daily for 31 days. More than 9,250 dozen oranges were sold during the time period. The researchers found that people preferred the Florida oranges but were very sensitive to price differences. A small price increase would cause consumers to purchase California rather than Florida oranges.

2.c. Example: Location

Researchers from Arizona State University and Harvard University investigated whether it made a difference to product sales whether the product was located near the front of the store in a display by itself or placed on shelves with other products. The researchers set up various displays and then introduced a select group of customers to the displays. The focus groups—the groups of potential customers—indicated that they would purchase more of the product when it was placed in a display by itself and the display was located near the front of the store than if it were located on shelves mixed in with other products.

RECAP

1. Firms utilize several methods to gather information about their customers—that is, to learn about demand.
2. Surveys, opinion polls, telemarketing, and focus groups all provide information related to what people say they will do in various circumstances.
3. Actual data based on experience may be used to infer information about demand.
4. Instantaneous information such as that provided by scanning devices connected to computers can provide useful information about demand.

3. KNOWING THE CUSTOMER

We've talked about how demand provides useful information to a business about revenue. But we've only touched the surface. Demand provides a great deal more information about revenue than we've discussed to this point.

Suppose you are in charge of setting the price of McDonald's Big Mac. McDonald's has not been doing well lately. Burger King has been grabbing more and more of the fast-food hamburger market. You have correctly reasoned that you should lower the price of the Big Mac to increase sales. The

In the past decade, U.S. consumers have dramatically switched their consumption from beef to fish. The doubling of the amount of fish consumed has led to an expansion of the fish-producing industry. Most fish consumed are not caught in oceans or rivers but are grown on farms, such as this one in Caldwell, Idaho. As demand rises, prices rise, and existing producers earn above-normal profits. Entry is relatively easy in the industry, so new farms are built and existing farms expand.

problem is you don't know how much to lower it. Should the price be $.99 or $.85 or $.55? The answer depends on how consumers respond to the price change. Economists have devised a measure of how much consumers alter their purchases in response to price changes. This measure is called the price elasticity of demand.

3.a. The Price Elasticity of Demand

■ **price elasticity of demand:**
the percentage change in quantity demanded divided by the percentage change in price

The **price elasticity of demand** is a measure of the magnitude by which consumers alter the quantity of some product they purchase in response to a change in the price of that product. The more price-elastic demand is, the more responsive consumers are to a price change—that is, the more consumers will adjust their purchases of a product when the price of that product changes. Conversely, the less price-elastic demand is, the less responsive consumers are to a price change.

The price elasticity of demand is defined as the percentage change in the quantity demanded of a product divided by the percentage change in the price of that product.

$$e_d = \frac{\text{percent change in quantity demanded}}{\text{percent change in price}}$$

■ **elastic:**
price elasticity greater than 1

■ **unit elastic:**
price elasticity equal to 1

■ **inelastic:**
price elasticity less than 1

Demand can be **elastic**, **unit elastic**, or **inelastic**. Because the price elasticity is always a negative number, we ignore the negative sign. Thus, we say that when the price elasticity of demand is greater than 1, demand is elastic. For instance, if the quantity of videotapes that are rented falls by 3 percent whenever the price of a videotape rental rises by 1 percent, the price elasticity of demand for videotape rentals is 3.

$$e_d = \frac{3 \text{ percent}}{1 \text{ percent}} = 3$$

When the price elasticity of demand is 1, demand is said to be unit elastic. For example, if the price of private education rises by 1 percent and the quantity of private education purchased falls by about 1 percent, the price elasticity of demand is 1.

$$e_d = \frac{1 \text{ percent}}{1 \text{ percent}} = 1$$

When the price elasticity of demand is less than 1, demand is said to be inelastic. In this case, a 1 percent rise in price brings forth a smaller than 1 percent decline in quantity demanded. For example, if the price of gasoline rises by 1 percent and the quantity of gasoline purchased falls by .2 percent, the price elasticity of demand is .2.

$$e_d = \frac{.2 \text{ percent}}{1 \text{ percent}} = .2$$

■ **perfectly elastic:**
price elasticity is infinite

3.a.1. Price Elasticity and Shape of the Demand Curve The shape of a demand curve depends on the price elasticity of demand. A **perfectly elastic** demand curve is a horizontal line that shows that consumers can purchase any quantity they want at the single price (P_1) shown in Figure 2(a). An example of a perfectly elastic demand might be the demand for disk drives in PCs. There are quite a few disk drive manufacturers, and the PC manufacturers do not care which they install in their machines; consumers have no idea which disk drive company produced their drives. As a result, if the price of one brand of disk drives is increased, the PC manufacturers are likely to move to another brand of disk drive. A perfectly elastic demand means that even the smallest price change will cause consumers to change their consumption by a huge amount, in fact, totally switching purchases to the producer with the lowest prices.

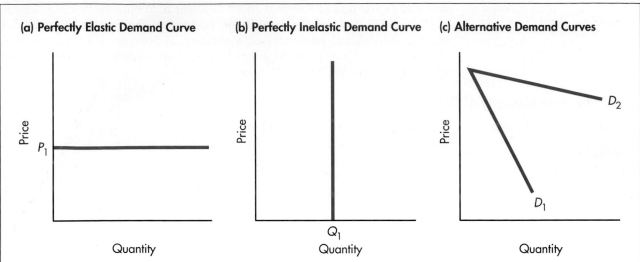

(a) Perfectly Elastic Demand Curve   **(b) Perfectly Inelastic Demand Curve**   **(c) Alternative Demand Curves**

Price

P_1

Quantity

Price

Q_1

Quantity

Price

D_2

D_1

Quantity

Figure 2(a)
Perfectly Elastic Demand
The quantity demanded varies from zero to infinity at the one price. At any other price there is no quantity demanded. Demand is so sensitive to price that even an infinitesimal change leads to a total change in quantity demanded.

Figure 2(b)
Perfectly Inelastic Demand
The quantity demanded is the same no matter the price. Demand is completely insensitive to price.

Figure 2(c)
Alternative Demand Curves
D_1 and D_2 represent straight, downward-sloping demand curves. The price elasticity of demand varies along a straight line curve. D_2 is said to be more elastic than D_1 because at every single price the elasticity of demand is higher at D_2 than at D_1.

■ **perfectly inelastic:**
price elasticity is zero

A **perfectly inelastic** demand curve is a vertical line, illustrating the idea that consumers cannot or will not change the quantity of a product they purchase when the price of the product is changed. Perhaps insulin to a person inflicted with diabetes is a reasonably vivid example of a product whose demand is perfectly inelastic. The diabetic would pay almost any price to get the quantity (Q_1) needed to remain healthy. Figure 2(b) shows a perfectly inelastic demand curve.

In between the two extreme shapes of demand curves are the demand curves for most products. Figure 2(c) illustrates two demand curves. One is a relatively flat line (D_2), and the other is a relatively steep line (D_1). D_2 is said to be more price-elastic than D_1.

3.b. Price Elasticity and Revenue

Why is the price elasticity of demand an important piece of information? It tells us how consumers will react to a price change. This means it also tells us what will happen to revenue as the price is increased or decreased.

The price elasticity of demand tells us if a price change will increase or decrease revenue. We know that total revenue (*TR*) is the price of a product multiplied by the quantity sold: $TR = P \times Q$. We also know that when the price goes up the quantity demanded declines and vice versa. So, whether total revenue increases or decreases when the price changes depends on which changes more, the price or the quantity demanded.

If *P* rises by 10 percent and *Q* falls by more than 10 percent, then total revenue declines as a result of the price rise. If *P* rises by 10 percent and *Q* falls by less than 10 percent, then total revenue rises as a result of the price rise. If *P* increases by 10 percent and *Q* falls by 10 percent, total revenue does not change as the price changes. *Thus, total revenue increases as price is*

Does Money Buy Happiness?

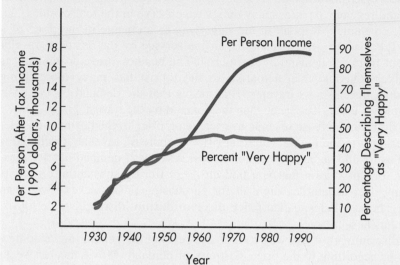

Are the rich happier than the poor? Would you be happier if you had more money? These questions have been asked by economists as long as economics has been a science. Economists have attempted to confirm or disprove the idea that additional money makes people happier, but doing so has proven difficult. Experiments have been carried out on the topic in laboratories using animals. In one experiment, laboratory rats were trained to work for pay. They had to hit a bar several times to get a piece of food or a drink of water. After obtaining a certain amount of food and water, the rats reduced their work efforts, choosing leisure instead of more food and water. Thus, the rats did react as if their income—food and water—had a diminishing importance to them.

Economists have also turned to psychology for answers. Psychologists have carried out many surveys to measure whether people are more or less happy under various circumstances. One survey asked people in different income brackets whether they were unhappy, pretty happy, or very happy. The results indicated that the higher income is, the happier people are. Another study found that although citizens of the more wealthy nations tend to be happier than citizens of the less wealthy nations, this relationship is not very strong. More important than wealth is the history of democracy; the longer a nation has been democratic, the happier are its citizens. Within any one country, there is only a modest link between well-being and being well-off. Once we're comfortable, more money doesn't make us increasingly happy. The second helping never tastes as good as the first. The second $50,000 of income provides less happiness than the first $50,000.

A graph measuring income and happiness each year illustrates the survey results. It shows that initially people's happiness and income rise closely together. But, eventually, people have enough money and find that they prefer to do other things. Income rises, but people's happiness does not continue rising with it.

Source: David G. Myers, *The Pursuit of Happiness* (New York: William Morrow and Co., Inc., 1992) and John Stossel, "The Mystery of Happiness: Who Has It and How to Get It," April 15, 1996, ABC.

---

increased if demand is inelastic, decreases as price is increased if demand is elastic, and does not change as price is increased if demand is unit elastic.

For example, if the price elasticity of demand for gasoline is .02, then a 10 percent increase in price, say from $1.20 per gallon to $1.32 per gallon, will result in a decline of quantity demanded by only 2 percent. Thus, total revenue will rise. As long as demand is inelastic, then increasing the price raises revenue.

On the other hand, if the price elasticity of demand is 2.0, such as is the case for video rentals, then a 10 percent increase in price, from $1.99 to 2.19, will lead to a 20 percent reduction in quantity demanded. This means that total revenue will decline. As long as demand is elastic, increasing the price reduces revenue.

Total revenue and price move in opposite directions when demand is elastic and move in the same direction when demand is inelastic. When demand is elastic, a price rise leads to a decline in total revenue while a price decrease causes total revenue to rise. When demand is inelastic, a price rise leads to an increase in total revenue while a price decline leads to a total revenue decrease. Thus, to increase revenue, a firm will increase price when demand is inelastic and reduce price when demand is elastic.

3.b.1. Price Discrimination The relationship between the price elasticity of demand and revenue explains many things we observe in the real world.

■ **price discrimination:** different prices charged to different customers

Not all consumers respond in the same way to a change in the price of a product. For instance, the demand for airline service by the business traveler is different from the demand by the tourist. The business traveler typically is on a tighter schedule than a tourist, so the tourist has many more flying options than the business traveler. This means that the demand by the business traveler is less price-elastic than the demand by the tourist.

The airline can increase revenue by increasing price to the business traveler and lowering it to the tourist. (Increase price to increase revenue if demand is price inelastic; and decrease price to increase revenue if demand is price elastic.) It is for this reason that you find airlines offering substantial discounts for staying over a Saturday night or for purchasing tickets several weeks in advance. These policies, called **price discrimination**, distinguish the tourist from the business traveler.

Price discrimination is a way to increase revenue by separating customers into groups according to the price elasticity of demand. Movie theaters separate customers into different groups—children, senior citizens, and others. Senior citizens' demand for movies has a higher price elasticity than the rest of the population's demand for movies. Thus, the movie theater discriminates by charging a higher price to the rest of the population than it does to senior citizens. Children's demand for movies also has a higher price elasticity, partly because their parents have to attend the movie with them, which raises the amount spent and thus the sensitivity to price.

Warehouse-type stores, like Price Club, CostCo, and Sam's, cater to the customers who are willing to purchase larger quantities of a product to get a lower price. Their demand for certain products has a higher price elasticity than those not willing to purchase in large quantities. In this case, firms lower their prices for large quantities of goods to attract the type of customer that cares less about ambiance or service than lower prices.

3.c. Determinants of Price Elasticity

If you're going to use the price elasticity of demand to set the price on the Big Mac, you've got to know what things influence the elasticity. In general,

1. the more substitutes for a product, the higher the price elasticity of demand;

2. the greater the importance of the product in the consumer's total budget, the higher the price elasticity of demand; and

3. the longer the time period under consideration, the higher the price elasticity of demand.

Consumers who can easily switch from one product to another without losing quality or some other attribute associated with the original product will be very sensitive to a price change. Their demand will be very elastic. A senior citizen discount is offered at movie theaters because senior citizens who are retired have many more substitutes than do working people. The retirees have more time to seek out alternative entertainment and to attend movies at different times. In contrast, business travelers have few substitutes for the times they need to travel; they have to take the airline at that time. As a result, their demands for airline seats are relatively inelastic.

When there are fewer close substitutes for a product, the firm can increase the price without losing significant business and revenue. It is for this reason that firms attempt to create brand names and customer loyalty. Increasing brand name recognition and customer loyalty toward that brand means that fewer close substitutes exist and thus that the price elasticity of demand is lower. It is because of brand name recognition that Coca-Cola is priced higher than Safeway brand cola and Bayer aspirin is priced higher than Walgreen's aspirin.

The greater the portion of the consumer's budget a good constitutes, the more price-elastic is the demand for the good. Because a new car and a European vacation are quite expensive, even a small percentage change in their prices can take a significant portion of a household's income. As a result, a 1 percent increase in price may cause many households to delay the purchase of a car or vacation. Coffee, on the other hand, accounts for such a small portion of a household's total weekly expenditures that a large percentage increase in the price of coffee will probably have little effect on the quantity of coffee purchased. The demand for vacations is usually more price-elastic than the demand for coffee.

The longer the period under consideration the more price-elastic is the demand for any product. The demand for most goods and services over a short period of time, say, a few hours or a few days, is less price-elastic. However, over a period of a year or several years, the demand for most products will be more price-elastic. For instance, the demand for gasoline is almost perfectly inelastic over a period of a month. No good substitutes are available in so brief a period. Over a 10-year period, however, the demand for gasoline is much more price-elastic. The additional time allows consumers to alter their behavior to make better use of gasoline and to find substitutes for gasoline.

RECAP

1. The price elasticity of demand is a measure of how sensitive consumers are to price changes. An elastic demand is one for which a 1 percent change in price leads to a greater than 1 percent change in the quantity demanded. An inelastic demand is one for which a 1 percent change in price leads to a less than 1 percent change in quantity demanded.

2. When demand is elastic, a 1 percent price decrease will lead to a greater than 1 percent increase in the quantity demanded. This means that total revenue rises when the price is decreased in the elastic region of demand.

3. When demand is inelastic, a 1 percent decrease in price leads to a smaller than 1 percent increase in quantity demanded. As a result, total revenue declines whenever price is decreased in the inelastic region of a demand curve.

4. Price discrimination is a pricing strategy whereby different customers are charged different prices for identical products. Price discrimination is based on different consumers having different price elasticities of demand. The customers with the higher price elasticities are charged lower prices than those with lower price elasticities.

5. The determinants of the price elasticity of demand include the availability of substitutes, the relative cost of the good or service (relative to income), and the time period being considered.

4. WHAT'S TO COME?

Once a firm has information about the demand for its goods and services, it is part of the way toward knowing the price to charge and the quantities to produce and try to sell. From demand a firm can determine revenue. But can it make a profit? For this, a firm must have both demand information and cost information. We'll turn to the cost information in the next chapter.

What did you decide about the Big Mac? Are you lowering the price? How much?

SUMMARY

What are total, average, and marginal revenue?

1. Total revenue is price times quantity sold.

2. Marginal revenue is the incremental revenue that comes from increasing or decreasing the quantity of a good or service that is sold.

3. Average revenue is per unit revenue. It is the same thing as demand.

4. Marginal revenue is less than average revenue. The marginal-revenue curve lies below the average-revenue (demand) curve.

Do consumers respond to price changes?

5. The price elasticity of demand is a measure of the responsiveness of consumers to changes in price. It is defined as the percentage change in the quantity demanded of a good divided by the percentage change in the price of the good.

6. Demand is price-elastic when the price elasticity is greater than 1; it is price-inelastic when the price elasticity is less than 1; it is unit elastic when the price elasticity is 1.

7. The price elasticity of demand is always a negative number because of the law of demand; when price goes up, quantity demanded goes down, and vice versa. As a result, we typically ignore the negative sign when speaking of the price elasticity of demand.

What is the relationship between revenue and price elasticity of demand?

8. If the price elasticity of demand is greater than 1, demand is price-elastic. In this case, total revenue and price changes move in opposite directions. An increase in price causes a decrease in total revenue and vice versa. If demand is inelastic, then price changes and total revenue move in the same direction.

9. Firms use price elasticity to set prices. In some cases, a firm will charge different prices to different sets of customers. This is called price discrimination.

10. The greater the number of close substitutes, the greater the price elasticity of demand.

11. The greater the proportion of a household's budget a good constitutes, the greater the household's elasticity of demand for that good.

12. The demand for most products over a longer time period has a greater price elasticity than the same product demand over a short time period.

KEY TERMS

total revenue
average revenue (*AR*)
marginal revenue (*MR*)
price elasticity of demand
elastic

unit elastic
inelastic
perfectly elastic
perfectly inelastic
price discrimination

EXERCISES

1. Use the table in the left column of page 73 to complete the following exercise.
   a. Determine the price elasticity of demand at each quantity demanded. Go from $5 to $10, then from $10 to $15, then from $15 to $20, and so on.
   b. Plot the price and quantity data. Indicate the price elasticity value at each point.

What happens to the elasticity value as you move down the demand curve?

PRICE	QUANTITY DEMANDED
$5	100
10	80
15	60
20	40
25	20
30	10

PRICE	QUANTITY SOLD
$100	200
90	250
80	300
70	350
60	400
50	450
40	500
30	550
20	600

2. Below the demand curve plotted in exercise 1, plot the total revenue curve measuring total revenue on the vertical axis and quantity on the horizontal axis.

3. What would a 10 percent increase in the price of movie tickets mean for the revenue of a movie theater if the price elasticity of demand was, in turn, .1, .5, 1.0 and 5.0?

4. Suppose the price elasticity of demand for movies by teenagers is .2 and that by adults is 2.0. What policy would the movie theater implement to increase total revenue?

5. Explain why senior citizens often obtain special discounts.

6. Using the following data, calculate total, average and marginal revenue.

7. In recent years, U.S. car manufacturers have charged lower car prices in western states in an effort to offset the competition by the Japanese cars. This two-tier pricing scheme has upset many car dealers in the eastern states. Many have called it discriminatory and illegal. Can you provide another explanation for the two-tier pricing scheme?

INTERNET EXERCISE

This chapter focuses on elasticity. One of the determinants of the price elasticity of demand is the number of substitutes for a particular good or service. Use the Internet to examine the substitutes for pharmaceuticals. Go to the Boyes/Melvin *Fundamentals of Economics* Web site at http://www.hmco.com/college/ and click on the Internet Exercise link for Chapter 4. Now answer the questions that appear on the Boyes/Melvin Web site.

5

Costs and Profit Maximization

1. What is the relationship between costs and output in the short run?

2. What is the law of diminishing marginal returns?

3. What do the owners of firms want the firm to do?

4. What is the difference between economic profit and accounting profit?

5. What is the profit-maximizing rule?

Preview

We'd all enjoy getting the things we purchase at lower prices. But a firm can't supply goods and services for very long if it can't sell them for more than it costs the firm to supply them. A firm hires labor, purchases or leases equipment, buildings, and land, and acquires raw materials. What it pays for these resources are the firm's costs. The firm must decide how many resources it needs and then what is the least cost to acquire and use these resources. Once the firm figures out its costs, it can compare the costs with the revenues to see if it can make a profit.

In this chapter, we first discuss costs, and then we'll combine costs and revenue to see how the firm earns a profit. ■

1. COSTS

The costs of producing and/or selling goods and services are the costs of the resources used (i.e., the cost of land, labor, and capital). Total cost is $C \times Q$—the cost of each quantity of output supplied multiplied by the quantity supplied.

What happens to costs as output rises? Since more resources are required to sell more output, it would seem logical that costs would rise as output rises. This is the case—costs do rise as output rises; but each unit increase in output does not increase costs the same amount. As output rises, costs rise relatively slowly at first but then increase more and more rapidly. The reason is that at first one additional resource can do a lot. For example, hiring another employee can allow the firm to deal with several more customers. But eventually it takes an increasing amount of additional resources to increase output another unit. With too many salespeople, each customer has to wait until his or her salesperson can get access to a cash register, for example. Thus, if there is only 1 salesclerk, to increase sales by $100 an hour might require only 1 additional salesclerk. But, if there are 20 clerks around the store, to increase sales by $100 an hour might require 10 more clerks. This means that costs rise by increasingly large amounts for each additional $100 of sales.

1.a. Total, Average, and Marginal Costs

■ **average total costs:** per unit costs, total costs divided by quantity

■ **marginal costs:** incremental costs, change in total costs divided by change in quantity

Let's use the table in Figure 1 to discuss costs for the same bicycle store from Chapter 4. The costs for the bicycle firm, Pacific Bikes, to sell bicycles each week are shown. Column 1 lists the total quantity (Q) of output—the number of bikes offered for sale each week. Column 2 lists the total costs (TC) of providing each output level; it is the total cost schedule.

Column 3 lists **average total costs** (**ATC**). Average total cost is derived by dividing the corresponding total costs by the quantity of output, in this case the number of bicycles. Average total costs inform the manager what the costs of producing each unit of output are.

Marginal cost (**MC**), the additional costs that come from selling an additional unit of output, is listed in column 4. Marginal costs are the incremental costs, the change in costs resulting from a small decline or increase in output. Marginal cost informs the manager whether the last unit of output offered for sale increased costs a huge amount, a small amount, or not at all.

The average and marginal cost schedules are plotted in the graph in Figure 1. The ATC curve declines until 7 bicycles and then rises. The MC curve begins below the ATC curve and declines until 5 bicycles, where it begins to climb. The MC curve passes through the ATC curve at the minimum point of the ATC curve.

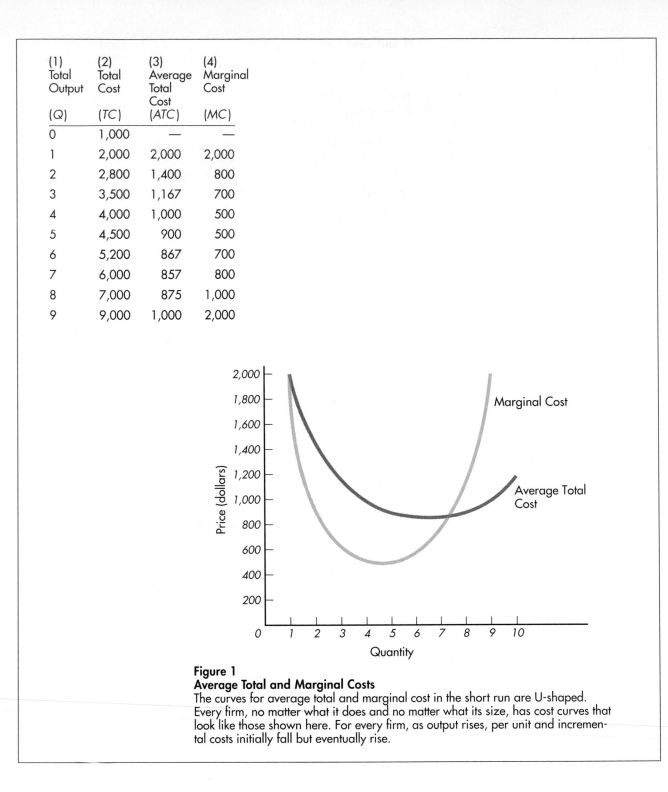

(1) Total Output (Q)	(2) Total Cost (TC)	(3) Average Total Cost (ATC)	(4) Marginal Cost (MC)
0	1,000	—	—
1	2,000	2,000	2,000
2	2,800	1,400	800
3	3,500	1,167	700
4	4,000	1,000	500
5	4,500	900	500
6	5,200	867	700
7	6,000	857	800
8	7,000	875	1,000
9	9,000	1,000	2,000

Figure 1
Average Total and Marginal Costs
The curves for average total and marginal cost in the short run are U-shaped. Every firm, no matter what it does and no matter what its size, has cost curves that look like those shown here. For every firm, as output rises, per unit and incremental costs initially fall but eventually rise.

1.b. Why Are the Cost Curves U-Shaped?

■ **short run:**
a period of time just short enough that at least one resource is fixed

Both the curves for average total and marginal cost are described as U-shaped—as output rises, per unit and incremental costs initially fall but eventually rise. The shape of these curves is quite important because every firm, no matter what it does and no matter its size, has cost curves that look like those in Figure 1 in the short run. The **short run** is a period of time just short enough that at least one of the resources can't be changed. How long is this? It depends on the type of business. An airline may have year-long leases on equipment and year-long contracts with employees. The short run would be anything less than one year. A basket weaver may have no leases and may be able to alter all of its resources within a week's time. The short run would be anything less than one week.

It is important to distinguish between the short run and the long run. In the short run, the firm has fewer options. It cannot expand or contract its entire operation. It can change only some of the resources, the resources referred to as variable. For instance, for the bike shop, the number of employees can be changed quite readily, probably within a day or two. But the size of the building and the number of cash registers, display areas, and repair stations cannot be changed for at least a few months. It is this fact that gives us the U-shaped cost curves. To understand why, let's look more closely at the operations of the bicycle shop.

The number of bicycles that can be assembled or repaired and then offered for sale during 1 week is shown in Table 1. One employee can put together and sell 3 bicycles if the bike store has 1 station for assembling the bikes, 10 bicycles if the bike store has 2 stations, 25 bicycles if the bike store has 3 repair stations, and so on. With a second employee, output is increased with each quantity of repair stations: 2 employees and 1 repair station now generate 6 bicycles, and so on.

Pacific Bikes could offer for sale about the same amount, say 34 to 36 bikes, with several different combinations of employees and stations— 3 employees with 2 stations, 2 employees with 3 stations, or 1 employee with 4 stations. And several other output levels can be offered with a number of different combinations of employees and repair stations. Which combination does the bike store choose? In the short run, the choices open to the firm are limited.

Suppose that Pacific Bikes had previously constructed one repair station and cannot change the number for at least a year. In this case, the fixed resource is the number of repair stations. The options open to Pacific Bikes in the short run are only those under column 1. Pacific Bikes can vary the number of employees but not the number of repair stations in the short run.

As the first units of the variable resource (employees) are hired, each additional employee can prepare and sell many bicycles. But after a time, there are too many employees in the store ("too many chefs stirring the broth") and each additional employee adds only a little to total bicycles offered for sale. If the employees must stand around waiting for tools or room to work on the bikes, then an additional employee will allow few, if any, additional bicycles

TABLE 1
Output with Different Combinations of Resources

Number of Employees	Capital (number of repair stations and cash registers)						
	1	2	3	4	5	6	7
0	0	0	0	0	0	0	0
1	3	10	25	34	41	40	39
2	6	25	36	45	52	53	50
3	10	36	48	57	61	62	61
4	13	44	58	64	69	70	69
5	13	50	65	71	76	77	77
6	11	54	70	76	80	82	84
7	10	55	72	79	82	85	89
8	8	54	68	80	83	86	90

This assembly line, on which gingerbread houses are constructed, involves workers and three moving sidewalks. The *variable* resources are the supplies—gingerbread, sugar, and other confection items—and the workers. The *fixed* resources are the moving sidewalks. A new platform would have to be constructed to increase the number of moving sidewalks. This would take several months.

■ **law of diminishing marginal returns:**
as quantity of variable resources is increased, output initially rises rapidly, then more slowly, and eventually may decline

to be repaired or assembled and sold. Eventually, adding another employee may actually detract from the productivity of the existing employees as they bump into each other and mix their tools up. The limited capacity of the fixed resources—the number of repair stations, repair stands, cash registers, and building space—causes the efficiency of the variable resource—the employees—to decline.

This relationship between quantities of a variable resource and quantities of output is called the **law of diminishing marginal returns**. According to the law of diminishing marginal returns, when successive equal amounts of a variable resource are combined with a fixed amount of another resource, output will initially increase rapidly, then increase more slowly, and eventually decline. Looking at Table 1, you can see the law of diminishing marginal returns at each quantity of repair stations. Just increase the number of employees for any given quantity of repair stations and output will rise rapidly at first, but then more slowly. Similarly, if the number of employees is fixed and the number of repair stations is variable, you would also observe the law of diminishing marginal returns. With 1 employee, for instance, as the number of repair stations is increased, output rises from 30 to 100 to 250 to 340 and so on. The first increases are large, but output rises less rapidly and eventually declines as the number of repair stations is increased.

Diminishing marginal returns is not unique to the bicycle industry. In every instance where increasing amounts of one resource are combined with fixed amounts of other resources, the additional output initially increases but eventually decreases. A classic example is putting increasing amounts of water on a potted plant. Initially the water helps the plant grow. Eventually, the water drowns the plant.

The law of diminishing marginal returns also applies to studying. During the first hour you study a subject you probably get a great deal of information. During the second hour you may also learn a large amount of new material, but eventually another hour of studying will provide no benefits and could be counterproductive.

Every firm (and every individual and nation as well) is faced with the law of diminishing marginal returns. The law is, in fact, a physical property, something that is inescapable. It is important in economics because it defines the relationship between costs and output in the short run for every firm no matter what the firm does, no matter how large the firm is, no matter where the firm is located. For every firm, as it increases the amount of a variable resource it uses along with a fixed resource, the firm is able to get a great deal of additional output initially, but eventually the additional output increases more slowly and may actually decline. And since the firm has to pay for each employee or each unit of variable resource, its costs rise slowly at first as output increases, but then rise more and more rapidly as output rises. This fact gives us the U-shaped curves of the average total and marginal cost.

RECAP

1. Average total costs (*ATC*) are total costs divided by the total quantity of the good offered for sale (*Q*). Average total costs are per unit costs.

$$ATC = \frac{\text{total costs}}{\text{quantity of output}}$$

2. Marginal costs (*MC*) are the incremental costs that come from producing one more or one less unit of output:

$$MC = \frac{\text{change in total costs}}{\text{change in quantity of output}}$$

3. The short run is a period of time just short enough that at least one of the resources is fixed.

4. The law of diminishing marginal returns applies only to the short run as variable resources are combined with a fixed resource.

5. According to the law of diminishing marginal returns, as successive units of a variable resource are added to the fixed resources, the additional output will initially rise but will eventually decline.

6. Diminishing marginal returns occur because the efficiency of variable resources depends on the quantity of the fixed resources.

7. The law of diminishing marginal returns results in the U-shaped curves of the average total and marginal cost.

2. MAXIMIZING PROFIT

We've now discussed revenue and cost. In this section we put the two together to determine profit. A firm's decision to supply a good or service depends on whether the firm expects to make a profit. An entrepreneur or manager of a firm looks at the demand for the firm's product and at its costs of doing business and determines what price to charge and what quantity to sell to earn maximum profit. To analyze the firm's decisions, we must put the demand for the firm's products together with the firm's costs.

A firm is a combination of resources used to sell a good or service. The firm *adds value* to the resources it uses if it pays for the use of the resources and still has something left over. In 1996 Microsoft bought materials worth $5.25 billion. Its wage and salary bill was around $1.12 billion, and the cost of the capital that the company used (premises, factories, machinery, and equipment) was about $250 million. Thus, it cost Microsoft $6.65 billion to sell its output. Sales were $8.75 billion—$2.1 billion more than it cost to sell the output. This figure of $2.1 billion is a measure of the value that Microsoft added. In other words, the **added value** is the difference between the value of output and the full cost of inputs.

■ **added value:**
the difference between the value of output and the full costs of inputs

2.a. Economic Profit

Recall from Chapter 1 that resources consist of three general groups: land, labor, and capital, and the cost of each is:

rent to land owners,

wages and salaries to workers for their labor, and

interest to the owners of capital (investors).

In each case, the cost is an opportunity cost—the amount necessary to keep the resource owners from moving the resources to an alternative use. For instance, if a landowner can rent her land to another firm at a higher rate, then she will. She has to be paid at least as much to keep her land in its current use. Similarly, if you could earn more for doing the same job elsewhere, you'd take that job. An employee must be paid at least what he could earn elsewhere if he is to stay in the current job.

■ **cost of capital:**
the opportunity cost of the funds used to purchase capital; the cost of debt plus the cost of equity

The **cost of capital** is also an opportunity cost. Capital (equipment, machinery, and buildings) is either acquired through loans (**debt**) or provided by the owner(s) of the business (**equity**). (If the business is publicly held, the owners are shareholders, or investors.) The cost of debt is the interest that is paid on the debt. The cost of equity is the alternative returns that the owners (or investors) could have gotten had they not chosen to invest in the particular activity or company. This is the investors' opportunity cost. For instance, since shareholders of Microsoft could invest in other businesses, the expected return from these alternative investments, a return that was foregone when Microsoft stock was purchased, is the cost of investing in Microsoft. And Microsoft must pay these shareholders at least what they expect to get from alternative investments, or the shareholders will take their money elsewhere.

■ **debt:**
loans; funds owed to lenders by borrowers

■ **equity:**
value of a firm less debt

■ **economic profit:**
revenue less all costs, including opportunity costs of owner's capital

This opportunity cost of equity capital (not debt capital) is considered by economists as the element that distinguishes **economic profit** from **accounting profit**. The profit figure reported in annual reports, income statements, and other financial statements is accounting profit. Accounting profit is the value of output less the cost of inputs but *not including* the opportunity of the owner's equity capital. Economic profit is the difference between the value of output and the opportunity costs of all inputs, *including* the opportunity cost of the owner's equity capital. Recall that added value is the difference between the value of a firm's output and the *full* cost of its inputs. Therefore, added value is economic profit.

■ **accounting profit:**
revenue less costs except opportunity costs of owner's capital

accounting profit = revenue (value of output) −
costs of labor, land, and debt capital (inputs)

economic profit = accounting profit −
opportunity cost of equity capital

Wal-Mart, for instance, reported a profit of $3,056 million in 1996. This is Wal-Mart's accounting profit. Subtracting Wal-Mart's cost of capital from its accounting profit indicates that economic profit was $306 million, only 10 percent of its accounting profit.

Coca-Cola had $3.5 billion in accounting profits in 1996. It had $16 billion of investor-supplied capital and its cost of capital was 12 percent. The economic profit for Coca-Cola in 1996 was:

Economic Profit = Accounting Profit − Opportunity Cost of Capital
= $3.5 billion − $16 billion (.12)
= $3.5 billion − $1.9 billion
= $1.6 billion.

■ **negative economic profit:**
revenue does not pay for all opportunity costs

2.a.1. Negative Economic Profit Economists refer to a firm where cost of equity capital is greater than its accounting profit as having **negative economic profit**. Negative economic profit means the resources would have a

Part II / Consumers, Firms, and Social Issues

higher value in another use. A firm that continually subtracts value will not exist in the long run. Suppose you were an investor in General Motors Corporation (GM). Having experienced 4 percent annual returns over the last ten years (lower returns than you anticipated), you look at your alternatives. You realize that you could have earned more by selling your shares of stock in GM and purchasing shares in another firm. If many GM shareholders did this, GM could no longer acquire the use of resources. It would have to go out of business. Why hasn't GM gone out of business? Because not enough investors have decided they could do better investing in another firm. However, for more than 1 percent of the total firms in the United States each year, investors choose to invest elsewhere and the firms do go out of business.

For a short period, firms can earn negative economic profit and remain in business. In 1996, such well known companies as Pepsico, BellSouth, Eli Lilly, Mobil, DuPont, Bell Atlantic, Amoco, Chevron, Boeing, Time Warner, and Turner Broadcasting had negative economic profit. If their owners anticipated a continuing pattern of negative economic profit, they would take their money elsewhere. In fact, these firms earned positive economic profits in 1997.

2.a.2. Zero Economic Profit

A firm that has sufficient revenue to pay the cost of inputs but with nothing left over is said to have **zero economic profit** or **normal accounting profit**. If Microsoft had revenue of \$8.75 billion and costs of \$6.75 billion, it would have had an accounting profit of \$2 billion. But if the shareholders expected to have been able to earn 10 percent in an alternative activity and they have invested \$20 billion in Microsoft, then Microsoft's economic profit would be zero.

Zero economic profit might sound bad, but it is not. A zero economic profit simply means that the owners could not do better elsewhere; a firm with zero economic profit is earning a positive accounting profit. The investors have no incentive to sell Microsoft and purchase something else since they would expect to earn no more than they do with Microsoft.

2.a.3. Positive Economic Profit

If a firm is returning more to its owners than the owners' opportunity cost, the firm is said to be earning **positive economic profit**. Positive economic profit is a powerful signal in the marketplace. Other investors see the positive economic profit and want to get in on it as well. As a result, they take their funds from whatever use they are currently in and invest in existing and new firms that will compete with the profitable firm.

Recall the example of the Miata selling in Detroit and L.A. at different prices. People bought the Miata in Detroit and sold it in L.A. as long as they could make a profit doing it. But once the price of the Miata rose in Detroit and fell in L.A. enough that there was no profit, the arbitrage process ended. No more people took the cars from the Detroit market to the L.A. market. The point is that entry occurs only as long as economic profit is positive. When opportunity costs are just covered, that is, when economic profit is zero, there is no incentive for investors to take their funds out of some other activity and invest in this one.

2.a.4. Accountants and Economic Profit

Accountants do not present economic profit in financial statements, and firms usually don't report it in their annual reports. Why not? Partly because they have not been convinced it is necessary and partly because of the difficulty of calculating the cost of capital. The cost of (equity) capital is the amount that the investors would have to be paid not to move their funds to another firm—that is, the opportunity cost to investors of leaving their money with a particular firm. That amount is sure to vary from investor to investor. My opportunity cost is not the same as yours. This problem could be ignored by focusing on the average investor; however, until the last four or five years, few firms have thought that reporting

■ **zero economic profit:** revenue just pays all opportunity costs

■ **normal accounting profit:** zero economic profit

■ **positive economic profit:** revenue exceeds all opportunity costs

Social Responsibility and Profits

In 1970, Nobel Prize-winning economist Milton Friedman upset many people with his statement that the social responsibility of business is to increase its profits. Some saw Friedman's statement again in the movie *Wall Street* with Michael Douglas when Douglas' character proclaimed, "Greed is Good."

What does it mean to say that the corporate executive has a social responsibility in his capacity as a business person? Perhaps it means that he is to refrain from increasing the price of the product in order to contribute to the social objective of preventing inflation, even though a price increase would be in the best interests of the corporation. Or that he is to make expenditures on reducing pollution beyond the amount that is in the best interests of the corporation in order to contribute to the social objective of improving the environment. Or that, at the expense of corporate profits, he is to hire the hardened unemployed rather than better-qualified workers.

In each of these cases, the executive would be spending someone else's money for what he perceives to be a general social interest. When his actions reduce returns to stockholders, he is spending their money. When his actions raise the price to customers, he is spending the customers' money. When his actions lower the wages of some employees, he is spending their money. Perhaps these people have different views of social responsibility. Perhaps they would choose to spend their money differently.

By seeking to maximize profit, firms will do what customers, and thus society, want. If customers want to protect the environment, to employ the unemployable, to provide amenities to communities, then businesses will offer these things in order to attract the customers. For years, The Body Shop customers flocked to the stores to purchase Body Shop cosmetics, not only because they liked the cosmetics, but because the products were environmentally safe, as

well. For years, ice cream lovers purchased Ben & Jerry's both because they liked the ice cream and because they liked Ben & Jerry's environmental and social policies.

Businesses are not individuals. Businesses do not have responsibilities. Only people can have responsibilities. Business people have responsibilities, but their responsibilities are to their employers and typically that responsibility is to earn as much profit as they can for their employers.

Seeking to maximize profits ensures that businesses will do what customers want them to do. Seeking to earn the most they can, businesses will provide the products customers want at the lowest possible prices. Businesses will be socially responsible when customers want and are willing to pay for social responsibility. And seeking maximum profit means that the social responsibility will be fulfilled most efficiently and most quickly.

economic profits was important. In the past few years, investors have begun to realize that having some information about economic profit helps to distinguish among successful and not so successful firms. As a result, more and more firms are beginning to offer investors some information on economic profit.

RECAP

1. Added value is the difference between the value of output and the cost of inputs.

2. Added value is the same as economic profit.

3. Adding value is the objective of a firm's owners.

4. Accounting profit is total revenue less total costs. It does not include the opportunity cost of the owner's capital, however.

5. Economic profit is accounting profit less the opportunity cost of the owner's capital.

6. Economic profit can be positive, negative, or zero. A positive economic profit means that the revenue exceeds the full cost of inputs; that is, that inputs are earning more than their opportunity cost. A negative economic profit means

Consumers have many choices. They can purchase the lowest-priced items, the highest-quality items, items with different colors or shapes, items that cause pollution when they are produced, or items that are biodegradable. Believing that the environment is important to the consumers of the industrial nations, The Body Shop sells only "green" products. "Green" refers to environmentally safe products. The British company has branched to several nations with its bodycare products that are environmentally safe and are not tested on animals. Although the products are more expensive than many substitute products, enough consumers prefer green products that The Body Shop has been very successful.

that the inputs are not earning their opportunity costs. A zero economic profit means that the inputs are just earning their opportunity costs.

7. Economic profit is not straightforward to measure because the opportunity cost of capital depends on investor alternatives.

8. The cost of capital is the amount a firm would have to pay investors to have them invest in this firm rather than another.

3. THE PROFIT-MAXIMIZING RULE: *MR = MC*

We know what profit is. The question now facing us is how do we know what quantity to sell and what price to charge in order to maximize profit. As we'll see in this section, the answer is quite simple; all we have to do is find the price and quantity where marginal revenue equals marginal cost.

3.a. Graphical Derivation of the *MR = MC* Rule

Profit is maximized at the price and quantity where $MR = MC$. Marginal cost is the additional cost of producing one more unit of output. Marginal revenue is the additional revenue obtained from selling one more unit of output. If the production of one more unit of output increases costs less than it increases revenue—that is, if marginal cost is less than marginal revenue—then producing (and selling) that unit of output will increase profit. Conversely, if the production of one more unit of output costs more than the revenue obtained from the sale of that unit, then producing that unit of output will decrease profit. *When marginal revenue is greater than marginal cost, producing more will increase profit. Conversely, when marginal revenue is less than marginal cost, producing more will lower profit. Thus, profit is at a maximum when marginal revenue equals marginal cost: MR = MC.*

Consider Figure 2, in which the curves of average total and marginal cost from Figure 1 are drawn along with the curves of demand and marginal revenue from the previous chapter. Figure 2 illustrates the fundamental decisions

(1) Total Output (Q)	(2) Price (P)	(3) Total Revenue (TR)	(4) Average Revenue (AR)	(5) Marginal Revenue (MR)	(6) Total Cost (TC)	(7) Average Total Cost (ATC)	(8) Marginal Cost (MC)	(9) Total Profit (TR − TC)	
0	0	0	0	0	$1,000	—	—	−$1,000	
1	$1,700	1,700	1,700	1,700	2,000	2,000	2,000	−300	
2	1,600	3,200	1,600	1,500	2,800	1,400	800	400	
3	1,500	4,500	1,500	1,300	3,500	1,167	700	1,000	
4	1,400	5,600	1,400	1,100	4,000	1,000	500	1,600	
5	1,300	6,500	1,300	900	4,500	900	500	2,000	
6	1,200	7,200	1,200	700	5,200	867	700	2,000	Profit Maximum
7	1,100	7,700	1,100	500	6,000	857	800	1,700	
8	1,000	8,000	1,000	300	7,000	875	1,000	1,000	
9	900	8,100	900	100	9,000	1,000	2,000	−900	

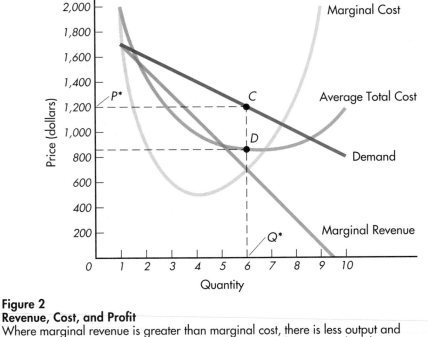

Figure 2
Revenue, Cost, and Profit
Where marginal revenue is greater than marginal cost, there is less output and some profit that could be earned is not. Where marginal revenue is less than marginal cost, there is more output and profit is reduced.

made by all business managers and owners. The profit-maximizing rule, *MR* = *MC*, is illustrated in the table of Figure 2, which lists output, total revenue, total cost, marginal revenue, marginal cost, and profit for Pacific Bikes. The first column is the total quantity (*Q*) of bikes sold. In column 2 is the price (*P*) of each bike. Column 3 is the total revenue (*TR*) generated by selling each quantity. In column 4 is average revenue (*AR*) (which is the same as demand)—total revenue divided by quantity. Column 5 lists marginal revenue (*MR*)—the change in total revenue that comes with the sale of an additional bike.

Total cost (*TC*) is listed in column 6. You might note that costs are $1,000 even when no bikes are sold. Costs that have to be paid even when production is zero are called **fixed costs**. Fixed costs are items like the lease on the building and the payment on the loans used to construct repair stations. Other costs, referred to as **variable costs**, change as output changes. Variable costs include the costs of employees, electricity, water, and materials—items that change as quantity changes.

■ **fixed costs:**
costs of fixed resources; costs that do not change as output changes

■ **variable costs:**
costs that vary as output varies

Average total cost (*ATC*) is listed in column 7; it is total cost divided by quantity. Marginal cost (*MC*), the additional cost of selling an additional bike, is listed in column 8. The marginal cost of the first bike is the additional cost of offering the first bike for sale, $1,000; the marginal cost of the second bike is the increase in costs that results from offering a second bike for sale, $800. Total profit, the difference between total revenue and total cost (*TR* − *TC*), is listed in the last column.

The first bike costs an additional $1,000 to sell; the marginal cost (additional cost) of the first bike is $1,000. When sold, the bike brings in $1,700 in revenue, so the marginal revenue is $1,700. Since marginal revenue is greater than marginal cost, the firm is better off selling that first bike than not selling it.

The second bike costs an additional $800 (column 8) to sell and brings in an additional $1,500 (column 5) in revenue when sold. With the second bike, marginal revenue exceeds marginal cost. Thus the firm is better off producing two bikes than none or one.

Profit continues to rise until the sixth bike is sold. The marginal cost of selling the seventh bike is $800 while the marginal revenue is $500. Thus, marginal cost is greater than marginal revenue. Profit declines if the seventh bike is sold. The firm can maximize profit by selling six bikes, the quantity at which marginal revenue and marginal cost are equal.

We can easily find the profit-maximizing price and quantity in Figure 2. Profit is maximized at the point at which *MR* = *MC*. The quantity the firm should sell to maximize profit is given by dropping a line down to the horizontal axis from the *MR* = *MC* point, a quantity of *Q** = 6. The price that the firm should charge to sell this quantity is given by extending the vertical line from the *MR* = *MC* point up to the demand curve. The demand curve tells us how much consumers are willing and able to pay for the quantity *Q**. Then, we draw a horizontal line over to the vertical axis, the price axis, at *P** = $1,200.

Total revenue is given by the rectangle *06CP**. The total cost is found by multiplying average total cost by quantity. We draw a vertical line from *Q** = 6 up to the average-total-cost curve, point *D*. This gives us the per unit costs of selling six bikes. We then draw a horizontal line over to the vertical axis; this represents multiplying *ATC* by *Q** = 6. The resulting rectangle *06D$867* is the total cost. Total profit, then, is the difference between total revenue and total cost. Total profit is given by the rectangle *$867DCP**.

Figure 2 provides a great deal of information about business behavior. The demand curve may be different (steeper or flatter) depending on the price elasticity of demand, or the position of the cost curves might be different depending on cost conditions; but irrespective, profit is maximized when *MR* = *MC*. Every decision a manager or owner makes comes down to comparing marginal revenue and marginal cost. Should the firm increase advertising expenditures? If the *MR* from doing so is greater than the *MC*, then yes. Should the firm hire another employee? If the *MR* from doing so exceeds the

MC, then yes. This decision-making approach shouldn't be any surprise to you. It is how you make decisions as well. You compare your marginal revenue (your additional benefits) of doing something to your marginal costs. If your marginal revenue exceeds your marginal cost, you do it. Nike used to have a slogan, "Just Do It." What they ought to have said is, "If *MR* exceeds *MC*, then do it."

3.b. What Have We Learned?

We have covered a great deal of territory. We have learned how firms select the price to charge and quantity to sell to maximize profit. A firm will supply the quantity and charge a price given by the point where *MR* = *MC*. Marginal revenue depends on demand, that is, on consumers. The firm must know what the consumer likes, what prices the consumer is willing and able to pay, and must supply its goods and services at those prices if it is to maximize its profit.

For-profit firms behave so as to maximize profit and thus sell a quantity and set a price determined by the point where *MR* = *MC*. So if we know marginal revenue and marginal cost, determining the quantity to sell and the price to charge is trivial. The problem is that marginal revenue and marginal cost are typically not known. All opportunity costs are not reported in accounting statements. Moreover, accountants allocate costs among activities or across departments; they do not calculate the *incremental* cost of producing one more unit or the *incremental* revenue from selling one more unit. As a result, it is often said that marginal cost and marginal revenue are not really useful. Why, then, do we pay so much attention to the rule *MR* = *MC*?

Although accountants do not provide marginal cost information and although executives say they pay no attention to marginal cost or marginal revenue, these concepts are critical aspects of their decision making. Consider, for instance, how an airline decides to price its services. The price of seats varies considerably depending on the time one flies, whether a Saturday night stay occurs, and when one purchases a ticket. Often an airline flying with some empty seats will sell the seats at the last moment very inexpensively. In fact, the price of the seat is often below the average cost of flying the plane. The average total cost (per passenger cost) for Southwest Airlines is about $.07 per mile. Yet, Southwest will often sell some of its seats on distances of 1,000 miles for $25. Why? Because $25 is significantly more than $0. The marginal cost of adding one more passenger is nearly zero. Thus, the additional (marginal) revenue of the seat, $25, is greater than the marginal cost. The executives of Southwest know that they are better off selling the seat than not selling it. They know this not because they have calculated marginal revenue and marginal cost but because they know they make more profit by doing so. The profit-maximizing rule, *MR* = *MC*, may not be on executives' lips nor in their manuals, but it does describe their behavior. It provides a framework for understanding business behavior. Thus, it is a very important part of understanding why the world looks and acts as it does.

RECAP

1. The profit-maximizing rule is to set a price and sell a quantity where marginal revenue equals marginal cost: *MR* = *MC*.

SUMMARY

What is the relationship between costs and output in the short run?

1. The short run is a period of time just short enough that the quantity of at least one of the resources cannot be altered.

2. Average total costs are the costs per unit of output—total costs divided by the quantity of output sold.

3. As quantity rises, total cost rises. Initially as quantity rises, total cost rises slowly. Eventually, as quantity rises, total cost rises more and more rapidly.

What is the law of diminishing marginal returns?

4. According to the law of diminishing marginal returns, when successive equal amounts of a variable resource are combined with a fixed amount of another resource, the additional output will initially rise but will eventually decline.

5. The U-shape of short-run, average-total-cost curves is due to the law of diminishing marginal returns.

What do the owners of firms want the firm to do?

6. The objective of firms is to add value. Added value is measured as the difference between the sales or value of output and the input costs (including the opportunity costs). It is called economic profit.

What is the difference between economic profit and accounting profit?

7. Accountants do not measure all opportunity costs. Accounting profit does not include the opportunity cost of the owner's equity capital. Economists take into account all opportunity costs.

8. Normal accounting profit is a zero economic profit. Positive economic profit occurs when revenue is greater than all opportunity costs. Negative economic profit occurs when revenue is less than total opportunity costs.

What is the profit-maximizing rule?

9. Profit is maximized at the output level where total revenue exceeds total costs by the greatest amount; at the point where $MR = MC$.

10. The supply rule for all firms is to supply the quantity at which the firm's marginal revenue and marginal cost are equal and to charge a price given by the demand curve at that quantity.

KEY TERMS

average total costs (ATC)

marginal costs (MC)

short run

law of diminishing marginal returns

added value

debt

equity

cost of capital

economic profit

accounting profit

negative economic profit

zero economic profit

normal accounting profit

positive economic profit

fixed costs

variable costs

EXERCISES

1. Use the table below and find average total costs and marginal costs.

OUTPUT	COSTS	ATC	MC
0	$100		
1	150		
2	225		
3	230		
4	300		
5	400		

2. Use the completed table to answer the questions listed below.

   a. Plot each of the cost curves.

   b. At what quantity of output does marginal cost equal average total cost?

3. Describe the relation between marginal and average total costs.

4. In the following figure, if the firm has average total costs ATC_1, which rectangle measures total profit? If the firm has average costs ATC_2, what is total profit?

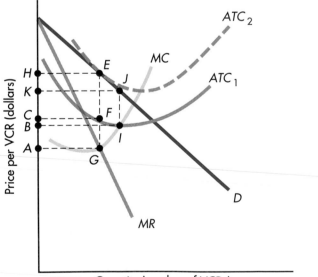

5. Consider the following demand schedule. Compute marginal and average revenue.

PRICE	$100	95	88	80	70	55	40	22
QUANTITY	1	2	3	4	5	6	7	8

6. Suppose the marginal cost of producing the good in question 5 is a constant $10 per unit of output. What quantity of output will the firm sell?

7. What follows is some accounting information for each of the firms shown. Can you tell which firm is the most successful? Explain.

	BOEING	GOODYEAR	LIZ CLAIBORNE	CIRCUIT CITY
Sales	5601	423	622	1767
Profits	254	26.9	56.2	31.6

8. A cost of capital figure for each of the firms is listed below. Explain what this figure means.

Motorola	11.6
Hershey Foods	12.8
Home Depot	12.2
Dillard Department Stores	10.5
Coca-Cola	12.0

9. Can accounting profit be positive and economic profit negative? Can accounting profit be negative and economic profit positive? Explain.

10. Use the following information to calculate accounting profit and economic profit.

    Sales $100

    Employee expenses $40

    Inventory expenses $20

    Value of owner's labor in any other enterprise $40

 **INTERNET EXERCISE**

This chapter focuses on the costs of doing business. In this chapter we discussed the costs that faced a hypothetical company. Use the Internet to examine an actual firm's costs in more detail. Go to the Boyes/Melvin *Fundamentals of Economics* Web site at **http://www.hmco.com/college/** and click on the Internet Exercise link for Chapter 5. Now answer the questions that appear on the Boyes/Melvin Web site.

6

Competition

FUNDAMENTAL QUESTIONS

1. What do barriers to entry have to do with competition?

2. How do firms create profits?

3. How do firms keep profits?

The profit-maximizing rule, *MR* = *MC*, applies to every profit-maximizing firm no matter the firm, the selling environment, or the decisions being considered. But, although all firms set a price and sell a quantity where *MR* = *MC*, firms do behave differently. Some offer a good or service without any marketing or advertising, while others devote more than half of their resources to marketing. Some behave as if they are in cutthroat competition with rivals, while others cooperate with rivals. In this chapter we'll consider many differences among firms and examine why firms engage in these behaviors. ■

1. PROFIT MAXIMIZATION AND THE MARKET PROCESS REVISITED

In the previous chapter we discovered the profit maximizing rule, *MR* = *MC*. We also learned how to illustrate the revenue, costs, and profit graphically. In Figure 1, repeated from Figure 2 of the previous chapter, profit is the rectangle *ADCB*, and it is a positive economic profit. If a firm is making a positive economic profit, the owners of the firm are doing better than they could expect to do putting their money into any other activity. In fact, other investors want to get in on the good thing. They start new firms to compete with the profitable firm.

When a new firm begins competing with the incumbent firm, the new firm takes some business away from the incumbent. This causes the demand curve for the incumbent firm to shift down. New firms continue to enter the market as economic profits are positive. Each entry causes the incumbent firm's demand curve to shift down further. Eventually, profits are driven down to the point

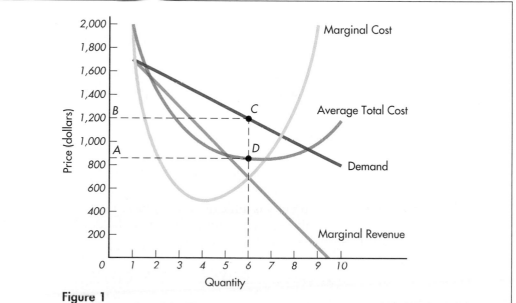

Figure 1
Revenue, Cost, and Profit
This figure is the same as Figure 2 in the previous chapter. Profit is maximized at the point where the marginal revenue and marginal cost are equal. If there were less output, marginal revenue would exceed marginal cost, and some profit that could be earned would not be earned. If there were greater output, marginal cost would exceed marginal revenue, and profit would be reduced.

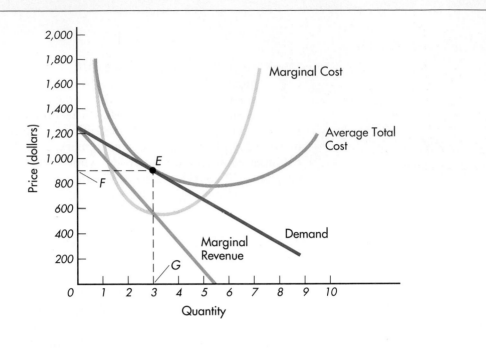

Figure 2
Entry and Profit
Profit is maximized at the point where marginal revenue and marginal cost are equal. In this case, entry has reduced this firm's demand and driven its economic profits to zero.

where only a normal accounting profit (zero economic profit) is earned. This is shown in Figure 2 where, at $900 for 3 units, the average revenue (demand) equals average total cost, and total revenue is equal to total cost, rectangle *0GEF.* At this point there is no reason for additional firms to enter.

The point is that a firm cannot earn positive economic profit very long when there is free entry. Free entry drives the economic profits to zero. If new firms cannot enter very easily or at all, then the story is different. The demand curve is not forced down, and economic profits do not decline. The incumbent firm can earn positive economic profit as long as entry is restricted.

RECAP

1. If entry occurs readily, firms are unable to keep or sustain positive economic profit.
2. If entry is difficult, firms in these market structures are able to earn positive economic profits until entry takes place.

2. THE BENEFITS OF COMPETITION

Competition depends on entry. With free entry, no firm can get away with anything. Any time consumers don't like a product or a service, they can switch to another firm. Any time a firm earns positive economic profit, other firms will copy that firm, drive the price down, and take some business away from the incumbent firm. Competition benefits consumers and society in general.

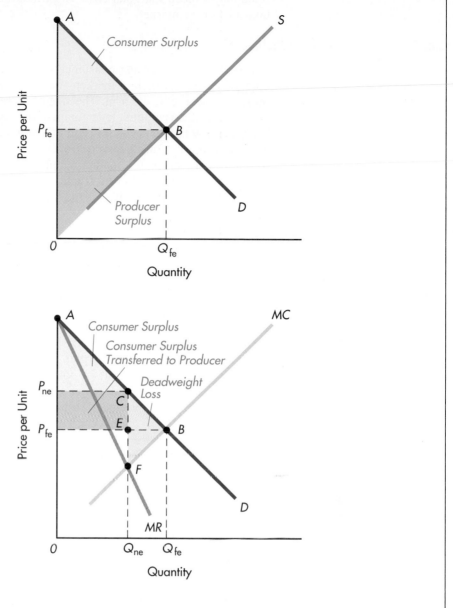

Figure 3
A Market Without Barriers to Entry
Figure 3 shows a market in which there are no barriers to entry. As a result, the firms produce where the market demand and supply intersect. The quantity produced by the total industry is Q_{fe}, and the price at which the products are sold is P_{fe}.

Figure 4
A Market With High Barriers to Entry
Figure 4 shows a single firm operating without any entry by rival firms. The single firm faces the demand curve D, which is the market demand curve (since it is the only firm in the market) and has the marginal-revenue curve MR. The intersection of the marginal-cost curve and the marginal-revenue curve indicates the quantity that will be produced in order to maximize profit, Q_{ne}. The price charged for that quantity is P_{ne}. The firm with barriers to entry produces less and charges more than the market where there are no barriers to entry. Consumer surplus is $P_{ne}CA$, smaller than consumer surplus when entry occurs, and producer surplus is $OFCP_{ne}$, larger than producer surplus when entry occurs. The loss to society of no entry, the deadweight loss, is the area CFB.

2.a. Consumer and Producer Surplus

A demand curve measures the price that buyers are willing and able to pay for each quantity of a good or service. Buyers need not pay the full amount they are willing to pay, however. The market system determines an equilibrium price, and it is that price buyers pay to purchase a good or service. In Figure 3, the equilibrium price is P_{fe}. This is the price buyers have to pay to purchase a unit of the good. All those buyers measured on the demand curve above the equilibrium price are willing to pay more than P_{fe}, which means that the market system provides a bonus to these consumers. This bonus is called **consumer surplus**.

Consumer surplus is a measure of the benefits consumers receive from market exchange. A similar measure exists for the firm. It is called **producer surplus**. Producer surplus is the difference between the price firms would have been willing to accept for their products and the price they actually receive. A firm is willing to sell its good or service for a price that is equal to the marginal cost of producing and selling its good or service, but the market

consumer surplus:
the difference between what consumers would be willing to pay and what they have to pay to purchase some item

producer surplus:
the difference between what suppliers would require to supply some item and the price they actually receive

price may exceed marginal cost. Thus, like the consumer, the firm receives a bonus from the market.

2.b. Deadweight Loss: Inefficiency

The sum of producer and consumer surplus represents the total benefits that come from exchange in a market—benefits that accrue to the consumer plus those that accrue to the firm. The size of these benefits depends on how easy entry is. To illustrate this, let's compare the result of competition in two markets: one in which entry is free and one in which there is just one firm. Figure 3 shows a market (not a single firm) in which free entry occurs. The market demand curve is D; the market supply curve is S. The market price determined by the intersection of D and S is P_{fe}, and the quantity produced and sold is Q_{fe}. Consumer surplus is the triangle $P_{fe}BA$. Producer surplus is the triangle $0BP_{fe}$.

Now, let's take that same market and transfer it to a situation where there is just one firm and entry cannot take place. Since the single firm is the entire market, the market demand curve is its demand, and the market supply curve is its marginal-cost curve. This is illustrated in Figure 4. The single firm produces where $MR = MC$ and thus produces less (Q_{ne} compared to Q_{fe}) and charges a higher price (P_{ne} compared to P_{fe}) than the market in which there is free entry.

Consumer surplus, when entry cannot take place (triangle $P_{ne}CA$), is smaller than the consumer surplus when entry does occur (triangle $P_{fe}BA$). The rectangle $P_{fe}ECP_{ne}$, part of consumer surplus when entry can occur, is transferred to the firm and becomes part of producer surplus when entry is restricted. The total producer surplus when entry is restricted is the area $0FCP_{ne}$.

Consumers are worse off by area $P_{fe}BCP_{ne}$, and firms are better off by area $P_{fe}ECP_{ne}$ less area EFB. Society as a whole is worse off. The triangle CFB is the reduction in consumer surplus and producer surplus when entry cannot occur: it is called a **deadweight loss**. Deadweight loss is the loss of the benefits of market exchange to society—an inefficiency resulting from restrictions to entry.

The greater the barriers to entry, the more economic profit the firm can earn, the longer the firm can continue to earn that positive economic profit, and the fewer the benefits that the consumer can gain. It is entry and competition that generate the benefits of the market system. It is barriers to entry that transfer consumer surplus to producers and create deadweight losses.

■ **deadweight loss:**
the loss of consumer and producer surplus when entry is restricted

RECAP

1. Consumer surplus is a bonus of the market system. It is the difference between what consumers would be willing and able to pay for a good or service and the amount they actually have to pay for that good or service.

2. Producer surplus is a bonus of the market system that goes to firms. It is the difference between the price at which the producers would be willing and able to supply a good or service and the price the producers actually receive.

3. Consumer surplus is higher when entry is free than when entry is restricted.

4. Restrictions on entry lead to some deadweight loss. The degree of loss depends on how strict the barriers to entry are.

3. CREATING BARRIERS TO ENTRY

Positive economic profit will not last long simply by doing the same thing others do. Over time, the only way that positive economic profit will continue to be earned is if others cannot copy the unique activity or product that creates the profit. Only if businesses create barriers to entry will they maintain positive economic profits over time.

In this section we'll discuss several business practices intended to create barriers to entry.

3.a. Product Differentiation: Reputation and Brand Name

The more distinct a product is, the lower is the price elasticity of demand. If a firm can reduce the price elasticity of demand for its products, the firm can increase the price and increase revenue. Thus, firms want to distinguish themselves and their products from their rivals.

A well-known company can have a real advantage over newcomers. Reputation is valuable in the market when the customers cannot easily judge product quality. If consumers know everything—have perfect information—producers have no incentive to create brand names or to differentiate products other than by actual physical characteristics. Aspirin would simply be aspirin, not Bayer. But Bayer Aspirin is much more expensive than generic aspirin. Why? Because of the brand name. To many people, the brand name is a signal of quality or reliability.

A business may create a reputation or brand name by having been around for a long time or by advertising extensively. Some businesses create a brand name by renting an established reputation in one market to use in a different market. Endorsement by famous personalities is a clear example. Everyone knows that celebrities give their endorsement, not because they have scoured the market for the best product, but because they have canvassed potential sponsors for the highest fee. So why are consumers influenced by the endorsement? The endorser is, to some degree, putting his or her reputation at risk. If the product is of poor quality, the celebrity's reputation and value to other sponsors can be damaged. For the firm, payment of the endorsement fee is a demonstration of its commitment to the market. Willingness to pay the endorsement fee is therefore actually a measure of product quality. If one company gets an endorsement from a well-known person, other companies must also come up with someone to endorse their products. Nike employs Michael Jordan; Reebok, Shaquille O'Neal.

In addition to creating a brand name or reputation, these expenditures on the creation of brand name raise the costs to firms entering the market. Potential entrants have to consider undertaking expenditures that are even more than those made by existing firms. If those expenditures are sunk, then the barrier to entry is even higher. A **sunk cost** is an expenditure that cannot be recouped. What a firm spends on advertising can't be recouped. The firm cannot sell the advertising to another firm. A firm that builds a sign or golden arches cannot then sell that sign or those arches to another firm. Sunk costs can serve as effective barriers to entry since they tell a potential new firm that it has to throw just as much money away on similar sunk expenditures if it is going to compete.

■ **sunk cost:**
cost that cannot be recouped

Advertising expenditures may be the most significant sunk costs of competition. When a firm advertises, it is saying, "We have just spent millions of dollars drawing your attention to our product. If we intended to disappoint your expectations, to withdraw from the market, or to produce a poor-quality product, spending that money would be a foolish thing for us to have done."

The advertisement assures the reader that the product is good, but not because it says that the product is good. Rather, the assurance that the product is good comes from the mere fact that the firm has the sunk costs of advertising.

Consider the case of a sidewalk vendor who sells neckties on the streets of a large city. If such a "firm" tells customers that it will guarantee the quality of its ties, customers will certainly question the validity of the guarantee, since, if the firm decides to go out of business, it can do so instantaneously. It has no headquarters, no brand name, no costly capital equipment, and no loyal customers to worry about. A firm with no obvious stake in the future has a difficult time persuading potential customers it will make good on its promises. In contrast, a firm that has devoted significant resources to items that have no liquidation value, such as advertising campaigns or expenditures on physical structures like McDonald's golden arches, is not as likely to pick up and leave at a moment's notice.

If the costs of entering a business are high and if the costs are sunk, then firms are likely to be more reluctant to enter an industry. If to compete with Microsoft, firms must also have interests in a film studio, then the costs to enter Microsoft's business will have risen considerably. If, to compete with Nike, a firm has to spend twice as much enlisting endorsements and on advertising, firms may be reluctant to enter the athletic shoe market.

3.b. Guarantees

Guarantees and warranties can serve as barriers to entry. When Japanese automobile companies first entered the U.S. market in the 1960s, they faced the difficulty of convincing consumers of the quality of the cars. Although the manufacturers knew that their products were of high quality, their potential customers did not. In fact, many believed that Japanese goods were shoddy imitations of Western products. "Made in Japan" had become synonymous with cheap and crummy. Accordingly, Japanese manufacturers offered more extensive warranties than had been usual in the market.

Guarantees are difficult to fake. A low-quality product would break down frequently, making the guarantee quite costly for the firm. Thus, the higher the quality of the product, the better the guarantee offered by the firm.

If a firm establishes a warranty policy, then other firms must either follow or admit to having a lower-quality product. If a potential rival is unable to imitate the existing warranty of its rivals, it may decide not to enter the market in the first place. This is what the Japanese auto producers did to the U.S. auto producers. U.S. auto producers did not offer warranties as extensive as Japan's. As a result, customers soon came to see that "Made in Japan" meant quality.

3.c. Unique Resources

If all firms in a market have the same resources and capabilities, no strategy for earning economic profit is available to one firm that would not also be available to all other firms in the market. Any strategy that confers advantage could be immediately imitated by any other firm. However, if a firm has a unique resource, that resource may serve as a barrier to entry. A single family owned the only mine producing desiccant clay, an important ingredient in inhibiting humidity in packaging. For years, this clay was the only material that could meet certain necessary standards for inhibiting the accumulation of humidity in packaging.

DeBeers controlled about 80 percent of the diamonds in the world when the Russian economy was tightly controlled by the government. DeBeers had a unique resource—acquisition and distribution of the diamonds. With the breakdown of the Soviet empire, DeBeers has had to fear a flood of diamonds and a reduction in the uniqueness of its resource.

Beginning in 1992, government regulation has been relaxed so that utilities must compete or prepare for competition from other electricity-generating companies. It is expected that within a decade or more, customers will be able to switch from one electric utility to another, just as they do in purchasing long-distance telephone service. Will electricity sellers be large firms or small enterprises?

Microsoft has hired as many of the best scientists as it can. This stock of top scientists is expected to allow Microsoft to maintain its advantage in the software market. These scientists are a unique resource.

RECAP

1. Economic profit induces entry and new competition.
2. Entry drives economic profit to zero.
3. Entry occurs unless there are barriers.
4. Barriers to entry include:
    a. brand name and reputation
    b. guarantees and warranties
    c. unique resources

4. FIRM SIZE AS A BARRIER TO ENTRY

An important barrier to entry can be the size of the firm relative to the market. If a firm must be large in order to enter an industry and begin offering a good or service, then the costs of being large may be too much and entry might be very difficult, if not impossible. In this case, the incumbent firm may be able to earn positive economic profits. To understand how size can be an advantage we need to discuss a concept called economies of scale.

4.a. Economies of Scale

■ **long run:**
period of time just long enough that all resources are variable

■ **economies of scale:**
per unit costs decline when all resources are increased

Remember the distinction between the short run and the long run? The short run is a period of time just short enough that at least one of the resources cannot be changed. The relationship between output and costs *in the short run* is defined by the law of diminishing marginal returns. In the **long run**, everything is variable. This means that the law of diminishing marginal returns does not apply. The relationship between output and costs *in the long run* is defined by whether there are economies or diseconomies of scale. **Economies** of scale mean that as the size of a firm increases (all of its resources are increased), its per unit costs decline. If economies of scale exist, a larger firm can produce a product at a lower per unit cost than a smaller firm can. This means that a new entrant would have to enter as a big firm in order to compete with existing firms.

Economies of scale could arise because a larger size allows more specialization; an employee can focus on one activity rather than trying to do everything. Economies of scale also can result because larger machines are more efficient than smaller ones; large blast furnaces produced many more tons of steel than the smaller, open-hearth furnaces in the same time and for about the same cost.

4.b. Diseconomies of Scale

Larger size does not automatically improve efficiency. The specialization that comes with large size often requires the addition of specialized managers. A 10 percent increase in the number of employees may require an increase greater than 10 percent in the number of managers. A manager to supervise the other managers is needed. Paperwork increases. Meetings are held more often. The amount of time and labor that are not devoted to producing output grows. It may become increasingly difficult for the CEO to coordinate the activities of each division head and for the division heads to communicate with one another. Larger machines are not always more efficient than smaller ones. A larger building may not allow a more efficient production than a smaller building. When increasing size leads to higher per unit costs, we say that there are **diseconomies of scale**.

■ **diseconomies of scale:** per unit costs rise when all resources are increased

4.c. Large Firm Advantage and the Extent of the Market

It might seem that a large firm would always have an advantage over smaller firms, if there are economies of scale. In fact, it would seem that the market would have to be just one firm—a monopoly—since the largest firm would be able to drive the others out of business, but appearances can be deceiving.

Most industries experience both economies and diseconomies of scale. Consider the fresh-cookie industry. Mrs. Fields Cookies trains the managers of all Mrs. Fields outlets at its headquarters in Park City, Utah. The training period is referred to as Cookie College. By spreading the cost of Cookie College over more than 700 outlets, Mrs. Fields Cookies is able to achieve economies of scale. However, the company faces some diseconomies because the cookie dough is produced at one location and distributed to the outlets in premixed packages. The dough factory can be large, but the distribution of dough produces diseconomies of scale that worsen as outlets are opened farther and farther away from the factory.

When long-run costs are characterized by economies of scale for smaller sizes and then by diseconomies of scale for larger sizes, the larger firm may or may not have a cost advantage over the smaller firm. It depends on demand. If demand is very large, then the firm will produce only an amount that allows it to experience economies of scale. Once diseconomies of scale begin, that is, once per unit costs begin to rise, the firm will not produce any more. In this case, the very large firm would not have an advantage over the smaller firm. When demand is sufficient only for a firm to experience economies of scale, then the larger firm has an advantage over the smaller firm. When demand is so large that a firm would experience diseconomies of scale trying to supply all of demand, then the large firm does not have an advantage over a smaller firm. When only diseconomies of scale occur, small firms have an advantage over larger firms.

5. WHAT'S TO COME?

It is more likely that a large firm will be able to create a cost advantage that serves as a barrier to entry than a small firm. In the next chapter we'll discuss some of the ways that firms, particularly larger firms, attempt to create advantages for themselves. We'll also discuss how the government attempts to define the rules of behavior for large firms.

RECAP

1. Size can serve as a barrier to entry in certain circumstances.
2. The long run is a period just long enough that all resources are variable; there are no fixed resources.
3. Economies of scale occur when the per unit costs decline as all resources (the size of the firm) increase in the long run.
4. If an industry is characterized by economies of scale, then the large firm can produce at a lower per unit cost than the smaller firm can. To enter this industry requires that a firm be large.
5. Whether economies of scale give a cost advantage to a large firm depends on the extent of the market. If demand is sufficiently large that a large firm can realize economies of scale, then firm size is a distinct advantage.
6. Diseconomies of scale occur when as the size of the firm increases, the per unit costs rise.

SUMMARY

1. Entry defines whether a firm can keep or sustain the positive economic profit it earns. If entry occurs, competition will drive the profit down to a normal accounting profit, or zero economic profit.

2. Consumer surplus is the bonus the market provides to consumers. It is the difference between the price the consumer would be willing and able to pay for a product and the price the consumer actually has to pay.

3. Producer surplus is the bonus market exchange provides to firms. It is the difference between the price at which the firm would be willing and able to supply a good or service and the price the firm actually receives for selling the good or service.

4. Deadweight loss is the benefits of market exchange that are lost when entry is restricted.

■■ **How do firms create profits?**

5. Firms create profits by doing something others don't do.

■■ **How do firms keep profits?**

6. Firms attempt to create barriers to entry. Activities such as advertising, brand name creation, and sunk cost expenditures may be effective barriers.

7. Size can serve as a barrier to entry in certain circumstances. Those circumstances depend on whether there are economies or diseconomies of scale.

8. The long run is a period just long enough that all resources are variable; there are no fixed resources.

9. Economies of scale occur when the per unit costs decline as all resources (the size of the firm) increase in the long run.

10. If an industry is characterized by economies of scale, then the large firm can produce at a lower per unit cost than the smaller firm can. To enter this industry requires that a firm be large.

11. Whether economies of scale give a cost advantage to a large firm depends on the extent or size of the market and whether the industry also experiences diseconomies of scale. If demand is sufficiently large that a large firm can realize economies of scale, then firm size is a distinct advantage.

KEY TERMS

consumer surplus
producer surplus
deadweight loss
sunk cost

long run
economies of scale
diseconomies of scale

EXERCISES

1. If a firm has no competitors producing close substitutes, will it set exorbitantly high prices?

2. Draw a perfectly elastic demand curve on top of a standard U-shaped, average-total-cost curve. Now add in the marginal-cost and marginal-revenue curves. Find the profit-maximizing point, $MR = MC$. Indicate the firm's total revenues and total cost.

3. Describe profit maximization in terms of marginal revenue and marginal cost.

4. Use the information below to calculate total revenue, marginal revenue, and marginal cost. Indicate the profit-maximizing level of output. At what level of output would the firm produce?

OUTPUT	PRICE	TOTAL COST
1	$5	$10
2	5	12
3	5	15
4	5	19
5	5	24
6	5	30
7	5	45

5. Using demand curves, illustrate the effect of product differentiation on the part of hair-cutters.

6. Why might society prefer a situation where entry can occur to a situation where entry is restricted?

7. Under what circumstances would a large size provide an advantage to a firm? How could it serve as a barrier to entry?

8. Texas Instruments once announced a price for random access memories that wouldn't be available for two years after the announcement. A few days later, Bowmar announced that it would produce this product and sell it at a lower price than Texas Instruments. A few weeks later, Motorola said it too would produce this product and sell it below the Bowmar price. A few weeks after this, Texas Instruments announced a price that was one half of Motorola's. The other two firms announced that, after reconsidering their decision, they would not produce the product.

   a. What was Texas Instruments' reason for announcing the price of a product two years before it was actually for sale?

   b. Under what conditions would Motorola not have rescinded its production decision?

9. Explain how a strategy of increasing expenditures on advertising could deter entry.

INTERNET EXERCISE

This chapter focuses on entry and barriers to entry. In this chapter we discussed the idea that advertising can be a barrier to entry. Use the Internet to examine the amount of advertising different firms carry out. Go to the Boyes/Melvin *Fundamentals of Economics* Web site at **http://www.hmco.com/college/** and click on the Internet Exercise link for Chapter 6. Now answer the questions that appear on the Boyes/Melvin Web site.

7

How Firms Behave

---

1. What is a large firm?

2. What is a pricing strategy?

3. Do firms ever cooperate with rivals?

4. Why does the government interfere with the behavior of firms?

$\mathcal{P}\!reveiw$

irms may be organized as sole proprietorships, partnerships, or corporations. A **sole proprietorship** is a business owned by one person. This type of firm may be a one-person operation or a large enterprise with many employees. In either case, the owner receives all the profits and is responsible for all the debts incurred by the business. A **partnership** is a business owned by two or more partners who share both the profits of the business and responsibility for the firm's losses. The partners could be individuals, estates, or other businesses. A **corporation** is a business whose identity in the eyes of the law is distinct from the identity of its owners. A corporation is an economic entity that, like a person, can own property and borrow money in its own name. The owners of a corporation are shareholders. Although there are many small firms, large firms and corporations account for the greatest share of business revenue. There are only about one-third as many corporations as sole proprietorships, but corporations have more than fifteen times the revenue of sole proprietorships. Most new enterprises are small businesses. Thus, an industry in which entry is free is likely to be one in which the businesses are small. In many industries, one or a few companies dominate the market. We refer to these as large firms. They may not be large in an absolute sense, but the fact that they dominate a market means they are large relative to the market.

In most cases, larger firms are large because they have created barriers to entry. Having barriers to entry enables the firms to behave differently than if entry is free. If entry is free, the firm has to set the price where all other firms set theirs. With barriers to entry, the firm has some flexibility to set the price independently of other firms. But being one among a few large firms may also mean having to be acutely aware of what others are doing. A small firm may be able to operate in isolation, responding to the market and trying to be as efficient as possible, and essentially ignoring all the other small firms in the industry. The larger firm may have to react to other firms in order not to lose sales.

In this chapter we'll discuss some of the ways that large firms behave. We'll also discuss the rules of behavior that the government prescribes for large firms. We begin with some pricing strategies. ■

■ **business firm:**
an entity in which resources are combined to produce an output

■ **sole proprietorship:**
a business firm owned by one person

■ **partnership:**
a business firm owned by two or more persons

■ **corporation:**
a business firm owned by many shareholders; owners are not liable for debts of a corporation

1. PRICE STRATEGIES

Firms maximize profit by charging a price and selling a quantity where $MR = MC$. This is a straightforward strategy and holds for every firm no matter the market structure in which it operates. But this simple rule gets complicated as firms sell more than one product, operate in more than one market, deal with varied consumers, and interact with rivals.

1.a. Price Discrimination

Price discrimination is the practice of charging different buyers different prices for the same good or service where the different prices are not associated with difference in costs. The seller must be able to separate buyers into distinct groups, each having different price elasticities of demand. It is relatively easy for a movie theater to separate customers by age. Similarly, it is easy for airlines to separate buyers into business travelers and tourists. The seller must also be able to keep those buyers who get the lower prices from selling their good or service to the buyers who pay the higher prices. A senior citizen could not sell his or her ticket to a middle-aged adult; the tickets are different colors. Travelers cannot change names on airline tickets; IDs are required.

When the price elasticity of demand differs from buyer to buyer, then the firm will maximize profit by charging each customer a different price. Profit maximization occurs when $MR = MC$. There is a different MR for each buyer. The firm thus equates MC with each MR; $MC = MR_1$, MR_2, and so on, depending on how many buyers there are. The buyers with higher price elasticities get lower prices.

Price discrimination is a strategy used by many firms that sell their products in different countries. A derogatory name for this policy is **dumping**. Dumping occurs when an identical good is sold to foreign buyers for a lower price than is charged to domestic buyers.

One famous case involved Sony Corporation of Japan. In the United States, Sony was selling Japanese-made TV sets for $180 while charging buyers in Japan $333 for the same model. U.S. television producers claimed that Sony was dumping TV sets in the U.S. market and seriously damaging U.S. television manufacturers. (Although U.S. producers disliked the low price of Japanese competitors, U.S. consumers benefited.) The U.S. government threatened to place high tariffs on Japanese television sets entering the United States unless Japan raised the price of Japanese televisions sold in the United States. The threat worked, and the price of Japanese TVs exported to the United States increased.

Charges of dumping make good news stories, but it is also true that price discrimination in international markets is to be expected when producers face different sets of buyers each with a different price elasticity of demand. Conceptually, price discrimination in international markets is no different from what happens when a car dealer charges one buyer a higher price than another for the same car. If both buyers were aware of the range of prices at which the dealer would sell the car or if both buyers had exactly the same price elasticity of demand, they would pay exactly the same price.

Price discrimination can be effective only if different sets of customers have different price elasticities of demand and the various sets of customers can be separated and easily distinguished. Suppose a movie theater decided to give a discount to people with an Irish ancestry but not to people with an eastern European ancestry. This would be an impossible task. It would cost the movie theater too much to force the customers to prove their ancestry.

What is the purpose of price discrimination? It is to enable a firm to collect as much of the consumer surplus as possible. If a firm could sell each customer a product at the highest price the customer was willing and able to pay, the firm would collect the entire consumer surplus. This would be perfect price discrimination—each customer pays a different price. This is what some selling tactics are designed to do. Many purchases of automobiles involve hours of negotiation between dealer and customer. The dealer is trying to find the very highest price the customer is willing and able to pay. That price will differ from customer to customer—so the dealer is price discriminating.

1.b. Peak Load Pricing

Peak load pricing involves charging a higher price to customers who purchase the product during periods of *peak* demand and a lower price for those who purchase during periods of *off-peak* demand.

The pricing of long-distance telephone calls is a good example of peak load pricing. Most long-distance calls are placed on weekday afternoons, while fewer calls are placed late at night and on weekends. In addition, just as the demand for telephone calls differs by the time of day, so does the cost of producing them. The switching facilities and lines provided by the telephone companies are designed to meet demand during peak times. As a result, marginal cost is low during off-peak times when much of the firm's capacity sits idle and high during peak times when capacity is strained. The firm equates MR and MC for the two time periods, generating higher prices during peak times and lower prices during off-peak times. Electric utilities use peak load pricing. They charge a higher rate for electrical use during seasons and times of the day when the usage is greatest. Peak load pricing is a commonly used pricing strategy in tourism businesses as well. Resort hotels charge more during busy times than during the off-season. Renegade Golf Course in Phoenix, Arizona, has green fees of $250 in February and $80 in July.

1.c. Discount Coupons

In 1996, American businesses distributed 300 billion coupons with a face value of $200 billion. Of these, consumers redeemed only 6 billion coupons worth about $4 billion. If only a small percentage of the coupons are redeemed, why do firms offer coupons? Why don't sellers simply cut the price? One reason is that the coupon is a way to discriminate among buyers. The more valuable a consumer's time, the higher the cost of redeeming a coupon will be. By issuing coupons, a seller can provide a lower price to those with higher price elasticities of demand—people willing to spend the time collecting coupons.

1.d. Bundling

Bundling is the combining of two or more products and selling the bundle for a single price. Cable television providers make extensive use of bundling in their pricing. The cable television providers offer a set of channels for a single price. The channels are bundled; a consumer cannot simply buy one of the channels. Why does the cable provider bundle the channels together rather than offer each one at a distinct price? The reason is primarily cost. The marginal cost of providing separate channels or separate packages of channels to each and every customer would be very high, but different customers prefer different channels. The cable company determines which set of channels satisfies most of the customers. It then determines the marginal revenue on the bundle and sets price where $MR = MC$.

1.e. Rebates and Other Price Strategies

Let's begin this section with a quiz.

1. *Who is happier: Person A, who wins the office football pool for $100 on the same day she ruins the carpet in her apartment and must pay the landlord $75, or Person B, who wins the office football pool for $25?*

2. *Who is happier: Person A, who ruins the carpet in her apartment and must pay the landlord $100, or Person B, who ruins the carpet in his apartment and must pay the landlord $75 and also scratches the front door and must pay the landlord $25?*

In both cases, most people believe Person A is happier even though A and B end up with the same gain or loss. The difference in the two cases is the way the gains and losses are presented. In the first case, A has a gain ($100) and a loss ($75) together, while B has just a gain ($25). In the second case, A has a loss ($100), while B has two losses ($25 + $75). If a comparison of alternatives involves a gain, people prefer to have the results of the actions presented separately—a $100 gain and a $25 loss rather than a $75 gain. This result is characterized by the lesson: "Don't wrap all the Christmas presents in one box." But if the comparison involves losses, people prefer to have the losses combined or shown just once—a $100 loss rather than separate losses of $25 and $75.

The quiz shows that prospective buyers are happier if multiple gains are offered separately and if multiple losses are combined. Instead of offering an additional discount for new subscribers, a sports magazine will add a video of sports highlights. The television shopping networks encourage you to buy now, and if you do, you get several other attachments and related products.

The separate gain means more to prospective buyers than a larger price discount on the subscription would or a reduction of the price of the item being sold on television.

Automobile manufacturers use price rebates to stimulate sales. Why don't the manufacturers simply discount the price instead? Because buyers seem to prefer a separate rebate payment—separating gains from losses.

Whereas consumers like their gains to be separated, they do not like to have losses offered separately. The price elasticity of demand is higher for separate purchases than if the same purchases are bundled together. For instance, it is easier to induce someone to buy a car stereo or other options at the time of a car purchase than to make the same sale separately. Most computer and appliance stores and most automobile dealerships offer extended warranty plans at the time the product is purchased. People are more likely to purchase savings bonds and insurance through payroll deductions. Paying for these by slightly reducing a large gain is much more palatable than incurring the cost outright.

RECAP

1. Pricing strategies involve the determination of prices.
2. All pricing strategies are based on equating *MR* and *MC*.
3. Price discrimination is offering different prices to different sets of customers for an identical product.
4. Peak load pricing is a form of price discrimination. It is the practice of charging a higher price during periods when demand is higher.
5. Discount coupons provide a means of discriminating among consumers on the basis of price elasticity of demand.
6. Bundling is the practice of combining products and selling the bundle for a single price.
7. Other pricing practices we observe in the real world occur because they appeal to consumers. Rebates allow firms to separate a gain (the rebate) from losses (the expenditure on the item), and consumers like gains to be separated.

2. INTERDEPENDENCE

The strategies we've discussed so far focus on a firm in isolation not really considering how other firms behave. Most firms have to consider the behavior of other firms when choosing their own strategies; most firms are interdependent. Interdependence between firms occurs when what is best for A depends on what B does and what is best for B depends on what A does. The setting is much like a card game—bridge, say—in which strategies are designed depending on the cards the players are dealt. Underbidding, overbidding, bluffing, deceit, and other strategies are carried out. This is what much of business is about. In this section, we discuss some of the ways that firms interact.

2.a. The Kinked Demand Curve

Firms often have to predict how their competitors will respond to a price change in order to know what their demand curve looks like. Let's consider the auto industry. Suppose General Motors' costs have fallen (its marginal-cost curve has shifted down), and the company is deciding whether to lower the prices on its cars. If GM did not have to consider how the other car companies would respond, it would simply lower the price from P_1 to P_2, as illustrated in Figure 1(a). But GM suspects that the demand and marginal-revenue

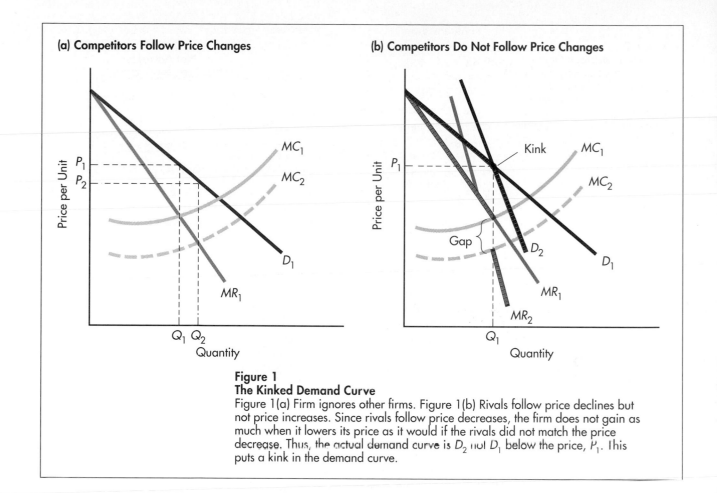

(a) Competitors Follow Price Changes

(b) Competitors Do Not Follow Price Changes

Figure 1
The Kinked Demand Curve
Figure 1(a) Firm ignores other firms. Figure 1(b) Rivals follow price declines but not price increases. Since rivals follow price decreases, the firm does not gain as much when it lowers its price as it would if the rivals did not match the price decrease. Thus, the actual demand curve is D_2 not D_1 below the price, P_1. This puts a kink in the demand curve.

curves in Figure 1(a) do not represent its true market situation. GM believes that if it lowers the prices on its cars from their current level of P_1, the other auto companies will follow suit. In other words, GM does not capture the market, as indicated in Figure 1(b) by D_1, but instead finds the quantity demanded increasing along D_2 (below price P_1). GM also suspects that should it increase the price of its cars, none of the other auto companies would raise theirs. In this case, the price increase would mean substantially reduced sales. The quantity demanded decreases, as indicated along D_1. Consequently, the demand curve for GM is a combination of D_1 and D_2. It is D_1 above P_1 and D_2 below P_1—a demand curve with a kink.

What should GM do? It should price where $MR = MC$. But the resulting marginal-revenue curve is given by a combination of MR_1 and MR_2. MR_1 slopes down gently until reaching the quantity associated with the kink. As we move below the kink, MR_2 becomes the appropriate marginal-revenue curve. Thus, the striped portions of the two marginal-revenue curves combine to give the firm's marginal-revenue curve. Notice how GM's marginal-cost curves, MC_1 and MC_2, intersect the combined MR curves at the same price and quantity, P_1 and Q_1. Thus, GM's strategy is to do nothing: to not change price even though costs have changed.

2.b. Dominant Strategy

Consider the situation in which firms must decide whether to devote more resources to advertising. When a firm in any given industry advertises its product, its demand increases for two reasons. First, people who had not used that type of product before learn about it, and some will buy it. Second, other people who already consume a different brand of the same product may switch brands. The first effect boosts sales for the industry as a whole, whereas the second redistributes existing sales within the industry.

Figure 2
Dominant Strategy Game

Figure 2
Dominant Strategy Game
The dominant strategy for firm A is to advertise. No matter what firm B does, firm A is better off advertising. Similarly, firm B is better off advertising no matter what firm A does. Both A and B have dominant strategies—to advertise.

	Firm A Advertise	Firm A Not Advertise
Firm B Advertise	Firm A 70 / Firm B 80	Firm A 40 / Firm B 100
Firm B Not Advertise	Firm A 100 / Firm B 50	Firm A 80 / Firm B 90

■ dominant strategy:
When one alternative is better than other alternatives no matter what rivals do

Consider the cigarette industry as an example and assume that the matrix in Figure 2 illustrates the possible actions that two firms might undertake and the results of those actions. The top left rectangle represents the payoffs, or results, if both A and B advertise; the bottom left is where A advertises but B does not; the top right represents when B advertises but A does not; and the bottom right shows the payoffs if neither advertises. If firm A can earn higher profits by advertising than by not advertising, whether or not firm B advertises, then firm A will surely advertise. This is referred to as a **dominant strategy**—a strategy that produces the best results no matter what strategy the opposing player follows. Firm A compares the left side of the matrix to the right side and sees that it earns more by advertising no matter what firm B does. If B advertises and A advertises, then A earns 70; but if A does not advertise, it earns 40. If B does not advertise, then A earns 100 by advertising and only 80 by not advertising. The dominant strategy for firm A is to advertise.

The dominant strategy for firm B also is to advertise, according to Figure 2. Firm B will earn 80 by advertising and 50 by not advertising, if A advertises. Firm B will earn 100 advertising but only 90 not advertising, if A does not advertise. But notice that both firms would be better off if neither advertised; firm A would earn 80 instead of 70, and firm B would earn 90 instead of 80. Yet the firms cannot afford to not advertise because they would lose more if the other firm advertised and they did not. This situation is known as the **prisoner's dilemma**.

■ prisoner's dilemma:
a situation in which the best outcome is not selected because actions depend on other firms

None of the cigarette manufacturers wants to do much advertising, yet they must. Firm A advertises, so firm B does also. Each ups the advertising ante. Using a dominant strategy involving advertising shows how firms are interdependent.

2.c. Cooperation

If the firms could come to some cooperative agreement, they would all be better off. For instance, the cigarette companies might spend no additional money and agree to share the market—agree not to advertise. Cooperation is an integral part of business when a few firms dominate the market.

2.c.1. Price Leadership
One way for firms to cooperate is to allow one firm to be the leader in changes in price or advertising activities. Once the leader makes a change, the others duplicate what the leader does. This action enables all firms to know exactly what the rivals will do. It eliminates a kink in the demand curve because both price increases and price decreases will be followed, and it avoids the situation in which excessive expenses are made on advertising or other activities. This type of behavior is called *price leadership*.

The steel industry in the 1960s is an example of a dominant-firm price leadership. For many years, steel producers allowed United States Steel to set prices for the entire industry. The cooperation of the steel companies probably led to higher profits than would have occurred with rivalry. However, the absence of rivalry is said to be one reason for the decline of the steel industry in the United States. Price leadership removed the need for the firms to compete by maintaining and upgrading equipment and materials and by developing new technologies. As a result, foreign firms that chose not to behave as price followers emerged as more sophisticated producers of steel than U.S. firms.

For many years, airlines also relied on a price leader. In many cases, the price leader in the airlines was not the dominant airline but one of the weaker or new airlines. In recent years, airlines have communicated less through a price leader and more through their computerized reservation system.

2.c.2. Collusion, Cartels, and Other Cooperative Mechanisms
Acting jointly allows firms to earn more profits than if they act independently or against each other. Firms may collude or come to some agreement about price and output levels. Typically these agreements provide the dominant firms in the market higher profits and thus raise prices to consumers. Collusion, which leads to secret cooperative agreements, is illegal in the United States, although it is acceptable in many other nations.

■ cartel:
An organization of independent producers that dictates the quantities produced by each member of the organization

A **cartel** is an organization of independent firms whose purpose is to control and limit production and maintain or increase prices and profits. A cartel can result from either formal or informal agreement among members. Like collusion, cartels are illegal in the United States but occur in other countries. The cartel most people are familiar with is the Organization of Petroleum Exporting Countries (OPEC), a group of nations rather than a group of independent firms. During the 1970s, OPEC was able to coordinate oil production in such a way that it drove the market price of crude oil from $1.10 to $32 a barrel. For nearly eight years, each member of OPEC agreed to produce a certain limited amount of crude oil as designated by the OPEC production committee. Then in the early 1980s, the cartel began to fall apart as individual members began to cheat on the agreement. Members began to produce more than their allocation in an attempt to increase profit. As each member of the cartel did this, the price of oil fell, reaching $12 per barrel in 1988. Oil prices rose again in 1990 when Iraq invaded Kuwait, causing widespread damage to Kuwait's oil fields. But as repairs have been made to Kuwait's oil wells, Kuwait has increased production and oil prices have dropped.

Production quotas are not easy to maintain among different firms or different nations. Most cartels do not last very long because the members cheat on the agreements. If each producer thinks that it can increase its own production, and thus its profits, without affecting what the other producers do, all producers end up producing more than their assigned amounts; the price of the product declines and the cartel falls apart.

Even though cartels are illegal in the United States, a few have been sanctioned by the government. The National Collegiate Athletic Association (NCAA) is a cartel of colleges and universities. It sets rules of behavior and enforces those rules through a governing board. Member schools are placed on probation or their programs are dismantled when they violate the agreement. The citrus cartel, composed of citrus growers in California and Arizona, enforces its actions through its governing board. Sunkist Growers, Inc., a cooperative of many growers, represents more than half of the California and Arizona production and also plays an important role in enforcing the rules of the cartel.

■ facilitating practices:
actions that lead to cooperation among rivals

2.c.3. Facilitating Practices
Actions by firms can contribute to cooperation and collusion even though the firms do not formally agree to cooperate. Such actions are called **facilitating practices**. Pricing policies can leave the impression that firms are explicitly fixing prices, or cooperating, when in fact they are merely following the same strategies. For instance, the use of

■ **cost-plus markup pricing:**
a price set by adding an amount
to the per unit cost of producing
and supplying a good or service

cost-plus markup pricing tends to bring about similar if not identical pricing behavior among rival firms. If firms set prices by determining the average cost of an item and adding a 50 percent markup to the cost, they would be cost-plus pricing. If all firms face the same cost curves, then all firms will set the same prices. If costs decrease, then all firms will lower prices the same amount and at virtually the same time. Such pricing behavior is common in the grocery business.

Another practice that leads to implicit cooperation is the most-favored-customer policy. Often the time between purchase and delivery of a product is quite long. To avoid the possibility that customer A purchases a product at one price and then learns that customer B purchased the product at a lower price or benefited from product features unavailable to customer A, a producer will guarantee that customer A will receive the lowest price and all features for a certain period of time. Customer A is thus a **most-favored customer (MFC)**.

■ **most-favored customer:**
a commitment that the customer
will receive a lower price if anyone else receives a lower price

The most-favored-customer policy actually gives firms an incentive not to lower prices even in the face of reduced demand. A firm that lowers the price of its product must then give rebates to all most-favored customers, which forces all other firms with most-favored-customer policies to do the same. In addition, the MFC allows a firm to collect information on what its rivals are doing. Customers will return products for a rebate when another firm offers the same product for a lower price.

Consider the behavior of firms that produced antiknock additives for gasoline from 1974 to 1979. Lead-based antiknock compounds had been used in the refining of gasoline since the 1920s. From the 1920s until 1948, the Ethyl Corporation was the sole domestic producer of the compounds. In 1948, Du Pont entered the industry. PPG Industries followed in 1961, and Nalco in 1964. Beginning in 1973, the demand for lead-based antiknock compounds decreased dramatically. However, because each company had most-favored-customer clauses, high prices were maintained even as demand for the product declined.

A most-favored-customer policy discourages price decreases because it requires producers to lower prices retroactively with rebates. If all rivals provide all buyers with most-favored-customer clauses, a high price is likely to be stabilized in the industry.

2.d. Summary: Business Behavior

Business behavior consists of the search for economic profit. Once that profit has been created, businesses want to keep it. This requires that barriers to entry be created. Having some type of barrier means that existing firms can earn positive economic profits for as long as the barriers are effective. This does not mean that business behavior stops. Businesses develop strategies to earn economic profit and then to keep that profit. Strategic behavior takes place when there are just a few firms competing with each other.

RECAP

1. Most business is carried out by large firms.
2. The shape of the demand curve and the marginal-revenue curve may depend on how rival firms react to changes in price and product.
3. The kinked demand curve is one example of how firms may react to price changes. The kink occurs because rivals follow price cuts but not price increases.
4. Price leadership occurs when one firm determines the price and quantity, knowing that all other firms will follow suit. The price leader is usually the dominant firm in the industry.

Judo and Business

Competition is often considered a game, like chess or bridge, whereby rivals initiate moves, respond to moves, bid, bluff, and carry out various strategies. It is also often compared to the martial arts, such as judo. A central principle of judo is to use your opponent's size and strength against him. This is what Netscape attempted when it announced on January 22, 1998, that it planned to make the source code of its next-generation browser, Communicator 5.0, freely available on the Internet. This allowed anyone with the requisite skills to extend, modify, customize, and enhance the program. The judo move was aimed at Microsoft.

Microsoft's strength is its dominance of the markets in operating systems and office applications. Netscape is using this strength against Microsoft. By providing an opportunity for diversity, Netscape is countering the uniformity created by Microsoft's dominance. Within minutes of Netscape's announcement, computer science students were exchanging e-mail about the features they wanted to add to the browser. In the Internet environment, an application that can change rapidly, like Communicator, in the hands of thousands of programmers may have a big advantage over an application that changes only when its manufacturer issues a new release.

Netscape's move was considered an act of desperation by many, and nearly simultaneously with the announcement Netscape was being shopped as a partner for many other high-tech firms. Yet the announcement could also have been judo in operation. Netscape gave its customers a fully customizable browser, something Microsoft, because of its huge size and dominance of the market, will have a hard time matching. In judo, the prize goes not to the biggest player but to the one who is most nimble and has the best moves.

5. Firms often have incentives to cooperate. Collusion, making a secret cooperative agreement, is illegal in the United States. Cartels, also illegal in the United States, rest on explicit cooperation achieved through formal agreement.

6. Facilitating practices implicitly encourage cooperation in an industry.

3. GOVERNMENT AND FIRMS

In the previous chapter, we saw that the large firm could have a cost advantage over smaller firms. When a firm dominates a market and does not fear entry, it can charge higher prices and earn higher profits. In the previous sections, we discussed several business strategies. The objective of the strategies is to take the consumer surplus and collect it as producer surplus—to earn positive economic profit. Are these behaviors fair? Are they legal?

■ antitrust laws:
rules of behavior prescribed by the government

The government makes the rules that define behavior. **Antitrust laws**, enforced by the Justice Department and the Federal Trade Commission (FTC), determine what types of contracts are legal, who can participate in certain markets, when firms can merge, and in general how firms *should* behave. These rules focus primarily on the large firm because of the potential of the large firm to charge excessive prices and earn excessive profits.

3.a. Antitrust Laws

The government—specifically the Justice Department and the Federal Trade Commission—attempts to maintain competition in markets by monitoring and controlling the activities of large firms and by setting the rules of behavior for large businesses. The government may not allow large firms to merge or to carry out certain activities. The government may take large firms to

Bill Gates, founder of Microsoft, has been under attack by rivals and the federal government in recent years because of Microsoft's dominance of the market. The most recent criticism of Microsoft has involved the practice of including the Microsoft Internet browser in each Office 98 software package. The Justice Department maintains that this is an act of anticompetition—a monopolization of the market.

■ **monopolization of a market:**
market dominance by one firm gained unfairly

court and attempt to penalize them for what is called **monopolization of a market**—the attempt to unfairly restrict or bar entry by rivals. The government carries out hundreds of activities limiting the behavior of large firms each year, although we usually hear about just a few high-profile cases.

In the 1960s, computers were sold or leased as complete systems, combinations of central processing units and peripherals—tape drives, disk drives, programs, and other components. A Control Data disk drive did not provide direct competition for an IBM disk drive because the Control Data unit would not work with the IBM central processing unit and software. In the late 1960s, several companies developed tape and disk drives that were compatible with the IBM units. This allowed the companies to sell the peripherals in direct competition with IBM, forcing IBM to respond to competition on each piece of equipment as well as on the entire system. IBM's ability to control price and output in the peripherals market was reduced, but because the peripheral companies could not produce a compatible central processing unit, IBM retained the ability to control price and output in the systems market. IBM dropped the price of its peripherals to the point at which the other firms could not compete and retained its higher price on the central processing unit. IBM was taken to court for its actions. After several years and millions of dollars, IBM won the right to continue its actions. By this time, the compatible peripherals had been manufactured by several companies.

The traditional telephone market is divided into long-distance and local. The long-distance market is a competitive market today, with many firms entering and offering service. In fact, there are about 400 long-distance telephone companies operating in the United States today. This was not always the case. Prior to 1984, the long-distance market was controlled by a single firm, AT&T, and that firm was regulated by the government. The government dictated telephone rates and service. In 1984, the government decreed that AT&T had to be broken into what is now AT&T (the long-distance company) and seven regional local calling companies, known today as the Regional Bell Operating Companies. The long-distance market was deregulated. The government allowed any firm that wanted to offer long-distance to enter the market and offer the service. The government gave up trying to dictate rates and service. As a result, hundreds of new companies entered the market, and long-distance prices have declined by about 70 percent.

In each of the seven regions, the Regional Bell Operating Company has over 90 percent of the local calling market. State governments regulate the regional Bell company operating in the state and dictate prices and service requirements. The success of deregulating the long-distance market induced Congress to attempt to deregulate the local market. The Telecommunications Act of 1996 was supposed to create a competitive market in local calling, but to date local calling remains dominated by the Regional Bell Operating Companies.

In February 1986, Coca-Cola Company declared its intention to purchase the Dr Pepper Company and merge the operations of the two companies. Just weeks earlier, PepsiCo had announced its intention to purchase the Seven-Up Company, a subsidiary of Philip Morris. These two mergers would have meant the consolidation of the first and fourth and the second and third largest sellers of concentrate for carbonated soft drinks in the United States. Government policymakers determined that these mergers would be anticompetitive and did not allow them.

In the 1980s and again in the late 1990s, Microsoft came under government scrutiny. The 1980s scrutiny of Microsoft was based on the claim that the operating system owned by Microsoft was so dominant that it allowed Microsoft to charge much higher prices than would occur in a competitive market with free entry. The 1990s argument against Microsoft was that Microsoft required computer manufacturers and retailers to include its Internet browser with each personal computer, thereby precluding competing firms like Netscape from competing in the market. In each case, Microsoft agreed to stop its behavior, but the agreement did not seem to alter the market.

The government also scrutinizes the price strategies of large firms. In recent years, a major controversy has been over the question whether a franchisor can dictate the prices that a franchisee can charge. Kodak sells its film products to independent retail outlets. Does Kodak have the right to tell the firms what prices they must charge for the Kodak products? Although both the yes and no sides have won arguments in court, the sentiment today in the Justice Department and FTC is that the answer is yes.

Another price strategy questioned in recent years by the government has involved bundling. Microsoft bundled its Internet access software with its Office 97 and 98 packages. Consumers cannot purchase the Office 97 or 98 without also getting the Internet access. Is this an unfair strategy? The debate continues.

The government has been involved in several cases of predatory pricing. It is argued that a firm will sell a product below its costs to try to drive another out of business for the sole purpose of then raising the price to excessive levels later. Predatory pricing has proven to be a difficult case for the government to win. Not only must the firm sell below its own cost, but it must then create significant barriers to entry if it is to raise its price to "excessive" levels. Without the barriers to entry, once the predatory firm earns positive economic profit, other firms will enter and again compete with the predatory firm.

Price discrimination comes under international scrutiny on a regular basis. The World Trade Organization, the international agency involved in business behavior, has examined many cases in which an industry in one country accuses competitors in another country of dumping. For instance, United States industries have filed claims of dumping against South African manufacturers of steel plate; against German, Italian, and French winemakers; against Japanese manufacturers of semiconductors; against Singapore; and against 19 steel-producing nations.

3.b. Regulation

Antitrust laws set rules of behavior for large firms. In many industries, the government does more than simply set the rules of behavior. Often it intervenes in the operation of the business, dictating the price that can be charged

The Botswana, Zimbabwe, and South African governments allow individuals to own elephants. These elephant "farmers" ensure that the elephants breed and reproduce so they can be sold for their tusks, for hunting in special hunting parks, or to zoos in developed nations. This has led to a revival of the elephant population in these nations. Most other nations have created national parks in which hunting is forbidden, but the results have not stemmed the tide of extinction of the species. These orphaned elephants are being cared for at a wildlife preserve in Kenya.

■ **regulation:**
the control of some aspect of business by the government

■ **natural monopolies:**
when economies of scale lead to just one firm

or the areas that can be or have to be served. In some cases, the government actually pays for and produces the good or service—public education, for instance. These types of intervention are referred to as **regulation**.

The government has regulated some industries because of the argument that the industries are **natural monopolies**. A natural monopoly is one that would arise because the industry consists only of economies of scale. Economies of scale would mean that the largest firm could set a price below that which any smaller firm would need to stay in business. The market would have just one firm—a monopoly. For many years following the industrial revolution, it was argued that the railroads were natural monopolies. Thus, the government has been involved in the railroad industry for more than 100 years. Electric utilities have been regulated because of the argument that they are natural monopolies. Until 1984, the FCC also regulated the telecommunications industry, controlling entry and some prices. The purpose of telecommunication regulation was to make high-quality service available to everyone in the country at reasonable prices and to control what was considered to be a natural monopoly held by AT&T.

The argument for regulating airlines was to create orderly growth and avoid a natural monopoly. From the mid-1930s to the mid-1970s, the Civil Aeronautics Authority and its successor, the Civil Aeronautics Board (CAB), controlled entry into the airline industry. Each airline was restricted to specific routes. For example, United Air Lines was authorized to serve north-south routes on the West Coast, and Delta and Eastern served such routes on the East Coast.

The argument for the government regulation of airwaves is to avoid chaos. If just anyone could broadcast radio or TV signals on any of the airwaves, the broadcast spectrum might become so crowded that a clear signal could not be obtained. Television and radio broadcasting rights are granted by the Federal Communications Commission (FCC).

Although economists debate the costs and benefits of regulation, the amount of regulation has grown steadily since the Great Depression. Most of this growth has been due to what is called **social regulation**, rather than economic regulation. Social regulation is concerned with the conditions under which goods and services are produced and the impact of these goods on the public. The following government agencies are concerned with social regulation:

■ **social regulation:**
government regulation of health, safety, the environment, and employment policies

The Occupational Safety and Health Administration (OSHA), which is concerned with protecting workers against injuries and illnesses associated with their jobs

The Consumer Product Safety Commission (CPSC), which specifies minimum standards for safety of products

The Food and Drug Administration (FDA), which is concerned with the safety and effectiveness of food, drugs, and cosmetics

The Equal Employment Opportunity Commission (EEOC), which focuses on the hiring, promotion, and discharge of workers

The Environmental Protection Agency (EPA), which is concerned with air, water, and noise pollution

3.c. Why Does the Government Intervene?

The argument in favor of the antitrust laws is that if the government does not limit the behavior of large firms, these firms will create barriers to entry and then be able to charge excessive prices and earn excessive profits. Although there are cases in which government intervention did lead to a favorable outcome for consumers and society in general, there also are cases in which it is the government intervention itself that creates a barrier to entry.

Seeking advantages from the government is a commonly used business strategy. Businesses seek government restrictions on imports, ask for limits on the entry of new firms, request price floors for their products, seek the imposition of costs on rivals, and devote resources to obtaining many other benefits. These types of activities are called **rent or benefit seeking**. Such activities do not create or produce goods and service. They simply take resources from one group and transfer them to another.

■ **rent or benefit seeking:** resources used to gain benefits from the government

If rent seeking is unproductive, why does it occur? It occurs because it can be extremely profitable. A firm may be able to secure more profit by enlisting the aid of government than by being innovative. A single cable TV firm is allowed to offer services in each region without any competitive firms offering cable services. A patent issued by the government enables the patent holder to be the sole provider of the good that is patented. Often a license or permit issued by the government is required in order to operate a business at a particular location. Until the mid-1980s in the United States, banks could not operate in more than one state; interstate banking was prohibited. In some states, banks could not have branches. These restrictions provided existing banks an advantage. As noted previously, until the mid-1970s, airlines were restricted from entering the market and from flying specific routes once they had entered. To be allowed to fly between major cities such as L.A. and New York was a real advantage. The government will often restrict the sales of foreign-made products. Harley-Davidson was able to get the U.S. government to protect it from competition from Japanese firms. Japanese motorcycle companies were allowed to sell only small motorcycles in the United States, leaving the large machines for the Harley-Davidson company.

Clearly some businesses gain from government intervention. Does the consumer? There is a debate among economists over this issue. On one side, it is argued that without the government monitoring and limiting the behavior of large firms, markets would be dominated by one or a few firms and consumer surplus would be minimal. On the other side, it is argued that the government intervenes not to improve efficiency but to provide benefits to special interest groups. Opponents of regulation argue that the natural monopoly and chaos arguments are not valid. They point out that most government regulation has been undertaken to protect special interests—the railroad barons, for example. When trucking became a direct competitor to the railroad, the government placed the trucking industry under regulation. Trucking was regulated not because it was a natural monopoly, but because years of regulation had put railroads at a disadvantage relative to trucking.

It appears that the second argument has been winning the day in recent years. The government has stopped controlling or regulating the transportation and long-distance telephone markets and is attempting to do the same with local calling and electricity. Yet the first argument, that in favor of government intervention, appears to be dominant in the social arena of business activities. The government has become increasingly involved with the health and safety of the workplace, the human resource policies of business (compensation, pensions, harassment, evaluation, stress, etc.), and the environmental consequences of business activities.

Most of the arguments made in support of social regulation are based on the idea that the regulation will aid the public. Over 10,000 workers die in job-related accidents in the United States each year. Air pollution is an increasing problem in many cities, leading to cancer and other diseases, which in turn mean increased demands on healthcare agencies. Hundreds of children are killed each year as a result of poorly designed toys. Unfair discharges from jobs, discrimination, and sexual harassment occur frequently. It is argued that without government regulation, these events would be much more serious and would impose tremendous costs on society.

There are costs to the regulation, however. It is expensive to administer the agencies and enforce the rules and regulations. The annual administrative costs of federal regulatory activities exceed $15 billion. The cost to business of complying with the rules and regulations has been estimated to exceed $300 billion per year. Complying with environmental regulations alone costs business more than $200 billion per year.

Added to the direct costs of regulations are the opportunity costs. For instance, the lengthy process for approving new biotechnology has stymied advances in agriculture. Regulatory restrictions on the telecommunications industry have resulted in the United States lagging behind Japan in the development of fiber optics and high-definition television. The total cost imposed on the U.S. economy from federal government regulations is estimated to be more than $600 billion a year, $6,000 per household.

Are the regulations worth the costs? To answer this question we need to compare the costs and benefits of each regulation. But this can be a difficult proposition. It may require us to answer the question: How much is a life worth? Simply asking the question offends many people. But answering the question is what economists think is necessary if regulation is not to benefit only special interest groups. To economists, life is worth what people are willing to pay to stay alive. Of course, that differs from person to person, but the values could be used to place limits on what regulations to implement. For instance, using the extra pay that people require to take dangerous jobs or calculating the total value of expenditures on smoke detectors and safer cars could provide estimates of how much people value life. Although the estimates vary widely, none exceed $10 million. Some economists thus argue that any regulation costing more than $10 million per life saved should not be implemented. For instance, rules on unvented space heaters save lives for just $130,000 each whereas regulations on asbestos removal exceed $100 million per life saved. According to a comparison of costs and benefits, the first rule should be implemented, but the second should not.

The cost-benefit test for regulation would limit regulations designed to benefit a very few at the cost of many. However, the cost-benefit test also should include the opportunity costs implied by interfering with the free market, according to many economists. If labeling is desired by the public, won't the public voluntarily pay the higher price for it? Why, then, is regulation necessary unless it is to benefit some special interest group? If seat belts and antilock braking systems are desired by the public, won't the public voluntarily pay the price to have these safety systems?

RECAP

1. The government can serve as a barrier to entry.

2. The government through the Justice Department and the Federal Trade Commission prescribes rules of behavior for business. These rules are referred to as antitrust laws.

3. Large firms come under the scrutiny of the government because of their potential to dominate a market.

4. The government intervenes in the market ostensibly to control the behavior of firms, but often the real story is to provide benefits to special interest groups.

5. Whereas antitrust laws prescribe the rules of behavior for large firms, with regulation the government may dictate specific behavior.

6. There are two general categories of regulation. One is the regulation of a specific business or industry. The second is social regulation—the regulation of all business for some social purpose.

7. Whereas regulation of specific businesses may not be in favor, social regulation has grown tremendously during the past two decades or so.

SUMMARY

■■ What is a large firm?

1. Most businesses are small proprietorships or partnerships, but total business activity is dominated by large firms.

2. A large firm is one that is large relative to the market.

3. Typically, if entry is free there are many small firms in the market.

■■ What is a pricing strategy?

4. A pricing strategy is a way to ensure that $MR = MC$ under different circumstances.

5. Price discrimination involves using different price elasticities to set different prices. The higher a consumer's price elasticity of demand, the lower the price that consumer receives.

6. Price discrimination is an effective strategy only if the customers have different price elasticities and the customers cannot resell to each other.

7. Interdependence is characterized as what is good for A depends on what B does and what B does depends on what A does.

8. The kinked demand curve illustrates one type of interdependence. The kink occurs because rivals follow price decreases but not price increases.

9. The prisoner's dilemma represents another type of interdependence. In the dilemma, firms select a less than first best strategy because of what they anticipate their rivals will do.

■■ Do firms ever cooperate with rivals?

10. Often cooperation enables firms to retain their economic profits better than cutthroat competition would.

11. Cooperation may take many forms: price leadership, collusion, cartels, and implicit actions such as cost-plus pricing or most-favored-customer practices.

■■ Why does the government interfere with the behavior of firms?

12. Antitrust laws are the rules the government sets on business behavior.

13. The units of government most involved with the activities of business are the Justice Department and the Federal Trade Commission.

14. The FTC and Justice Department focus primarily on the large firm.

15. The government does more than set the rules of behavior, it regulates some businesses.

16. Arguments for regulation are to control the excesses of a natural monopoly and to prevent chaos.

17. Regulations in the operation of business have been declining in recent years. Social regulation, however, has increased significantly.

18. The two arguments as to why the government intervenes in the activities of business are (1) to ensure that markets are essentially competitive; and (2) to provide benefits to special interest groups.

KEY TERMS

business firm

sole proprietorship

partnership

corporation

dumping

dominant strategy

prisoner's dilemma

cartel

facilitating practices

cost-plus markup pricing

most-favored customer (MFC)

antitrust laws

monopolization of a market

regulation

natural monopolies

social regulation

rent or benefit seeking

EXERCISES

1. Suppose you are the manager of a firm that has discovered an innovation that enhances the power of a microchip 1,000 times. What would you do with that unique resource—your innovation? Would you sell the chip to Intel and Motorola and allow them to market the chip under their own brand? Would you sell the chip directly to manufacturers like IBM and Macintosh under your own firm's label?

2. Explain when it might make sense to bundle two products together and charge a single price for the two. Would you charge more or less than the total of each one separately?

3. Explain how negotiating over the price of an automobile is an attempt by the auto dealer to extract your consumer surplus.

4. Time-of-day pricing is a strategy of charging a different price for a good or service depending on the time of day. Explain what this and peak load pricing have in common.

5. In a situation that occurs only once, if you advertise and your rival advertises, you will each earn $5 million in profits. If neither of you advertises, your rival will make $4 million and you will make $2 million. If you advertise and your rival does not, you will make $10 million and your rival will make $3 million. If your rival advertises and you do not, you will make $1 million and your rival will make $3 million.

   a. Set up the situation in a matrix form.

   b. Do you have a strategy that you will choose no matter what your rival does?

   c. Does your rival have a strategy that he will choose no matter what you do?

   d. What is the solution or equilibrium?

   e. How much would you be willing to pay your rival not to advertise?

   f. Find the equilibrium when there are no repeated transactions.

   g. Now, suppose there are repeated transactions. If the interest rate is 10 percent, what will be the outcome?

6. You and your rival must simultaneously decide what price to advertise in the weekly newspaper. If you each charge a low price, you each earn zero profits. If you each charge a high price, you each earn profits of $3. If you charge different prices, the one charging the higher price loses $5 and the one charging the lower price makes $5. Explain what you do in this case.

7. You are the owner-operator of a gas station in a small town. Over the past 20 years you and your rival have successfully kept prices at a very high level. You recently learned that your rival is retiring and closing his station in two weeks. What should you do today?

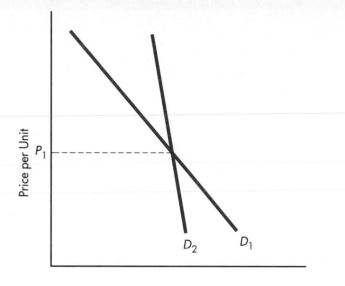

Price per Unit

P_1

D_2 D_1

Quantity

8. What is meant by interdependence? How does the kinked demand curve describe interdependence?

9. What is the cost of a firm that fails to take rivals' actions into account? Suppose the firm operates along demand curve D_1, shown at left, as if no firms will follow its lead in price cuts or price increases. In fact, however, other firms do follow the price cuts and the true demand curve below price P_1 lies below D_1. If the firm sets a price lower than P_1, what happens?

10. The payoff matrix below shows the profit two firms earn if both advertise, neither advertises, or one advertises while the other does not. Profits are reported in millions of dollars. Does either firm have a dominant strategy?

Firm 1

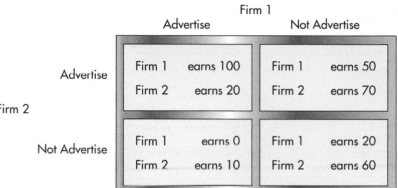

		Advertise	Not Advertise
Firm 2	**Advertise**	Firm 1 earns 100 Firm 2 earns 20	Firm 1 earns 50 Firm 2 earns 70
	Not Advertise	Firm 1 earns 0 Firm 2 earns 10	Firm 1 earns 20 Firm 2 earns 60

 INTERNET EXERCISE

This chapter discusses the behavior of large firms and the government's role in regulating business. Use the Internet to explore the Federal Trade Commission. Go to the Boyes/Melvin *Fundamentals of Economics* Web site at http://www.hmco.com/college/ and click on the Internet Exercise link for Chapter 7. Now answer the questions that appear on the Boyes/Melvin Web site.

8

Social Issues

---

1. How does the market for natural resources function?

2. Why might a market not allocate goods and services efficiently?

3. How do global environmental problems differ from domestic environmental problems?

4. Why are illicit drugs such a problem?

5. What is discrimination?

6. Are discrimination and freely functioning markets compatible?

7. What are minimum wages?

8. Who bears the negative effects of a minimum wage?

9. Are incomes distributed equally in the United States?

10. How is poverty measured, and does poverty exist in the United States?

11. Who are the poor?

A re you concerned with global warming, saving the rain forests, and reducing pollution? Have you noticed the number of homeless people on the streets these days? Are there more than in the past? Have you ever been discriminated against because of your age, race, or sex? Have you been touched by illegal drugs, or by gang wars, drive-by shootings, or other drug-related crimes? Let's discuss some of these issues using the knowledge we've gained regarding firms, consumers, and markets. In this chapter, we'll use our knowledge of economics to discuss environmental issues, the problems of illicit drugs, discrimination, minimum wages, and income distribution and poverty. ■

1. THE ENVIRONMENT

Global warming, the destruction of the rain forests, the depletion of the ozone, the extinction of animal species, and other environmental issues are of great concern to many people. So are the costs that people have to pay in the name of the environment—higher prices on cars due to emission control equipment, annual fees to test for emissions from cars, higher gas prices due to refining requirements, higher taxes to pay for cleaning up the environment, and so on.

When speaking of the environment, we are actually referring to natural resources—**renewable natural resources**, like trees, plants, and animals, and **nonrenewable natural resources**, resources that can be used only once and cannot be replaced, like coal, natural gas, and oil. To understand environmental issues, it is necessary to examine the markets for renewable and nonrenewable natural resources.

1.a. The Market for Natural Resources

Let's consider the nonrenewable natural resources first. Only a fixed amount of oil or coal exists, so the more that is used in any given year, the less that remains for future use. As some of the resource is used today, less is available next year. This is shown in Figure 1. The vertical line along the right side of the figure illustrates the idea that there is a fixed amount of the resource.

■ **renewable natural resources:**
resources that can renew themselves

■ **nonrenewable natural resources:**
resources that cannot replenish themselves

Oil poured from a transport vessel after the vessel ran aground. The oil covered nearby beaches, caught several species of wildlife in its sticky sludge, and led to a very expensive cleanup process.

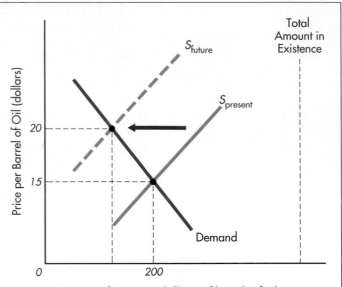

Figure 1
The Market for Nonrenewable Resources
Supply curve $S_{present}$ represents the quantity that resource owners are willing to extract and offer for sale during any particular year. As the price rises, more is extracted now, leaving less available in the future, $S_{present}$ to S_{future}. The demand for a nonrenewable natural resource is the value of that resource to the firm and to consumers—what the resource contributes to the firm's revenue and consumers' enjoyment. Equilibrium occurs in the market for a nonrenewable natural resource when the demand and supply curves intersect.

Although there is a fixed amount in total, at any given time there is a varying amount depending on the price of the resource. For example, supply curve $S_{present}$ represents the quantity that resource owners are willing to extract and offer for sale during any particular year. As the price rises, more is extracted now, leaving less available in the future. This causes the supply curve of the resource in the future to shift up, as shown in Figure 1 by the move from $S_{present}$ to S_{future}. The shift occurs because the cost of acquiring or extracting the resource rises as the amount of the resource in existence falls. For instance, in the late 1800s, oil became an important resource. At first, it was extracted with small pumps that gathered up the oil seeping out of the ground. Once that extremely accessible source was gone, wells had to be dug. Over time, wells had to be deeper and be placed in progressively more difficult terrain. From land, to the ocean off California, to the rugged waters off Alaska, to the wicked North Sea, the search for oil has progressed. Each progression is more difficult and thus more costly.

The demand for a nonrenewable natural resource is determined in the same way as the demand for any other resource. Demand is the value of that resource to the firm and to consumers—what the resource contributes to the firm's revenue and consumers' enjoyment.

Equilibrium occurs in the market for a nonrenewable natural resource when the demand for and supply of that resource are equal, as shown in Figure 1 at $15 and 200 billion barrels. The equilibrium price, $15, and equilibrium quantity, 200 billion barrels, represent the price and quantity today. Extracting and selling the equilibrium quantity of 200 billion barrels today reduces the quantity available in the future by 200 billion barrels. This means that extracting the resource tomorrow is probably going to be more costly than extracting it today. Thus, the supply curve for the resource in the future lies above the supply curve for the present, S_{future} rather than $S_{present}$, if any of the resource is being consumed today. With a higher supply curve and the same demand, the price is higher, $20 rather than $15. Thus, the price in the future is likely to be higher than the price today if some of the resource is extracted and sold today.

The resource owner must decide whether to extract and sell the resource today or leave it in the ground for future use. Suppose that by extracting and selling the oil that lies below someone's land today, the landowner can make a profit of $10 per barrel after all costs have been paid. With that $10 the owner could buy stocks or bonds to put the money into a savings account or use it to acquire education or marketable skills. If the owner could earn 10 percent doing one of these alternatives, then, in essence, the owner would realize $11 one year from now from the $10 profit obtained today. Should the oil be extracted today? The answer depends on how much profit the resource owner expects to earn on the oil one year from now, and this depends on what the price of oil and the cost of extraction are one year from now.

You can probably understand why economists argue that it is unlikely the world will ever run out of nonrenewable resources. As the total amount of oil or any other nonrenewable resource in existence is reduced, its price in the future will rise. It will continue rising as the supply dwindles until it is so high that no one would extract the oil today, thus, saving it for the future.

Renewable natural resources are different from nonrenewable resources in the sense that renewable (nonexhaustible) natural resources can be used repeatedly without depleting the amount available for future use. Plants and animals can replenish themselves, if there are enough of a species available to do that. The problem is not that there is a fixed quantity but that a resource will be consumed too rapidly for it to reproduce. The role of the market for renewable resources is to determine a price at which the quantity of the resource used is just sufficient to enable the resource to renew itself at a rate that best satisfies society's wants. For instance, the rate at which trees are harvested depends on comparing the rate at which the value of the forests increases over time and the rate that could be earned by razing the forests, selling the trees, and placing the money into another activity today. A large harvest one year means fewer trees available in the future and a longer time for renewal to occur. This would suggest a lower price for the trees today and a higher price in the future, which would induce some tree owners to hold off harvesting their trees.

The markets for nonrenewable and renewable resources operate to ensure that current and future wants are satisfied in the least costly manner and that resources are used in their highest-valued alternative now and in the future. When a nonrenewable resource is being rapidly depleted, its future price rises so that less of the resource is used today. When a renewable resource is being used at a rate that does not allow the resource to replenish itself, the future price rises so that less of the resource is used today.

1.b. Environmental Problems

If the market for natural resources allocates resources to their most highly valued use today and in the future, why do we hear so much about global warming, the depletion of the ozone layer, the destruction of the rain forest, the pollution of the oceans and rivers, and the extinction of wildlife? Part of the answer may be that the markets for resources do not work as well as we have just described.

1.b.1. Externalities Problems may arise in markets when private individuals and businesses do not have to bear the full costs of transactions they undertake. A business firm knows how much it costs to employ workers, and it knows the costs of purchasing materials or constructing buildings. An individual who buys a new car or pays for a pizza knows exactly what the cost of these items will be. Such costs are **private costs**—costs borne solely by the

■ **private costs:**
costs borne solely by the individuals involved in a transaction

individuals involved in the transaction that created the costs. Many environmental problems arise, however, because the costs of an individual's actions are not borne directly by that individual. When a firm pollutes the air or water or a tourist leaves trash in a park, the costs of these actions are not easily determined and are not borne by the individual or firm creating them. This situation represents a market problem because the price of the good and the equilibrium quantity produced and consumed do not reflect the full costs of producing or consuming the good. In this sense, "too much" or "too little" is produced.

Consider an oil tanker that runs aground and dumps crude oil into a pristine ocean area teeming with wildlife, or a public beach where people litter, or even your classrooms where people leave their cups, used papers, and food wrappers on the floor. A cost is involved in these actions. The crude oil may kill wildlife and ruin fishing industries; the garbage may discourage families from using the beach and harm wildlife; and the trash in the classroom may distract from the discussions and lectures. But in none of these cases is the cost of the action borne solely by the individuals who took the action. Instead, the cost is also borne by those who were not participants in the activity. The fishermen, the fish, and other wildlife did not spill the oil, yet they have to bear the cost. The beachgoers who encounter trash and broken bottles were not the litterers, yet they must bear the cost of the litter. You do not create the garbage and yet must wade through the trash. The cost is external to the activity that created it and is thus called an externality, in this case, a **negative externality**. The total cost of a transaction or activity includes the external costs and the private costs. The total cost is called the **social cost**.

Externalities can be negative or positive. A **positive externality** may result from an activity in which benefits are received by consumers or firms not involved directly in the activity. For instance, inoculations for mumps, measles, and other communicable diseases provide benefits to all of society. Society benefits, but individuals are the ones who pay for the inoculations.

When there is a divergence between social costs and private costs, the result is either too much or too little production and consumption. In either case, resources are not being used in their highest-valued activity. Consider a gas station selling gasoline with pumps that have no emission control equipment. Each time a consumer pumps gas, a certain quantity of pollutants is released into the air. The consumer demands gasoline at various prices as reflected by the demand curve. The gas station prices the gasoline in order to maximize profit—by setting prices as given by the demand curve at the quantity where marginal revenue and marginal cost are equal, as illustrated in Figure 2.

The actual cost of the gasoline to society—including the marginal cost and the externality—is given by the marginal-social-cost curve, *MSC*. The price ought to be P_{MSC} rather than P_{MC} and the quantity purchased ought to be Q_{MSC} rather than Q_{MC} if all costs are to be accounted for. According to society's desires, "too much" gasoline is purchased.

In contrast to negative externalities, private costs exceed social costs when external benefits are created. In the case of a positive externality, the *MSC* curve would lie below the *MC* curve and "too little" of the good or service would be produced and purchased. From society's viewpoint, too few people are vaccinated against communicable diseases when individuals have to pay all the costs of inoculations.

1.b.2. Private Property Rights
Market problems may also result because of the absence of well-defined private property rights. A **private property right** is the right to claim ownership of an item. It is well defined if there is a clear owner and if the right is recognized and enforced by society. The lack of private property ownership or rights is a common one in the natural resources area. No one has a private property right to the ocean or air. No one owns the

■ negative externality:
costs that are not borne by the individuals involved in the transaction creating the costs

■ social cost:
private costs plus external costs

■ positive externality:
benefits that are not borne by the individuals involved in the transaction creating the benefits

■ private property right:
the right to claim ownership of an item

Figure 2
Externalities
A firm selling a product whose consumption generates a social cost would sell the amount given by $MR = MC$, ignoring the social costs. Society would prefer the price and quantity given by $MR = MSC$ in order to take into account the social cost.

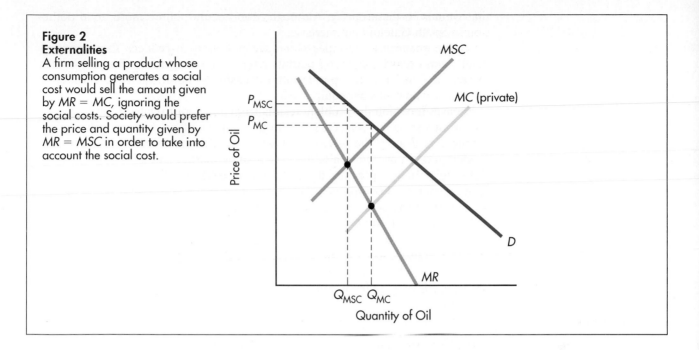

fish in the sea; no one owns the elephants that roam the African plains; no one owns the rain forest; and no one owned the American buffalo or bald eagle. Because no one owns these natural resources, the natural resource market cannot function to ensure that the correct or optimal amount of the resource is used.

The resource markets would solve the problem of harvesting now or in the future if someone owned the forests, oceans, and animals. Without private ownership, however, no one has the incentive to sell the resources at the profit-maximizing rate. A fishing crew has no incentive to harvest the "right" amount of fish, since leaving fish until the future simply leaves them for other fishing crews today. If someone owned the fish, that resource owner would sell the fish only up to the point that the value of fish caught in the future would equal the future value of the revenue obtained from the fish caught today.

1.c. Solutions to Environmental Problems

Is there any way that these market problems can be resolved? Typically, the government is called on to reduce the externality or define the property right. For instance, in the United States, the government agency known as the Environmental Protection Agency (EPA) defines emission levels around the country and requires firms to meet its standards. In some areas of the United States, the EPA is relying on the market to solve the externality problem. The EPA used to define the amount of pollution that could be created by each generator, boiler, baking oven, or other piece of equipment. This was a very costly and inefficient procedure for both the firms involved and the government. In many instances, the EPA now allows a company to choose how it wants to pollute as long as total pollution does not exceed some assigned level. Each business gets a certificate indicating the amount of pollution it is permitted each year; each is given a property right to that amount of pollution. These permits can then be bought and sold in a market, which is referred to as a "smog" market. A firm easily meeting its standards can sell its excess to a firm having some difficulty meeting its standards. For example, Mobil Corporation purchased permission to spew out an additional 900 pounds of noxious gas vapors each day for about $3 million from the city of South Gate, California. South Gate had acquired the credits from General Motors, which closed a plant there and sold the city the property and the pollution permits that went with the property. Although Mobil could pollute more, total pollution in South Gate did not increase.

As the government decides to reduce pollution, it reduces the permitted levels, and the price of smog permits rises. Firms then must choose whether to continue polluting and purchasing increasingly more expensive permits or to purchase new, cleaner equipment.

In cases in which the problem results from a lack of private property rights, the problem can be corrected by the assignment of private property rights. Again it is usually the government who is called on to assign and enforce property rights. In addition to creating a smog market and assigning property rights to pollution permits, the government assigns property rights to many other resources. For instance, broadcast frequencies are assigned to companies by the FCC, and the Department of the Interior assigns private property rights to some forest lands.

In Africa, a few nations have assigned ownership of elephants to individuals. The individuals are able to raise the elephants and then sell them. The elephant population in these countries has actually increased since private property rights were instituted.

1.d. Global Problems

Global environmental problems are complicated by the simple fact that the individuals involved live in many nations. Sulfur dioxide and nitrogen dioxide emitted by factories in the United States are blown to Canada, where they mix with moisture and fall as acid rain. Manufacturing plants located along the Mexican side of the U.S.-Mexico border emit pollutants that flow across the border into the United States. Because one nation cannot impose its wishes on another, it is difficult for either government to assign property rights.

The ozone layer poses another international challenge. Many scientists claim that the stratospheric ozone layer has been damaged by the use of CFCs and other chemicals. The problem is that no one government can claim ownership of the ozone. As a result, property rights cannot be assigned. No one has an incentive to stop using CFCs or other chemicals that might harm the ozone.

The approach nations have taken to reduce these problems has been ineffective; multinational, nonbinding agreements have been drafted and signed. These agreements promise a reduction in emissions or pollution but, in reality, have no substance.

RECAP

1. Nonrenewable natural resources are natural resources whose supply is fixed. Renewable natural resources are natural resources that can be replenished.

2. The gap between the equilibrium price today and the equilibrium price at some point in the future generates a rate of return on resources. When that rate of return exceeds what is currently available elsewhere, then the resource is not extracted or used. When that return is less than what can be earned elsewhere, the resource is extracted and sold.

3. Under ideal economic conditions, the harvest rate of renewable resources is such that the amount used meets society's demands and allows the resources to reproduce.

4. Environmental problems may arise either because of an externality or because of the lack of private property rights.

5. An externality occurs when not all the costs and benefits of a transaction are borne by the transacting parties. A negative externality means that

social costs exceed private costs. A positive externality means private costs exceed social costs.

6. When a resource is not privately owned, too much of the resource may be used. No one has an incentive to ensure that the resource is available in the future.

7. A solution to the lack of private property rights is to create such rights and to assign them.

8. Global environmental issues are particularly difficult to solve because no one government can claim ownership of the resource.

2. ILLICIT DRUGS

The market for illicit or illegal drugs is complicated and large and a very interesting illustration of how markets function. Worldwide trade in illicit drugs constitutes 4 percent of total world trade, as much as textiles and steel. The biggest share of the trade occurs in the United States. Americans spend nearly $60 billion a year on illegal drugs—$38 billion on cocaine, $10 billion on heroin, $7 billion on marijuana, and $3 billion on other illegal drugs—about 60 percent of all illicit drugs consumed in the world. Let's discuss some aspects of the illicit drug market.

2.a. The Market

We'll begin with a simple demand and supply diagram representing the market for illicit drugs. It is not unrealistic to suppose that the demanders consist of two segments: those who are hard-core users (addicts) and those who might be tempted to experiment with the drug at the right price. In this case, there are two demands; the one for the addicts is very price-inelastic, and the one for the experimental users is quite price-elastic.

Like any firm with two distinct groups of buyers, the supplier of the drugs would devise a strategy to appeal to both groups of consumers. The supplier's costs are the same for supplying either group of buyers. This is illustrated in Figure 3 with the one marginal-cost curve. Knowing that the price elasticity of demand for the hard-core users is different than it is for the experimental

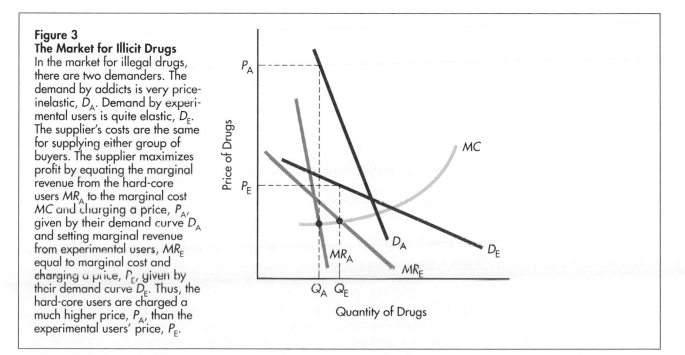

Figure 3
The Market for Illicit Drugs
In the market for illegal drugs, there are two demanders. The demand by addicts is very price-inelastic, D_A. Demand by experimental users is quite elastic, D_E. The supplier's costs are the same for supplying either group of buyers. The supplier maximizes profit by equating the marginal revenue from the hard-core users MR_A to the marginal cost MC and charging a price, P_A, given by their demand curve D_A and setting marginal revenue from experimental users, MR_E equal to marginal cost and charging a price, P_E, given by their demand curve D_E. Thus, the hard-core users are charged a much higher price, P_A, than the experimental users' price, P_E.

users, the supplier would price discriminate. The supplier maximizes profit by equating the marginal revenue from the hard-core users, MR_A, to the marginal cost, MC, and charging a price, P_A, given by their demand curve, D_A.

For the experimental users, the supplier sets marginal revenue from them, MR_E, equal to marginal cost and charges a price, P_E, given by their demand curve, D_E. Thus, the hard-core users are charged a much higher price, P_A, than the experimental users, P_E.

If the supplier is earning a positive economic profit, other suppliers want to get in on the business. The ease or difficulty of entry depends on the type of illicit drugs. It is not difficult to enter the market for the so-called "designer" drugs like amphetamines and crystal ice. A few over-the-counter chemicals and an abandoned building are sufficient to manufacture the drugs. The markets for cocaine and heroin are more difficult to enter. A supplier must have access to the resources (cocoa and poppies) as well as the refining facilities and transportation and distribution channels to get the product to the market.

Since there are few suppliers in the cocaine and heroin markets, what each one does affects the others. If one attempts to increase its market area, the others respond. If one lowers the price, the others respond. In situations in which there are just a few suppliers, the suppliers often decide it is better to cooperate than engage in cutthroat competition. Thus, drug cartels have been formed, such as Medellin, Sinaloa, Belarussa, and so forth. The cartels assign members' territories and dictate quantities and prices.

As with most cartels, there is an enforcer, ensuring that other members follow the rules. In the Organization of Petroleum Exporting Countries (OPEC) Saudi Arabia serves as the enforcer. Whenever one of the member nations decides to increase oil production above its quota, Saudi Arabia will open its facilities and flood the market with oil. The cheating nation ends up with lower revenues than if it had remained within its quota. In the National College Athletic Association (NCAA) whenever a school athletic department cheats, the NCAA administration penalizes it with forfeiture of prize money and sanctions.

The enforcer in the drug cartel literally destroys the errant supplier; drive-by shootings, bombings, and so on are the cartel's enforcer ensuring that cheating by members of the cartel won't occur.

As with all profit-maximizing firms, drug suppliers want to alter the demand curves for their products, making them more price-inelastic and shifting them out. Since the demand by the hard-core user is very price-inelastic already, the suppliers focus on the experimenter's demand. By offering discounts, higher-quality drugs, and even free samples, the suppliers hope to change the price elasticity of demand.

The suppliers would also like to reduce their costs. The primary cost of the drug suppliers is the cost of avoiding having products confiscated, employees arrested, and facilities destroyed. Suppliers attempt to reduce the probability of such costs by bribing or, in some cases, assassinating officials.

Although operating in an illegal market means there are costs of avoiding detection, would the existing suppliers like to see drugs legalized? The answer is a resounding NO. Legalization would reduce the costs of entry to potential new suppliers and drive down economic profits.

2.b. The War on Drugs

The United States devotes enormous resources to fighting illicit drugs. U.S. federal government spending on drug control has risen from \$4.7 billion in 1987 to nearly \$20 billion in 1998. Each state spends millions more. What is the effect of the government's war against drugs?

In the market for illicit drugs, the government's war means that the supplier's costs are raised. In Figure 4, we examine just one demand curve and show the increased costs as an upward shift of the average-cost curves from

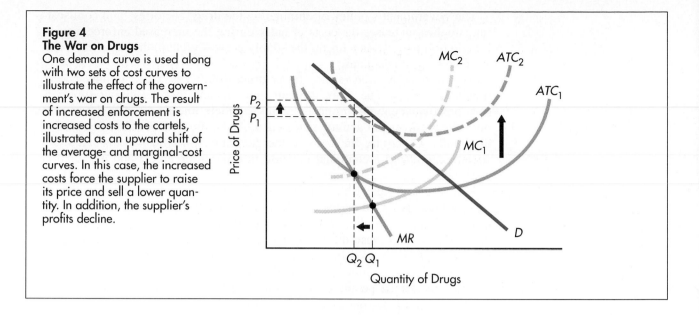

Figure 4
The War on Drugs
One demand curve is used along with two sets of cost curves to illustrate the effect of the government's war on drugs. The result of increased enforcement is increased costs to the cartels, illustrated as an upward shift of the average- and marginal-cost curves. In this case, the increased costs force the supplier to raise its price and sell a lower quantity. In addition, the supplier's profits decline.

ATC_1 to ATC_2 and marginal-cost curves from MC_1 to MC_2. In this case, the increased costs force the supplier to raise its price from P_1 to P_2 and sell a lower quantity, Q_2 rather than Q_1.

The rising costs mean that the supplier's profits decline, but this is most likely only a temporary setback. Aggressive marketing by the cartels has attracted more young people and created more hard-core users. During the 1990s, drug use among junior high and high school students increased dramatically. Illicit drug use rose to 40 percent from 29 percent among high school students. The percentage of the population addicted to illicit drugs today is three times greater than before drug prohibition was implemented in 1920. Thus, although enforcement increased supplier costs, the demand for the drugs rose, leading to even higher profits.

The result of the war on drugs has been to reduce the number of suppliers and to increase the barriers to entry, thereby ensuring that the remaining cartels control the market and earn positive economic profit.

2.c. Free Drugs?

Is there an alternative to illicit drug control other than the war on drugs? The Swiss government provides heroin to hard-core users free and has a very liberal policy regarding drug use by others. Is this the appropriate policy? The user need not commit crimes to obtain the funds with which to purchase the heroin. The Swiss have found that drug-related crime has declined since they initiated their policy of free heroin to hard-core users. On the other hand, reducing the price to the experimenters increases the quantity demanded by them. This could lead to an increasing number of hard-core users. The Swiss policy has not been in force long enough to test this implication, but it is the likely outcome. If so, different policies are needed for the hard-core users and the experimental users.

2.d. Designer Drugs

What about policy regarding the so-called designer drugs, the easily manufactured drugs? Entry into the market for designer drugs is easy. This means that economic profit is driven to zero and there is no incentive for new suppliers to enter. Suppliers might try to differentiate their product in an attempt to reduce the price elasticity of demand, but the cost of differentiating typically exceeds the possible benefits.

The government's policy of eliminating the drug "factories" and confiscating supplies increases the costs of entry during the increased enforcement or interdiction period. As a result, the supply curve shifts up, the price rises, and the quantity sold declines.

Isn't this the desired result—fewer drugs sold? Yes, but it is only a very temporary result. The more difficult entry means that remaining suppliers earn positive economic profit. Potential suppliers line up to enter the market once the enforcement activity is lessened. And enforcement has to be reduced eventually. Otherwise the costs to the government would rise unabated. No society can afford a continual increase in drug enforcement and interdiction activities.

Rather than focusing on supply, perhaps it would be more productive to focus on demand. One means of reducing the quantity demanded is to raise the price. Licensing suppliers and imposing a tax, much like that on cigarettes, could serve to increase the price and reduce quantity demanded, unless this creates an illegal market in untaxed drugs. When taxes are increased on cigarettes too rapidly, an illegal market for untaxed cigarettes develops. It might be possible to change people's tastes with an educational program. If potential consumers could be convinced that the drugs are unhealthy, dangerous, antisocial, or whatever, it might change tastes and thus shift the demand curve in.

RECAP

1. The market for illicit drugs consists of two markets: one for heroin and cocaine and another for the so-called designer drugs.

2. The market for cocaine and heroin is difficult to enter.

3. The market for designer drugs is easy to enter, and the products are identical.

4. The cocaine and heroin market has few suppliers, who usually co-operate. Cartels dominate the market, dictating prices, quantities, and location.

5. Government policy attempting to control illicit drugs has been flawed in both markets. In the cocaine and heroin market, the government has failed to differentiate between the addict and the experimental user. In the designer drug market, the government has failed to realize what the market is and that it must focus on changing demand, not supply.

3. DISCRIMINATION

■ **discrimination:**
the practice of treating people differently in a market, based on a characteristic having nothing to do with that market

We've talked about price discrimination many times in this book. Price discrimination is the practice of charging different customers different prices for an identical item. Price discrimination occurs because the different customers have different price elasticities of demand. **Discrimination**, in general, is somewhat different from price discrimination. Discrimination is the practice of treating different people differently in a market, based on some characteristic that has nothing to do with the market. In the labor market, discrimination occurs when someone or some group is receiving favorable treatment for a reason having nothing to do with that person's or group's job performance.

3.a. The Market

Discrimination on the basis of characteristics that have nothing to do with one's job performance is costly in a market in which entry is easy. Suppose, for instance, that customers preferred to be served by only a certain kind of individual. Customers would then have to be willing to pay higher prices to be served by the preferred group. This is illustrated in Figure 5.

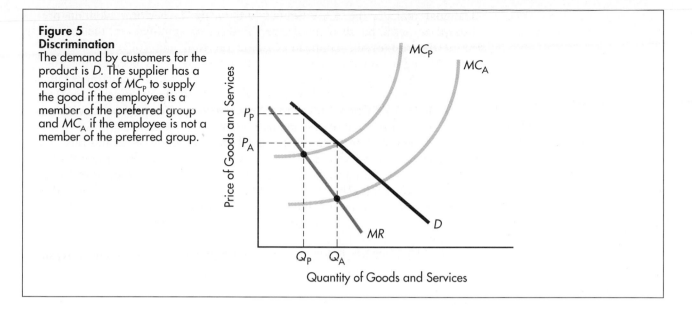

Figure 5
Discrimination
The demand by customers for the product is *D*. The supplier has a marginal cost of MC_P to supply the good if the employee is a member of the preferred group and MC_A if the employee is not a member of the preferred group.

The firm can supply the good using the services of any employee, along cost curve MC_A. The firm can also use the preferred employees, but then the cost of supplying the good is higher, MC_P. Those customers who want the product, but only if served by the preferred group, have to pay P_P, whereas those customers choosing to be served by anyone would have to pay only P_A.

Discrimination requires paying a premium to associate with certain groups or not to associate with certain groups. As we know from prior chapters, any firm not using resources efficiently will be driven out of the market if entry is easy. When entry is easy, having higher costs due to discrimination could drive the discriminating firm out of the market. If customers are not willing to pay the premium (the difference between P_P and P_A), then the firm cannot discriminate.

If a firm has erected strict barriers to entry, then the discrimination may not be costly. A monopoly or even a government agency that does not have to compete with another firm could get away with using resources less efficiently. Managers, employees, and even customers of monopolies or government agencies may be able to discriminate without having more efficient firms drive them out of the market. Indeed, studies have shown that most discrimination takes place in government agencies, firms that do business with the government, and regulated monopolies.

3.b. Statistical Discrimination

Discrimination may occur because of a lack of information rather than a taste for or against certain groups. For instance, employers must try to predict the potential value of job applicants to the firm, but rarely do they know what a worker's actual value will be. Often, the only information available when they hire someone is information that may be imperfectly related to value in general and may not apply to a particular person at all. Using characteristics like education, experience, age, and test scores as the basis for selecting among job applicants may keep some very good people from getting a job and may result in the hiring of some unproductive people.

Suppose two types of workers apply for a word-processing job: those who can process 80 words per minute and those who can process only 40 words per minute. The problem is that these actual productivities are unknown to the employer. The employer can observe only the results of a five-minute word-processing test given to all applicants. How can the employer decide who is lucky or unlucky on the test and who can actually process 80 words per minute? Suppose the employer discovers that applicants from a particular vocational college, the AAA School, are taught to perform well on pre-employment tests, but their overall performance as employees is the same as that of the rest of the applicants—some do well and some do not. The employer might decide to reject all applicants from AAA because the good and bad ones can't be differentiated. Is the employer discriminating against AAA? The answer is yes. The employer is **statistically discriminating**. Statistical discrimination can cause a systematic preference for one group over another at the expense of some individuals in the group.

■ **statistically discriminating:** using characteristics that apply to a group, although not all individual members of that group may have those characteristics, as an allocation device

What is the effect of a ban on statistical discrimination? It would raise the firm's costs. The firm would have to either collect information about each applicant or risk hiring some of the lower-quality word processors. Since costs rise, profits fall. This would induce the firm to reduce its output and to reduce the number of resources used, including labor.

So, would a ban on statistical discrimination be a good law even if it raises costs and creates job losses? The answer is determined by comparing the costs and benefits to society of allowing statistical discrimination versus the costs and benefits to society of outlawing statistical discrimination.

RECAP

1. Discrimination is costly in a market economy when entry into markets is easy.

2. Statistical discrimination occurs due to a lack of information. When the characteristics of a group are imposed on each member of that group whether they apply or not, statistical discrimination occurs.

4. MINIMUM WAGES

■ **minimum wage:** a government-imposed wage defining the least someone can be paid

A **minimum wage** is a government policy that requires firms to pay at least a certain wage—the minimum wage. The minimum wage in the United States (in 1998) is $5.15 per hour. The arguments in favor of the minimum wage are that a worker must earn at least the minimum wage in order to have a decent standard of living. At $5.15 per hour, 40 hours per week, 50 weeks per year, you would earn $10,300 per year. Currently, the government defines the poverty level of income for a family of four to be about $16,000. Thus, at the minimum wage, a family of four with a single wage-earner would be far below the poverty level. The arguments opposed to minimum wages claim that implementation of such minimums will increase unemployment, particularly among the unskilled—teenagers, minorities, and women—and lead to worse cases of poverty.

In a competitive labor market, a worker's wages are equal to the value he or she contributes to the firm. A minimum wage set above the equilibrium wage creates a labor surplus (unemployment). In Figure 6, setting the minimum wage (W_M) at $5.15, above the equilibrium wage (W) of $4, creates a labor surplus of $Q_S - Q_D$. In other words, all the people willing and able to work at $5.15 are unable to get jobs. At the $5.15 per hour wage, Q_S are willing and able to work, but only Q_D are able to find jobs. A surplus of $Q_S - Q_D$ workers is created. Notice also that employment falls from the equilibrium level of Q_e to Q_D.

Who is most affected by the surplus? It is those who have the least value to the firm. Studies show that the minimum wage adversely affects teenagers and other low-skilled workers, causing increased unemployment among these groups. A 10 percent increase in the minimum wage is estimated to result in a 1 to 3 percent decrease in teenage employment. The last increase in the minimum wage from $4.35 to $5.15 per hour was an 18 percent increase. This

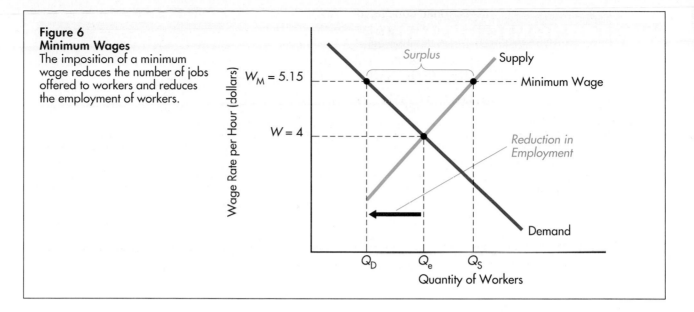

Figure 6
Minimum Wages
The imposition of a minimum wage reduces the number of jobs offered to workers and reduces the employment of workers.

caused somewhere between a 1.8 percent to 5.4 percent reduction in teenage employment. To reduce the adverse effects on teens, the government has allowed firms to pay a wage to teens that is lower than the minimum wage. The lower wage reduces the negative effects on teenagers. Still, any time an above equilibrium or minimum wage is imposed, some job loss occurs.

RECAP

1. A minimum wage is a government policy requiring firms to pay at least that wage—a wage that is above the equilibrium wage.
2. The effect of a minimum wage is to reduce employment.
3. A minimum wage has the greatest negative effects on the unskilled—usually teenagers, minorities, and women.

5. INCOME INEQUALITY AND POVERTY

In a market system, incomes are distributed according to the ownership of resources. Those who own the most highly valued resources have the highest incomes. One consequence of a market system, therefore, is that incomes are distributed unequally. In the United States, as in every country, there are rich and there are poor.

Equal incomes among members of a population can be illustrated by drawing a 45-degree line that is equidistant from the axes, as in Figure 7. The horizontal axis measures the total population in cumulative percentages; as we move along the horizontal axis, we are counting a larger and larger percentage of the population. The numbers end at 100, which designates 100 percent of the population. The vertical axis measures total income in cumulative percentages. As we move up the vertical axis, the percentage of total income being counted rises to 100 percent. The 45-degree line splitting the distance between the axes is called the line of income equality. At each point on the line, the percentage of total population and the percentage of total income are equal. The line of income equality indicates that 10 percent of the population earns 10 percent of the income, 20 percent of the population earns 20 percent of the income, and so on, until we see that 90 percent of the population earns 90 percent of the income, and 100 percent of the population earns 100 percent of the income.

Does the Minimum Wage Really Cause Unemployment Among Teens?

Economists were virtually unanimous regarding the effects of a minimum wage until just a few years ago when a study carried out by two economists, David Card and Alan Krueger, questioned the effects of minimum wages on teenage employment. Their study compared the effect on teenage employment of a New Jersey statewide increase in the minimum wage to teenage employment in Pennsylvania, which did not change its minimum wage. The economists found that employment actually increased in New Jersey following the minimum wage increase.

The study was so contrary to the economic theory of the minimum wage that it gathered quite a bit of attention. The Clinton administration referred to it in its efforts to increase the federal minimum wage to $5.15 per hour. As economists began to examine the study more carefully, they came to the conclusion that there were problems with the results. The biggest problem was that the New Jersey minimum wage increase of 1992 followed increases in the federal minimum wage in 1991. If teenage employment following the 1991 federal law is examined, it is found that a much larger drop in

New Jersey's teenage employment occurred than in Pennsylvania's. Employers in New Jersey seemed to anticipate that their state was going to raise the minimum wage even further. So when New Jersey did raise it own state minimum in 1992, there was very little additional effect. The New Jersey employers had already made the cuts in teenage employment that were caused by a higher minimum wage.

Source: David Card and Alan Krueger, *Myth and Measurement*, (Princeton: Princeton University Press, 1995); Gary S. Becker, "It's Simple: Hike the Minimum Wage and You Put People Out of Work," *Business Week*, March 6, 1995.

■ **income distribution:**
the ways in which a society's income is divided

■ **Lorenz curve:**
a diagram illustrating the degree of income inequality

Points off the line of income equality indicate an **income distribution** that is unequal. Figure 7 shows the line of income equality and a curve that bows down below the income-equality line. The bowed curve is called a **Lorenz curve**. The Lorenz curve in Figure 7 is for the United States. In the U.S., 20 percent of the population receives only 3.6 percent of total income, seen at point A. The second 20 percent accounts for another 9.6 percent of income, shown as point B, so the bottom 40 percent of the population has 12.8 percent of the income (3.6 percent owned by the first 20 percent of the population plus the additional 9.6 percent owned by the second 20 percent). The third 20 percent accounts for another 15.7 percent of income, so point C is plotted at a population of 60 percent and an income of 28.4 percent. The fourth 20 percent accounts for another 23.4 percent of income, shown as point D, where 80 percent of the population receives 51.8 percent of the income. The richest 20 percent accounts for the remaining 48.2 percent of income, shown as point E. With the last 20 percent of the population and the last 48.2 percent of income, 100 percent of population and 100 percent of income are accounted for. Point E, therefore, is plotted where both income and population are 100 percent.

The farther the Lorenz curve bows down, away from the line of income equality, the greater the inequality of the distribution of income. From 1929 to 1995, the Lorenz curve for the United States moved closer to the line of income equality as incomes became more equally distributed. But from 1995 to 1998, the curve moved further away from the line of income equality, and the distribution of income became less equal.

Many people argue that the increasing inequality of income in recent years is the result of the increased demand for skilled labor. With skills, people are earning relatively more; without skills, they are earning relatively less. Professional, technical, and managerial jobs accounted for just one-sixth of the work force in 1950. By 1995, that had risen to one in three. This increased demand for skilled labor has placed a much higher premium on educational attainment; generally speaking, workers who have spent more time in training

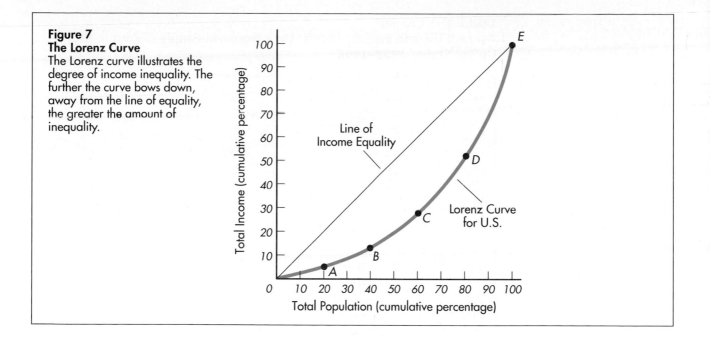

Figure 7
The Lorenz Curve
The Lorenz curve illustrates the degree of income inequality. The further the curve bows down, away from the line of equality, the greater the amount of inequality.

and education earn significantly higher wages. Between 1984 and 1995, employees with post high school education and training gained about 11 percent in income, while high school dropouts' earnings fell 1.5 percent.

The most unequal distributions of income are found in less developed countries. On average, the richest 20 percent of the population receives more than 50 percent of income, and the poorest 20 percent receives less than 4 percent. Figure 8 shows two Lorenz curves: one for the United States and one for Mexico. The curve for Mexico bows down far below the curve for the United States, indicating the greater inequality in Mexico.

5.a. Poverty

■ **poverty:**
an arbitrary level of income chosen to provide a measure of how well basic human needs are being met

Unequal income means some people are relatively well-off and some relatively poor. The poorest in the United States are those in **poverty**. Poverty is an arbitrary level of income that is supposed to provide a measure of how well basic human needs are being met. The poverty level in the U.S., as specified by the federal government, is listed in Table 1. Currently, a family

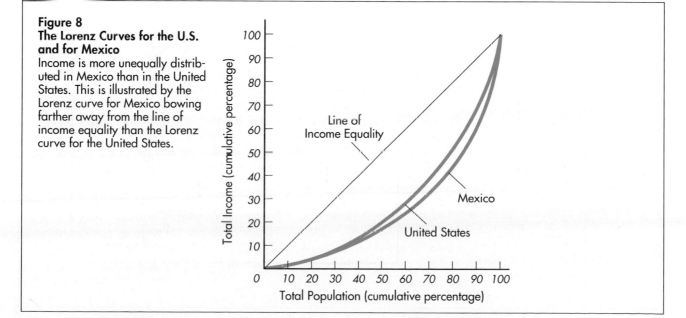

Figure 8
The Lorenz Curves for the U.S. and for Mexico
Income is more unequally distributed in Mexico than in the United States. This is illustrated by the Lorenz curve for Mexico bowing farther away from the line of income equality than the Lorenz curve for the United States.

TABLE 1
Average Income Poverty Cutoffs for a Nonfarm Family of Four in the United States, 1959–1996

Year	Poverty Level	Year	Poverty Level
1959	$ 2,973	1984	$10,609
1960	3,022	1985	10,989
1966	3,317	1986	11,203
1969	3,743	1987	11,611
1970	3,968	1988	12,090
1975	5,500	1989	12,675
1976	5,815	1990	13,359
1977	6,191	1991	13,924
1978	6,662	1992	13,950
1979	7,412	1993	14,764
1980	8,414	1994	15,200
1981	9,287	1995	15,600
1982	9,862	1996	16,036
1983	10,178		

Sources: U.S. Bureau of the Census, *Current Population Reports,* series P-60, no 174 (Washington, D.C.: U.S. Government Printing Office, 1996), and *Social Security Bulletin,* Spring 1997.

of four with an income less than $16,036 is in poverty. Yet an income of $16,036 per year would be a very high level of income in some countries. Ethiopia, for instance, has a per capita income of only $150 per year.

How many Americans fall below the poverty line? In 1997, more than 36 million U.S. residents received incomes that were lower than the cutoff.

Figure 9
The Trends of Poverty Incidence
The number of people classified as living in poverty is measured on the left vertical axis. The percentage of the population classified as living in poverty is measured on the right vertical axis. The number and the percentage declined steadily throughout the 1960s, rose during the recessions of 1969, 1974, 1981, and 1990 and fell during the economic growth between 1983 and 1989.
Sources: U.S. Bureau of the Census, *Current Population Reports* (Washington, D.C.: U.S. Government Printing Office, 1998); *Economic Report of the President,* 1998.

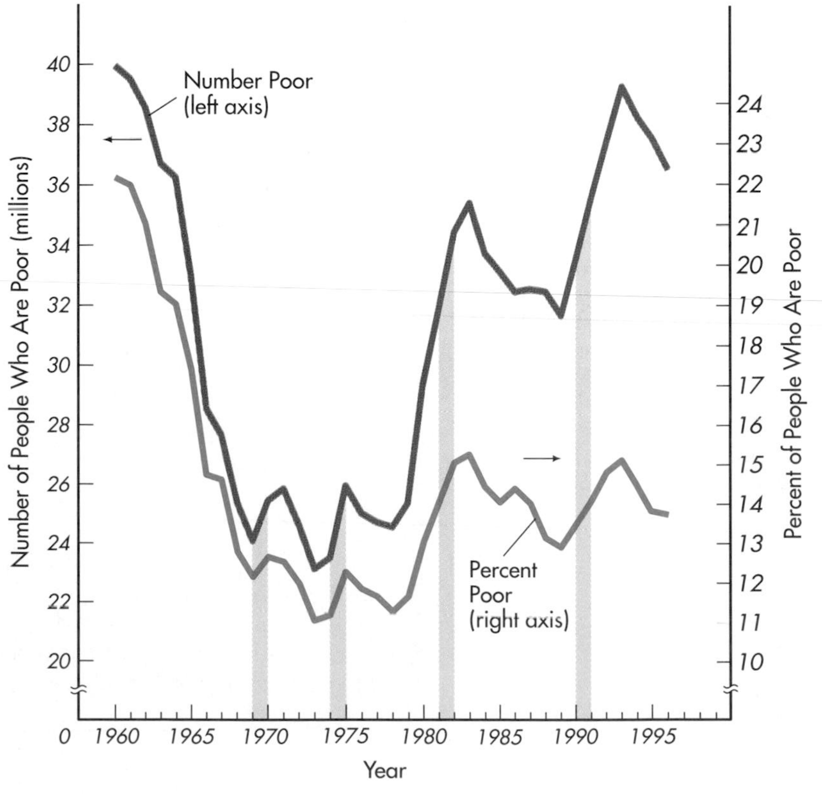

Part II / Consumers, Firms, and Social Issues

Homeless people are present in most every city in the country. Pushing their carts of discarded materials, the homeless wander the streets, rest on park benches, and build shelters in alleys and under highway bridges. Many of the homeless are people who have lost jobs and have been unable to maintain residences or to support their families.

Figure 9 compares the *number* of people living in poverty and the *percentage* of the total population living in poverty (the incidence of poverty) for each year from 1960 to 1996. From 1960 to the late 1970s, the incidence of poverty declined rapidly. From the late 1970s until the early 1980s, the incidence of poverty rose; it then began to decline again after 1982. Small upswings in the incidence of poverty occurred in 1968 and 1974, and a large rise occurred between 1978 and 1982. It then fell until 1990, when the U.S. once again dipped into recession. It continued to rise even as the economy grew in 1993 and 1994 and then fell slightly thereafter.

Studies indicate that approximately 25 percent of all Americans fall below the poverty line at some time in their lives. Many of these spells of poverty are relatively short; nearly 45 percent last less than a year. However, more than 50 percent of those in poverty at a particular time remain in poverty for at least 10 years.

The primary reason for poverty is a lack of a job. Since the young have more trouble finding a job than the middle-aged, a young person has a much greater chance of falling into poverty. The highest incidence of poverty occurs among those under 18 years old. The second highest occurs among those between 18 and 24.

Because a job is the determining factor as to whether one is in poverty, the greatest impact on poverty is the health of the economy. The economy grew at a fairly sustained rate between 1960 and 1969 and from 1982 through 1990. During both growth periods, the poverty rate fell. But from 1992 to 1994, the poverty rate rose even as the economy improved. People are generally made better off by economic growth, so this experience was a surprise. Typically, economic stagnation and recession throw the relatively poor out of their jobs and into poverty, while economic growth increases the number of jobs and draws people out of poverty and into the mainstream of economic progress. What seemed to occur between 1992 and 1994 was that the economic growth only helped those with technical skills. Those without skills were left behind; in fact, their wages actually fell during those years, while those with skills had large wage increases.

To understand the fluctuations of poverty, it is necessary to understand why the economy dips into recessions at some times or expands during other times. We'll turn to this topic in the next few chapters.

RECAP

1. Income is determined by who owns resources.
2. Since not everyone owns the same resources, incomes are not equal.
3. Income distribution is illustrated with a Lorenz curve.
4. Poverty is defined relative to a society. Someone in poverty in the United States would be well-off in Ethiopia.
5. The primary factor leading to poverty is a lack of a job; that is partly determined by whether the economy is growing or is in a recession.

SUMMARY

How does the market for natural resources function?

1. Renewable resources are resources that can replenish themselves.
2. Nonrenewable resources are resources whose total amount in existence is limited.
3. The market for resources determines prices at which the rate of use of renewable resources allows the resources to replenish and limits the rate at which the nonrenewable resources are consumed.

Why might a market not allocate goods and services efficiently?

4. When an externality occurs, private costs and benefits differ from social costs. Either too much or too little is consumed or produced relative to the quantities that would occur if all costs and benefits were included.
5. An externality may result from the lack of private property rights.
6. Possible solutions to environmental problems include the government reducing externalities and assigning private property rights.

How do global environmental problems differ from domestic environmental problems?

7. Global environmental problems are more difficult to resolve than domestic ones because of the lack of property rights. When no one government owns the resource being damaged by an externality, then the externality cannot be resolved by any one government.

Why are illicit drugs such a problem?

8. The market for illicit drugs is actually two types of markets: one with barriers to entry, and one with free entry.
9. The cocaine and heroin market consists of few suppliers, who usually cooperate. Cartels dominate the market, dictating prices, quantities, and location.
10. The market for designer drugs is characterized by easy entry.
11. Government policy attempting to control illicit drugs has been flawed in both markets. In the cocaine and heroin market, the government has failed to differentiate between the addict and the experimental user. In the designer drug market, the government has failed to realize the market is one with free entry; that it must focus on changing demand not on supply.

What is discrimination?

12. Discrimination occurs when some factor not related to an individual's value to the firm affects the wage rate someone receives.

Are discrimination and freely functioning markets compatible?

13. Discrimination is costly to those who discriminate and should not last in a market economy, at least when entry is easy.
14. Statistical discrimination is the result of imperfect information and can occur as long as information is imperfect.

What are minimum wages?

15. A minimum wage is a wage imposed by government that is greater than the equilibrium wage.

16. In the United States, the current minimum wage is $5.15 per hour.

17. A minimum wage reduces employment.

Who bears the negative effects of a minimum wage?

18. The unskilled bear the costs—usually teenagers, minorities, and women.

Are incomes distributed equally in the United States?

19. The Lorenz curve illustrates the degree of income inequality.

20. If the Lorenz curve corresponds with the line of income equality, then incomes are distributed equally. If the Lorenz curve bows down below the line of income equality, then income is distributed in such a way that more people earn low incomes than earn high incomes.

21. As a rule, incomes are distributed more unequally in less developed countries than in developed countries.

How is poverty measured, and does poverty exist in the United States?

22. Poverty is an arbitrary level of income chosen to provide a measure of how well basic human needs are being met.

23. The incidence of poverty decreases as the economy grows and increases as the economy falls into recession.

Who are the poor?

24. Many people fall below the poverty line for a short time only. However, a significant core of people remain in poverty for at least 10 years.

25. The poor are primarily those without jobs. These tend to be people without skills and the youngest members of society.

KEY TERMS

renewable natural resources
nonrenewable natural resources
private costs
negative externality
social cost
positive externality
private property right

discrimination
statistically discriminating
minimum wage
income distribution
Lorenz curve
poverty

EXERCISES

1. What is a Lorenz curve? What would the curve look like if income were equally distributed? Could the curve ever bow upward above the line of income equality?

2. Why does the health of the economy affect the number of people living in poverty?

3. What would it mean if the poverty income level of the United States were applied to Mexico?

4. Use the following information to plot a Lorenz curve.

Percent of Population	Percent of Income
20	5
40	15
60	35
80	65
100	100

5. If the incidence of poverty decreases during periods when the economy is growing and increases during periods when the economy is in recession, what government policies might be used to reduce poverty most effectively?

6. Explain what is meant by discrimination. Explain what statistical discrimination is.

7. Why do economists say that discrimination is inherently inefficient and therefore will not occur in general?

8. Use the following information to answer the questions listed below.

    a. What is the external cost per unit of output?

    b. What level of output will be produced?

    c. What level of output should be produced to achieve economic efficiency?

    d. What is the value to society of correcting the externality?

Quantity	Marginal Cost MC	Marginal Social Cost MSC	Marginal Revenue MR
1	$ 2	$ 4	$12
2	4	6	10
3	6	8	8
4	8	10	6
5	10	12	4

9. If, in question 9, the MC and MSC columns were reversed, you would have an example of what? Would too much or too little of the good be produced?

10. Overfishing refers to catching fish at a rate that does not allow the fish to repopulate. What is the fundamental problem associated with overfishing of the oceans? What might lead to underfishing?

11. Elephants eat 300 pounds of food per day. They flourished in Africa when they could roam over huge areas of land, eating the vegetation in one area and then moving on so that the vegetation could renew itself. Now, the area over which elephants can roam is declining. Without some action, the elephants will become extinct. What actions might save the elephants? What are the costs and benefits of such actions?

12. What could explain why the value of pollution permits in one area of the country is rising 20 percent per year while in another it is unchanged from year to year? What would you expect to occur as a result of this differential?

▢ INTERNET EXERCISE

In this chapter we examined, among other things, environmental issues and natural resources. The Sierra Club has been at the forefront of environmental issues during the past thirty years. Use the Internet to explore the Sierra Club in more detail. Go to the Boyes/Melvin *Fundamentals of Economics* Web site at http://www.hmco.com/college/ and click on the Internet Exercise link for Chapter 8. Now answer the questions that appear on the Boyes/Melvin Web site.

III

The National and Global Economies

9

An Overview of the National and International Economies

FUNDAMENTAL QUESTIONS

1. What is a household, and what is household income and spending?

2. What is a business firm, and what is business spending?

3. How does the international sector affect the economy?

4. What does government do?

5. How do the three private sectors—households, businesses, and the international sector—interact in the economy?

6. How does the government interact with the other sectors of the economy?

You decide to buy a new Toyota, so you go to a Toyota dealer and exchange money for the car. The Toyota dealer has rented land and buildings and hired workers in order to make cars available to you and other members of the public. The employees earn income paid by the Toyota dealer and then use their incomes to buy food from the grocery store. This transaction generates revenue for the grocery store, which hires workers and pays them incomes that they then use to buy groceries and Toyotas. Your expenditure for the Toyota is part of a circular flow. Revenue is received by the Toyota dealer, who pays employees, who, in turn, buy goods and services.

Of course, the story is complicated by the fact that the Toyota is originally manufactured and purchased in Japan and then shipped to the United States before it can be sold by the local Toyota dealer. Your purchase of the Toyota creates revenue for the local dealer as well as for the manufacturer in Japan, who pays Japanese autoworkers to produce Toyotas. Furthermore, when you buy your Toyota, you must pay a tax to the government, which uses tax revenues to pay for police protection, national defense, the legal system, and other services. Many people in different areas of the economy are involved.

An economy is made up of individual buyers and sellers. Economists could discuss the neighborhood economy that surrounds your university, the economy of the city of Chicago, or the economy of the state of Massachusetts. But typically it is the national economy, the economy of the United States, that is the center of their attention. To clarify the operation of the national economy, economists usually group individual buyers and sellers into sectors: households, businesses, government, and the international sector. Since the U.S. economy affects, and is affected by, the rest of the world, to understand how the economy functions we must include the international sector. In this chapter we examine basic data and information on each individual sector and examine how the sectors interact. ■

1. HOUSEHOLDS

■ **household:**
one or more persons who occupy a unit of housing

A **household** consists of one or more persons who occupy a unit of housing. The unit of housing may be a house, an apartment, or even a single room, as long as it constitutes separate living quarters. A household may consist of related family members, like a father, mother, and children, or it may comprise unrelated individuals, like three college students sharing an apartment. The person in whose name the house or apartment is owned or rented is called the *householder.*

1.a. Number of Households and Household Income

In 1996, there were more than 98 million households in the United States. The breakdown of households by age of householder is shown in Figure 1. Householders between 35 and 44 years old make up the largest number of households. Householders between 45 and 54 years old have the largest median income. The *median* is the middle value—half of the households in an age group have an income higher than the median and half have an income lower than the median. Figure 1 shows that households in which the householder is between 45 and 54 years old have a median income of about $48,000, substantially higher than the median incomes of other age groups. Typically, workers in this age group are at the peak of their earning power. Younger households are gaining experience and training; older households include retired workers.

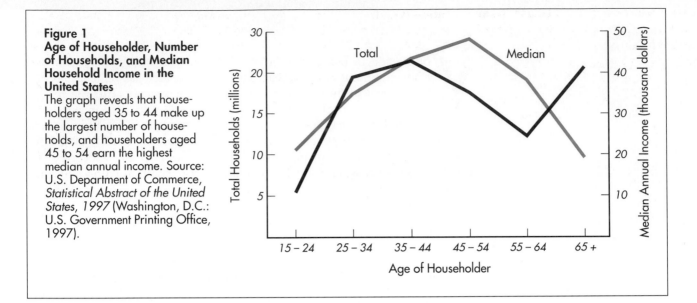

Figure 1
Age of Householder, Number of Households, and Median Household Income in the United States
The graph reveals that householders aged 35 to 44 make up the largest number of households, and householders aged 45 to 54 earn the highest median annual income. Source: U.S. Department of Commerce, *Statistical Abstract of the United States, 1997* (Washington, D.C.: U.S. Government Printing Office, 1997).

Thirty-two percent of all households, or 31,880,000, are two-person households. The stereotypical household of husband, wife, and two children accounts for only 16 percent of all households. There are relatively few large households in the United States. Of the more than 98 million households in the country, only 996,000 (1 percent) have seven or more persons.

1.b. Household Spending

■ **consumption:**
household spending

Household spending is called **consumption**. Householders consume housing, transportation, food, entertainment, and other goods and services. Household spending (also called *consumer spending*) per year in the United States between 1959 and 1997 is shown in Figure 2, along with household income. The pattern is one of steady increase. Spending by the household sector is the largest component of total spending in the economy—rising to nearly $6 trillion in 1997.

RECAP

1. A household consists of one or more persons who occupy a unit of housing.
2. An apartment or house is rented or owned by a householder.
3. As a group, householders between the ages of 45 and 54 have the highest median incomes.
4. Household spending is called consumption.

2. BUSINESS FIRMS

A business firm is a business organization controlled by a single management. The firm's business may be conducted at more than one location. The terms *company, enterprise*, and *business* are used interchangeably with *firm*.

2.a. Forms of Business Organizations

Firms are organized as sole proprietorships, partnerships, or corporations. A sole proprietorship is a business owned by one person. This type of firm may be a one-person operation or a large enterprise with many employees. In

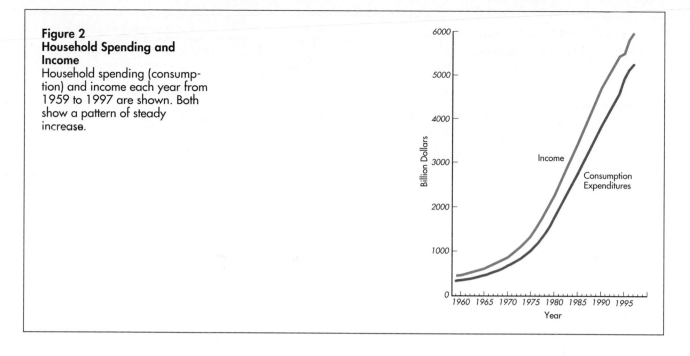

Figure 2
Household Spending and Income
Household spending (consumption) and income each year from 1959 to 1997 are shown. Both show a pattern of steady increase.

either case, the owner receives all the profits and is responsible for all the debts incurred by the business.

A partnership is a business owned by two or more partners who share both the profits of the business and responsibility for the firm's losses. The partners could be individuals, estates, or other businesses.

State law allows the formation of corporations. A corporation is a business whose identity in the eyes of the law is distinct from the identity of its owners. A corporation is an economic entity that, like a person, can own property and borrow money in its own name. The owners of a corporation are shareholders. If a corporation cannot pay its debts, creditors cannot seek payment from the shareholders' personal wealth. The corporation itself is responsible for all its actions. The shareholders' liability is limited to the value of the stock they own.

Many firms are global in their operations even though they may have been founded and may be owned by residents of a single country. Firms typically first enter the international market by selling products to foreign countries. As revenues from these sales increase, the firms realize advantages by locating subsidiaries in foreign countries. A **multinational business** is a firm that owns and operates producing units in foreign countries. The best-known U.S. corporations are multinational firms. Ford, IBM, PepsiCo, and McDonald's all own operating units in many different countries. Ford Motor Company, for instance, is the parent firm of sales organizations and assembly plants located around the world. As transportation and communication technologies progress, multinational business activity will grow.

■ **multinational business:**
a firm that owns and operates producing units in foreign countries

2.b. Business Statistics

Figure 3(a) shows that in the United States there are far more sole proprietorships than partnerships or corporations. Figure 3(a) also compares the revenues earned by each type of business. The great majority of sole proprietorships are small businesses, with revenues under $25,000 a year. Similarly, over half of all partnerships also have revenues under $25,000 a year, but only 24 percent of the corporations are in this category.

Figure 3(b) shows that the 67 percent of sole proprietorships that earn less than $25,000 a year account for only 10 percent of the revenue earned by proprietorships. The 0.004 percent of proprietorships with revenue of $1 million

Figure 3
Number and Revenue of Business Firms

Most sole proprietorships and partnerships are small firms, with nearly 70 percent of all proprietorships falling into the less-than-$25,000 revenue category, and over 60 percent of all partnerships falling into the same lowest revenue category. Corporations are more likely to be larger—17 percent have revenues exceeding $1 million.

Most sole proprietorship revenues are earned by the larger proprietorships, those in the $100,000 to $499,000 category. By contrast, the small number of partnerships in the top revenue category is enough to account for 84 percent of all partnership revenues. Source: *Statistical Abstract of the United States, 1997* (Washington, D.C.: U.S. Government Printing Office, 1997).

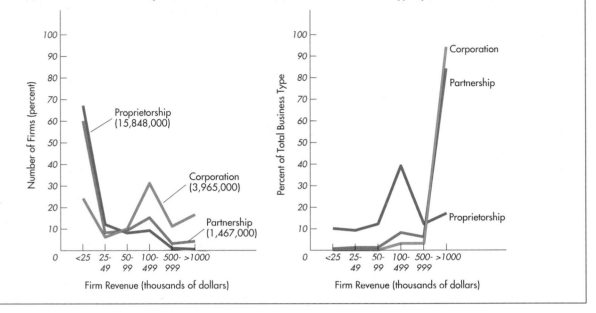

(a) Number of Business Firms by Revenue Amount

(b) Percent of Total Business Type by Revenue Amount

or more account for 17 percent. Even more striking are the figures for partnerships and corporations. The 60 percent of partnerships with the smallest revenue account for only 0.5 percent of the total revenue earned by partnerships. At the other extreme, the 4 percent of partnerships with the largest revenue account for 84 percent of total partnership revenue. The 24 percent of corporations in the smallest range account for less than 0.1 percent of total corporate revenue, while the 17 percent of corporations in the largest range account for 94 percent of corporate revenue.

The message of Figure 3 is that big business is important in the United States. There are many small firms, but large firms and corporations account for the greatest share of business revenue. Although there are only about one-third as many corporations as sole proprietorships, corporations have more than fifteen times the revenue of sole proprietorships.

2.c. Firms Around the World

Big business is a dominant force in the United States. Many people believe that because the United States is the world's largest economy, U.S. firms are the largest in the world. Figure 4 shows that this is not true. Of the ten largest corporations in the world (measured by sales), six are Japanese. Big business is not just an American phenomenon.

2.d. Business Spending

■ **investment:**
spending on capital goods to be used in producing goods and services

Investment is the expenditure by business firms for capital goods—machines, tools, and buildings—that will be used to produce goods and services. The economic meaning of *investment* is different from the everyday meaning,

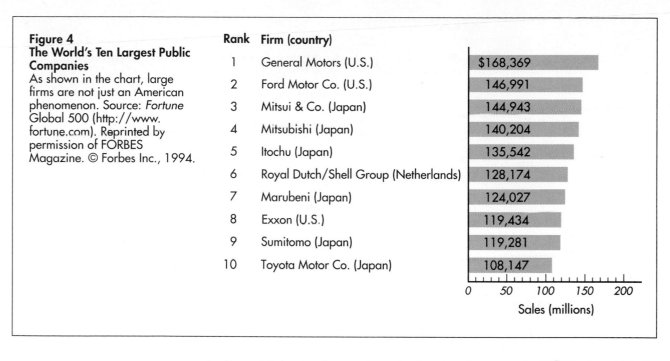

Figure 4
The World's Ten Largest Public Companies
As shown in the chart, large firms are not just an American phenomenon. Source: *Fortune Global 500* (http://www.fortune.com). Reprinted by permission of FORBES Magazine. © Forbes Inc., 1994.

Rank	Firm (country)	Sales (millions)
1	General Motors (U.S.)	$168,369
2	Ford Motor Co. (U.S.)	146,991
3	Mitsui & Co. (Japan)	144,943
4	Mitsubishi (Japan)	140,204
5	Itochu (Japan)	135,542
6	Royal Dutch/Shell Group (Netherlands)	128,174
7	Marubeni (Japan)	124,027
8	Exxon (U.S.)	119,434
9	Sumitomo (Japan)	119,281
10	Toyota Motor Co. (Japan)	108,147

"a financial transaction such as buying bonds or stocks." In economics, the term *investment* refers to business spending for capital goods.

Investment spending in 1997 was $1,205 billion, an amount equal to roughly one-fifth of consumption, or household spending. Investment spending between 1959 and 1997 is shown in Figure 5. Compare Figures 2 and 5 and notice the different patterns of spending. Investment increases unevenly, actually falling at times and then rising very rapidly. Even though investment spending is much smaller than consumption, the wide swings in investment spending mean that business expenditures are an important factor in determining the economic health of the nation.

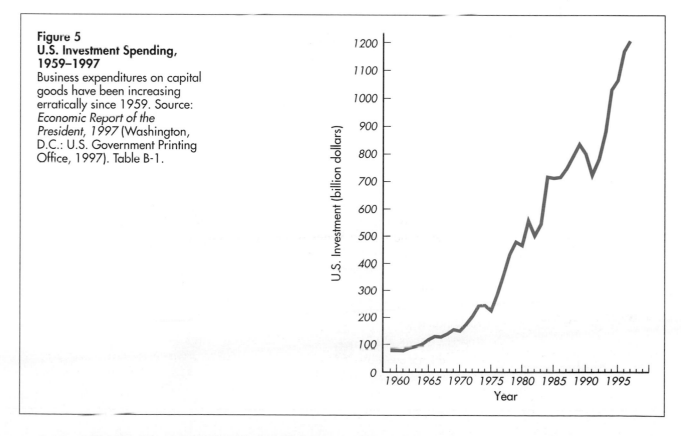

Figure 5
U.S. Investment Spending, 1959–1997
Business expenditures on capital goods have been increasing erratically since 1959. Source: *Economic Report of the President, 1997* (Washington, D.C.: U.S. Government Printing Office, 1997). Table B-1.

RECAP

1. Business firms may be organized as sole proprietorships, partnerships, or corporations.

2. Large corporations account for the largest fraction of total business revenue.

3. Business investment spending fluctuates widely over time.

3. THE INTERNATIONAL SECTOR

Today, foreign buyers and sellers have a significant effect on economic conditions in the United States, and developments in the rest of the world often influence U.S. buyers and sellers. We saw in previous chapters, for instance, how exchange rate changes can affect the demand for and supply of U.S. goods and services.

3.a. Types of Countries

The nations of the world may be divided into two categories: industrial countries and developing countries. Developing countries greatly outnumber industrial countries (see Figure 6). The World Bank (an international organization that makes loans to developing countries) groups countries according

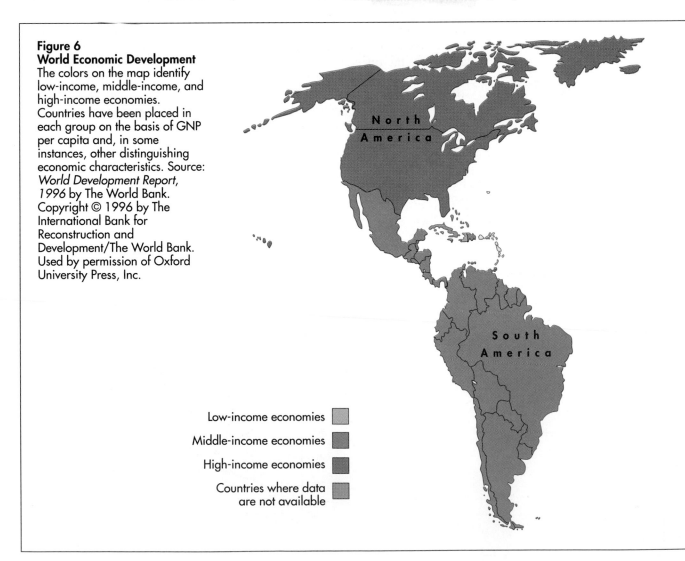

Figure 6
World Economic Development
The colors on the map identify low-income, middle-income, and high-income economies. Countries have been placed in each group on the basis of GNP per capita and, in some instances, other distinguishing economic characteristics. Source: *World Development Report, 1996* by The World Bank. Copyright © 1996 by The International Bank for Reconstruction and Development/The World Bank. Used by permission of Oxford University Press, Inc.

Low-income economies
Middle-income economies
High-income economies
Countries where data are not available

to per capita income (income per person). Low-income economies are those with per capita incomes of $750 or less. Middle-income economies have per capita incomes of $750–$8,260. High-income economies—oil exporters and industrial market economies—are distinguished from the middle-income economies and have per capita incomes of greater than $8,260. Some countries are not members of the World Bank and so are not categorized, and information about a few small countries is so limited that the World Bank is unable to classify them.

It is readily apparent from Figure 6 that low-income economies are heavily concentrated in Africa and Asia. Countries in these regions have a low profile in U.S. trade, although they may receive aid from the United States. U.S. trade is concentrated with its neighbors Canada and Mexico, along with the major industrial powers. Nations in each group present different economic challenges to the United States.

3.a.1. The Industrial Countries
The World Bank uses per capita income to classify twenty-three countries as "industrial market economies." They are listed in the bar chart in Figure 7. The twenty-three countries listed in Figure 7 are among the wealthiest countries in the world. Not appearing on the list are the high-income oil-exporting nations like Libya, Saudi Arabia, Kuwait, and the United Arab Emirates.

The economies of the industrial nations are highly interdependent. As conditions change in one nation, business firms and individuals looking for the best return or interest rate on their funds may shift large sums of money

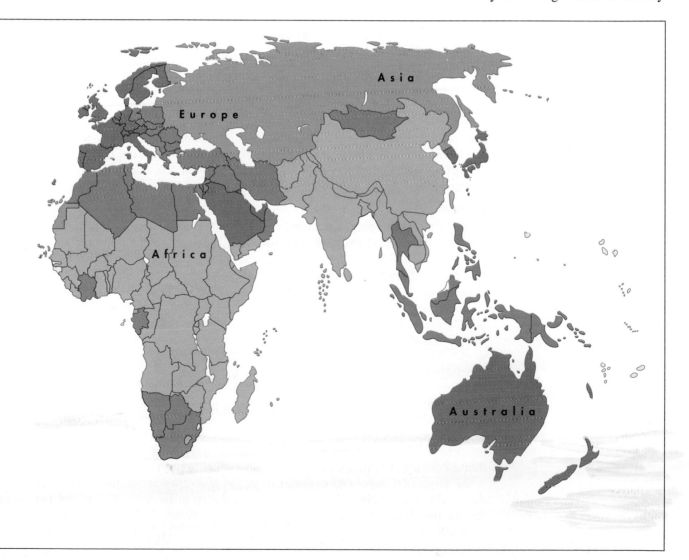

Figure 7
The Industrial Market Economies
The bar chart lists some of the wealthiest countries in the world. Ironically, high-income oil-exporting countries such as Libya, Saudi Arabia, Kuwait, and the United Arab Emirates do not appear on the list because the World Bank still considers them to be developing. Source: World Bank, *World Development Report, 1996.* Used by permission of Oxford University Press, Inc.

Country	Income per Person (thousands of 1994 U.S. dollars)
Switzerland	$37,930
Japan	34,630
Denmark	27,970
Norway	26,390
United States	25,880
Germany	25,580
Austria	24,630
Sweden	23,530
France	23,420
Belgium	22,870
Singapore	22,500
Netherlands	22,010
Hong Kong	21,650
Canada	19,510
Italy	19,300
Finland	18,850
United Kingdom	18,340
Australia	18,000
Israel	14,530
Ireland	13,530
Spain	13,440
New Zealand	13,350
Portugal	9,320

between countries. As the funds flow from one country to another, economic conditions in one country spread to other countries. As a result, the industrial countries, particularly the major economic powers like the United States, Germany, and Japan, are forced to pay close attention to each other's economic policies.

3.a.2. The Developing Countries The developing countries (sometimes referred to as less developed countries, or LDCs) provide a different set of problems for the United States than do the industrial countries. In the 1980s, the debts of the developing countries to the developed nations reached tremendous heights. For instance, at the end of 1989, Brazil owed foreign creditors $111.3 billion, Mexico owed $95.6 billion, and Argentina owed $64.7 billion. In each case, the amounts owed were more than several times the annual sales of goods and services by those countries to the rest of the world. The United States had to arrange loans at special terms and establish special trade arrangements in order for those countries to be able to buy U.S. goods.

The United States tends to buy, or *import*, primary products such as agricultural produce and minerals from the developing countries. Products that a country buys from another country are called **imports**. The United States tends to sell, or *export*, manufactured goods to developing countries. Products that a country sells to another country are called **exports**. The United States is the largest producer and exporter of grains and other agricultural output in the world. The efficiency of U.S. farming relative to farming in much of the rest of the world gives the United States a comparative advantage in many agricultural products.

■ **imports:**
products that a country buys from other countries

■ **exports:**
products that a country sells to other countries

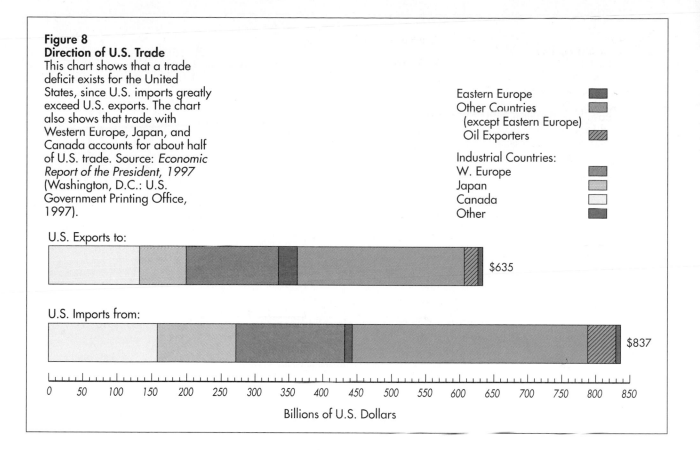

Figure 8
Direction of U.S. Trade
This chart shows that a trade deficit exists for the United States, since U.S. imports greatly exceed U.S. exports. The chart also shows that trade with Western Europe, Japan, and Canada accounts for about half of U.S. trade. Source: *Economic Report of the President, 1997* (Washington, D.C.: U.S. Government Printing Office, 1997).

Eastern Europe
Other Countries
  (except Eastern Europe)
Oil Exporters

Industrial Countries:
W. Europe
Japan
Canada
Other

U.S. Exports to:

$635

U.S. Imports from:

$837

0   50   100   150   200   250   300   350   400   450   500   550   600   650   700   750   800   850

Billions of U.S. Dollars

3.b. International Sector Spending

trade surplus:
the situation that exists when imports are less than exports

trade deficit:
the situation that exists when imports exceed exports

net exports:
the difference between the value of exports and the value of imports

U.S. economic activity with the rest of the world includes U.S. spending on foreign goods and foreign spending on U.S. goods. Figure 8 shows how U.S. exports and imports are spread over different countries. Notice that two countries, Canada and Japan, account for roughly one-third of U.S. exports and more than one-third of U.S. imports. Trade with Eastern Europe is trivial.

When exports exceed imports, a **trade surplus** exists. When imports exceed exports, a **trade deficit** exists. Figure 8 shows that the United States is importing much more than it exports.

The term **net exports** refers to the difference between the value of exports and the value of imports: net exports equals exports minus imports. Figure 9 traces U.S. net exports for the period 1959 to 1997. Positive net exports represent trade surpluses; negative net exports represent trade deficits. The trade deficits (indicated by negative net exports) of the 1980s were unprecedented. Reasons for this pattern of international trade are discussed in later chapters.

RECAP

1. The majority of U.S. trade is with the industrial market economies.
2. Exports are products sold to foreign countries; imports are products bought from foreign countries.
3. Exports minus imports equals net exports.
4. Positive net exports signal a trade surplus; negative net exports signal a trade deficit.

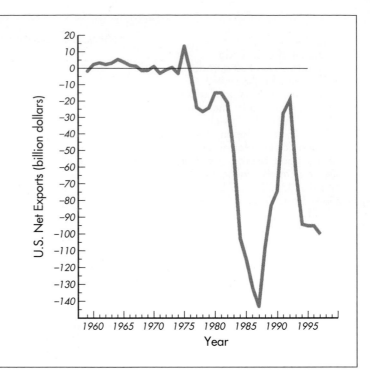

Figure 9
U.S. Net Exports, 1959–1997
Prior to the late 1960s, the United States generally exported more than it imported and had a trade surplus. Since 1976, net exports have been negative, and the United States has had a trade deficit. Source: *Economic Report of the President, 1997* (Washington, D.C.: U.S. Government Printing Office, 1997).

4. OVERVIEW OF THE UNITED STATES GOVERNMENT

When Americans think of government policies, rules, and regulations, they typically think of Washington, D.C., because their economic lives are regulated and shaped more by policies made there than by policies made at the local and state levels.

Who actually is involved in economic policymaking? Important government institutions that shape U.S. economic policy are listed in Table 1. This list is far from inclusive, but it includes the agencies with the broadest powers and greatest influence. Economic policy involves macroeconomic issues like government spending and control of the money supply and microeconomic issues aimed at providing public goods like police and military protection and correcting problems such as pollution.

4.a. Government Policy

The government has been given many functions in the economy. These include providing some goods, regulating some firm behaviors, and promoting competition via laws restricting the ability of business firms to engage in certain practices.

Most attention is given to the government's monetary and fiscal policy. **Monetary policy** is policy directed toward control of money and credit. The major player in this policy arena is the Federal Reserve, commonly called "the Fed." The **Federal Reserve** is the central bank of the United States. It serves as a banker for the U.S. government and regulates the U.S. money supply.

The Federal Reserve System is run by a seven-member Board of Governors. The most important member of the Board is the chairman, who is appointed by the president for a term of four years. The Board meets regularly (from ten to twelve times a year) with a group of high-level officials to review the current economic situation and set policy for the growth of U.S. money and credit. The Federal Reserve exercises a great deal of influence on U.S. economic policy.

■ **monetary policy:**
policy directed toward control of money and credit

■ **Federal Reserve:**
the central bank of the United States

TABLE 1

U.S. Government Economic Policymakers and Related Agencies

Institution	Role
Fiscal policymakers	
President	Provides leadership in formulating fiscal policy
Congress	Sets government spending and taxes and passes laws related to economic conduct
Monetary policymaker	
Federal Reserve	Controls money supply and credit conditions
Related agencies	
Council of Economic Advisers	Monitors the economy and advises the president
Office of Management and Budget	Prepares and analyzes the federal budget
Treasury Department	Administers the financial affairs of the federal government
Commerce Department	Administers federal policy regulating industry
Justice Department	Enforces legal setting of business
Comptroller of the Currency	Oversees national banks
International Trade Commission	Investigates unfair international trade practices
Federal Trade Commission	Administers laws related to fair business practices and competition

■ **fiscal policy:**
policy directed toward government spending and taxation

Fiscal policy, the other area of macroeconomic policy, is policy directed toward government spending and taxation. In the United States, fiscal policy is determined by laws that are passed by Congress and signed by the president. The relative roles of the legislative and executive branches in shaping fiscal policy vary with the political climate, but usually it is the president who initiates major policy changes. Presidents rely on key advisers for fiscal policy information. These advisers include Cabinet officers such as the secretary of the treasury and the secretary of state as well as the director of the Office of Management and Budget. In addition, the president has a Council of Economic Advisers made up of three economists—usually a chair, a macroeconomist, and a microeconomist—who, together with their staff, monitor and interpret economic developments for the president. The degree of influence wielded by these advisers depends on their personal relationship with the president.

4.b. Government Spending

Federal, state, and local government spending for goods and services between 1959 and 1997 is shown in Figure 10. Except during times of war in the 1940s and 1950s, federal expenditures were roughly similar in size to state and local expenditures until 1969. Since 1969, state and local spending has been growing more rapidly than federal spending.

Combined government spending on goods and services is larger than investment spending but much smaller than consumption. In 1996, combined government spending was $1,419 billion, investment spending was $1,120 billion, and consumption was $5,200 billion.

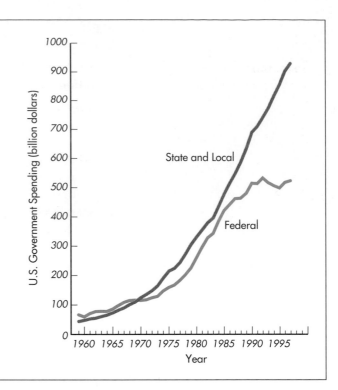

Figure 10
Federal, State, and Local Government Expenditures for Goods and Services, 1959–1997
In the 1950s and early 1960s, federal government spending was above state and local government spending. In 1969, state and local expenditures rose above federal spending and have remained higher ever since.
Source: Data are from the *Economic Report of the President, 1997* (Washington, D.C.: U.S. Government Printing Office, 1997).

■ **transfer payments:**
income transferred from one citizen who is earning income to another citizen who may not be

■ **budget surplus:**
the excess that results when government spending is less than revenue

■ **budget deficit:**
the shortage that results when government spending is greater than revenue

Besides government expenditures on goods and services, government also serves as an intermediary, taking money from taxpayers with higher incomes and transferring this income to those with lower incomes. Such **transfer payments** are a part of total government expenditures, so that the total government budget is much larger than the expenditures on goods and services reported in Figure 10. In 1996, total expenditures of federal, state, and local government for goods and services was $1,419 billion. In this same year, transfer payments paid by all levels of government were $1,085 billion.

The magnitude of federal government spending relative to federal government revenue from taxes has become an important issue in recent years. Figure 11 shows that the federal budget was roughly balanced until the early 1970s. The budget is a measure of spending and revenue. A balanced budget occurs when federal spending is approximately equal to federal revenue. This was the case through the 1950s and 1960s. If federal government spending is less than tax revenue, a **budget surplus** exists. Until 1997, the U.S. government last had a budget surplus in 1969. By the early 1980s, federal government spending was much larger than revenue, so a large **budget deficit** existed. The federal budget deficit grew very rapidly to around $200 billion by the mid-1980s. When spending is greater than revenue, the excess spending must be covered by borrowing, and this borrowing can have effects on investment and consumption as well as on economic relationships with other countries. In the late 1990s, the budget deficit dropped rapidly as strong economic growth generated tax revenues that grew more rapidly than expenditures.

RECAP

1. The microeconomic functions of government focus on issues aimed at providing public goods like police and military protection and correcting problems like pollution.

2. Macroeconomic policy attempts to control the economy through monetary and fiscal policy.

3. The Federal Reserve conducts monetary policy. Congress and the president formulate fiscal policy.

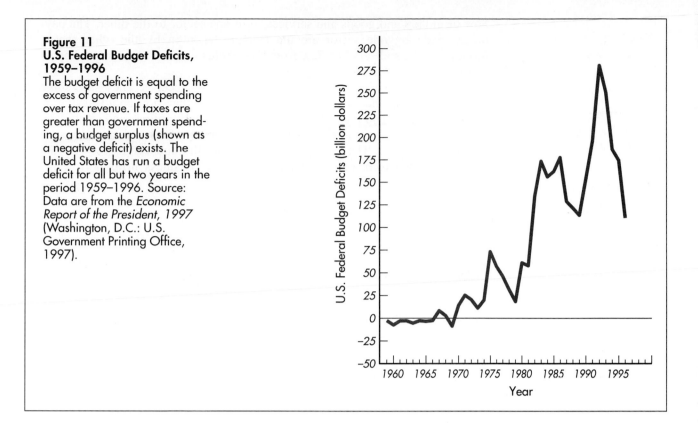

Figure 11
U.S. Federal Budget Deficits, 1959–1996
The budget deficit is equal to the excess of government spending over tax revenue. If taxes are greater than government spending, a budget surplus (shown as a negative deficit) exists. The United States has run a budget deficit for all but two years in the period 1959–1996. Source: Data are from the *Economic Report of the President, 1997* (Washington, D.C.: U.S. Government Printing Office, 1997).

4. Government spending is larger than investment spending but much smaller than consumption spending.

5. When government spending exceeds tax revenue, a budget deficit exists. When government spending is less than tax revenue, a budget surplus exists.

■ **private sector:**
households, businesses, and the international sector

■ **public sector:**
the government

5. LINKING THE SECTORS

Now that we have an idea of the size and structure of each of the **private sectors**—households, businesses, and international—and the government, also known as the **public sector**, let's discuss how the sectors interact.

5.a. The Private Sector

Households own all the basic resources, or factors of production, in the economy. Household members own land and provide labor, and they are the entrepreneurs, stockholders, proprietors, and partners who own business firms.

Households and businesses interact with each other by means of buying and selling. Businesses employ the services of resources in order to produce goods and services. Business firms pay households for their services of resources.

Households sell their resource services to businesses in exchange for money payments. The flow of resource services from households to businesses is shown by the blue arrow beneath the sectors of households, government, and firms shown in Figure 12. The flow of money payments from firms to households is shown by the gold arrow under Resource Services. Households use the money payments to buy goods and services from firms. These money payments are the firms' revenues. The flow of money payments from households to firms is shown by the gold arrow near the top of the diagram. The flow of goods and services from firms to households is shown by the blue arrow under Payments for Goods and Services. There is, therefore, a flow of money and goods and services from one sector to the other. The payments made by one sector are the receipts taken in by the other sector. Money, goods, and services flow from households to firms and back to households in a circular flow.

Households do not spend all of the money they receive. They save some fraction of their income. In Figure 12, we see that household saving is deposited in financial intermediaries like banks, credit unions, and saving and loan firms. A financial intermediary accepts deposits from savers and makes loans to borrowers. The money that is saved by the households reenters the economy in the form of investment spending as business firms borrow for expansion of their productive capacity.

Figure 12
The Circular Flow: Households, Firms, Government, and Foreign Countries
The diagram assumes that households and government are not directly engaged in international trade. Domestic firms trade with firms in foreign countries. The government sector buys resource services from households and goods and services from firms. This government spending represents income for the households and revenue for the firms. The government uses the resource services and goods and services to provide government services for households and firms. Households and firms pay taxes to the government to finance government expenditures.

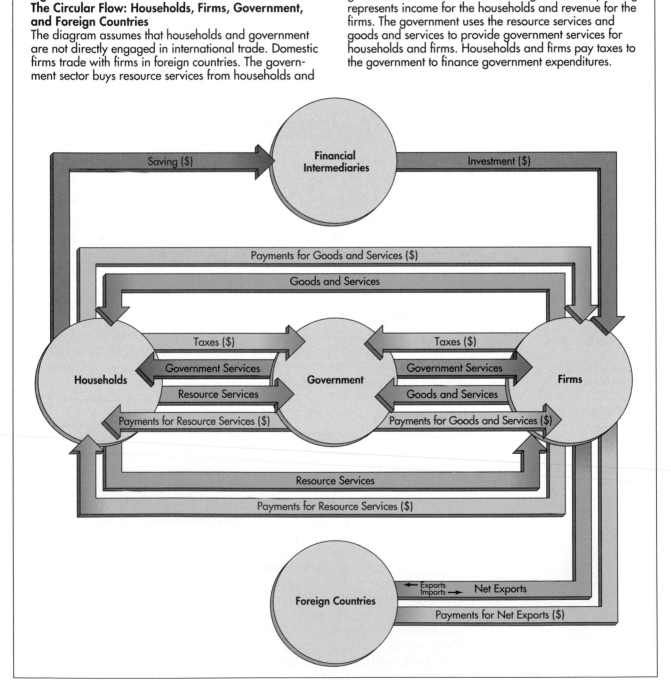

■ circular flow diagram:
a model showing the flow of output and income from one sector of the economy to another

To simplify this **circular flow diagram**, let's assume that households are not directly engaged in international trade and that only business firms are buying and selling goods and services across international borders. This assumption is not far from the truth for the industrial countries and for many developing countries. We typically buy a foreign-made product from a local business firm rather than directly from the foreign producer.

The lines Net Exports and Payments for Net Exports connect firms and foreign countries in Figure 12. Notice that neither line has an arrow indicating the direction of flow as do the other lines in the diagram. The reason is that net exports of the home country may be either positive (a trade surplus) or negative (a trade deficit). When net exports are positive, there is a net flow of goods from the firms of the home country to foreign countries and a net flow of money from foreign countries to the firms of the home country. When net exports are negative, the opposite occurs. A trade deficit involves a net flow of goods from foreign countries to the firms of the home country and a net flow of money from the home country firms to the foreign countries. If exports and imports are equal, net exports are zero because the value of exports is offset by the value of imports.

5.b. The Public Sector

Government at the federal, state, and local levels interacts with both households and firms. Because the government employs factors of production to produce government services, households receive payments from the government in exchange for the services of the factors of production. The flow of resource services from households to government is illustrated by the blue arrow flowing from the households to government in Figure 12. The flow of money from government to households is shown by the gold arrow flowing from government to households. We assume that government, like a household, does not trade directly with foreign countries but obtains foreign goods from domestic firms who do trade with the rest of the world.

Households pay taxes to support the provision of government services, such as national defense, education, and police and fire protection. In a sense, then, the household sector is purchasing goods and services from the government as well as from private businesses. The flow of tax payments from households and businesses to government is illustrated by the gold arrows flowing from households and businesses to government, and the flow of government services to households and businesses is illustrated by the purple lines flowing from government.

The addition of government brings significant changes to the model. Households have an additional place to sell their resources for income, and businesses have an additional market for goods and services. The value of private production no longer equals the value of household income. Households receive income from government in exchange for providing resource services to government. The total value of output in the economy is equal to the total income received, but government is included as a source of income and a producer of services.

RECAP

1. The circular flow diagram illustrates how the main sectors of the economy fit together.

2. Government interacts with both households and firms. Households get government services and pay taxes; they provide resource services and receive income. Firms sell goods and services to government and receive income.

3. The circular flow diagram shows that the value of output is equal to income.

SUMMARY

■■■ **What is a household, and what is household income and spending?**

1. A household consists of one or more persons who occupy a unit of housing.

2. Household spending is called consumption and is the largest component of spending in the economy.

■■■ **What is a business firm, and what is business spending?**

3. A business firm is a business organization controlled by a single management.

4. Businesses may be organized as sole proprietorships, partnerships, or corporations.

5. Business investment spending—the expenditure by business firms for capital goods—fluctuates a great deal over time.

■■■ **How does the international sector affect the economy?**

6. The international trade of the United States occurs predominantly with the other industrial economies.

7. Exports are products sold to the rest of the world. Imports are products bought from the rest of the world.

8. Exports minus imports equals net exports. Positive net exports mean that exports are greater than imports and a trade surplus exists. Negative net exports mean that imports exceed exports and a trade deficit exists.

■■■ **What does the government do?**

9. The government carries out microeconomic and macroeconomic activities. The microeconomic activities involve providing public goods and correcting problems. The macroeconomic activities attempt to control the economy through monetary and fiscal policy.

10. In the United States, monetary policy is the province of the Federal Reserve, and fiscal policy is up to the Congress and the president.

■■■ **How do the three private sectors—households, businesses, and the international sector—interact in the economy?**

11. Money, goods, and services flow from households to firms and back in a circular flow.

12. Some household income is not spent but saved in financial intermediaries where firms borrow for expansion of their productive capacity.

13. The circular flow diagram assumes that households are not directly engaged in international trade, but, rather, business firms only buy and sell goods and services across international borders.

■■■ **How does the government interact with the other sectors of the economy?**

14. The circular flow diagram illustrates the interaction among all sectors of the economy—households, businesses, the international sector, and the public sector.

KEY TERMS

household	monetary policy
consumption	Federal Reserve
multinational business	fiscal policy
investment	transfer payments
imports	budget surplus
exports	budget deficit
trade surplus	private sector
trade deficit	public sector
net exports	circular flow diagram

EXERCISES

1. Is a family a household? Is a household a family?

2. Which sector (household, business, or international) spends the most? Which sector spends the least? Which sector, because of volatility, has importance greater than is warranted by its size?

3. What does it mean if net exports are negative?

4. Why does the value of output always equal the income received by the resources that produced the output?

5. Total spending in the economy is equal to consumption plus investment plus government spending plus net exports. If households want to save and thus do not use all of their income for consumption, what will happen to total spending? Because total spending in the economy is equal to total income and output, what will happen to the output of goods and services if households want to save more?

6. People sometimes argue that imports should be limited by government policy. Suppose a government quota on the quantity of imports causes net exports to rise. Using the circular flow diagram as a guide, explain why total expenditures and national output may rise after the quota is imposed. Who is likely to benefit from the quota? Who will be hurt?

7. Draw the circular flow diagram linking households, business firms, and the international sector. Use the diagram to explain the effects of a decision by the household sector to increase saving.

8. Suppose there are three countries in the world. Country A exports $11 million worth of goods to country B and $5 million worth of goods to country C; country B exports $3 million worth of goods to country A and $6 million worth of goods to country C; and country C exports $4 million worth of goods to country A and $1 million worth of goods to country B.

   a. What are the net exports of countries A, B, and C?

   b. Which country is running a trade deficit? A trade surplus?

9. The chapter provides data indicating that there are many more sole proprietorships than corporations or partnerships. Why are there so many sole proprietorships? Why is the revenue of the average sole proprietorship less than that of the typical corporation?

10. Using the circular flow diagram, illustrate the effects of an increase in taxes imposed on the household sector.

🖥 INTERNET EXERCISE

In this chapter we learned about government budget deficits and surpluses. Use the Internet to determine the current state of the federal, state, and local government budgets. Go to the Boyes/Melvin *Fundamentals of Economics* Web site at http://www.hmco.com/college/ and click on the Internet Exercise link for Chapter 9. Now answer the questions that appear on the Boyes/Melvin Web site.

10

Macroeconomic Measures

FUNDAMENTAL QUESTIONS

1. How is the total output of an economy measured?

2. What is the difference between nominal and real GDP?

3. What is a price index?

4. How is money traded internationally?

5. How do nations record their transactions with the rest of the world?

*J*ust as we use a thermometer and degrees of temperature as a measure of a person's health, we must use economic data to analyze the health of an economy. Since we prefer more goods and services to less, we need a good way to measure how much is produced to see if the economy is providing more goods and services and, if so, how much more. Since we like prices to rise slower rather than faster, we need a good way to monitor how prices change in the economy. Since we trade goods, services, and money with the rest of the world, we need good measures of how much is traded and what things cost. In this chapter, we will learn how economists measure things like output and inflation. We will also find out how trade with the rest of the world is counted. This will allow a solid foundation upon which future chapters will build as we use this information in further analysis of business conditions both at home and abroad. ■

1. MEASURES OF OUTPUT AND INCOME

■ **national income accounting:** the framework that summarizes and categorizes productive activity in an economy over a specific period of time, typically a year

In this chapter we discuss gross domestic product, real GDP, and other measures of national productive activity by making use of the **national income accounting** system used by all countries. National income accounting provides a framework for discussing macroeconomics. It measures the output of an entire economy as well as the flows between sectors. It summarizes the level of production in an economy over a specific period of time, typically a year. In practice, the process *estimates* the amount of activity that occurs. It is beyond the capability of government officials to count every transaction that takes place in a modern economy. Still, national income accounting generates useful and fairly accurate measures of economic activity in most countries, especially wealthy industrial countries that have comprehensive accounting systems.

1.a. Gross Domestic Product

Modern economies produce an amazing variety of goods and services. To measure an economy's total production, economists combine the quantities of oranges, golf balls, automobiles, and all the other goods and services produced, into a single measure of output. Of course, simply adding up the number of things produced—the number of oranges, golf balls, and automobiles—does not reveal the *value* of what is being produced. If a nation produces 1 million more oranges and 1 million fewer automobiles this year than it did last year, the total number of things produced remains the same. But because automobiles are much more valuable than oranges, the value of output has dropped substantially. Prices reflect the value of goods and services in the market, so economists use the money value of things to create a measure of total output, a measure that is more meaningful than the sum of units produced.

The most common measure of a nation's output is gross domestic product. **Gross domestic product (GDP)** is the market value of all final goods and services produced in a year within a country's borders. A closer look at three parts of this definition—*market value*, *final goods and services*, and *produced in a year*—will make clear what the GDP does and does not include.

■ **gross domestic product (GDP):** the market value of all final goods and services produced in a year within a country

Market Value The *market value* of final goods and services is their value at market price. The process of determining market value is straightforward where prices are known and transactions are observable. However, there are cases where prices are not known and transactions are not observable. For instance, illegal drug transactions are not reported to the government, which

The Value of Homemaker Services

One way GDP underestimates the total value of a nation's output is by failing to record nonmarket production. A prime example is the work homemakers do. Of course, people are not paid for their work around the house, so it is difficult to measure the value of their output. But notice that we say *difficult*, not impossible. Economists can use several methods to assign value to homemaker services.

One is an opportunity cost approach. This approach measures the value of a homemaker's services by the forgone market salary the homemaker could have earned if he or she worked full time outside the home. The rationale is that society loses the output the homemaker would have produced in the market job in order to gain the output the homemaker produces in the home.

Another alternative is to estimate what it would cost to hire workers to produce the goods and services that the homemaker produces. For example, what would it cost to hire someone to prepare meals, iron, clean, and take care of the household? It has been estimated that the average homemaker spends almost 8 hours a day, 7 days a week, on household work. This amounts to over 50 hours a week. At a rate of $10 an hour, the value of the homemaker's services is over $500 a week.

Whichever method we use, two things are clear. The value of homemaker services to the household and the economy is substantial. And by failing to account for those services, the GDP substantially underestimates the value of the nation's output.

means they are not included in GDP statistics. In fact, almost any activity that is not traded in a market is not included. For example, production that takes place in households, such as homemakers' services (as discussed in the Economic Insight "The Value of Homemaker Services"), is not counted, nor are unreported barter and cash transactions. For instance, if a lawyer has a sick dog and a veterinarian needs some legal advice, by trading services and not reporting the activity to the tax authorities, each can avoid taxation on the income that would have been reported had they sold their services to each other. If the value of a transaction is not recorded as taxable income, it generally does not appear in the GDP. There are some exceptions, however. Contributions toward GDP are estimated for *in-kind wages*, nonmonetary compensation like room and board. GDP values also are assigned to the output consumed by a producer—for example, the home consumption of crops by a farmer.

Final Goods and Services The second part of the definition of GDP limits the measure to *final goods and services*, the goods and services available to the ultimate consumer. This limitation avoids double-counting. Suppose a retail store sells a shirt to a consumer for $20. The value of the shirt in the GDP is $20. But the shirt is made of cotton that has been grown by a farmer, woven at a mill, and cut and sewn by a manufacturer. What would happen if we counted the value of the shirt at each of these stages of the production process? We would overstate the market value of the shirt.

■ **intermediate good:**
a good that is used as an input in the production of final goods and services

Intermediate goods are goods that are used in the production of a final product. For instance, the ingredients for a meal are intermediate goods to a restaurant. Similarly, the cotton and the cloth are intermediate goods in the production of the shirt. The stages of production of the $20 shirt are shown in Figure 1. The value-of-output axis measures the value of the product at each stage. The cotton produced by the farmer sells for $1. The cloth woven by the textile mill sells for $5. The shirt manufacturer sells the shirt wholesale to the retail store for $12. The retail store sells the shirt—the final good—to the ultimate consumer for $20.

Remember that GDP is based on the market value of final goods and services. In our example, the market value of the shirt is $20. That price already

**Figure 1
Stages of Production and Value Added in Shirt Manufacturing**
A cotton farmer sells cotton to a textile mill for $1, adding $1 to the value of the final shirt. The textile mill sells cloth to a shirt manufacturer for $5, adding $4 to the value of the final shirt. The manufacturer sells the shirt wholesale to the retail store for $12, adding $7 to the value of the final shirt. The retail store sells the final shirt to a consumer for $20, adding $8 to the value of the final shirt. The sum of the prices received at each stage of production equals $38, which is greater than the price of the final shirt. The sum of the value added at each stage of production equals $20, which equals the market value of the shirt.

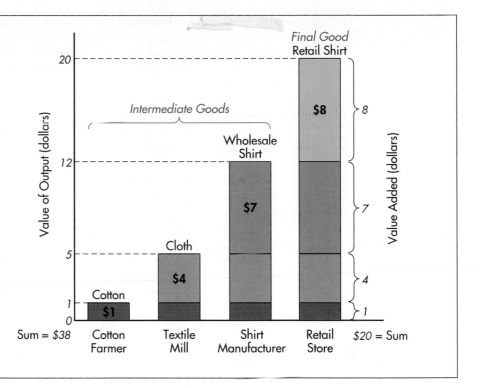

■ **value added:**
the difference between the value of output and the value of the intermediate goods used in the production of that output

includes the value of the intermediate goods that were used to produce the shirt. If we add to it the value of output at every stage of production, we would be counting the value of the intermediate goods twice, and we would be overstating the GDP.

It is possible to compute GDP by computing the **value added** at each stage of production. Value added is the difference between the value of output and the value of the intermediate goods used in the production of that output. In Figure 1, the value added by each stage of production is listed at the right. The farmer adds $1 to the value of the shirt. The mill takes the cotton worth $1 and produces cloth worth $5, adding $4 to the value of the shirt. The manufacturer uses $5 worth of cloth to produce a shirt it sells for $12, so the manufacturer adds $7 to the shirt's value. Finally, the retail store adds $8 to the value of the shirt: it pays the manufacturer $12 for the shirt and sells it to the consumer for $20. The sum of the value added at each stage of production is $20. The total value added, then, is equal to the market value of the final product.

Economists can compute GDP using two methods: the final goods and services method uses the market value of the final good or service; the value-added method uses the value added at each stage of production. Both methods count the value of intermediate goods only once. This is an important distinction: GDP is not based on the market value of *all* goods and services, but on the market value of all *final* goods and services.

Produced in a Year GDP measures the value of output *produced in a year*. The value of goods produced last year is counted in last year's GDP; the value of goods produced this year is counted in this year's GDP. The year of production, not the year of sale, determines allocation to GDP. Although the value of last year's goods is not counted in this year's GDP, the value of services involved in the sale is. This year's GDP does not include the value of a house built last year, but it does include the value of the real estate broker's fee; it does not include the value of a used car, but it does include the income earned by the used-car dealer in the sale of that car.

To determine the value of goods produced in a year but not sold in that year, economists calculate changes in inventory. **Inventory** is a firm's stock

■ **inventory:**
the stock of unsold goods held by a firm

of unsold goods. If a shirt that is produced this year remains on the retail store's shelf at the end of the year, it increases the value of the store's inventory. A $20 shirt increases that value by $20. Changes in inventory allow economists to count goods in the year in which they are produced whether or not they are sold.

Changes in inventory can be planned or unplanned. A store may want a cushion above expected sales (*planned inventory changes*), or it may not be able to sell all the goods it expected to sell when it placed the order (*unplanned inventory changes*). For instance, suppose Jeremy owns a surfboard shop, and he always wants to keep 10 surfboards above what he expects to sell. This is done so that in case business is surprisingly good, he does not have to turn away customers to his competitors and lose those sales. At the beginning of the year, Jeremy has 10 surfboards and then builds as many new boards during the year as he expects to sell. Jeremy *plans* on having an inventory at the end of the year of 10 surfboards. Suppose Jeremy expects to sell 100 surfboards during the year, so he builds 100 new boards. If business is surprisingly poor so that Jeremy sells only 80 surfboards, how do we count the 20 new boards that he made but did not sell? We count the change in his inventory. He started the year with 10 surfboards and ends the year with 20 more unsold boards for a year-end inventory of 30. The change in inventory of 20 (equal to the ending inventory of 30 minus the starting inventory of 10) represents output that is counted in GDP. In Jeremy's case, the inventory change is unplanned since he expected to sell the 20 extra surfboards that he has in his shop at the end of the year. But whether the inventory change is planned or unplanned, changes in inventory will count output that is produced but not sold in a given year.

1.a.1. GDP as Output

GDP is a measure of the market value of a nation's total output in a year. Remember that economists divide the economy into four sectors: households, businesses, government, and the international sector. The total value of economic activity equals the sum of the output produced in each sector. Since GDP counts the output produced in the United States, U.S. GDP is produced in business firms, households, and government located within the boundaries of the United States. Not unexpectedly in a capitalist country, privately owned businesses account for the largest percentage of output: in the United States, 84 percent of the GDP is produced by private firms. Government produces 11 percent of the GDP, and households 5 percent.

In terms of output, GDP is the value of final goods and services produced by domestic households, businesses, and government units. If some of the firms producing in the United States are foreign-owned, their output produced in the United States is counted in U.S. GDP.

1.a.2. GDP as Expenditures

Here we look at GDP in terms of what each sector pays for goods and services it purchases. The dollar value of total expenditures—the sum of the amount each sector spends on final goods and services—equals the dollar value of output. Household spending is called *consumption*. Households spend income on goods and services to be consumed. Business spending is called *investment*. Investment is spending on capital goods that will be used to produce other goods and services. The two other components of total spending are *government spending* and *net exports*. Net exports are the value of *exports* (goods and services sold to the rest of the world) minus the value of *imports* (goods and services bought from the rest of the world).

GDP – consumption + investment + government spending + net exports

■ $GDP = C + I + G + X$

Or, in the shorter form commonly used by economists,

$$GDP = C + I + G + X$$

where X is net exports.

Consumption, or household spending, accounts for 68 percent of national expenditures. Government spending represents 18 percent of expenditures, and business investment, 15 percent. Net exports are negative (−1 percent), which means that imports exceed exports. To determine total national expenditures on *domestic* output, the value of imports, spending on foreign output, are subtracted from total expenditures.

1.a.3. GDP as Income The total value of output can be calculated by adding up the expenditures of each sector. And because one sector's expenditures are another's income, the total value of output also can be computed by adding up the income of all sectors.

Business firms use factors of production to produce goods and services. The income earned by factors of production is classified as wages, interest, rent, and profits. *Wages* are payments to labor, including fringe benefits, social security contributions, and retirement payments. *Interest* is the net interest paid by businesses to households plus the net interest received from foreigners (the interest they pay us minus the interest we pay them). *Rent* is income earned from selling the use of real property (houses, shops, farms). Finally, *profits* are the sum of corporate profits plus proprietors' income (income from sole proprietorships and partnerships).

In terms of income, wages account for 58 percent of the GDP. Interest and profits account for 5 percent and 10 percent of the GDP, respectively. Proprietors' income accounts for 7 percent. Rent (2 percent) is very small in comparison. *Net factor income from abroad* is income received from U.S.-owned resources located in other countries minus income paid to foreign-owned resources located in the United States. Since U.S. GDP refers only to income earned within U.S. borders, we must deduct this kind of income to arrive at GDP (−.2 percent).

GDP also includes two income categories that we have not discussed: capital consumption allowance and indirect business taxes. **Capital consumption allowance** is not a money payment to a factor of production; it is the estimated value of capital goods used up or worn out in production plus the value of accidental damage to capital goods. The value of accidental damage is relatively small, so it is common to hear economists refer to capital consumption allowance as **depreciation**. Machines and other capital goods wear out over time. The reduction in the value of capital stock due to its being used up or worn out over time is called depreciation. A depreciating capital good loses value each year of its useful life until its value is zero.

Even though capital consumption allowance does not represent income received by a factor of production, it must be accounted for in GDP as income. Otherwise the value of GDP measured as output would be higher than the value of the GDP as income. Depreciation is a kind of resource payment, part of the total payment to the owners of capital. All of the income categories—wages, interest, rent, profits, and capital consumption allowance—are expenses incurred in the production of output.

Indirect business taxes, like capital consumption allowances, are not payments to a factor of production. They are taxes collected by businesses that then are turned over to the government. Both excise taxes and sales taxes are forms of indirect business taxes.

For example, suppose a motel room in Florida costs $80 a night. A consumer would be charged $90. Of that $90, the motel receives $80 as the value of the service sold; the other $10 is an excise tax. The motel cannot keep the $10; it must turn it over to the state government. (In effect, the motel is acting as the government's tax collector.) The consumer spends $90; the motel earns $80. To balance expenditures and income, we have to allocate the $10 difference to indirect business taxes.

■ **capital consumption allowance:**
the estimated value of depreciation plus the value of accidental damage to capital stock

■ **depreciation:**
a reduction in the value of capital goods over time due to their use in production

■ **indirect business tax:**
a tax that is collected by businesses for a government agency

To summarize, GDP measured as income includes the four payments to the factors of production: wages, interest, rent, and profits. These income items represent expenses incurred in the production of GDP. To these we must subtract net factor income from abroad in order for the total to sum to GDP. Along with these payments are two nonincome items: capital consumption allowance and indirect business taxes.

$$\text{GDP} = \text{wages} + \text{interest} + \text{rent} + \text{profits} - \text{net factor income from abroad}$$
$$+ \text{capital consumption allowance} + \text{indirect business taxes}$$

GDP is the total value of output produced in a year, the total value of expenditures made to purchase that output, and the total value of income received by the factors of production. Because all three are measures of the same thing—GDP—all must be equal.

1.b. Other Measures of Output and Income

GDP is the most common measure of a nation's output, but it is not the only measure. Economists rely on a number of others in analyzing the performance of components of an economy.

■ **gross national product (GNP):**
gross domestic product plus receipts of factor income from the rest of the world minus payments of factor income to the rest of the world

1.b.1. Gross National Product
Gross national product (GNP) equals GDP plus receipts of factor income from the rest of the world minus payments of factor income to the rest of the world. If we add to GDP the value of income earned by U.S. residents from factors of production located outside the United States and subtract the value of income earned by foreign residents from factors of production located inside the United States, we have a measure of the value of output produced by U.S.-owned resources—GNP.

Figure 2 shows the national income accounts in the United States in 1997. The figure begins with the GDP and then shows the calculations necessary to obtain the GNP and other measures of national output. In 1997, the U.S. GNP was $8,060.1 billion.

■ **net national product (NNP):**
gross national product minus capital consumption allowance

1.b.2. Net National Product
Net national product (NNP) equals GNP minus capital consumption allowance. NNP measures the value of goods and services produced in a year less the value of capital goods that became obsolete or were used up during the year. Because NNP includes only net additions to a nation's capital, it is a better measure of the expansion or contraction of current output than is GNP. Remember how we defined GDP in terms of expenditures in section 1.a.2:

$$\text{GDP} = \text{consumption} + \text{investment} + \text{government spending} + \text{net exports}$$

■ **gross investment:**
total investment, including investment expenditures required to replace capital goods consumed in current production

■ **net investment:**
gross investment minus capital consumption allowance

The investment measure in GDP (and GNP) is called **gross investment**. Gross investment is total investment, which includes investment expenditures required to replace capital goods consumed in current production. NNP does not include investment expenditures required to replace worn-out capital goods; it includes only net investment. **Net investment** is equal to gross investment minus capital consumption allowance. Net investment measures business spending over and above that required to replace worn-out capital goods.

Figure 2 shows that in 1997, the U.S. NNP was $7,192.2 billion. This means that the U.S. economy produced well over $7 trillion worth of goods and services above those required to replace capital stock that had depreciated. Over $867 billion in capital was "worn out" in 1997.

■ **national income (NI):**
net national product minus indirect business taxes

1.b.3. National Income
National income (NI) equals the NNP minus indirect business taxes, plus or minus a couple of other small adjustments. NI captures the costs of the factors of production used in producing output. Remember that GDP includes two nonincome expense items: capital consumption allowance and indirect business taxes (section 1.a.3). Subtracting

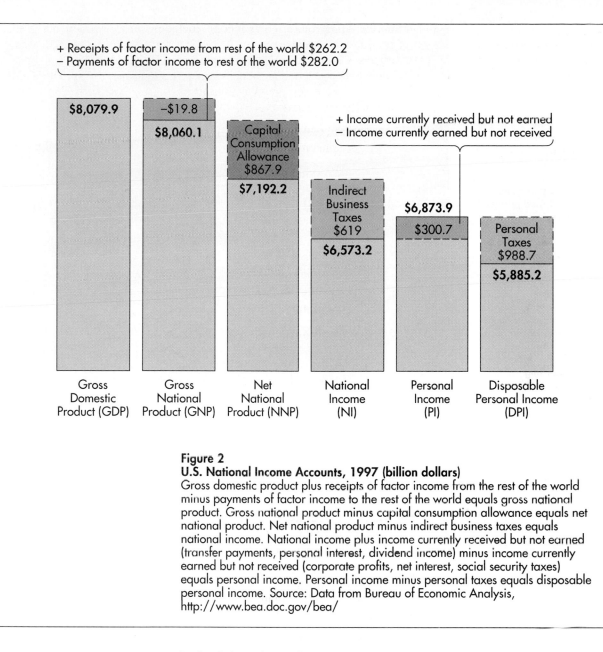

Figure 2
U.S. National Income Accounts, 1997 (billion dollars)
Gross domestic product plus receipts of factor income from the rest of the world minus payments of factor income to the rest of the world equals gross national product. Gross national product minus capital consumption allowance equals net national product. Net national product minus indirect business taxes equals national income. National income plus income currently received but not earned (transfer payments, personal interest, dividend income) minus income currently earned but not received (corporate profits, net interest, social security taxes) equals personal income. Personal income minus personal taxes equals disposable personal income. Source: Data from Bureau of Economic Analysis, http://www.bea.doc.gov/bea/

both of these items from the GDP leaves the income payments that actually go to resources.

Because the NNP equals the GNP minus capital consumption allowance, we can subtract indirect business taxes from the NNP to find NI, as shown in Figure 2. This measure helps economists analyze how the costs of (or payments received by) resources change.

■ **personal income (PI):**
national income plus income currently received but not earned, minus income currently earned but not received

1.b.4. Personal Income Personal income (PI) is national income adjusted for income that is received but not earned in the current year and income that is earned but not received in the current year. Social security and welfare benefits are examples of income that is received but not earned in the current year. As you learned in Chapter 9, they are called transfer payments. An example of income that is currently earned but not received is profits that are retained by a corporation to finance current needs rather than paid out to stockholders. Another is social security (FICA) taxes, which are deducted from workers' paychecks.

■ **disposable personal income (DPI):**
personal income minus personal taxes

1.b.5. Disposable Personal Income Disposable personal income (DPI) equals personal income minus personal taxes—income taxes, excise and real estate taxes on personal property, and other personal taxes. DPI is the income

All final goods and services produced in a year are counted in GDP. For instance, the value of a rafting trip down the Colorado River through the Grand Canyon is part of the national output of the United States. The value of the rafting trip would be equal to the amount that travelers would have to pay the guide company in order to take the trip. This price would reflect the value of the personnel, equipment, and food provided by the guide company.

that individuals have at their disposal for spending or saving. The sum of consumption spending plus saving must equal disposable personal income.

RECAP

1. Gross domestic product (GDP) is the market value of all final goods and services produced in an economy in a year.

2. GDP can be calculated by summing the market value of all final goods and services produced in a year, by summing the value added at each stage of production, by adding total expenditures on goods and services (GDP = consumption + investment + government spending + net exports), and by using the total income earned in the production of goods and services (GDP = wages + interest + rent + profits) and subtracting net factor income from abroad, and adding depreciation, and indirect business taxes.

3. Other measures of output and income include gross national product (GNP), net national product (NNP), national income (NI), personal income (PI), and disposable personal income (DPI).

National Income Accounts

GDP = consumption + investment + government spending
      + net exports
GNP = GDP + receipts of factor income from the rest of the world
      − payments of factor income to the rest of the world
NNP = GNP − capital consumption allowance
 NI = NNP − indirect business taxes
 PI = NI − income earned but not received
      + income received but not earned
DPI = PI − personal taxes

2. NOMINAL AND REAL MEASURES

GDP is the market value of all final goods and services produced within a country in a year. Value is measured in money terms, so the U.S. GDP is reported in dollars, the German GDP in marks, the Mexican GDP in pesos, and so on. Market value is the product of two elements: the money price and the quantity produced.

2.a. Nominal and Real GDP

■ **nominal GDP:**
a measure of national output based on the current prices of goods and services

■ **real GDP:**
a measure of the quantity of final goods and services produced, obtained by eliminating the influence of price changes from the nominal GDP statistics

Nominal GDP measures output in terms of its current dollar value. **Real GDP** is adjusted for changing price levels. In 1980, the U.S. GDP was $2,784 billion; in 1997, it was $8,079.9 billion—an increase of 190 percent. Does this mean that the United States produced 190 percent more goods and services in 1997 than it did in 1980? If the numbers reported are for nominal GDP, we cannot be sure. Nominal GDP cannot tell us whether the economy produced more goods and services, because nominal GDP changes when prices change *and* when quantity changes.

Real GDP measures output in constant prices. This allows economists to identify the changes in actual production of final goods and services: real GDP measures the quantity of goods and services produced after eliminating the influence of price changes contained in nominal GDP. In 1980, real GDP in the United States was $4,612 billion; in 1997, it was $7,188.8 billion, an increase of just 56 percent. The 190 percent increase in nominal GDP in large part reflects increased prices, not increased output.

Since we prefer more goods and services to higher prices, it is better to have nominal GDP rise because of higher output than because of higher prices. We want nominal GDP to increase as a result of an increase in real GDP.

Consider a simple example that illustrates the difference between nominal GDP and real GDP. Suppose a hypothetical economy produces just three goods: oranges, coconuts, and pizzas. The dollar value of output in three different years is listed in the table in Figure 3.

As shown in Figure 3, in year 1, 100 oranges were produced at $.50 per orange, 300 coconuts at $1 per coconut, and 2,000 pizzas at $8 per pizza. The total dollar value of output in year 1 is $16,350. In year 2, prices are constant at the year 1 values, but the quantity of each good has increased by 10 percent. The dollar value of output in year 2 is $17,985, 10 percent higher than the value of output in year 1. In year 3, the quantity of each good is back at the year 1 level, but prices have increased by 10 percent. Oranges now cost $.55, coconuts $1.10, and pizzas $8.80. The dollar value of output in year 3 is $17,985.

Notice that in years 2 and 3, the dollar value of output ($17,985) is 10 percent higher than it was in year 1. But there is a difference here. In year 2, the increase in output is due entirely to an increase in the production of the three goods. In year 3, the increase is due entirely to an increase in the prices of the goods.

Because prices did not change between years 1 and 2, the increase in nominal GDP is entirely accounted for by an increase in real output, or real GDP. In years 1 and 3, the actual quantities produced did not change, which means that real GDP was constant; only nominal GDP was higher, a product only of higher prices.

2.b. Price Indexes

The total dollar value of output or income is equal to price multiplied by the quantity of goods and services produced:

$$\text{dollar value of output} = \text{price} \times \text{quantity}$$

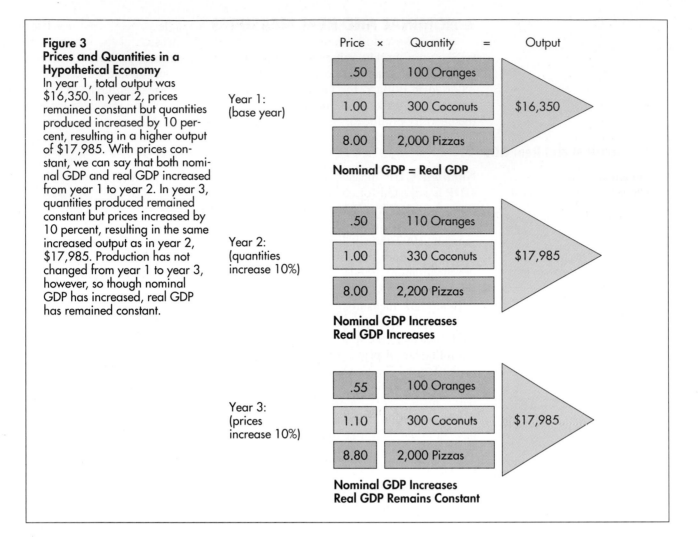

Figure 3
Prices and Quantities in a Hypothetical Economy
In year 1, total output was $16,350. In year 2, prices remained constant but quantities produced increased by 10 percent, resulting in a higher output of $17,985. With prices constant, we can say that both nominal GDP and real GDP increased from year 1 to year 2. In year 3, quantities produced remained constant but prices increased by 10 percent, resulting in the same increased output as in year 2, $17,985. Production has not changed from year 1 to year 3, however, so though nominal GDP has increased, real GDP has remained constant.

By dividing the dollar value of output by price, you can determine the quantity of goods and services produced:

$$\text{quantity} = \frac{\text{dollar value of output}}{\text{price}}$$

In macroeconomics, a **price index** measures the average level of prices in an economy and shows how prices, on average, have changed. Prices of individual goods can rise and fall relative to one another, but a price index shows the general trend in prices across the economy.

2.b.1. Base Year The example in Figure 3 provides a simple introduction to price indexes. The first step is to pick a **base year**, the year against which other years are measured. Any year can serve as the base year. Suppose we pick year 1 in Figure 3. The value of the price index in year 1, the base year, is defined to be 100. This simply means that prices in year 1 are 100 percent of prices in year 1 (100 percent of 1 is 1). In the example, year 2 prices are equal to year 1 prices, so the price index also is equal to 100 in year 2. In year 3, every price has risen 10 percent relative to the base-year (year 1) prices, so the price index is 10 percent higher in year 3, or 110. The value of the price index in any particular year indicates how prices have changed relative to the base year. A value of 110 indicates that prices are 110 percent of base-year prices, or that the average price level has increased 10 percent.

price index in any year = 100 + (or −) percentage change in prices from the base year

2.b.2. Types of Price Indexes The price of a single good is easy to determine. But how do economists determine a single measure of the prices of the millions of goods and services produced in an economy? They have constructed price indexes to measure the price level; there are several different price indexes used to measure the price level in any economy. Not all prices rise or fall at the same time or by the same amount. This is why there are several measures of the price level in an economy.

The price index used to estimate constant dollar real GDP is the **GDP price index (GDPPI)**, a measure of prices across the economy that reflects all of the categories of goods and services included in GDP. The GDPPI is a very broad measure. Economists use other price indexes to analyze how prices change in more specific categories of goods and services.

Probably the best-known price index is the **consumer price index (CPI)**. The CPI measures the average price of consumer goods and services that a typical household purchases. The CPI is a narrower measure than the GDPPI because it includes fewer items. However, because of the relevance of consumer prices to the standard of living, news reports on price changes in the economy typically focus on consumer price changes. In addition, labor contracts sometimes include provisions that raise wages as the CPI goes up. Social security payments also are tied to increases in the CPI. These increases are called **cost of living adjustments (COLAs)**, because they are supposed to keep nominal income rising along with the cost of items purchased by the typical household.

The **producer price index (PPI)** measures average prices received by producers. At one time this price index was known as the *wholesale price index (WPI)*. Because the PPI measures price changes at an earlier stage of production than the CPI, it can indicate a coming change in the CPI. If producer input costs are rising, we can expect the price of goods produced to go up as well.

Figure 4 illustrates how the three different measures of prices have changed over time. Notice that the PPI is more volatile than the GDPPI or the CPI. This is because there are smaller fluctuations in the equilibrium prices of final goods than in those of intermediate goods.

■ **GDP price index:**
a broad measure of the prices of goods and services included in the gross domestic product

■ **consumer price index (CPI):**
a measure of the average price of goods and services purchased by the typical household

■ **cost of living adjustment (COLA):**
an increase in wages that is designed to match increases in prices of items purchased by the typical household

■ **producer price index (PPI):**
a measure of average prices received by producers

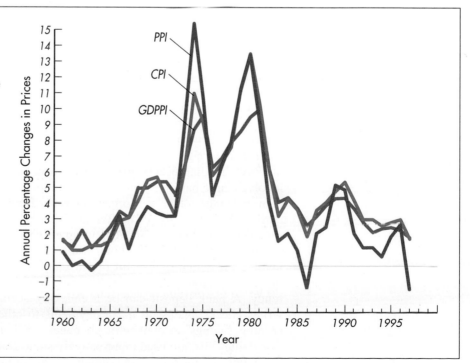

Figure 4
The GDP Price Index, the CPI, and the PPI
The graph plots the annual percentage change in the GDP price index (GDPPI), the consumer price index (CPI), and the producer price index (PPI). The GDPPI is used to construct constant dollar real GDP. The CPI measures the average price of consumer goods and services that a typical household purchases. The PPI measures the average price received by producers; it is the most variable of the three because fluctuations in equilibrium prices of intermediate goods are much greater than for final goods. Source: *Economic Report of the President, 1997* (Washington, D.C.: U.S. Government Printing Office, 1997).

RECAP

1. Nominal GDP is measured using current dollars.
2. Real GDP measures output with price effects removed.
3. The GDP price index, the consumer price index, and the producer price index are all measures of the level of prices in an economy.

3. FLOWS OF INCOME AND EXPENDITURES

GDP is both a measure of total expenditures on final goods and services and a measure of the total income earned in the production of those goods and services. The idea that total expenditures equal total income is clearly illustrated in the circular flow diagram of Chapter 9.

The figure links the four sectors of the economy: households, firms, government, and foreign countries. The arrows between the sectors indicate the direction of the flows. The money flows are both income and expenditures. Because one sector's expenditures represent another sector's income, the total expenditures on goods and services must be the same as the total income from selling goods and services, and those must both be equal to the total value of the goods and services produced.

RECAP

1. Total spending on final goods and services equals the total income received in producing those goods and services.
2. The circular flow model shows that one sector's expenditures represent the income of other sectors.

4. THE FOREIGN EXCHANGE MARKET

■ **foreign exchange:**
currency and bank deposits that are denominated in foreign money

■ **foreign exchange market:**
a global market in which people trade one currency for another

Foreign exchange is foreign money, including paper money and bank deposits like checking accounts that are denominated in foreign currency. When someone with U.S. dollars wants to trade those dollars for Japanese yen, the trade takes place in the **foreign exchange market**, a global market in which people trade one currency for another. Many financial markets are located in a specific geographic location. For instance, the New York Stock Exchange is a specific location in New York City where stocks are bought and sold. The Commodity Exchange is a specific location in New York City where contracts to deliver agricultural and metal commodities are bought and sold. The foreign exchange market is not in a single geographic location, however. Trading occurs all over the world by telephone. Most of the activity involves large banks in New York, London, and other financial centers. A foreign exchange trader at Morgan Guaranty Bank in New York can buy or sell currencies with a trader at Barclays Bank in London by calling the other trader on the telephone or exchanging e-mail.

Only tourism and a few other transactions in the foreign exchange market involve the actual movement of currency. The great majority of transactions involve the buying and selling of bank deposits denominated in foreign currency. A bank deposit can be a checking account that a firm or individual writes checks against to make payments to others, or it may be an interest-earning savings account with no check-writing privileges. Currency notes, like dollar bills, are used in a relatively small fraction of transactions. When a large corporation or a government buys foreign currency, it buys a bank deposit denominated in the foreign currency. Still, all exchanges in the market require that monies have a price.

4.a. Exchange Rates

An exchange rate is the price of one country's money in terms of another country's money. Exchange rates are needed to compare prices quoted in two different currencies. Suppose a shirt that has been manufactured in Canada sells for 20 U.S. dollars in Seattle, Washington, and for 25 Canadian dollars in Vancouver, British Columbia. Where would you get the better buy? Unless you know the exchange rate between U.S. and Canadian dollars, you can't tell. The exchange rate allows you to convert the foreign currency price into its domestic currency equivalent, which then can be compared to the domestic price.

Table 1 lists exchange rates for February 24, 1998. The rates are quoted in U.S. dollars per unit of foreign currency in the second column, and units of foreign currency per U.S. dollar in the last column. For instance, the Canadian dollar was selling for $.7033, or a little more than 70 U.S. cents. The same day, the U.S. dollar was selling for 1.4218 Canadian dollars (1 U.S. dollar would buy 1.4218 Canadian dollars).

If you know the price in U.S. dollars of a currency, you can find the price of the U.S. dollar in that currency by taking the reciprocal. To find the reciprocal of a number, write it as a fraction and then turn the fraction upside down. Let's say that 1 British pound sells for 2 U.S. dollars. In fraction form, 2 is 2/1. The reciprocal of 2/1 is 1/2, or .5. So 1 U.S. dollar sells for .5 British pounds. The table shows that the actual dollar price of the pound was 1.6504. The *reciprocal exchange rate*—the number of pounds per dollar—is .6059 (1/1.6504), which was the pound price of 1 dollar that day.

Let's go back to comparing the price of the Canadian shirt in Seattle and Vancouver. The symbol for the U.S. dollar is $. The symbol for the Canadian dollar is C$. The shirt sells for $20 in Seattle and C$25 in Vancouver. Suppose the exchange rate between the U.S. dollar and the Canadian dollar is .8. This means that C$1 costs .8 U.S. dollars, or 80 U.S. cents.

TABLE 1
Exchange Rates
February 24, 1998

Country	U.S. $ per currency	Currency per U.S. $
Argentina (peso)	1.0001	.9999
Australia (dollar)	.6566	1.5024
Britain (pound)	1.6504	.6059
Canada (dollar)	.7033	1.4218
China (renminbi)	.1208	8.2789
France (franc)	.1660	6.0240
Germany (mark)	.5567	1.7964
Israel (shekel)	.2779	3.5980
Italy (lira)	.00056	1,773
Japan (yen)	.0078	127.98
Mexico (peso)	.1166	8.5800
New Zealand (dollar)	.5759	1.7364
Russia (ruble)	.1649	6.0660
Singapore (dollar)	.6126	1.6325
Switzerland (franc)	.6891	1.4511

To find the domestic currency value of a foreign currency price, multiply the foreign currency price by the exchange rate:

domestic currency value = foreign currency price × exchange rate

In our example, the U.S. dollar is the domestic currency:

U.S. dollar value = C$25 × .8 = $20

If we multiply the price of the shirt in Canadian dollars (C$25) by the exchange rate (.8), we find the U.S. dollar value ($20). After adjusting for the exchange rate, then, we can see that the shirt sells for the same price when the price is measured in a single currency.

4.b. Exchange Rate Changes and International Trade

Because exchange rates determine the domestic currency value of foreign goods, changes in those rates affect the demand for and supply of goods traded internationally. Suppose the price of the shirt in Seattle and in Vancouver remains the same, but the exchange rate changes from .8 to .9 U.S. dollars per Canadian dollar. What happens? The U.S. dollar price of the shirt in Vancouver increases. At the new rate, the shirt that sells for C$25 in Vancouver costs a U.S. buyer $22.50 (C$25 × .9).

A rise in the value of a currency is called *appreciation*. In our example, as the exchange rate moves from $.8 = C$1 to $.9 = C$1, the Canadian dollar appreciates against the U.S. dollar. As a country's currency appreciates, international demand for its products falls, other things equal.

Suppose the exchange rate in our example moves from $.8 = C$1 to $.7 = C$1. Now the shirt that sells for C$25 in Vancouver costs a U.S. buyer $17.50 (C$25 × .7). In this case the Canadian dollar has *depreciated* in value relative to the U.S. dollar. As a country's currency depreciates, its goods sell for lower prices in other countries and the demand for its products increases, other things equal.

When the Canadian dollar is appreciating against the U.S. dollar, the U.S. dollar must be depreciating against the Canadian dollar. For instance, when the exchange rate between the U.S. dollar and the Canadian dollar moves from $.8 = C$1 to $.9 = C$1, the reciprocal exchange rate—the rate between the Canadian dollar and the U.S. dollar—moves from C$1.25 = $1 (1/.8 = 1.25) to C$1.11 = $1 (1/.9 = 1.11). At the same time that Canadian goods are becoming more expensive to U.S. buyers, U.S. goods are becoming cheaper to Canadian buyers.

RECAP

1. The foreign exchange market is a global market in which foreign money, largely bank deposits, is bought and sold.

2. An exchange rate is the price of one money in terms of another.

3. Foreign demand for domestic goods decreases as the domestic currency appreciates and increases as the domestic currency depreciates.

5. THE BALANCE OF PAYMENTS

The U.S. economy does not operate in a vacuum. It affects and is affected by the economies of other nations. This point was brought home to Americans in the 1980s and 1990s as newspaper headlines announced the latest trade deficit and politicians denounced foreign countries for running trade surpluses against the United States. It seemed as if everywhere there was talk of the balance of payments.

TABLE 2

Balance of Payments Entries for Sale of U.S. Tractor to French Buyer

Activity	Credit	Debit
U.S. firm exports tractor and receives $50,000 from French buyer	$50,000	
French buyer imports tractor and transfers $50,000 from U.S. bank account to U.S. firm		$50,000
	$50,000	$50,000

■ balance of payments:
a record of a country's trade in goods, services, and financial assets with the rest of the world

The **balance of payments** is a record of a country's trade in goods, services, and financial assets with the rest of the world. This record is divided into categories, or accounts, that summarize the nation's international economic transactions. For example, one category measures transactions in merchandise; another measures transactions involving financial assets (bank deposits, bonds, stocks, loans). These accounts distinguish between private transactions (by individuals and businesses) and official transactions (by governments). Balance of payments data are reported quarterly for most developed countries.

5.a. Accounting for International Transactions

■ double-entry bookkeeping:
a system of accounting in which every transaction is recorded in at least two accounts and in which the debit total must equal the credit total for the transaction as a whole

The balance of payments is an accounting statement based on **double-entry bookkeeping**, a system in which every transaction is recorded in at least two accounts. Suppose a U.S. tractor manufacturer sells a $50,000 tractor to a resident of France. The transaction is recorded twice: once as the tractor going from the United States to France, and then again as the payment of $50,000 going from France to the United States.

Double-entry bookkeeping means that for each transaction there is a credit entry and a debit entry. *Credits* record activities that bring payments into a country; *debits* record activities that involve payments to the rest of the world. Table 2 shows the entries in the U.S. balance of payments to record the sale of a $50,000 U.S. tractor to a French importer. The sale of the tractor represents a $50,000 credit entry in the balance of payments because U.S. exports earn foreign exchange for U.S. residents. To complete the record of this transaction, we must know how payment was made for the tractor. Let's assume that the French buyer paid with a $50,000 check drawn on a U.S. bank. Money that is withdrawn from a foreign-owned bank account in the United States is treated as foreign exchange moved out of the country. So we record the payment as a debit entry in the balance of payments. In fact, the money did not leave the country; its ownership was transferred from the French buyer to the U.S. seller. The tractor sale is recorded on both sides of the balance of payments. There is a credit entry, and there is a debit entry. For every international transaction, there must be both a credit entry and a debit entry. This means that the sum of total credits and the sum of total debits must be equal. Credits always offset, or balance, debits.

5.b. Balance of Payments Accounts

■ current account:
the sum of the merchandise, services, investment income, and unilateral transfers accounts in the balance of payments

The balance of payments uses several different accounts to classify transactions (Table 3). The **current account** is the sum of the balances in the merchandise, services, investment income, and unilateral transfers accounts.

TABLE 3

Simplified U.S. Balance of Payments, 1997 (millions of dollars)

Account	Credit	Debit	Net Balance
Merchandise	$678,348	$877,282	−$198,934
Services	$253,220	$167,929	$ 85,291
Investment income	$236,043	$250,320	−$ 14,277
Unilateral transfers			−$ 38,526
Current account			−$166,446
Capital account	$690,497	$426,938	$263,559
Statistical discrepancy			−$ 97,113

Source: Data from Bureau of Economic Analysis, http://www.bea.doc.gov/bea/

Merchandise   This account records all transactions involving goods. U.S. exports of goods are merchandise credits; U.S. imports of foreign goods are merchandise debits. When exports (or credits) exceed imports (or debits), the merchandise account shows a surplus. When imports exceed exports, the account shows a deficit. The balance on the merchandise account is frequently referred to as the **balance of trade**.

> **■ balance of trade:**
> the balance on the merchandise account in a nation's balance of payments

In 1997, the merchandise account in the U.S. balance of payments showed a deficit of $198,934 million. This means that the merchandise credits of $678,348 million created by U.S. exports were $198,934 million less than the merchandise debits of $877,282 million created by U.S. imports. In other words, the United States bought more goods from other nations than it sold to them.

Services   This account measures trade involving services. It includes travel and tourism, royalties, transportation costs, and insurance premiums. In 1997, the balance on the services account was a $85,291 million surplus.

Investment Income   The income earned from investments in foreign countries is a credit; the income paid on foreign-owned investments in the United States is a debit. Investment income is the return on a special kind of service: it is the value of services provided by capital in foreign countries. In 1997, there was a deficit of $14,277 million in the investment income account.

Unilateral Transfers   In a unilateral transfer, one party gives something but gets nothing in return. Gifts and retirement pensions are forms of unilateral transfers. For instance, if a farmworker in El Centro, California, sends money to his family in Guaymas, Mexico, this is a unilateral transfer from the United States to Mexico. Only the net balance on unilateral transfers is reported. In 1997, that balance was a deficit of $38,526.

> **■ capital account:**
> the record in the balance of payments of the flow of financial assets into and out of a country

The current account is a useful measure of international transactions because it contains all of the activities involving goods and services. The **capital account** is where trade involving financial assets and international investment is recorded. In 1997, the current account showed a deficit of $166,446 million. This means that U.S. imports of merchandise, services, investment income, and unilateral transfers were $166,446 million greater than exports of these items.

If we draw a line in the balance of payments under the current account, then all entries below the line relate to financing the movement of merchandise, services, investment income, and unilateral transfers into and out of the country. In the terminology of the balance of payments, *capital* refers to financial and investment flows—bank deposits, purchases of stocks and bonds, loans, land purchases, and purchases of business firms—not simply

Every nation uses its own currency: dollars in the United States, pesetas in Spain, kroner in Norway, and pounds in England. Trade between countries must involve buying and selling national currencies. Since U.S. exporters ultimately want U.S. dollars for their products, if they export goods to England, pounds must be exchanged for dollars. The foreign exchange market is where national currencies are bought and sold.

the factories and equipment that are defined as capital in the macroeconomic sense of the word. Credits to the capital account reflect foreign purchases of U.S. financial assets or real property like land and buildings, and debits reflect U.S. purchases of foreign financial assets and real property. In 1997, the U.S. capital account showed a surplus of $263,559 million.

The *statistical discrepancy* account, the last account listed in Table 3, could be called *omissions and errors*. Government cannot accurately measure all transactions that take place. Some international shipments of goods and services go uncounted or are miscounted, as are some international flows of capital. The statistical discrepancy account is used to correct for these omissions and errors. In 1997, measured credits exceeded measured debits, so the statistical discrepancy was $-97,113 million.

Over all of the balance of payments accounts, the sum of credits must equal the sum of debits. The bottom line—the *net balance*—must be zero. It cannot show a surplus or a deficit. When people talk about a surplus or a deficit in the balance of payments, they actually are talking about a surplus or a deficit in one of the balance of payments accounts. The balance of payments itself by definition is always in balance, a function of double-entry bookkeeping.

5.c. The Current Account and the Capital Account

The current account reflects the movement of goods and services into and out of a country. The capital account reflects the flow of financial assets into and out of a country. In Table 3, the current account shows a deficit balance of $166,446 million. Remember that the balance of payments must *balance*. If there is a deficit in the current account, there must be a surplus in the capital account that offsets that deficit.

What is important here is not the bookkeeping process, the concept that the balance of payments must balance, but rather the meaning of deficits and surpluses in the current and capital accounts. These deficits and surpluses tell us whether a country is a net borrower from or lender to the rest of the world. A

Figure 5
The U.S. Current Account Balance, 1960–1997
The current account of the balance of payments is the sum of the balances in the merchandise, services, investment income, and unilateral transfers accounts. The United States experienced very large current account deficits in the 1980s. Source: Data from the *Economic Report of the President, 1997.*

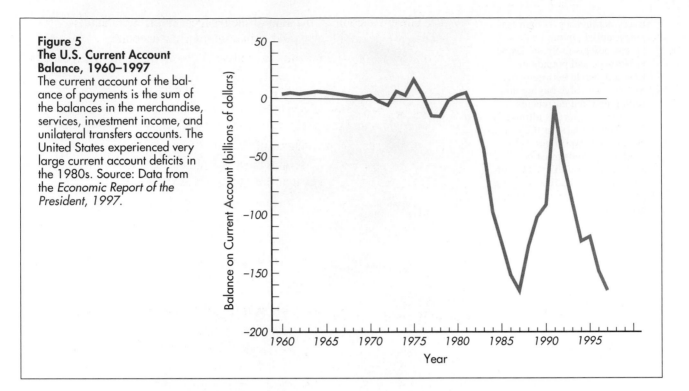

deficit in the current account means that a country is running a net surplus in its capital account. And it signals that a country is a net borrower from the rest of the world. A country that is running a current account deficit must borrow from abroad an amount sufficient to finance that deficit. A capital account surplus is achieved by selling more bonds and other debts of the domestic country to the rest of the world than the country buys from the rest of the world.

Figure 5 shows the current account balance in the United States for each year from 1960 to 1997. The United States experienced large current account deficits in the 1980s and then again in the mid-1990s. Such deficits indicate that the United States consumed more than it produced. This means that the United States sold financial assets and borrowed large amounts of money from foreign residents to finance its current account deficits. This large foreign borrowing made the United States the largest debtor in the world. A *net debtor* owes more to the rest of the world than it is owed; a *net creditor* is owed more than it owes. The United States was an international net creditor from the end of World War I until the mid-1980s. The country financed its large current account deficits in the 1980s by borrowing from the rest of the world. As a result of this accumulated borrowing, in 1985 the United States became an international net debtor for the first time in almost 70 years. Since that time, the net debtor status of the United States has grown steadily.

RECAP

1. The balance of payments is a record of a nation's international transactions.

2. Double-entry bookkeeping requires that every transaction be entered in at least two accounts, so that credits and debits are balanced.

3. In the balance of payments, credits record activities that represent payments into the country, and debits record activities that represent payments out of the country.

4. The current account is the sum of the balances in the merchandise, services, investment income, and unilateral transfers accounts.

5. A surplus exists when credits exceed debits; a deficit exists when credits are less than debits.

6. The capital account is where the transactions necessary to finance the movement of merchandise, services, investment income, and unilateral transfers into and out of the country are recorded.

7. The net balance in the balance of payments must be zero.

8. A deficit in the current account must be offset by a surplus in the capital account. It also indicates that the nation is a net borrower.

SUMMARY

▤ How is the total output of an economy measured?

1. National income accounting is the system economists use to measure both the output of an economy and the flows between sectors of that economy.

2. Gross domestic product (GDP) is the market value of all final goods and services produced in a year in a country.

3. GDP also equals the value added at each stage of production.

4. GDP as output equals the sum of the output of households, business firms, and government within the country.

5. GDP as expenditures equals the sum of consumption plus investment plus government spending plus net exports.

6. GDP as income equals the sum of wages, interest, rent, profits, proprietors' income, capital consumption allowance, and indirect business taxes less net factor income from abroad.

7. Other measures of national output include gross national product (GNP), net national product (NNP), national income (NI), personal income (PI), and disposable personal income (DPI).

▤ What is the difference between nominal and real GDP?

8. Nominal GDP measures output in terms of its current dollar values including the effects of price changes; real GDP measures output after eliminating the effects of price changes.

▤ What is a price index?

9. A price index measures the average level of prices across an economy.

10. Total expenditures on final goods and services equal total income.

▤ How is money traded internationally?

11. Foreign exchange is currency and bank deposits that are denominated in foreign currency.

12. The foreign exchange market is a global market in which people trade one currency for another.

13. Exchange rates, the price of one country's money in terms of another country's money, are necessary to compare prices quoted in different currencies.

14. The value of a good in a domestic currency equals the foreign currency price times the exchange rate.

15. When a domestic currency appreciates, domestic goods become more expensive to foreigners and foreign goods become cheaper to domestic residents.

16. When a domestic currency depreciates, domestic goods become cheaper to foreigners and foreign goods become more expensive to domestic residents.

▤ How do nations record their transactions with the rest of the world?

17. The balance of payments is a record of a nation's transactions with the rest of the world.

18. Credits record activities that bring payments into a country; debits record activities that take payments out of a country.

19. In the balance of payments, the sum of total credits and the sum of total debits must be equal.

20. The current account is the sum of the balances in the merchandise, services, investment income, and unilateral transfers accounts.

21. The capital account reflects the transactions necessary to finance the movement of merchandise, services, investment income, and unilateral transfers into and out of the country.

22. A deficit in the current account must be offset by a surplus in the capital account.

KEY TERMS

national income accounting

gross domestic product (GDP)

intermediate good

value added

inventory

capital consumption allowance

depreciation

indirect business tax

gross national product (GNP)

net national product (NNP)

gross investment

net investment

national income (NI)

personal income (PI)

disposable personal income (DPI)

nominal GDP

real GDP

price index

base year

GDP price index

consumer price index (CPI)

cost of living adjustment (COLA)

producer price index (PPI)

foreign exchange

foreign exchange market

balance of payments

double-entry bookkeeping

current account

balance of trade

capital account

EXERCISES

1. The following table lists the stages required in the production of a personal computer. What is the value of the computer in the GDP?

Stage	Value Added
Components manufacture	$ 50
Assembly	250
Wholesaler	500
Retailer	1,500

2. What is the difference between GDP and each of the following?

   a. Gross national product

   b. Net national product

   c. National income

   d. Personal income

   e. Disposable personal income

Use the following national income accounting information to answer questions 3–7:

Consumption	$400
Imports	10
Net investment	20
Government purchases	100
Exports	20
Capital consumption allowance	20
Indirect business taxes	5
Receipts of factor income from the rest of the world	12
Payments of factor income to the rest of the world	10

3. What is the GDP for this economy?

4. What is the GNP for this economy?

5. What is the NNP for this economy?

6. What is the national income for this economy?

7. What is the gross investment in this economy?

8. Why has nominal GDP increased faster than real GDP in the United States over time? What would it mean if an economy had real GDP increasing faster than nominal GDP?

9. If a surfboard is produced this year but not sold until next year, how is it counted in this year's GDP and not next year's?

10. What is the price of 1 U.S. dollar in terms of each of the following currencies, given the following exchange rates?

    a. 1 Austrian schilling = $.10

    b. 1 Chinese yuan = $.12

    c. 1 Israeli shekel = $.30

    d. 1 Kuwaiti dinar = $3.20

11. A bicycle manufactured in the United States costs $100. Using the exchange rates listed in Table 1, what would the bicycle cost in each of the following countries?

    a. Argentina

    b. Britain

    c. Canada

12. The U.S. dollar price of a Swedish krona changes from $.1572 to $.1730.

    a. Has the dollar depreciated or appreciated against the krona?

    b. Has the krona appreciated or depreciated against the dollar?

    Use the information in the following table on Mexico's 1996 international transactions to answer questions 13–15 (the amounts are the U.S. dollar values in millions):

Merchandise imports	$96,000
Merchandise exports	$89,469
Services exports	$10,901
Services imports	$10,819
Investment income receipts	$ 4,032
Investment income payments	$17,099
Unilateral transfers	$ 4,531

13. What is the balance of trade?

14. What is the current account?

15. Did Mexico become a larger international net debtor during 1996?

16. If the U.S. dollar appreciated against the German mark, what would you expect to happen to U.S. net exports with Germany?

17. Suppose the U.S. dollar price of a British pound is $1.50; the dollar price of a German mark is $.60; a hotel room in London, England, costs 120 British pounds; and a comparable hotel room in Hanover, Germany, costs 220 German marks.

    a. Which hotel room is cheaper to a U.S. tourist?

    b. What is the exchange rate between the German mark and the British pound?

🖳 INTERNET EXERCISE

In this chapter, we learned that GDP as expenditures equals the sum of consumption (*C*), investment (*I*), government spending (*G*), and net exports (*X*). To see how the U.S. economy has been doing, go to the Boyes/Melvin *Fundamentals of Economics* Web site at **http://www.hmco.com/college/** and click on the Internet Exercise link for Chapter 10. Now answer the questions that appear on the Boyes/Melvin Web site.

11

Unemployment, Inflation, and Business Cycles

FUNDAMENTAL QUESTIONS

1. What is a business cycle?

2. How is the unemployment rate defined and measured?

3. What is the cost of unemployed resources?

4. What is inflation?

5. Why is inflation a problem?

I f you were graduating from college today, what would your job prospects be? In 1932, they would have been bleak. A large number of people were out of work (about one in four workers), and a large number of firms had laid off workers or gone out of business. At any time, job opportunities depend not only on the individual's ability and experience, but also on the current state of the economy.

All economies have cycles of activity: periods of expansion, where output and employment increase, followed by periods of contraction, where output and employment decrease. For instance, during the expansionary period of the 1990s, less than 5 percent of U.S. workers had no job by 1997. But during the period of contraction of 1981–1982, 9.5 percent of U.S. workers had no job. When the economy is growing, the demand for goods and services tends to increase. To produce those goods and services, firms hire more workers. Economic expansion also has an impact on inflation. As the demand for goods and services goes up, the prices of those goods and services also tend to rise. By the late 1990s, following several years of economic growth, consumer prices in the United States were rising by about 3 percent a year. During periods of contraction, as more people are out of work, demand for goods and services tends to fall and there is less pressure for rising prices. During the period of the Great Depression in the 1930s in the United States, consumer prices fell by more than 5 percent in 1933. Both price increases and the fraction of workers without jobs are affected by business cycles in fairly regular ways. But their effects on individual standards of living, income, and purchasing power are much less predictable.

Why do certain events move in tandem? What are the links between unemployment and inflation? What causes the business cycle to behave as it does? What effect does government activity have on the business cycle—and on unemployment and inflation? Who is harmed by rising unemployment and inflation? Who benefits? Macroeconomics attempts to answer all of these questions. ∎

Preview

1. BUSINESS CYCLES

In this chapter we describe the business cycle and examine measures of unemployment and inflation. We talk about the ways in which the business cycle, unemployment, and inflation are related. And we describe their effects on the participants in the economy.

The most widely used measure of a nation's output is gross domestic product. When we examine the value of real GDP over time, we find periods in which it rises and other periods in which it falls.

1.a. Definitions

■ **business cycle:**
pattern of rising real GDP followed by falling real GDP

This pattern—real GDP rising, then falling—is called a **business cycle**. The pattern occurs over and over again, but as Figure 1 shows, the pattern over time is anything but regular. Historically the duration of business cycles and the rate at which real GDP rises or falls (indicated by the steepness of the line in Figure 1) vary considerably.

Looking at Figure 1, it is clear that the U.S. economy has experienced up-and-down swings in the years since 1959. Still, real GDP has grown at an average rate of approximately 3 percent per year. While it is important to recognize that periods of economic growth, or prosperity, are followed by periods of contraction, or **recession**, it is also important to recognize the presence of long-term economic growth—despite the presence of periodic recessions,

■ **recession:**
a period in which real GDP falls

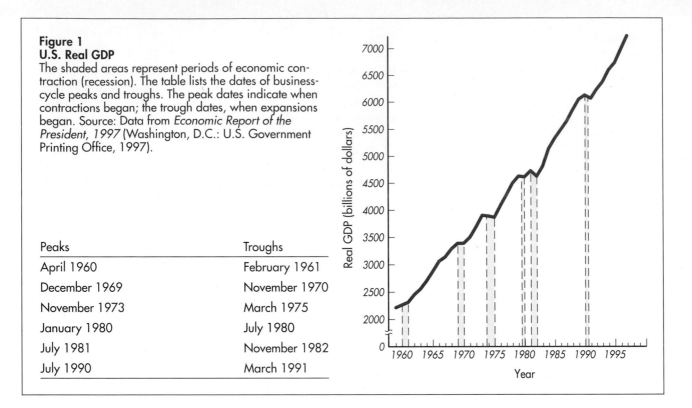

Figure 1
U.S. Real GDP
The shaded areas represent periods of economic contraction (recession). The table lists the dates of business-cycle peaks and troughs. The peak dates indicate when contractions began; the trough dates, when expansions began. Source: Data from *Economic Report of the President, 1997* (Washington, D.C.: U.S. Government Printing Office, 1997).

Peaks	Troughs
April 1960	February 1961
December 1969	November 1970
November 1973	March 1975
January 1980	July 1980
July 1981	November 1982
July 1990	March 1991

in the long run the economy produces more goods and services. The long-run growth in the economy depends on the growth in productive resources, like land, labor, and capital, along with technological advances. Technological change increases the productivity of resources so that output increases even with a fixed amount of inputs. In recent years there has been concern about the growth rate of U.S. productivity and its effect on the long-run growth potential of the economy.

Figure 2 shows how real GDP behaves over a hypothetical business cycle and identifies the stages of the cycle. The vertical axis on the graph measures the level of real GDP; the horizontal axis measures time in years. In year 1, real GDP is growing; the economy is in the *expansion* phase, or *boom* period, of the business cycle. Growth continues until the *peak* is reached, in year 2. Real GDP begins to fall during the *contraction* phase of the cycle, which continues until year 4. The *trough* marks the end of the contraction and the start of a new expansion. Even though the economy is subject to periodic ups and downs, real GDP, the measure of a nation's output, has risen over the long term, as illustrated by the upward-sloping line labeled *trend*.

If an economy is growing over time, why do economists worry about business cycles? Economists try to understand the causes of business cycles so that they can learn to moderate or avoid recessions and their harmful effects on standards of living.

1.b. Historical Record

The official dating of recessions in the United States is the responsibility of the National Bureau of Economic Research (NBER), an independent research organization. The NBER has identified the shaded areas in the graph in Figure 1 as recessions, the unshaded areas as expansions. Recessions are periods between cyclical peaks and the troughs that follow them. Expansions are periods between cyclical troughs and the peaks that follow them. There have been twelve recessions since 1929. The most severe was the Great Depression. Between 1929 and 1933, national output fell by 25 percent; this period is called the Great Depression. A **depression** is a prolonged period of

■ **depression:**
a severe, prolonged economic contraction

Figure 2
The Business Cycle
The business cycle contains four phases: the expansion (boom), when real GDP is increasing; the peak, which marks the end of an expansion and the beginning of a contraction; the contraction (recession), when real GDP is falling; and the trough, which marks the end of a contraction and the beginning of an expansion.

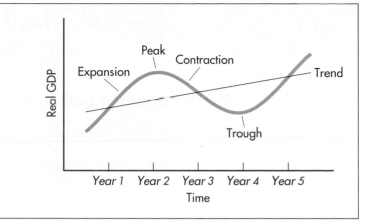

severe economic contraction. The fact that people refer to "the Depression" when speaking about the recession that began in 1929 indicates the severity of that contraction relative to others in recent experience. There was widespread suffering during the Depression. Many people were jobless and homeless, and many firms went bankrupt.

1.c. Indicators

■ leading indicator:
a variable that changes before real output changes

We have been talking about the business cycle in terms of real GDP. There are a number of other variables that move in a fairly regular manner over the business cycle. The Department of Commerce classifies these variables in three categories—leading indicators, coincident indicators, and lagging indicators—depending on whether they move up or down before, at the same time as, or following a change in real GDP (see Table 1).

Leading indicators generally change before real GDP changes. As a result, economists use them to forecast changes in output. Looking at Table 1, it is easy to see how some of these leading indicators could be used to forecast future output. For instance, new building permits signal new construction. If the number of new permits issued goes up, economists can expect the amount of new construction to increase. Similarly, if manufacturers receive more new orders, economists can expect more goods to be produced.

TABLE 1
Indicators of the Business Cycle

Leading Indicators

Average workweek	New building permits
Unemployment claims	Delivery times of goods
Manufacturers' new orders	Interest rate spread
Stock prices	Money supply
New plant and equipment orders	Consumer expectations

Coincident Indicators

Payroll employment
Industrial production
Personal income
Manufacturing and trade sales

Lagging Indicators

Labor cost per unit of output
Inventories to sales ratio
Unemployment duration
Consumer credit to personal income ratio
Outstanding commercial loans
Prime interest rate
Inflation rate for services

As real income falls, living standards go down. This 1937 photo of a Depression-era breadline indicates the paradox of the world's richest nation, as emphasized on the billboard in the background, having to offer public support to feed able-bodied workers who are out of work due to the severity of the business-cycle downturn.

WORLD'S HIGHEST STANDARD OF LIVING

There's no way like the American Way

Leading indicators are not infallible, however. The link between them and future output can be tenuous. For example, leading indicators may fall one month and then rise the next, while real output rises steadily. Economists want to see several consecutive months of a new direction in the leading indicators before forecasting a change in output. Short-run movements in the indicators can be very misleading.

Coincident indicators are economic variables that tend to change at the same time real output changes. For example, as real output increases, economists expect to see employment and sales rise. The coincident indicators listed in Table 1 have demonstrated a strong tendency over time to change along with changes in real GDP.

The final group of variables listed in Table 1, **lagging indicators**, do not change their value until after the value of real GDP has changed. For instance, as output increases, jobs are created and more workers are hired. It makes sense, then, to expect the duration of unemployment (the average time workers are unemployed) to fall. The duration of unemployment is a lagging indicator. Similarly, the inflation rate for services (which measures how prices change for things like dry cleaners, veterinarians, and other services) tends to change after real GDP changes. Lagging indicators are used along with leading and coincident indicators to identify the peaks and troughs in business cycles.

■ **coincident indicator:**
a variable that changes at the same time that real output changes

■ **lagging indicator:**
a variable that changes after real output changes

RECAP

1. The business cycle is a recurring pattern of rising and falling real GDP.
2. Although all economies move through periods of expansion and contraction, the duration of expansion and recession varies.
3. Real GDP is not the only variable affected by business cycles; leading, lagging, and coincident indicators also show the effects of economic expansion and contraction.

2. UNEMPLOYMENT

Recurring periods of prosperity and recession are reflected in the nation's labor markets. In fact, this is what makes understanding the business cycle so important. If business cycles signified only a little more or a little less profit for businesses, governments would not be so anxious to forecast or to control their swings. It is the human costs of lost jobs and incomes—the inability to maintain standards of living—that make an understanding of business cycles and of the factors that affect unemployment so important.

2.a. Definition and Measurement

■ **unemployment rate:**
the percentage of the labor force that is not working

The **unemployment rate** is the percentage of the labor force that is not working. The rate is calculated by dividing the number of people who are unemployed by the number of people in the labor force:

$$\text{unemployment rate} = \frac{\text{number unemployed}}{\text{number in labor force}}$$

This ratio seems simple enough, but there are several subtle issues at work here. First, the unemployment rate does not measure the percentage of the total population that is not working; it measures the percentage of the *labor force* that is not working. Who is in the labor force? Obviously, everybody who is employed is part of the labor force. But only some of those who are not currently employed are counted in the labor force.

The Bureau of Labor Statistics of the Department of Labor compiles labor data each month based on an extensive survey of U.S. households. All U.S. residents are potential members of the labor force. The Labor Department arrives at the size of the actual labor force by using this formula:

$$\text{labor force} = \text{all U.S. residents} - \text{residents under 16 years of age} - \text{institutionalized adults} - \text{adults not looking for work}$$

So the labor force includes those adults (an adult being 16 or older) currently employed or actively seeking work. It is relatively simple to see to it that children and institutionalized adults (for instance, those in prison or long-term care facilities) are not counted in the labor force. It is more difficult to identify and accurately measure adults who are not actively looking for work.

A person is actively seeking work if he or she is available to work, has looked for work in the past four weeks, is waiting for a recall after being laid off, or is starting a job within 30 days. Those who are not working and who meet these criteria are considered unemployed.

2.b. Interpreting the Unemployment Rate

Is the unemployment rate an accurate measure? The fact that the rate does not include those who are not actively looking for work is not necessarily a failing. Many people who are not actively looking for work—homemakers, older citizens, and students, for example—have made a decision to do housework, to retire, or to stay in school. These people rightly are not counted among the unemployed.

■ **discouraged workers:**
workers who have stopped looking for work because they believe no one will offer them a job

But there are people missing from the unemployment statistics who are not working and are not looking for work, yet would take a job if one was offered. **Discouraged workers** have looked for work in the past year but have given up looking for work because they believe that no one will hire them. These individuals are ignored by the official unemployment rate even though they are able to work and may have spent a long time looking for work. Estimates of the number of discouraged workers indicate that in 1998, about 1.5 million people were not counted in the labor force yet claimed that

Official unemployment data, like national income data, do not include activity in the underground economy. Obviously, drug dealers and prostitutes do not report their earnings. Nor do many of the people who supplement their unemployment benefits with part-time jobs. In addition, people like the waiter who reports a small fraction of his actual tips and the housecleaning person who requests payment in cash in order to avoid reporting taxable income are also part of the underground economy.

Because activity in the underground economy goes unreported, there is no exact way to determine its size. Estimates range from 5 to 33 percent of the gross domestic product. With the GDP at $8 trillion, this places the value of underground activity between $400 billion and $2.6 trillion.

We will never know the true size of the underground economy, but evidence suggests that it is growing. That evidence has to do with cash. The vast majority of people working in the underground economy are paid in cash. One indicator of the growth of that economy, then, is the rise in currency over time relative to checking accounts. Also, per capita holdings of $100 bills have increased substantially. Certainly, much of the demand for $100 bills is a product of inflation (as the prices of goods and services go up, it is easier to pay for them in larger-denomination bills). But there is also a substantial rise in real holdings of $100 bills as well.

The underground economy forces us to interpret government statistics carefully. We must remember that:

■ Official income statistics understate the true national income.

■ Official unemployment data overestimate true unemployment.

■ When the underground economy grows more rapidly than the rest of the economy, the true rate of growth is higher than reported.

■ underemployment:
the employment of workers in jobs that do not utilize their productive potential

they were available for work. Of this group, 25 percent, or 374,000 people, were considered to be discouraged workers. It is clear that the reported unemployment rate underestimates the true burden of unemployment in the economy because it ignores discouraged workers.

Discouraged workers are one source of hidden unemployment; underemployment is another. **Underemployment** is the underutilization of workers—employment in tasks that do not fully utilize their productive potential—including part-time workers who prefer full-time employment. Even if every worker has a job, substantial underemployment leaves the economy producing less than its potential GDP.

The effect of discouraged workers and underemployment is an unemployment rate that understates actual unemployment. In contrast, the effect of the *underground economy* is a rate that overstates actual unemployment. A sizable component of the officially unemployed is actually working. The unemployed construction worker who plays in a band at night may not report that activity because he or she wants to avoid paying taxes on his or her earnings as a musician. This person is officially unemployed but has a source of income. Many officially unemployed individuals have an alternate source of income. This means that official statistics overstate the true magnitude of unemployment. The larger the underground economy, the greater this overstatement. (See the Economic Insight "The Underground Economy.")

We have identified two factors, discouraged workers and underemployment, that cause the official unemployment rate to underestimate true unemployment. Another factor, the underground economy, causes the official rate to overestimate the true rate of unemployment. There is no reason to expect these factors to cancel one another out, and there is no way to know for sure which is most important. The point is to remember what the official data on unemployment do and do not measure.

2.c. Types of Unemployment

Economists have identified four basic types of unemployment:

Seasonal unemployment A product of regular, recurring changes in the hiring needs of certain industries on a monthly or seasonal basis.

Frictional unemployment A product of the short-term movement of workers between jobs and of first-time job seekers.

Structural unemployment A product of technological change and other changes in the structure of the economy.

Cyclical unemployment A product of business-cycle fluctuations.

In certain industries, labor needs fluctuate throughout the year. When local crops are harvested, farms need lots of workers; the rest of the year, they do not. (Migrant farmworkers move from one region to another, following the harvests, to avoid seasonal unemployment.) Ski resort towns like Park City, Utah, are booming during the ski season, when employment peaks, but need fewer workers during the rest of the year. In the nation as a whole, the Christmas season is a time of peak employment and low unemployment rates. To avoid confusing seasonal fluctuations in unemployment with other sources of unemployment, unemployment data are seasonally adjusted.

Frictional and structural unemployment exist in any dynamic economy. In terms of individual workers, frictional unemployment is short term in nature. Workers quit one job and soon find another; students graduate and soon find a job. This kind of unemployment cannot be eliminated in a free society. In fact, it is a sign of efficiency in an economy when workers try to increase their income or improve their working conditions by leaving one job for another. Frictional unemployment is often called *search unemployment* because workers take time to search for a job after quitting a job or leaving school.

Frictional unemployment is short term; structural unemployment, on the other hand, can be long term. Workers who are displaced by technological change (assembly line workers who have been replaced by machines, for example) or by a permanent reduction in the demand for an industry's output (cigar makers who have been laid off because of a decrease in demand for tobacco) may not have the necessary skills to maintain their level of income in another industry. Rather than accept a much lower salary, these workers

Seasonal unemployment is unemployment that fluctuates with the seasons of the year. For instance, these Santas in training will be employed from fall through Christmas. After Christmas they will be unemployed and must seek new positions. Other examples of seasonal unemployment include farmworkers who migrate to follow the harvest of crops, experiencing unemployment between harvests.

tend to prolong their job search. Eventually they adjust their expectations to the realities of the job market, or they enter the pool of discouraged workers.

Structural unemployment is very difficult for those who are unemployed. But for society as a whole, the technological advances that cause structural unemployment raise living standards by giving consumers a greater variety of goods at lower cost.

Cyclical unemployment is a result of the business cycle. As a recession occurs, cyclical unemployment increases, and as growth occurs, cyclical unemployment decreases. It is also a primary focus of macroeconomic policy. Economists believe that a greater understanding of business cycles and their causes may enable them to find ways to smooth out those cycles and swings in unemployment. Much of the analysis in future chapters is related to macroeconomic policy aimed at minimizing business-cycle fluctuations. In addition to macroeconomic policy aimed at moderating cyclical unemployment, other policy measures—for example, job training and counseling—are being used to reduce frictional and structural unemployment.

2.d. Costs of Unemployment

The cost of being unemployed is more than the obvious loss of income and status suffered by the individual who is not working. In a broader sense, society as a whole loses when resources are unemployed. Unemployed workers produce no output. So an economy with unemployment will operate inside its production possibilities curve rather than on the curve. Economists measure this lost output in terms of the *GDP gap*:

$$\text{GDP gap} = \text{potential real GDP} - \text{actual real GDP}$$

■ **potential real GDP:**
the output produced at the natural rate of unemployment

■ **natural rate of unemployment:**
the unemployment rate that would exist in the absence of cyclical unemployment

Potential real GDP is the level of output produced when nonlabor resources are fully utilized and unemployment is at its natural rate. The **natural rate of unemployment** is the unemployment rate that would exist in the absence of cyclical unemployment, so it includes seasonal, frictional, and structural unemployment. The natural rate of unemployment is not fixed; it can change over time. For instance, some economists believe that the natural rate of unemployment has risen in recent decades, a product of the influx of baby boomers and women into the labor force. As more workers move into the labor force (begin looking for jobs), frictional unemployment, increases, raising the natural rate of unemployment. The natural rate of unemployment is sometimes called the non-accelerating-inflation rate of unemployment, or NAIRU—the idea being that there would be upward pressure on wages and prices in a "tight" labor market where the unemployment rate fell below the NAIRU.

Potential real GDP measures what we are capable of producing at the natural rate of unemployment. If we compute potential real GDP and then subtract actual real GDP, we have a measure of the output lost as a result of unemployment, or the cost of unemployment.

The GDP gap in the United States for recent decades is shown in Figure 3(a). The gap widens during recessions and narrows during expansions. As the gap widens (as the output not produced increases), there are fewer goods and services available, and living standards are lower than they would be at the natural rate of unemployment. Figure 3(b) is a graph of the gap between potential and real GDP, taken from Figure 3(a).

Until recently economists used the term *full employment* instead of *natural rate of unemployment*. Today the term *full employment* is rarely used because it may be interpreted as implying a zero unemployment rate. If frictional and structural unemployment are always present, zero unemployment is impossible; there must always be unemployed resources in an economy. *Natural rate of unemployment* describes the labor market when the economy is producing what it realistically can produce in the absence of cyclical unemployment.

Figure 3
The GDP Gap
The GDP gap is the difference between what the economy can produce at the natural rate of unemployment (potential GDP) and actual output (actual GDP). When the unemployment rate is higher than the natural rate, actual GDP is less than potential GDP. The gap between potential and actual real GDP is a cost associated with unemployment. Recession years are shaded to highlight how the gap widens around recessions.

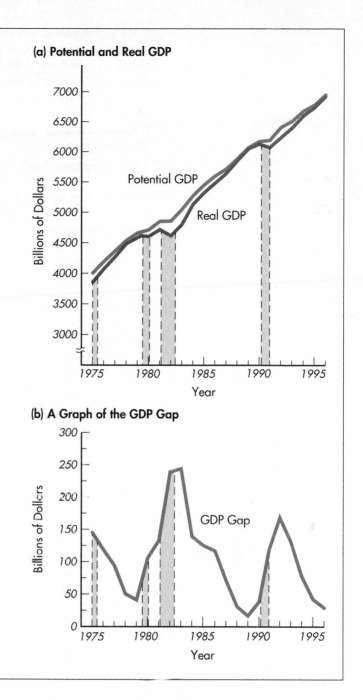

(a) Potential and Real GDP

(b) A Graph of the GDP Gap

What is the value of the natural rate of unemployment in the United States? In the 1950s and 1960s, economists generally agreed on 4 percent. By the 1970s, that agreed-on rate had gone up to 5 percent. In the early 1980s, many economists placed the natural rate of unemployment in the United States at 6 to 7 percent. By the late 1980s, some had revised their thinking, placing the rate back at 5 percent. In fact, economists do not know exactly what the natural rate of unemployment is. Over time it varies within a range from around 4 percent to around 7 percent. It will also vary across countries, as labor markets and macroeconomic policies differ.

2.e. The Record of Unemployment

Unemployment rates in the United States from 1951 to 1997 are listed in Table 2. Over this period, the unemployment rate for all workers reached a low of 2.8 percent in 1953 and a high of 9.5 percent in 1982 and 1983. The table shows some general trends in the incidence of unemployment across different demographic groups:

In most years, the unemployment rate for women is higher than it is for men. Several factors may be at work here. First, during this period, a large number of women entered the labor force for the first time. Second, discrimination against women in the workplace limited job opportunities for them, particularly early in this period. Finally, a large number of women move out of the labor force on temporary maternity leaves.

Teenagers have the highest unemployment rates in the economy. This makes sense because teenagers are the least-skilled segment of the labor force.

Whites have lower unemployment rates than nonwhites. Discrimination plays a role here. To the extent that discrimination extends beyond hiring practices and job opportunities for minority workers to the education that is necessary to prepare students to enter the work force, minority workers will have fewer opportunities for employment. The quality of education provided in many schools with large minority populations may not be as good as that provided in schools with large white populations. Equal opportunity programs and legislation are aimed at rectifying this inequality.

Although exact comparisons across countries are difficult to make because countries measure unemployment in different ways, it is interesting to look at the reported unemployment rates of different countries. Table 3 lists unemployment rates for seven major industrial nations. The rates have been adjusted to match as closely as possible the U.S. definition of unemployment. For instance, the official Italian unemployment data include people who have not looked for work in the past 30 days. The data for Italy in Table 3 have been adjusted to remove these people. If the data had not been adjusted, the Italian unemployment rates would be roughly twice as high as those listed.

Countries not only define unemployment differently, they also use different methods to count the unemployed. All major European countries except

TABLE 2
Unemployment Rates in the United States

		Unemployment Rate, Civilian Workers[1]				
Year	All Civilian Workers	Males	Females	Both Sexes 16–19 Years	White	Black and Other
1951	3.3	2.8	4.4	8.2	3.1	5.3
1955	4.4	4.2	4.9	11.0	3.9	8.7
1959	5.5	5.2	5.9	14.6	4.8	10.7
1963	5.7	5.2	6.5	17.2	5.0	10.8
1967	3.8	3.1	5.2	12.9	3.4	7.4
1971	5.9	5.3	6.9	16.9	5.4	9.9
1975	8.5	7.9	9.3	19.9	7.8	13.8
1979	5.8	5.1	6.8	16.1	5.1	11.3
1983	9.6	9.9	9.2	22.4	8.4	17.8
1987	6.2	6.2	6.2	16.9	5.3	11.6
1991	6.7	7.0	6.3	18.6	6.0	11.1
1995	5.6	5.6	5.6	17.3	4.9	9.6
1997	5.0	4.2	4.4	16.0	4.2	8.8

[1]Unemployed as a percentage of the civilian labor force in the group specified.

Source: *Economic Report of the President, 1995* (Washington, D.C.: U.S. Government Printing Office, 1998), p. 320.

TABLE 3
Unemployment Rates in Major Industrial Countries

				Civilian Unemployment Rate (percent)			
Year	United States	Canada	France	Italy	Japan	United Kingdom	Germany
1960	5.5	6.5	1.5	3.7	1.7	2.2	1.1
1965	4.5	3.6	1.6	3.5	1.2	2.1	.3
1970	4.9	5.7	2.5	3.2	1.2	3.1	.5
1975	8.5	6.9	4.1	3.4	1.9	4.6	3.4
1980	7.1	7.5	6.4	4.4	2.0	7.0	2.9
1985	7.2	10.5	10.4	6.0	2.6	11.2	7.5
1990	5.5	8.1	9.2	7.0	2.1	6.9	5.0
1995	5.6	9.5	11.7	12.0	3.2	8.8	6.5

Source: *Economic Report of the President, 1998* (Washington, D.C.: U.S. Government Printing Office, 1998.

Sweden use a national unemployment register to identify the unemployed. Only those people who register for unemployment benefits are considered unemployed. A problem with this method is that it excludes those who have not registered because they are not entitled to benefits and it includes those who receive benefits but would not take a job if one was offered. Other countries—among them the United States, Canada, Sweden, and Japan—conduct monthly surveys of households to estimate the unemployment rate. Surveys allow more comprehensive analysis of unemployment and its causes than does the use of a register. The Organization for Economic Cooperation and Development, an organization created to foster international economic cooperation, compared annual surveys of the labor force in Europe with the official register of unemployment data and found that only 80 to 85 percent of those surveyed as unemployed were registered in Germany, France, and the United Kingdom. In Italy, only 63 percent of those surveyed as unemployed were registered.

Knowing their limitations, we can still identify some important trends from the data in Table 3. Through the 1960s and early 1970s, European unemployment rates generally were lower than U.S. and Canadian rates. Over the next decade, European unemployment rates increased substantially, as did the rates in North America. But in the mid-1980s, while U.S. unemployment began to fall, European unemployment remained high. The issue of high unemployment rates in Europe has become a major topic of discussion at international summit meetings. Japanese unemployment rates, like those in Europe, were much lower than U.S. and Canadian rates in the 1960s and 1970s. However, unlike European rates, Japanese rates remained much lower in the 1980s and 1990s.

RECAP

1. The unemployment rate is the number of people unemployed as a percentage of the labor force.
2. To be in the labor force, one must either have or be looking for a job.
3. By its failure to include discouraged workers and the output lost because of underemployment, the unemployment rate understates real unemployment in the United States.

4. By its failure to include activity in the underground economy, the U.S. unemployment rate overstates actual unemployment.

5. Unemployment data are adjusted to eliminate seasonal fluctuations.

6. Frictional and structural unemployment are always present in a dynamic economy.

7. Cyclical unemployment is a product of recession; it can be moderated by controlling the period of contraction in the business cycle.

8. Economists measure the cost of unemployment in terms of lost output.

9. Unemployment data show that women generally have higher unemployment rates than men, that teenagers have the highest unemployment rates in the economy, and that blacks and other minority groups have higher unemployment rates than whites.

3. INFLATION

■ **inflation:**
a sustained rise in the average level of prices

Inflation is a sustained rise in the average level of prices. Notice the word *sustained*. Inflation does not mean a short-term increase in prices; it means prices are rising over a prolonged period of time. Inflation is measured by the percentage change in the price level. The inflation rate in the United States was 1.7 percent in 1997. This means that the level of prices increased 1.7 percent over the year.

3.a. Absolute Versus Relative Price Changes

In the modern economy, over any given period, some prices rise faster than others. To evaluate the rate of inflation in a country, then, economists must know what is happening to prices on average. Here it is important to distinguish between *absolute* and *relative* price changes.

Let's look at an example using the prices of fish and beef:

	Year 1	Year 2
1 pound of fish	$1	$2
1 pound of beef	$2	$4

In year 1, beef is twice as expensive as fish. This is the price of beef *relative* to fish. In year 2, beef is still twice as expensive as fish. The relative prices have not changed between years 1 and 2. What has changed? The prices of both beef and fish have doubled. The *absolute* levels of all prices have gone up, but because they have increased by the same percentage, the relative prices are unchanged.

Inflation measures changes in absolute prices. In our example, all prices doubled, so the inflation rate is 100 percent. There was a 100 percent increase in the prices of beef and fish. Inflation does not proceed evenly through the economy. Prices of some goods rise faster than others, which means that relative prices are changing at the same time that absolute prices are rising. The measured inflation rate records the *average* change in absolute prices.

3.b. Effects of Inflation

To understand the effects of inflation, you have to understand what happens to the value of money in an inflationary period. The real value of money is what it can buy, its *purchasing power:*

$$\text{real value of } \$1 = \frac{\$1}{\text{price level}}$$

The higher the price level, the lower the real value (or *purchasing power*) of the dollar. For instance, suppose an economy had only one good—milk. If a glass of milk sold for $.50, then one dollar would buy two glasses of milk. If the price of milk rose to $1, then a dollar would only buy one glass of milk. The purchasing power, or real value, of money falls as prices rise.

Table 4 lists the real value of the dollar in selected years from 1946 to 1997. The price level in each year is measured relative to the average level of prices over the 1982–1984 period. For instance, the 1946 value, .195, means that prices in 1946 were, on average, only 19.5 percent of prices in the 1982–1984 period. Notice that as prices go up, the purchasing power of the dollar falls. In 1946 a dollar bought five times more than a dollar bought in the early 1980s. The value 5.13 means that one could buy 5.13 times more goods and services with a dollar in 1946 than one could in 1982–1984.

Prices have risen steadily in recent decades. By 1997, they had gone up more than 61 percent above the average level of prices in the 1982–1984 period. Consequently, the purchasing power of a 1997 dollar was lower. In 1997, $1 bought just 62 percent of the goods and services that one could buy with a dollar in 1982–1984.

If prices and nominal income rise by the same percentage, it might seem that inflation is not a problem. It doesn't matter if it takes twice as many dollars now to buy fish and beef than it did before, if we have twice as many dollars in income available to buy the products. Obviously, inflation is very much a problem when a household's nominal income rises at a slower rate than prices. Inflation hurts those households whose income does not keep up with the prices of the goods they buy.

In the 1970s in the United States, the rate of inflation rose to near-record levels. Many workers believed that their incomes were lagging behind the rate of inflation, so they negotiated cost-of-living raises in their wage contracts. The typical cost-of-living raise ties salary to changes in the consumer price index. If the CPI rises 8 percent over a year, workers receive an 8 percent raise plus compensation for experience or productivity increases. As the U.S. rate of inflation fell during the 1980s, concern about cost-of-living raises subsided as well.

TABLE 4
The Real Value of a Dollar

Year	Average Price Level[1]	Purchasing Power of a Dollar[2]
1946	.195	5.13
1950	.241	4.15
1954	.269	3.72
1958	.289	3.46
1962	.302	3.31
1966	.324	3.09
1970	.388	2.58
1974	.493	2.03
1978	.652	1.53
1982	.965	1.04
1986	1.096	.91
1990	1.307	.77
1994	1.482	.67
1997	1.613	.62

[1]Measured by the consumer price index as given in http://stats.bls.gov/

[2]Found by taking the reciprocal of the consumer price index (1/CPI).

It is important to distinguish between expected and unexpected inflation. *Unexpectedly high inflation* redistributes income away from those who receive fixed incomes (like creditors who receive debt repayments of a fixed amount of dollars per month) toward those who make fixed expenditures (like debtors who make fixed debt repayments per month). For example, consider a simple loan agreement:

Maria borrows $100 from Ali, promising to repay the loan in one year at 10 percent interest. In one year, Maria will pay Ali $110—principal of $100 plus interest of $10 (10 percent of $100, or $10).

When Maria and Ali agree to the terms of the loan, they do so with some expected rate of inflation in mind. Suppose they both expect 5 percent inflation over the year. In one year it will take 5 percent more money to buy goods than it does now. Ali will need $105 to buy what $100 buys today. Because Ali will receive $110 for the principal and interest on the loan, he will gain purchasing power. However, if the inflation rate over the year turns out to be surprisingly high—say, 15 percent—then Ali will need $115 to buy what $100 buys today. He will lose purchasing power if he makes a loan at a 10 percent rate of interest.

Economists distinguish between nominal and real interest rates when analyzing economic behavior. The **nominal interest rate** is the observed interest rate in the market and includes the effect of inflation. The **real interest rate** is the nominal interest rate minus the rate of inflation:

$$\text{real interest rate} = \text{nominal interest rate} - \text{rate of inflation}$$

If Ali charges Maria 10 percent nominal interest and the inflation rate is 5 percent, the real interest rate is 5 percent (10% − 5% = 5%). This means that Ali will earn a positive real return from the loan. However, if the inflation rate is 10 percent, the real return from a nominal interest rate of 10 percent is zero (10% − 10% = 0). The interest Ali will receive from the loan will just compensate him for the rise in prices; he will not realize an increase in purchasing power. If the inflation rate is higher than the nominal interest rate, then the real interest rate is negative—the lender will lose purchasing power by making the loan.

Now you can see how unexpected inflation redistributes income. Borrowers and creditors agree to loan terms based on what they *expect* the rate of inflation to be over the period of the loan. If the *actual* rate of inflation turns out to be different from what was expected, then the real interest rate paid by the borrower and received by the lender will be different from what was expected. If Ali and Maria both expect a 5 percent inflation rate and agree to a 10 percent nominal interest rate for the loan, then they both expect a real interest rate of 5 percent (10% − 5% = 5%) to be paid on the loan. If the actual inflation rate turns out to be greater than 5 percent, then the real interest rate will be less than expected. Maria will get to borrow Ali's money at a lower real cost than she expected, and Ali will earn a lower real return than he expected. Unexpectedly high inflation hurts creditors and benefits borrowers because it lowers real interest rates.

Figure 4 shows the real interest rates on U.S. Treasury bills from 1970 through 1997. You can see a pronounced pattern in the graph. In the late 1970s, there was a period of negative real interest rates, followed by high positive real rates in the 1980s. The evidence suggests that nominal interest rates did not rise fast enough in the 1970s to offset high inflation. This was a time of severe strain on many creditors, including savings and loan associations and banks. These firms had lent funds at fixed nominal rates of interest. When those rates of interest turned out to be lower than the rate of inflation, the financial institutions suffered significant losses. In the early 1980s, the inflation rate dropped sharply. Because nominal interest rates did not drop nearly as fast as the rate of inflation, real interest rates were high. In this

■ **nominal interest rate:**
the observed interest rate in the market

■ **real interest rate:**
the nominal interest rate minus the rate of inflation

Figure 4
The Real Interest Rate on U.S. Treasury Bills
The real interest rate is the difference between the nominal rate (the rate actually observed) and the rate of inflation over the life of the bond. The figure shows the real interest rate in June and December for each year. For instance, in the first observation for June 1970, a six-month Treasury bill paid the holder 6.91 percent interest. This is the nominal rate of interest. To find the real rate of interest on the bond, we subtract the rate of inflation that existed over the six months of the bond's life (June to December 1970), which was 5.17 percent. The difference between the nominal interest rate (6.91 percent) and the rate of inflation (5.17 percent) is the real interest rate, 1.74 percent. Notice that real interest rates were negative during most of the 1970s and then turned highly positive (by historical standards) in the early 1980s.

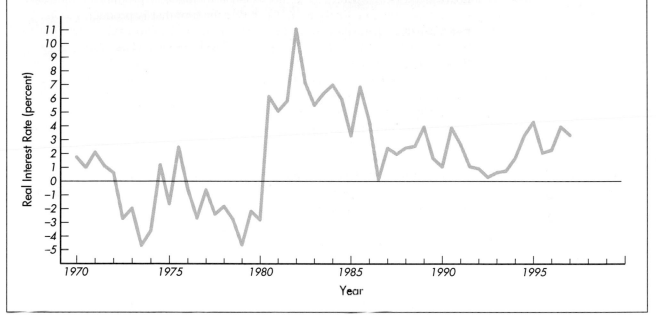

period many debtors were hurt by the high costs of borrowing to finance business or household expenditures.

Unexpected inflation affects more than the two parties to a loan. Any contract calling for fixed payments over some long-term period changes in value as the rate of inflation changes. For instance, a long-term contract that provides union members with 5 percent raises each year for five years gives the workers more purchasing power if inflation is low than if it is high. Similarly, a contract that sells a product at a fixed price over a long-term period will change in value as inflation changes. Suppose a lumber company promises to supply a builder with lumber at a fixed price for a two-year period. If the rate of inflation in one year turns out to be higher than expected, the lumber company will end up selling the lumber for less profit than it had planned. Inflation raises costs to the lumber company. Usually the company would raise its prices to compensate for higher costs. Because the company contracted to sell its goods at a fixed price to the builder, however, the builder benefits at the lumber company's expense. Again, unexpectedly high inflation redistributes real income or purchasing power away from those receiving fixed payments to those making fixed payments.

One response to the effects of unexpected inflation is to allow prices, wages, or interest rates to vary with the rate of inflation. Labor sometimes negotiates cost-of-living adjustments as part of new wage contracts. Financial institutions offer variable interest rates on home mortgages to reflect current market conditions. Any contract can be written to adjust dollar amounts over time as the rate of inflation changes.

3.c. Types of Inflation

Economists often classify inflation according to the source of the inflationary pressure. The most straightforward method defines inflation in terms of pres-

■ demand-pull inflation:
inflation caused by increasing demand for output.

■ cost-push inflation:
inflation caused by rising costs of production.

sure from the demand side of the market or the supply side of the market. **Demand-pull inflation** is caused by increasing demand for output. Increases in total spending that are not offset by increases in the supply of goods and services cause the average level of prices to rise. **Cost-push inflation** is caused by rising costs of production. Increases in production costs cause firms to raise prices to avoid losses.

Sometimes inflation is blamed on "too many dollars chasing too few goods." This is a roundabout way of saying that the inflation stems from demand pressures. Because demand-pull inflation is a product of increased spending, it is more likely to occur in an economy that is producing at maximum capacity. If resources are fully employed, in the short run it may not be possible to increase output to meet increased demand. The result: existing goods and services are rationed by rising prices.

Some economists claim that rising prices in the late 1960s were a product of demand-pull inflation. They believe that increased government spending for the Vietnam War caused the level of U.S. prices to rise.

Cost-push inflation can occur in any economy, whatever its output. If prices go up because the costs of resources are rising, the rate of inflation can go up regardless of demand.

For example, some economists argue that the inflation in the United States in the 1970s was largely due to rising oil prices. This means that decreases in the oil supply (a shift to the left in the supply curve) brought about higher oil prices. Because oil is so important in the production of many goods, higher oil prices led to increases in prices throughout the economy. Cost-push inflation stems from changes in the supply side of the market.

Cost-push inflation is sometimes attributed to profit-push or wage-push pressures. *Profit-push pressures* are created by suppliers who want to increase their profit margins by raising prices faster than their costs increase. *Wage-push pressures* are created by labor unions and workers who are able to increase their wages faster than their productivity. There have been times when "greedy" businesses and unions have been blamed for periods of inflation in the United States. The problem with these "theories" is that people have always wanted to improve their economic status and always will. In this sense, people have always been greedy. But inflation has not always been a problem. Were people less greedy in the early 1980s when inflation was low than they were in the late 1970s when inflation was high? Obviously, we have to look to other reasons to explain inflation. We discuss some of those reasons in later chapters.

3.d. The Inflationary Record

Many of our students, having always lived with inflation, are surprised to learn that inflation is a relatively new problem for the United States. From 1789, when the U.S. Constitution was ratified, until 1940, there was no particular trend in the general price level. At times prices rose, and at times they fell. The average level of prices in 1940 was approximately the same as it was in the late eighteenth century.

Since 1940, prices in the United States have gone up markedly. The price level today is eight times what it was in 1940. But the rate of growth has varied. Prices rose rapidly for the first couple of years following the Second World War, and then grew at a relatively slow rate through the 1950s and 1960s. In the early 1970s, the rate of inflation began to accelerate. Prices climbed quickly until the early 1980s, when inflation slowed.

Annual rates of inflation for several industrial and developing nations are shown in Table 5. In 1996, the average rate of inflation across all industrial countries was 2.3 percent; the average across all developing countries was 15.7 percent. Look at the diversity across countries: rates range from 0.1 percent in Japan to 659 percent in the Congo.

TABLE 5
Rates of Inflation for Selected Countries, 1996

Country	Inflation Rate (percent)
All industrial	2.3
All developing	15.7
Selected industrial:	
Canada	1.6
Germany	1.5
Italy	4.0
Japan	0.1
United Kingdom	2.4
United States	2.9
Selected developing:	
Botswana	10
Brazil	16
Chile	7
Congo	659
Egypt	7
Hong Kong, China	6
India	9
Israel	11
Mexico	34
Philippines	8
Poland	20
South Africa	7

Source: International Monetary Fund, *International Financial Statistics* (Washington, D.C.), December 1997. Reprinted by permission.

■ **hyperinflation:**
an extremely high rate of inflation

Hyperinflation is an extremely high rate of inflation. In most cases hyperinflation eventually makes a country's currency worthless and leads to the introduction of a new money. Argentina experienced hyperinflation in the 1980s. People had to carry large stacks of currency for small purchases. Cash registers and calculators ran out of digits as prices reached ridiculously high levels. After years of high inflation, Argentina replaced the old peso with the peso Argentino in June 1983. The government set the value of 1 peso Argentino equal to 10,000 old pesos (striking four zeros from all prices). A product that sold for 10,000 old pesos before the reform sold for 1 new peso after. But Argentina did not follow up its monetary reform with a noninflationary change in economic policy. In 1984 and 1985, the inflation rate exceeded 600 percent each year. As a result, in June 1985, the government again introduced a new currency, the austral, setting its value at 1,000 pesos Argentino. However, the economic policy associated with the introduction of the austral only lowered the inflation rate temporarily. By 1988, the inflation rate was over 300 percent, and in 1989 the inflation rate was over 3,000 percent. The rapid rise in prices associated with the austral resulted in the introduction of yet another currency, again named peso Argentino, in January 1992 with a value equal to 10,000 australes.

The most dramatic hyperinflation in modern times occurred in Europe after World War I. Table 6 shows how the price level rose in Germany between

TABLE 6
German Wholesale Prices, 1914–1924

Year	Price Index
1914	100
1915	126
1916	150
1917	156
1918	204
1919	262
1920	1,260
1921	1,440
1922	3,670
1923	278,500
1924	117,320,000,000,000

Source: J. P. Young, *European Currency and Finance* (Washington, D.C.: U.S. Government Printing Office, 1925).

1914 and 1924 in relation to prices in 1914. For instance, the value in 1915, 126, indicates that prices were 26 percent higher that year than in 1914. The value in 1919, 262, indicates that prices were 162 percent higher that year than in 1914. By 1924, German prices were more than 100 trillion times higher than they had been in 1914. At the height of the inflation, the mark was virtually worthless.

In later chapters, we will see how high rates of inflation generally are caused by rapid growth of the money supply. When a central government wants to spend more than it is capable of funding through taxation or borrowing, it simply issues money to finance its budget deficit. As the money supply increases faster than the demand to hold it, spending increases and prices go up.

RECAP

1. Inflation is a sustained rise in the average level of prices.
2. The higher the price level, the lower the real value (purchasing power) of money.
3. Unexpectedly high inflation redistributes income away from those who receive fixed-dollar payments (like creditors) toward those who make fixed-dollar payments (like debtors).
4. The real interest rate is the nominal interest rate minus the rate of inflation.
5. Demand-pull inflation is a product of increased spending; cost-push inflation reflects increased production costs.
6. Hyperinflation is a very high rate of inflation that often results in the introduction of a new currency.

SUMMARY

▪▪ What is a business cycle?

1. Business cycles are recurring changes in real GDP, in which expansion is followed by contraction.

2. The four stages of the business cycle are expansion (boom), peak, contraction (recession), and trough.

3. Leading, coincident, and lagging indicators are variables that change in relation to changes in output.

▪▪ How is the unemployment rate defined and measured?

4. The unemployment rate is the percentage of the labor force that is not working.

5. To be in the U.S. labor force, an individual must be working or actively seeking work.

6. Unemployment can be classified as seasonal, frictional, structural, or cyclical.

7. Frictional and structural unemployment are always present in a dynamic economy; cyclical unemployment is a product of recession.

▪▪ What is the cost of unemployed resources?

8. The GDP gap measures the output lost because of unemployment.

▪▪ What is inflation?

9. Inflation is a sustained rise in the average level of prices.

10. The higher the level of prices, the lower the purchasing power of money.

▪▪ Why is inflation a problem?

11. Inflation becomes a problem when income rises at a slower rate than prices.

12. Unexpectedly high inflation hurts those who receive fixed-dollar payments (like creditors) and benefits those who make fixed-dollar payments (like debtors).

13. Inflation can stem from demand-pull or cost-push pressures.

14. Hyperinflation—an extremely high rate of inflation—can force a country to introduce a new currency.

KEY TERMS

business cycle
recession
depression
leading indicator
coincident indicator
lagging indicator
unemployment rate
discouraged workers
underemployment

potential real GDP
natural rate of unemployment
inflation
nominal interest rate
real interest rate
demand-pull inflation
cost-push inflation
hyperinflation

EXERCISES

1. What is the labor force? Do you believe that the U.S. government's definition of the labor force is a good one—that it includes all the people it should include? Explain your answer.

2. Suppose you are able-bodied and intelligent, but lazy. You'd rather sit home and watch television than work, even though you know you could find an acceptable job if you looked.

   a. Are you officially unemployed?

   b. Are you a discouraged worker?

3. Does the GDP gap measure all of the costs of unemployment? Why or why not?

4. Why do teenagers have the highest unemployment rate in the economy?

5. Write an equation that defines the real interest rate. Use the equation to explain why unexpectedly high inflation redistributes income from creditors to debtors.

6. Many home mortgages in recent years have been made with variable interest rates. Typically, the interest rate is adjusted once a year based on current interest rates on government bonds. How do variable interest rate loans protect creditors from the effects of unexpected inflation?

7. The word *cycle* suggests a regular, recurring pattern of activity. Is there a regular pattern in the business cycle? Support your answer by examining the duration (number of months) of each expansion and contraction in Figure 1.

8. Suppose 500 people were surveyed, and of those 500, 450 were working full time. Of the 50 not working, 10 were full-time college students, 20 were retired, 5 were under sixteen years of age, 5 had stopped looking for work because they believed there were no jobs for them, and 10 were actively looking for work.

   a. How many of the 500 surveyed are in the labor force?

   b. What is the unemployment rate among the 500 surveyed people?

9. Consider the following price information:

	Year 1	Year 2
Cup of coffee	$ .50	$1.00
Glass of milk	$1.00	$2.00

   a. Based on the information given, what was the inflation rate between year 1 and year 2?

   b. What happened to the price of coffee relative to that of milk between year 1 and year 2?

10. Use a supply and demand diagram to illustrate:

   a. Cost-push inflation caused by a labor union successfully negotiating for a higher wage.

   b. Demand-pull inflation caused by an increase in demand for domestic products from foreign buyers.

INTERNET EXERCISE

In this chapter, the unemployment rate was defined as the number unemployed divided by the number in the labor force. This means that the unemployment rate will fluctuate as the number unemployed fluctuates or the size of the labor force fluctuates. To see recent data on the U.S. unemployment rate, go to the Boyes/Melvin *Fundamentals of Economics* Web site at **http://www.hmco.com/college/** and click on the Internet Exercise link for Chapter 11. Now answer the questions that appear on the Boyes/Melvin Web site.

12

Macroeconomic Equilibrium: Aggregate Demand and Supply

FUNDAMENTAL QUESTIONS

1. What factors affect aggregate demand?

2. What causes the aggregate demand curve to shift?

3. What factors affect aggregate supply?

4. Why does the short-run aggregate supply curve become steeper as real GDP increases?

5. Why is the long-run aggregate supply curve vertical?

6. What causes the aggregate supply curve to shift?

7. What determines the equilibrium price level and real GDP?

T otal output and income in the United States have grown over time. Each generation has experienced a higher living standard than the previous generation. Yet, as we learned in Chapter 11, economic growth has not been steady. Economies go through periods of expansion followed by periods of contraction or recession, and such business cycles have major impacts on people's lives, incomes, and living standards.

Economic stagnation and recession throw many, often those who are already relatively poor, out of their jobs and into real poverty. Economic growth increases the number of jobs and draws people out of poverty and into the mainstream of economic progress. To understand why economies grow and why they go through cycles, we must discover why firms decide to produce more or less and why buyers decide to buy more or less. The approach we take is similar to the approach we followed in the early chapters of the text using demand and supply curves. In Chapters 2 and 3, demand and supply curves were derived and used to examine questions involving the equilibrium price and quantities demanded and supplied of a single good or service. This simple yet powerful microeconomic technique of analysis has a macroeconomic counterpart—aggregate demand and aggregate supply, which are used to determine an equilibrium price level and quantity of goods and services produced for the *entire economy*. In this chapter we shall use aggregate demand and supply curves to illustrate the causes of business cycles and economic growth. ■

1. AGGREGATE DEMAND, AGGREGATE SUPPLY, AND BUSINESS CYCLES

What causes economic growth and business cycles? We can provide some answers to this important question using aggregate demand (AD) and aggregate supply (AS) curves. Suppose we represent the economy in a simple demand and supply diagram, as shown in Figure 1. Aggregate demand represents the total spending in the economy at alternative price levels. Aggregate supply represents the total output of the economy at alternative price levels. To understand the causes of business cycles and inflation, we must understand how aggregate demand and supply cause the equilibrium price level and real GDP, the nation's output of goods and services, to change. The intersection between the AD and AS curves defines the equilibrium level of real GDP and level of prices. The equilibrium price level is P_e and the equilibrium level of real GDP is Y_e. This price and output level represents the level of prices and output for some particular period of time, say 1999. Once that equilibrium is established, there is no tendency for prices and output to change until changes occur in either the aggregate demand curve or the aggregate supply curve. Let's first consider a change in aggregate demand and then look at a change in aggregate supply.

1.a. Aggregate Demand and Business Cycles

An increase in aggregate demand is illustrated by a shift of the AD curve to the right, like the shift from AD_1 to AD_2 in Figure 2. This represents a situation in which buyers are buying more at every price level. The shift causes the equilibrium level of real GDP to rise from Y_{e1} to Y_{e2}, illustrating the expansionary phase of the business cycle. As output rises, unemployment decreases. The increase in aggregate demand also leads to a higher price level, as shown by the change in the price level from P_{e1} to P_{e2}. The increase

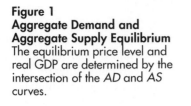

Figure 1
Aggregate Demand and
Aggregate Supply Equilibrium
The equilibrium price level and
real GDP are determined by the
intersection of the AD and AS
curves.

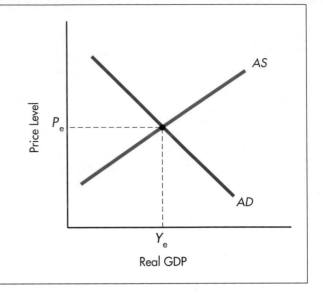

in the price level represents an example of demand-pull inflation, which you
may recall, is inflation caused by increasing demand for output.

If aggregate demand falls, like the shift from AD_1 to AD_3, then there is a
lower equilibrium level of real GDP, Y_{e3}. In this case, buyers are buying *less*
at every price level. The drop in real GDP caused by lower demand would
represent an economic slowdown or a recession, when output falls and unemployment rises.

1.b. Aggregate Supply and Business Cycles

Changes in aggregate supply can also cause business cycles. Figure 3 illustrates what happens when aggregate supply changes. An increase in aggregate
supply is illustrated by the shift from AS_1 to AS_2, leading to an increase in the
equilibrium level of real GDP from Y_{e1} to Y_{e2}. An increase in aggregate supply comes about when firms produce more at every price level. Such an
increase could result from an improvement in technology or a decrease in
costs of production.

If aggregate supply decreased, as in the shift from AS_1 to AS_3, then the
equilibrium level of real GDP would fall to Y_{e3} and the equilibrium price level
would increase from P_{e1} to P_{e3}. A decrease in aggregate supply could be

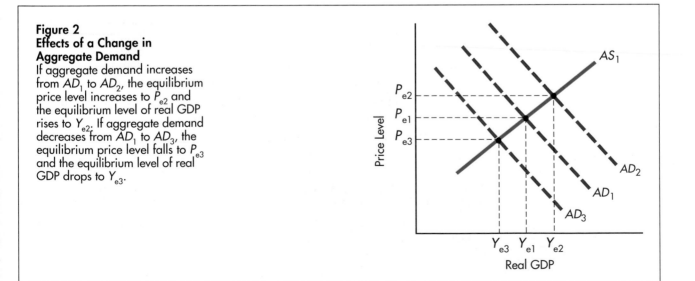

Figure 2
Effects of a Change in
Aggregate Demand
If aggregate demand increases
from AD_1 to AD_2, the equilibrium
price level increases to P_{e2} and
the equilibrium level of real GDP
rises to Y_{e2}. If aggregate demand
decreases from AD_1 to AD_3, the
equilibrium price level falls to P_{e3}
and the equilibrium level of real
GDP drops to Y_{e3}.

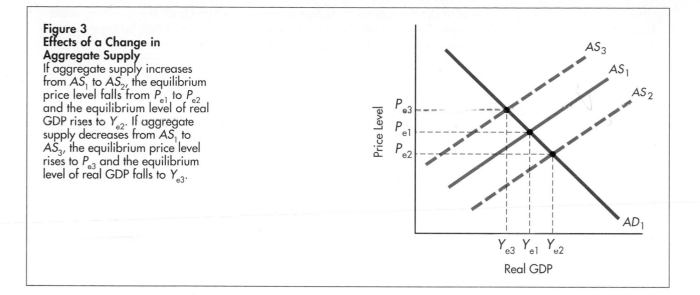

Figure 3
Effects of a Change in Aggregate Supply
If aggregate supply increases from AS_1 to AS_2, the equilibrium price level falls from P_{e1} to P_{e2} and the equilibrium level of real GDP rises to Y_{e2}. If aggregate supply decreases from AS_1 to AS_3, the equilibrium price level rises to P_{e3} and the equilibrium level of real GDP falls to Y_{e3}.

caused by higher production costs that lead producers to raise their prices. This is an example of cost-push inflation—where the price level rises due to increased costs of production and the associated decrease in aggregate supply.

1.c. A Look Ahead

Business cycles result from changes in aggregate demand, from changes in aggregate supply, and from changes in both AD and AS. The degree to which real GDP declines during a recession or increases during an expansion depends on the amount by which the AD and/or AS curves shift. The degree to which an expansion involves output growth or increased inflation depends on the shapes of the AD and AS curves. We need to consider why the curves have the shapes they do, and what causes them to shift.

The comparison we made earlier, between aggregate demand, aggregate supply, and their microeconomic counterparts, the supply and demand curves, is only superficial. As we examine the aggregate demand and supply curves, you will see that the reasons underlying the shapes and movements of AD and AS are in fact quite different from those explaining the shapes and movements of the supply and demand curves.

RECAP

1. Aggregate demand (AD) represents the total spending in the economy at alternative price levels.
2. Aggregate supply (AS) represents the total output of the economy at alternative price levels.
3. The intersection between the AD and AS curves defines the equilibrium level of real GDP and the level of prices.
4. Business cycles result from changes in AD and/or AS.

2. FACTORS THAT INFLUENCE AGGREGATE DEMAND

Aggregate demand is the relation between aggregate expenditures, or total spending, and the price level. Aggregate expenditures are the sum of expenditures of each sector of the economy: households (consumption), business firms (investment), government, and the rest of the world (net exports). Each sector of the economy has different reasons for spending; for instance, household spending depends heavily on household income, while business spending depends on the profits businesses expect to earn. Because each sector of the economy has a different reason for the amount of spending it undertakes, aggregate spending depends on all of these reasons. To understand aggregate demand, therefore, requires that we look at those factors that influence the expenditures of each sector of the economy.

2.a. Consumption

How much households spend depends on their income, wealth, expectations about future prices and incomes, demographics like the age distribution of the population, and taxes.

- Income: If current income rises, households purchase more goods and services.

- Wealth: Wealth is different from income. It is the value of assets owned by a household, including homes, cars, bank deposits, stocks, and bonds. An increase in household wealth will increase consumption.

- Expectations: Expectations regarding future changes in income or wealth can affect consumption today. If households expect a recession and worry about job loss, consumption tends to fall. On the other hand, if households become more optimistic regarding future increases in income and wealth, consumption rises today.

- Demographics: Demographic change can affect consumption in several different ways. Population growth is generally associated with higher consumption for an economy. Younger households and older households generally consume more and save less than middle-aged households. Therefore, as the age distribution of a nation changes, so will consumption.

- Taxes: Higher taxes will lower the disposable income of households and decrease consumption, while lower taxes will raise disposable income and increase consumption. Government policy may change taxes and thereby bring about a change in consumption.

2.b. Investment

Investment is business spending on capital goods and inventories. In general, investment depends on the expected profitability of such spending, so any factor that could affect the profitability will be a determinant of investment. Factors affecting the expected profitability of business projects include the interest rate, technology, the cost of capital goods, and capacity utilization.

- Interest rate: Investment is negatively related to the interest rate. The interest rate is the cost of borrowed funds. The greater the cost of borrowing, other things being equal, the fewer investment projects that offer sufficient profit to be undertaken. As the interest rate falls, investment is stimulated as the cost of financing the investment is lowered.

- Technology: New production technology stimulates investment spending as firms are forced to adopt new production methods to stay competitive.

- Cost of capital goods: If machines and equipment purchased by firms rise in price, then the higher costs associated with investment will lower profitability and investment will fall.

- Capacity utilization: The more excess capacity (unused capital goods) is available, the more firms can expand production without purchasing new capital goods, and the lower investment is. As firms approach full capacity, more investment spending is required to expand output further.

2.c. Government Spending

Government spending may be set by government authorities independent of current income or other determinants of aggregate expenditures.

2.d. Net Exports

Net exports are equal to exports minus imports. We assume exports are determined by conditions in the rest of the world, like foreign income, tastes, prices, exchange rates, and government policy. Imports are determined by similar domestic factors.

Income   As domestic income rises and consumption rises, some of this consumption includes goods produced in other countries. Therefore, as domestic income rises, imports rise and net exports fall. Similarly, as foreign income rises, foreign residents buy more domestic goods, and net exports rise.

Prices   Other things being equal, higher (lower) foreign prices make domestic goods relatively cheaper (more expensive) and increase (decrease) net exports. Higher (lower) domestic prices make domestic goods relatively more expensive (cheaper) and decrease (increase) net exports.

Exchange Rates   Other things being equal, a depreciation of the domestic currency on the foreign exchange market will make domestic goods cheaper to foreign buyers and make foreign goods more expensive to domestic residents so that net exports will rise. An appreciation of the domestic currency will have just the opposite effects.

Government Policy   Net exports may fall if foreign governments restrict the entry of domestic goods reducing domestic exports. If the domestic government restricts imports into the domestic economy, net exports may rise.

2.e. Aggregate Expenditures

You can see how aggregate expenditures, the sum of all spending on U.S. goods and services, must depend on prices, income, and all of the other determinants discussed in the previous sections. As with the demand curve for a specific good or service, with the aggregate demand curve we want to classify the factors that influence spending into the price and the nonprice determinants for the aggregate demand curves as well. The components of aggregate expenditures that change as the price level changes will lead to movements along the aggregate demand curve—changes in quantity demanded—while changes in aggregate expenditures caused by nonprice effects will cause shifts of the aggregate demand curve—changes in aggregate demand. In the following section we look first at the price effects, or movements along an aggregate demand curve. Following that discussion, we focus on the nonprice determinants of aggregate demand.

RECAP

1.   Aggregate expenditures are the sum of consumption, investment, government spending, and net exports.
2.   Consumption depends on household income, wealth, expectations, demographics, and taxation.
3.   Investment depends on the interest rate, technology, the cost of capital goods, and capacity utilization.
4.   Government spending is determined independent of current income.
5.   Net exports depend on foreign and domestic incomes, prices, government policies, and exchange rates.

3. THE AGGREGATE DEMAND CURVE

When we examined the demand curves in Chapter 2, we divided our study into two parts: the movement along the curves—changes in quantity demanded—and the shifts of the curve—changes in demand. We take the same approach here in examining aggregate demand. We first look at the movements along the aggregate demand curve caused by changes in the price level. We then turn to the nonprice determinants of aggregate demand that cause shifts in the curve.

3.a. Changes in Aggregate Quantity Demanded: Price-Level Effects

Aggregate demand curves are downward-sloping just like the demand curves for individual goods that were shown in Chapter 2, although for different reasons. Along the demand curve for an individual good, the price of that good changes while the prices of all other goods remain constant. This means that the good in question becomes relatively more or less expensive compared to all other goods in the economy. Consumers tend to substitute a less expensive good for a more expensive good. The effect of this substitution is an inverse relationship between price and quantity demanded. As the price of a good rises, quantity demanded falls. For the economy as a whole, however, it is not a substitution of a less expensive good for a more expensive good that causes the demand curve to slope down. Instead, aggregate quantity demanded, or total spending, will change as the price level changes due to the wealth effect, the interest rate effect, and the international trade effect of a price-level change on aggregate expenditures. We will discuss each of these effects in turn.

3.a.1. The Wealth Effect
Individuals and businesses own money, bonds, and other financial assets. The purchasing power of these assets is the quantity of goods and services the assets can be exchanged for. When the level of prices falls, the purchasing power of these assets increases, allowing households and businesses to purchase more. When prices go up, the purchasing power of financial assets falls, which causes households and businesses to spend less. This is the **wealth effect** (sometimes called the *real-balance effect*) of a price change: a change in the real value of wealth that causes spending to change when the level of prices changes. *Real values* are values that have been adjusted for price-level changes. Here *real value* means "purchasing power." When the price level changes, the purchasing power of financial assets also changes. When prices rise, the real value of assets and wealth falls, and aggregate expenditures tend to fall. When prices fall, the real value of assets and wealth rises, and aggregate expenditures tend to rise.

■ **wealth effect:**
a change in the real value of wealth that causes spending to change when the level of prices changes

3.a.2. The Interest Rate Effect
When the price level rises, the purchasing power of each dollar falls, which means more money is required to buy any particular quantity of goods and services (see Figure 4). Suppose that a family of three needs $100 each week to buy food. If the price level doubles, the same quantity of food costs $200. The household must have twice as much money to buy the same amount of food. Conversely, when prices fall, the family needs less money to buy food because the purchasing power of each dollar is greater.

When prices go up, people need more money. So they sell their other financial assets, like bonds, to get that money. The increase in supply of bonds lowers bond prices and raises interest rates. Since bonds typically pay fixed-dollar interest payments each year, as the price of a bond varies, the interest rate (or yield) will change. For instance, suppose you pay $1,000 for a bond that pays $100 a year in interest. The interest rate on this bond is found by dividing the annual interest payment by the bond price, or $100/$1,000 = 10 percent. If the price of the bond falls to $900, then the interest rate is equal to

Figure 4
The Interest Rate Effect

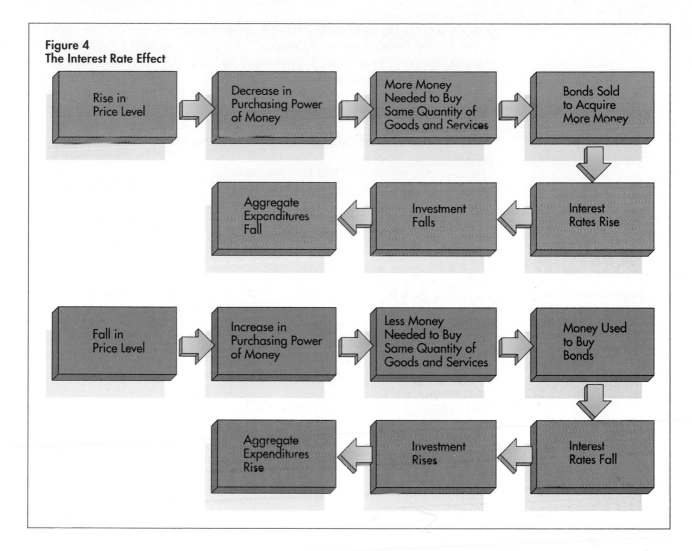

Rise in Price Level	→ Decrease in Purchasing Power of Money	→ More Money Needed to Buy Same Quantity of Goods and Services	→ Bonds Sold to Acquire More Money
Aggregate Expenditures Fall	← Investment Falls	← Interest Rates Rise	↓

Fall in Price Level	→ Increase in Purchasing Power of Money	→ Less Money Needed to Buy Same Quantity of Goods and Services	→ Money Used to Buy Bonds
Aggregate Expenditures Rise	← Investment Rises	← Interest Rates Fall	↓

the annual interest payment (which remains fixed at $100 for the life of the bond) divided by the new price of $900: $100/$900 = 11 percent. When bond prices fall, interest rates rise, and when bond prices rise, interest rates fall.

If people want more money and they sell some of their bond holdings to raise the money, bond prices will fall and interest rates will rise. The rise in interest rates is necessary to sell the larger quantity of bonds, but it causes investment expenditures to fall, which causes aggregate expenditures to fall.

When prices fall, people need less money to purchase the same quantity of goods. So they use their money holdings to buy bonds and other financial assets. The increased demand for bonds increases bond prices and causes interest rates to fall. Lower interest rates increase investment expenditures, thereby pushing aggregate expenditures up.

Figure 4 shows the **interest rate effect**, the relationship among the price level, interest rates, and aggregate expenditures. As the price level rises, interest rates rise and aggregate expenditures fall. As the price level falls, interest rates fall and aggregate expenditures rise.

3.a.3. The International Trade Effect The third channel through which a price-level change affects the quantity of goods and services demanded is called the **international trade effect**. A change in the level of domestic prices can cause net exports to change. If domestic prices rise while foreign prices and the foreign exchange rate remain constant, domestic goods become more expensive in relation to foreign goods.

Suppose the United States sells oranges to Japan. If the oranges sell for $1 per pound and the yen-dollar exchange rate is 100 yen = $1, a pound of U.S.

■ **interest rate effect:**
a change in interest rates that causes investment and therefore aggregate expenditures to change as the level of prices changes

■ **international trade effect:**
the change in aggregate expenditures resulting from a change in the domestic price level that changes the price of domestic goods in relation to foreign goods

oranges costs a Japanese buyer 100 yen. What happens if the level of prices in the United States goes up 10 percent? All prices, including the price of oranges, increase 10 percent. U.S. oranges sell for $1.10 a pound after the price increase. If the exchange rate is still 100 yen = $1, a pound of oranges now costs the Japanese buyer 110 yen (100 × 1.10). If orange prices in other countries do not change, some Japanese buyers may buy oranges from those countries. The increase in the level of U.S. prices makes U.S. goods more expensive relative to foreign goods and causes U.S. net exports to fall; a decrease in the level of U.S. prices makes U.S. goods cheaper in relation to foreign goods, which increases U.S. net exports.

When the price of domestic goods increases in relation to the price of foreign goods, net exports fall, causing aggregate expenditures to fall. When the price of domestic goods falls in relation to the price of foreign goods, net exports rise, causing aggregate expenditures to rise. The international trade effect of a change in the level of domestic prices causes aggregate expenditures to change in the opposite direction.

3.a.4. The Sum of the Price-Level Effects

The **aggregate demand curve** (*AD*) shows how the equilibrium level of expenditures for the economy's output changes as the price level changes. In other words, the curve shows the amount people spend at different price levels.

Figure 5 displays the typical shape of the *AD* curve. The price level is plotted on the vertical axis and real GDP is plotted on the horizontal axis. Suppose that initially the economy is at point *A* with prices at P_0. At this point, spending equals $500. If prices fall to P_1, expenditures equal $700 and the economy is at point *C*. If prices rise from P_0 to P_2, expenditures equal $300 at point *B*.

Because aggregate expenditures increase when the price level decreases, and decrease when the price level increases, the aggregate demand curve slopes down. The aggregate demand curve is drawn with the price level for the *entire economy* on the vertical axis. A price-level change here means that, on average, *all prices in the economy change*; there is no relative price change among domestic goods. The negative slope of the aggregate demand curve is a product of the wealth effect, the interest rate effect, and the international trade effect.

A lower domestic price level increases consumption (the wealth effect), investment (the interest rate effect), and net exports (the international trade effect). As the price level drops, aggregate expenditures rise.

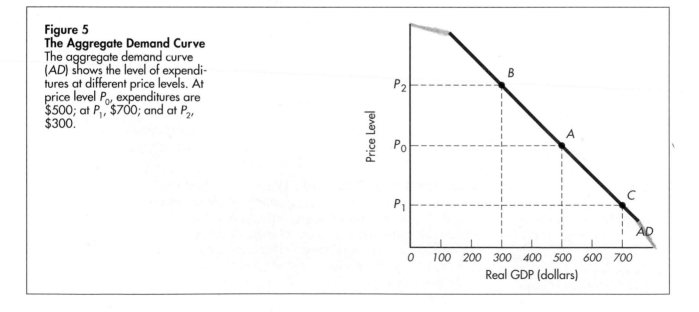

Figure 5
The Aggregate Demand Curve
The aggregate demand curve (*AD*) shows the level of expenditures at different price levels. At price level P_0, expenditures are $500; at P_1, $700; and at P_2, $300.

A higher domestic price reduces consumption (the wealth effect), investment (the interest rate effect), and net exports (the international trade effect). As prices rise, aggregate expenditures fall. These price effects are summarized in Figure 6.

3.b. Changes in Aggregate Demand: Nonprice Determinants

The aggregate demand curve shows the level of aggregate expenditures at alternative price levels. We draw the curve by varying the price level and finding out what the resulting total expenditures are, holding all other things constant. As those "other things"—the nonprice determinants of aggregate demand—change, the aggregate demand curve shifts. The nonprice determinants of aggregate demand include all of the factors covered in the discussion of the components of expenditures—income, wealth, demographics, expectations, taxes, the interest rate (interest rates can change for reasons other than price-level changes), the cost of capital goods, capacity utilization, foreign

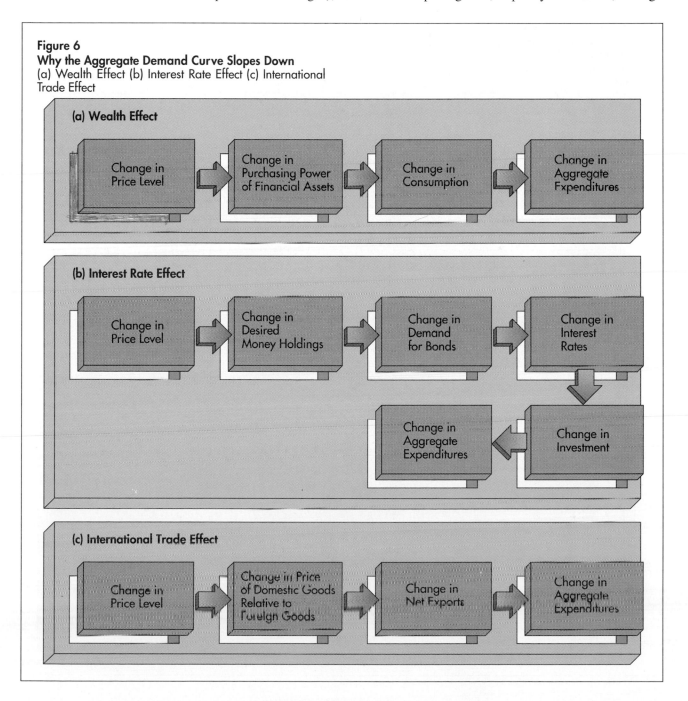

Figure 6
Why the Aggregate Demand Curve Slopes Down
(a) Wealth Effect (b) Interest Rate Effect (c) International Trade Effect

(a) Wealth Effect

Change in Price Level → Change in Purchasing Power of Financial Assets → Change in Consumption → Change in Aggregate Expenditures

(b) Interest Rate Effect

Change in Price Level → Change in Desired Money Holdings → Change in Demand for Bonds → Change in Interest Rates → Change in Investment → Change in Aggregate Expenditures

(c) International Trade Effect

Change in Price Level → Change in Price of Domestic Goods Relative to Foreign Goods → Change in Net Exports → Change in Aggregate Expenditures

income and price levels, exchange rates, and government policy. A change in any one of these can cause the *AD* curve to shift. In the discussions that follow, we will focus particularly on the effect of expectations, foreign income and price levels, and will also mention government policy, which will be examined in detail in Chapter 13. Figure 7 summarizes these effects, which are discussed next.

3.b.1. Expectations Consumption and business spending are affected by expectations. Consumption is sensitive to people's expectations of future income, prices, and wealth. For example, when people expect the economy to do well in the future, they increase consumption today at every price level. This is reflected in a shift of the aggregate demand curve to the right, from AD_0 to AD_1, as shown in Figure 8. When aggregate demand increases, aggregate expenditures increase at every price level.

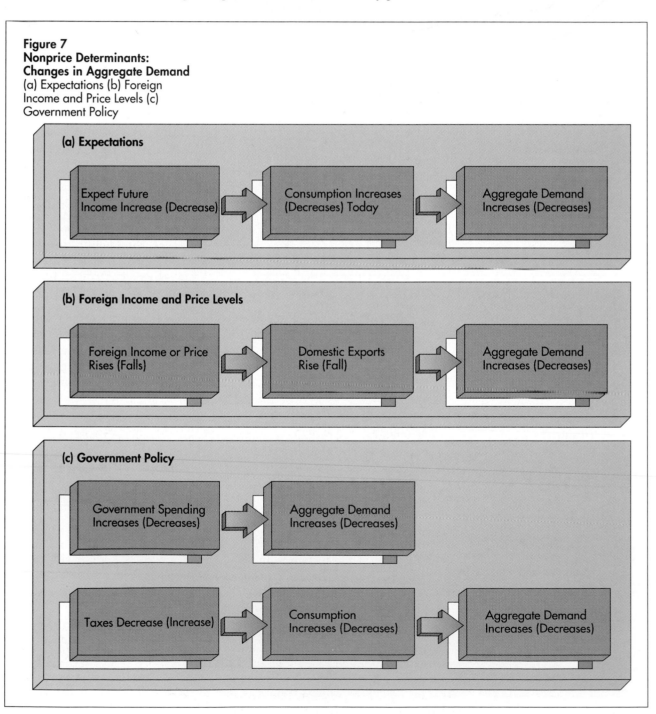

Figure 7
Nonprice Determinants:
Changes in Aggregate Demand
(a) Expectations (b) Foreign Income and Price Levels (c) Government Policy

(a) Expectations

Expect Future Income Increase (Decrease) → Consumption Increases (Decreases) Today → Aggregate Demand Increases (Decreases)

(b) Foreign Income and Price Levels

Foreign Income or Price Rises (Falls) → Domestic Exports Rise (Fall) → Aggregate Demand Increases (Decreases)

(c) Government Policy

Government Spending Increases (Decreases) → Aggregate Demand Increases (Decreases)

Taxes Decrease (Increase) → Consumption Increases (Decreases) → Aggregate Demand Increases (Decreases)

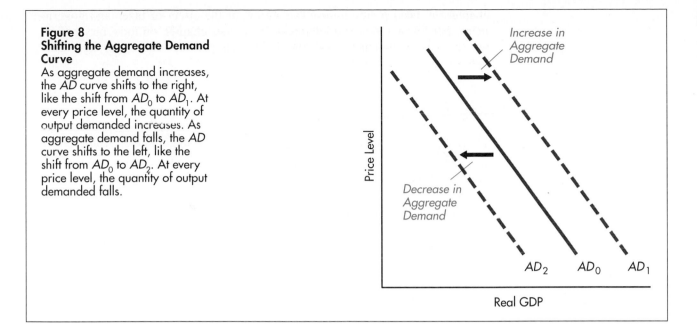

Figure 8
Shifting the Aggregate Demand Curve
As aggregate demand increases, the *AD* curve shifts to the right, like the shift from AD_0 to AD_1. At every price level, the quantity of output demanded increases. As aggregate demand falls, the *AD* curve shifts to the left, like the shift from AD_0 to AD_2. At every price level, the quantity of output demanded falls.

On the other hand, if people expect a recession in the near future, they tend to reduce consumption and increase saving in order to protect themselves against a greater likelihood of losing a job or a forced cutback in hours worked. As consumption drops, aggregate demand decreases. The *AD* curve shifts to the left, from AD_0 to AD_2. At every price level along AD_2, planned expenditures are less than they are along AD_0.

Expectations also play an important role in investment decisions. Before undertaking a particular project, businesses forecast the likely revenues and costs associated with that project. When the profit outlook is good—say, a tax cut is on the horizon—investment and therefore aggregate demand increase. When profits are expected to fall, investment and aggregate demand decrease.

3.b.2. Foreign Income and Price Levels

When foreign income increases, so does foreign spending. Some of this increased spending is for goods produced in the domestic economy. As domestic exports increase, aggregate demand rises. Lower foreign income has just the opposite effect. As foreign income falls, foreign spending falls, including foreign spending on the exports of the domestic economy. Lower foreign income, then, causes domestic net exports and domestic aggregate demand to fall.

If foreign prices rise in relation to domestic prices, domestic goods become less expensive relative to foreign goods, and domestic net exports increase. This means that aggregate demand rises, or the aggregate demand curve shifts up, as the level of foreign prices rises. Conversely, when the level of foreign prices falls, domestic goods become more expensive relative to foreign goods, causing domestic net exports and aggregate demand to fall.

Let's go back to the market for oranges. Suppose U.S. growers compete with Brazilian growers for the Japanese orange market. If the level of prices in Brazil rises while the level of prices in the United States remains stable, the price of Brazilian oranges to the Japanese buyer rises in relation to the price of U.S. oranges. What happens? U.S. exports of oranges to Japan should rise while Brazilian exports of oranges to Japan fall.

3.b.3. Government Policy

One of the goals of macroeconomic policy is to achieve economic growth without inflation. For GDP to increase, either *AD* or *AS* would have to change. Government economic policy can cause the aggregate demand curve to shift. An increase in government spending or a decrease in taxes will increase aggregate demand; a decrease in government spending or an increase in taxes will decrease aggregate demand. We devote an entire chapter on fiscal policy to an examination of the effect of taxes and government spending on aggregate demand. In another chapter, on monetary policy, we describe how changes in the money supply can cause the aggregate demand curve to shift.

RECAP

1. The aggregate demand curve shows the level of aggregate expenditures at different levels of price.

2. Aggregate expenditures are the sum of consumption, investment, government spending, and net exports.

3. The wealth effect, the interest rate effect, and the international trade effect are three reasons why aggregate demand slopes down. These effects explain movements along a given *AD* curve.

4. The aggregate demand curve shifts with changes in the nonprice determinants of aggregate demand: expectations, foreign income and price levels, and government policy.

4. AGGREGATE SUPPLY

■ **aggregate supply curve:**
a curve that shows the amount of real GDP produced at different price levels

The **aggregate supply curve** shows the quantity of real GDP produced at different price levels. The aggregate supply curve (*AS*) looks like the supply curve for an individual good, but, as with aggregate demand and the microeconomic demand curve, different factors are at work. The positive relationship between price and quantity supplied of an individual good is based on the price of that good changing in relation to the prices of all other goods. As the price of a single good rises relative to the prices of other goods, sellers are willing to offer more of the good for sale. With aggregate supply, on the other hand, we are analyzing how the amount of all goods and services produced changes as the level of prices changes. The direct relationship between prices and national output is explained by the effect of changing prices on profits, not by relative price changes.

4.a. Changes in Aggregate Quantity Supplied: Price-Level Effects

Along the aggregate supply curve, everything is held fixed except the price level and output. The price level is the price of output. The prices of resources, that is, the costs of production—wages, rent, and interest—are assumed to be constant, at least for a short time following a change in the price level.

If the price level rises while the costs of production remain fixed, business profits go up. As profits rise, firms are willing to produce more output. As the price level rises, then, the quantity of output firms are willing to supply increases. The result is the positively sloped aggregate supply curve shown in Figure 9.

As the price level rises from P_0 to P_1 in Figure 9, real GDP increases from $300 to $500. The higher the price level, the higher are profits, everything else held constant, and the greater is the quantity of output produced in the economy. Conversely, as the price level falls, the quantity of output produced falls.

4.b. Short-Run Versus Long-Run Aggregate Supply

The curve in Figure 9 is a *short-run* aggregate supply curve because the costs of production are held constant. Although production costs may not rise

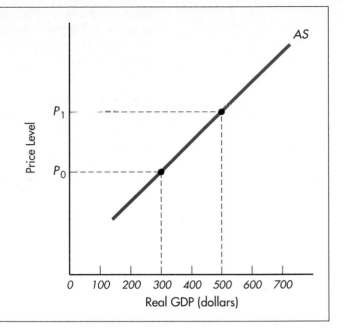

Figure 9
Aggregate Supply
The aggregate supply curve shows the amount of real GDP produced at different price levels. The *AS* curve slopes up, indicating that the higher the price level, the greater the quantity of output produced.

immediately when the price level rises, eventually they will. Labor will demand higher wages to compensate for the higher cost of living; suppliers will charge more for materials. The positive slope of the *AS* curve, then, is a short-run phenomenon. How short is the short run? It is the period of time over which production costs remain constant. (In the long run, all costs change or are variable.) For the economy as a whole, the short run can be months or, at most, a few years.

4.b.1. Short-Run Aggregate Supply Curve Figure 9 represents the general shape of the short-run aggregate supply curve. In Figure 10 you see a more realistic version of the same curve—its steepness varies. The steepness of the aggregate supply curve depends on the ability and willingness of producers to respond to price-level changes in the short run. Figure 10 shows the typical shape of the short-run aggregate supply curve.

Notice that as the level of real GDP increases in Figure 10, the *AS* curve becomes steeper. This is because each increase in output requires firms to hire more and more resources, until eventually full capacity is reached in some

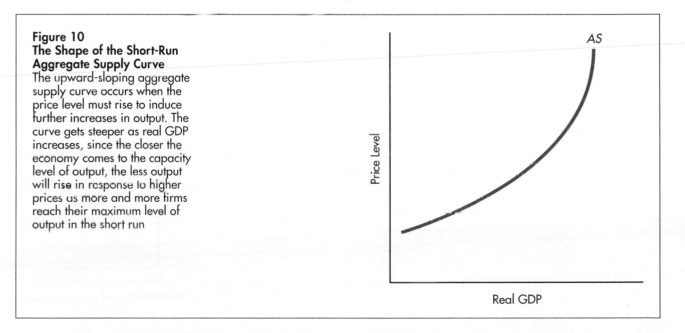

Figure 10
The Shape of the Short-Run Aggregate Supply Curve
The upward-sloping aggregate supply curve occurs when the price level must rise to induce further increases in output. The curve gets steeper as real GDP increases, since the closer the economy comes to the capacity level of output, the less output will rise in response to higher prices as more and more firms reach their maximum level of output in the short run

areas of the economy, resources are fully employed, and some firms reach maximum output. At this point, increases in the price level bring about smaller and smaller increases in output from firms as a whole. The short-run aggregate supply curve becomes increasingly steep as the economy approaches maximum output.

4.b.2. Long-Run Aggregate Supply Curve   Aggregate supply in the short run is different from aggregate supply in the long run (see Figure 11). That difference stems from the fact that quantities and costs of resources are not fixed in the long run. Over time, contracts expire and wages and other resource costs adjust to current conditions. The increased flexibility of resource costs in the long run has costs rising and falling with the price level and changes the shape of the aggregate supply curve. Lack of information about economic conditions in the short run also contributes to the inflexibility of resource prices as compared to the long run.

■ **long-run aggregate supply curve (LRAS):**
a vertical line at the potential level of national income

The **long-run aggregate supply curve (LRAS)** is viewed by most economists to be a vertical line at the potential level of real GDP or output (Y_p), as shown in Figure 11. Remember that the potential level of real GDP is the income level that is produced in the absence of any cyclical unemployment, or when the natural rate of unemployment exists. In the long run, wages and other resource costs fully adjust to price changes. The short-run AS curve slopes up because we assume that the costs of production, particularly wages, do not change to offset changing prices. In the short run, then, higher prices increase producers' profits and stimulate production. In the long run, because the costs of production adjust completely to the change in prices, neither profits nor production increase. What we find here are higher wages and other costs of production to match the higher level of prices.

4.c. Changes in Aggregate Supply: Nonprice Determinants

The aggregate supply curve is drawn with everything but the price level and real GDP held constant. There are several things that can change and cause the aggregate supply curve to shift. The shift from AS_0 to AS_1 in Figure 12 represents an increase in aggregate supply. AS_1 lies to the right of AS_0, which

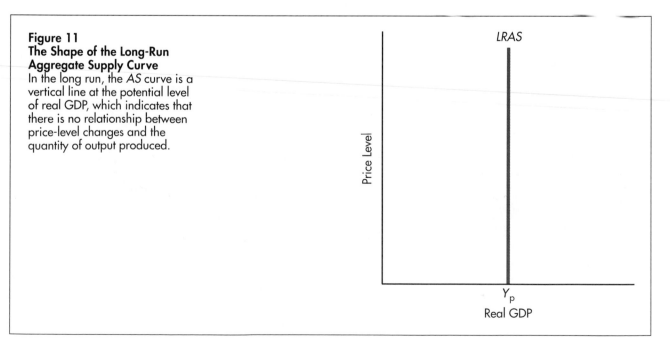

Figure 11
The Shape of the Long-Run Aggregate Supply Curve
In the long run, the AS curve is a vertical line at the potential level of real GDP, which indicates that there is no relationship between price-level changes and the quantity of output produced.

LRAS

Price Level

Y_p
Real GDP

Technological advance shifts the aggregate supply curve outward and increases output. An example of a technological advance that has increased efficiency in banking is the automated teller machine (or ATM). The photo shows an ATM in Brazil that allows the bank to offer the public a lower-cost way to make withdrawals and deposits than dealing with a bank employee. Such innovations can be important determinants of aggregate supply.

means that at every price level, production is higher on AS_1 than on AS_0. The shift from AS_0 to AS_2 represents a decrease in aggregate supply. AS_2 lies to the left of AS_0, which means that at every price level, production along AS_2 is less than along AS_0. The nonprice determinants of aggregate supply are resource prices, technology, and expectations. Figure 13 summarizes the nonprice determinants of aggregate supply, discussed in detail next.

4.c.1. Resource Prices

When the price of output changes, the costs of production do not change immediately. At first, then, a change in profits induces a change in production. Costs eventually change in response to the change in prices and production, and when they do, the aggregate supply curve shifts. When the cost of resources—labor, capital goods, materials—falls, the aggregate supply curve shifts to the right, from AS_0 to AS_1 in Figure 12. This means firms are willing to produce more output at any given price level. When the cost of resources goes up, profits fall and the aggregate supply curve shifts to the left, from AS_0 to AS_2. Here, at any given level of price, firms produce less output.

Figure 12
Changes in Aggregate Supply
The aggregate supply curve shifts with changes in resource prices, technology, and expectations. When aggregate supply increases, the curve shifts to the right, like the shift from AS_0 to AS_1, so that at every price level more is being produced. When aggregate supply falls, the curve shifts to the left, like the shift from AS_0 to AS_2, so that at every price level less is being produced.

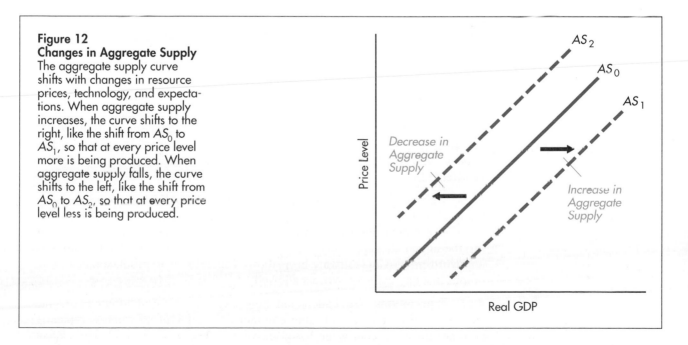

Figure 13
Determinants of Aggregate Supply
(a) Resource Prices (b) Technology (c) Expectations

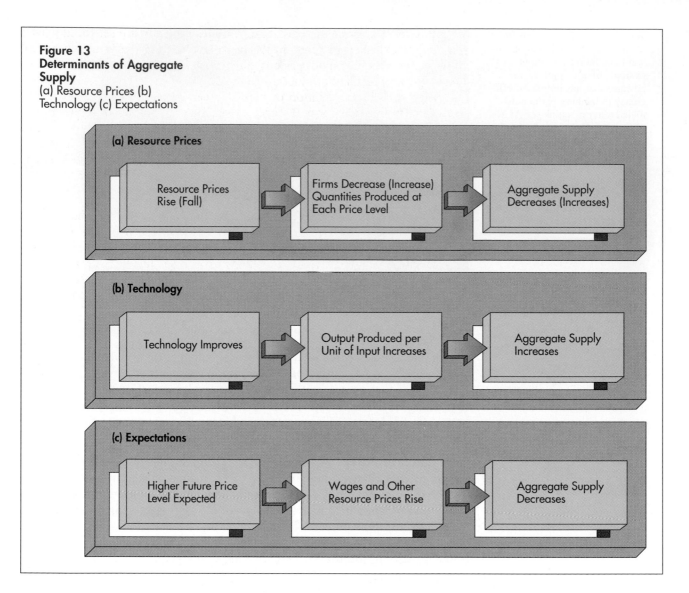

(a) Resource Prices

Resource Prices Rise (Fall) → Firms Decrease (Increase) Quantities Produced at Each Price Level → Aggregate Supply Decreases (Increases)

(b) Technology

Technology Improves → Output Produced per Unit of Input Increases → Aggregate Supply Increases

(c) Expectations

Higher Future Price Level Expected → Wages and Other Resource Prices Rise → Aggregate Supply Decreases

Remember that the vertical axis of the aggregate supply graph plots the price level for all goods and services produced in the economy. Only those changes in resource prices that raise the costs of production across the economy have an impact on the aggregate supply curve. For example, oil is an important raw material. If a new source of oil is discovered, the price of oil falls and aggregate supply increases. However, if oil-exporting countries restrict oil supplies and the price of oil increases substantially, aggregate supply decreases, a situation that occurred when OPEC reduced the supply of oil in the 1970s (see the Economic Insight "OPEC and Aggregate Supply"). If the price of only one minor resource changed, then aggregate supply would be unlikely to change. For instance, if the price of land increased in Las Cruces, New Mexico, we would not expect the U.S. aggregate supply curve to be affected.

4.c.2. Technology Technological innovations allow businesses to increase the productivity of their existing resources. As new technology is adopted, the amount of output that can be produced by each unit of input increases, moving the aggregate supply curve to the right. For example, personal computers and word-processing software have allowed secretaries to produce much more output in a day than typewriters allowed.

4.c.3. Expectations To understand how expectations can affect aggregate supply, consider the case of labor contracts. Manufacturing workers typically contract for a nominal wage based on what they and their employers expect the future level of prices to be. Because wages typically are set for at least a year, any unexpected increase in the price level during the year lowers real wages. Firms receive higher prices for their output, but the cost of labor stays the same. So profits and production go up.

If wages rise in anticipation of higher prices but prices do not go up, the cost of labor rises. Higher real wages caused by expectations of higher prices reduce current profits and production, moving the aggregate supply curve to the left. Other things being equal, anticipated higher prices cause aggregate supply to decrease; conversely, anticipated lower prices cause aggregate supply to increase. In this sense, expectations of price-level changes that shift aggregate supply actually bring about price-level changes.

4.c.4. Economic Growth: Long-Run Aggregate Supply Shifts The vertical long-run aggregate supply curve, as shown in Figure 11, does not mean that the economy is forever fixed at the current level of potential real gross domestic product. Over time, as new technologies are developed and the quantity and quality of resources increase, potential output also increases, shifting both the short- and long-run aggregate supply curves to the right. Figure 14 shows long-run economic growth by the shift in the aggregate supply curve from $LRAS$ to $LRAS_1$. The movement of the long-run aggregate supply curve to the right reflects the increase in potential real GDP from Y_p to Y_{p1}. Even though the price level has no effect on the level of output in the long run, changes in the determinants of the supply of real output in the economy do.

RECAP

1. The aggregate supply curve shows the quantity of output (real GDP) produced at different price levels.

2. The aggregate supply curve slopes up because, everything else held constant, higher prices increase producers' profits, creating an incentive to increase output.

3. The aggregate supply curve shifts with changes in resource prices, technology, and expectations. These are nonprice determinants of aggregate supply.

Figure 14
Shifting the Long-Run Aggregate Supply Curve
Changes in technology and the availability and quality of resources can shift the *LRAS* curve. For instance, a new technology that increases productivity would move the curve to the right, from *LRAS* to *LRAS₁*.

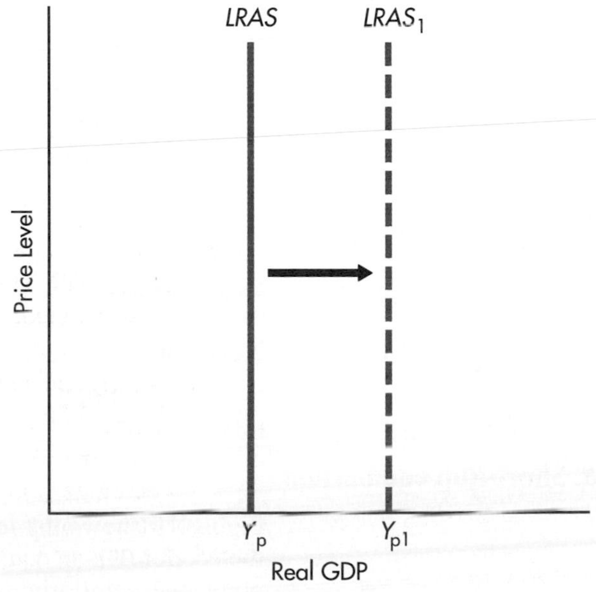

ECONOMIC INSIGHT

OPEC and Aggregate Supply

In 1973 and 1974, and again in 1979 and 1980, the Organization of Petroleum Exporting Countries (OPEC) reduced the supply of oil, driving the price of oil up dramatically. For example, the price of Saudi Arabian crude oil more than tripled between 1973 and 1974, and more than doubled between 1979 and 1980. Researchers estimate that the rapid jump in oil prices reduced output by 17 percent in Japan, by 7 percent in the United States, and by 1.9 percent in Germany.*

Oil is an important resource in many industries. When the price of oil increases due to restricted oil output, aggregate supply falls. You can see this in the graph. When the price of oil goes up, the aggregate supply curve falls from AS_1 to AS_2. When aggregate supply falls, the equilibrium level of real GDP (the intersection of the AS curve and the AD curve) falls from Y_1 to Y_2.

Higher oil prices due to restricted oil output would not only decrease short-run aggregate supply and current equilibrium real GDP, as shown in the figure, but also

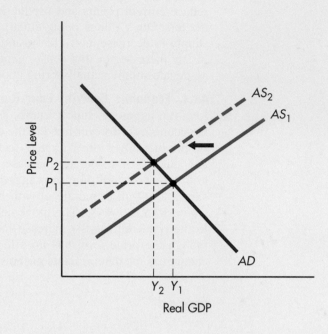

potential equilibrium income at the natural rate of unemployment. Unless other factors change to contribute to economic growth, the higher resource (oil) price reduces the productive capacity of the economy.

*These estimates were taken from "Energy Price Shocks, Aggregate Supply, and Monetary Policy: The Theory and the International Evidence," Robert H. Rasche and John A. Tatom, in Karl Brunner and Allan H. Meltzer, eds., *Carnegie-Rochester Conference Series on Public Policy* 14 (Spring 1981): pp. 9–93.

4. The short-run aggregate supply curve is upward-sloping, showing that increases in production are accompanied by higher prices.

5. The long-run aggregate supply curve is vertical at potential real GDP because, eventually, wages and the costs of other resources adjust fully to price-level changes.

5. AGGREGATE DEMAND AND SUPPLY EQUILIBRIUM

Now that we have defined the aggregate demand and aggregate supply curves separately, we can put them together to determine the equilibrium level of price and real GDP.

5.a. Short-Run Equilibrium

Figure 15 shows the level of equilibrium in a hypothetical economy. Initially the economy is in equilibrium at point 1, where AD_1 and AS_1 intersect. At this point, the equilibrium price is P_1 and the equilibrium real GDP is $500. At price P_1, the amount of output demanded is equal to the amount supplied. Suppose aggregate demand increases from AD_1 to AD_2. In the short run,

Figure 15
Aggregate Demand and Supply Equilibrium
The equilibrium level of price and real GDP is at the intersection of the AD and AS curves. Initially equilibrium occurs at point 1, where the AD_1 and AS_1 curves intersect. Here the price level is P_1 and real GDP is $500. If aggregate demand increases, moving from AD_1 to AD_2, in the short run there is a new equilibrium at point 2, where AD_2 intersects AS_1. The price level rises to P_2, and the equilibrium level of real GDP increases to $600. Over time, as the costs of wages and other resources rise in response to higher prices, aggregate supply falls, moving AS_1 to AS_2. Final equilibrium occurs at point 3, where the AS_2 curve intersects the AD_2 curve. The price level rises to P_3, but the equilibrium level of real GDP returns to its initial level, $500. In the long run, there is no relationship between prices and the equilibrium level of real GDP because the costs of resources adjust to changes in the level of prices.

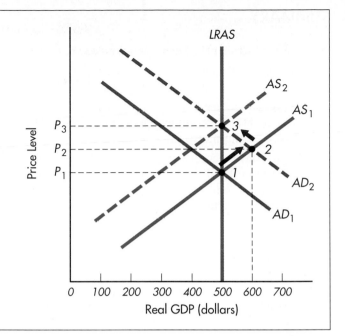

aggregate supply does not change, so the new equilibrium is at the intersection of the new aggregate demand curve, AD_2, and the same aggregate supply curve, AS_1, at point 2. The new equilibrium price is P_2, and the new equilibrium real GDP is $600. Note that in the short run, the equilibrium point on the short-run aggregate supply curve can lie to the right of the long-run aggregate supply curve (*LRAS*). This is because the *LRAS* represents the potential level of real GDP, not the capacity level. It is possible to produce more than the potential level of real GDP in the short run when the unemployment rate falls below the natural rate of unemployment.

5.b. Long-Run Equilibrium

Point 2 is not a permanent equilibrium because aggregate supply decreases to AS_2 once the costs of production rise in response to higher prices. Final equilibrium is at point 3, where the price level is P_3 and real GDP is $500. Notice that equilibrium here is the same as the initial equilibrium at point 1. Points 1 and 3 both lie along the long-run aggregate supply curve (*LRAS*). The initial shock to or change in the economy was an increase in aggregate demand. The change in aggregate expenditures initially led to higher output and higher prices. Over time, however, as resource costs rise and profit falls, output falls back to its original value.

We are not saying that the level of output never changes. The long-run aggregate supply curve shifts as technology changes and new supplies of resources are obtained. But the output change that results from a change in aggregate demand is a temporary, or short-run, phenomenon. The price level eventually adjusts, and output eventually returns to the potential level.

RECAP

1. The equilibrium level of price and real GDP is at the point where the aggregate demand and aggregate supply curves intersect.

2. In the short run, a shift in aggregate demand establishes a temporary equilibrium along the short-run aggregate supply curve.

3. In the long run, the short-run aggregate supply curve shifts so that changes in aggregate demand only affect the price level, not the equilibrium level of output or real GDP.

SUMMARY

■■ **What factors affect aggregate demand?**

1. Aggregate demand is the relation between aggregate expenditures and the price level.

2. Aggregate demand is the sum of consumption, investment, government spending, and net exports at alternative price levels.

3. Aggregate expenditures change with changes in the price level because of the wealth effect, the interest rate effect, and the international trade effect. These cause a movement along the *AD* curve.

■■ **What causes the aggregate demand curve to shift?**

4. The aggregate demand (*AD*) curve shows the level of expenditures for real GDP at different price levels.

5. Because expenditures and prices move in opposite directions, the *AD* curve is negatively sloped.

6. The nonprice determinants of aggregate demand include expectations, foreign income and price levels, and government policy.

■■ **What factors affect aggregate supply?**

7. The aggregate supply curve shows the quantity of real GDP produced at different price levels.

■■ **Why does the short-run aggregate supply curve become steeper as real GDP increases?**

8. As real GDP rises and the economy pushes closer to capacity output, the level of prices must rise to induce increased production.

■■ **Why is the long-run aggregate supply curve vertical?**

9. The long-run aggregate supply curve is a vertical line at the potential level of real GDP. The shape of the curve indicates that there is no effect of higher prices on output when an economy is producing at potential real GDP.

■■ **What causes the aggregate supply curve to shift?**

10. The nonprice determinants of aggregate supply are resource prices, technology, and expectations.

■■ **What determines the equilibrium price level and real GDP?**

11. The equilibrium level of price and real GDP is at the intersection of the aggregate demand and aggregate supply curves.

12. In the short run, a shift in aggregate demand establishes a new, but temporary, equilibrium along the short-run aggregate supply curve.

13. In the long run, the short-run aggregate supply curve shifts so that changes in aggregate demand determine the price level, not the equilibrium level of output or real GDP.

KEY TERMS

wealth effect

interest rate effect

international trade effect

aggregate demand curve

aggregate supply curve

long-run aggregate supply curve (*LRAS*)

EXERCISES

1. How is the aggregate demand curve different from the demand curve for a single good, like hamburgers?

2. Why does the aggregate demand curve slope down? Give real-world examples of the three effects that explain the slope of the curve.

3. How does an increase in foreign income affect domestic aggregate expenditures and demand? Draw a diagram to illustrate your answer.

4. How does a decrease in foreign price levels affect domestic aggregate expenditures and demand? Draw a diagram to illustrate your answer.

5. How is the aggregate supply curve different from the supply curve for a single good, like pizza?

6. There are several determinants of aggregate supply that can cause the aggregate supply curve to shift.
    a. Describe those determinants and give an example of a change in each.
    b. Draw and label an aggregate supply diagram that illustrates the effect of the change in each determinant.

7. Draw a short-run aggregate supply curve that gets steeper as real GDP rises.
    a. Explain why the curve has this shape.
    b. Now draw a long-run aggregate supply curve that intersects a short-run AS curve. What is the relationship between short-run AS and long-run AS?

8. Draw and carefully label an aggregate demand and supply diagram with initial equilibrium at P_0 and Y_0.
    a. Using the diagram, explain what happens when aggregate demand falls.
    b. How is the short run different from the long run?

9. Draw an aggregate demand and supply diagram for Japan. In the diagram, show how each of the following affects aggregate demand and supply.
    a. U.S. gross domestic product falls.
    b. The level of prices in Korea falls.
    c. Labor receives a large wage increase.
    d. Economists predict higher prices next year.

10. If the long-run aggregate supply curve gives the level of potential real GDP, how can the short-run aggregate supply curve ever lie to the right of the long-run aggregate supply curve?

11. What will happen to the equilibrium price level and real GDP if:
    a. aggregate demand and aggregate supply both increase?
    b. aggregate demand increases and aggregate supply decreases?
    c. aggregate demand and aggregate supply both decrease?
    d. aggregate demand decreases and aggregate supply increases?

12. During the Great Depression, the U.S. economy experienced a falling price level and declining real GDP. Using an aggregate demand and aggregate supply diagram, illustrate and explain how this could occur.

13. Suppose aggregate demand increases, causing an increase in real GDP but no change in the price level. Using an aggregate demand and aggregate supply diagram, illustrate and explain how this could occur.

14. Suppose aggregate demand increases, causing an increase in the price level but no change in real GDP. Using an aggregate demand and aggregate supply diagram, illustrate and explain how this could occur.

15. Use an aggregate demand and aggregate supply diagram to illustrate and explain how each of the following will affect the equilibrium price level and real GDP:
    a. Consumers expect a recession.
    b. Foreign income rises.
    c. Foreign price levels fall.
    d. Government spending increases.
    e. Workers expect higher future inflation and negotiate higher wages now.
    f. Technological improvements increase productivity.

🖥 INTERNET EXERCISE

In this chapter, we learned how changes in aggregate demand (*AD*) and aggregate supply (*AS*) are associated with business cycle fluctuations. An increase (decrease) in *AD* should be expansionary (contractionary) with rising (falling) GDP and prices. An increase (decrease) in *AS* should be expansionary (contractionary) with rising (falling) GDP and falling (rising) prices. The length of expansions and contractions is determined by the size and duration of shifts in *AD* and *AS*. We can see the history of U.S. business cycle fluctuations by going to the Boyes/Melvin *Fundamentals of Economics* Web site at **http://www.hmco.com/college/** and clicking on the Internet Exercise link for Chapter 12. Now answer the questions that appear on the Boyes/Melvin Web site.

13

Fiscal Policy

1. How can fiscal policy eliminate a GDP gap?

2. How has U.S. fiscal policy changed over time?

3. What are the effects of budget deficits?

4. How does fiscal policy differ across countries?

Macroeconomics plays a key role in national politics. When Jimmy Carter ran for the presidency against Gerald Ford in 1976, he created a "misery index" to measure the state of the economy. The index was the sum of the inflation rate and the unemployment rate, and Carter showed that it had risen during Ford's term in office. When Ronald Reagan challenged Carter in 1980, he used the misery index to show that inflation and unemployment had gone up during the Carter years. The implication is that presidents are responsible for the condition of the economy. If the inflation rate or the unemployment rate is relatively high coming into an election year, incumbent presidents are open to criticism by their opponents. For instance, many people believe that George Bush was defeated by Bill Clinton in 1992 because of the country's economic conditions. Clinton emphasized the recession that began in 1990—a recession that was not announced as having ended in March 1991 until after the election. As a result, Clinton's campaign made economic growth a focus of its attacks on Bush. Then in 1996, a healthy economy helped Bill Clinton defeat Bob Dole. This is more than campaign rhetoric, however. By law the government *is* responsible for the macroeconomic health of the nation. The Employment Act of 1946 states:

"It is the continuing policy and responsibility of the Federal Government to use all practical means consistent with its needs and obligations and other essential considerations of national policy to coordinate and utilize all its plans, functions, and resources for the purpose of creating and maintaining, in a manner calculated to foster and promote free competitive enterprise and the general welfare conditions under which there will be afforded useful employment opportunities, including self-employment for those able, willing, and seeking to work, and to promote maximum employment, production, and purchasing power."

Fiscal policy is one tool that government uses to guide the economy along an expansionary path. In this chapter we examine the role of fiscal policy—government spending and taxation—in determining the equilibrium level of income. Then we review the budget process and the history of fiscal policy in the United States. Finally we describe the difference in fiscal policy between industrial and developing countries. ■

1. FISCAL POLICY AND AGGREGATE DEMAND

The GDP gap is the difference between potential real GDP and the equilibrium level of real GDP. If the government wants to close the GDP gap so that the equilibrium level of real GDP reaches its potential, it must use fiscal policy to alter aggregate expenditures and cause the aggregate demand curve to shift.

Fiscal policy is the government's policy with respect to spending and taxation. Since aggregate demand includes consumption, investment, net exports, and government spending, government spending on goods and services affects the level of aggregate demand directly. Taxes affect aggregate demand indirectly by changing the disposable income of households, which alters consumption.

1.a. Shifting the Aggregate Demand Curve

Changes in government spending and taxes shift the aggregate demand curve. Remember that the aggregate demand curve represents combinations of equilibrium aggregate expenditures and alternative price levels. An increase in

Preview

government spending or a decrease in taxes raises the level of expenditures at every level of prices and moves the aggregate demand curve to the right.

Figure 1 shows an increase in aggregate demand that would result from an increase in government spending or a decrease in taxes. Only if the aggregate supply curve is horizontal do prices remain fixed as aggregate demand increases. In Figure 1(a), equilibrium occurs along the horizontal segment (the Keynesian region) of the AS curve. If government spending increases and the price level remains constant, aggregate demand shifts from AD to AD_1; it increases by the horizontal distance from point A to point B. Once aggregate demand shifts, the AD_1 and AS curves intersect at potential real GDP, Y_p.

But Figure 1(a) is not realistic. The AS curve is not likely to be horizontal all the way to the level of potential real GDP; it should begin sloping up well before Y_p. And once the economy reaches the capacity level of output, the AS curve should become a vertical line, as shown in Figure 1(b).

If the AS curve slopes up before reaching the potential real GDP level, as it does in part (b) of the figure, expenditures have to go up by more than the amount suggested in part (a) for the economy to reach Y_p. Why? Because when prices rise, the effect of spending on real GDP is reduced. This effect is shown in Figure 1(b). To increase the equilibrium level of real GDP from Y_e to Y_p, aggregate demand must shift by the amount from point A to C, a larger increase than that shown in Figure 1(a), where the price level is fixed.

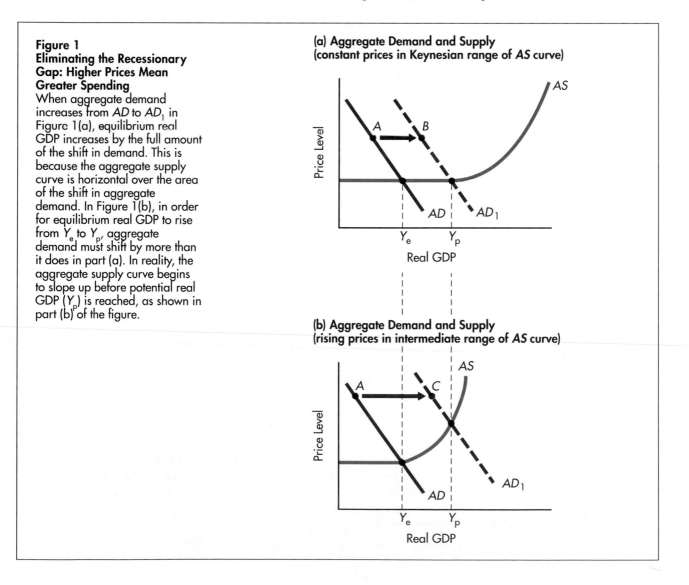

Figure 1
Eliminating the Recessionary Gap: Higher Prices Mean Greater Spending
When aggregate demand increases from AD to AD_1 in Figure 1(a), equilibrium real GDP increases by the full amount of the shift in demand. This is because the aggregate supply curve is horizontal over the area of the shift in aggregate demand. In Figure 1(b), in order for equilibrium real GDP to rise from Y_e to Y_p, aggregate demand must shift by more than it does in part (a). In reality, the aggregate supply curve begins to slope up before potential real GDP (Y_p) is reached, as shown in part (b) of the figure.

(a) Aggregate Demand and Supply (constant prices in Keynesian range of AS curve)

(b) Aggregate Demand and Supply (rising prices in intermediate range of AS curve)

1.b. Multiplier Effects

Changes in government spending may have an effect on real GDP that is a multiple of the original change in government spending; a $1 change in government spending may increase real GDP by more than $1. This is because the original $1 of expenditure is spent over and over again in the economy as it passes from person to person. The government spending multiplier measures the multiple by which an increase in government spending increases real GDP. Similarly, a change in taxes may have an effect on real GDP that is a multiple of the original change in taxes.

If the price level rises as real GDP increases, the multiplier effects of any given change in aggregate demand are smaller than they would be if the price level remains constant. In addition to changes in the price level modifying the effect of government spending and taxes on real GDP, there are other factors that affect how much real GDP will change following a change in government spending. One such factor is how the government pays for, or finances, its spending.

Government spending must be financed by some combination of taxing, borrowing, or creating money:

government spending = taxes + change in government debt
+ change in government-issued money

In Chapter 15 we discuss the effect of financing government spending by creating money. As you will see, this source of government financing is relied on heavily in some developing countries. Here we talk about the financing problem relevant for industrial countries: how taxes and government debt can modify the expansionary effect of government spending on national income.

1.c. Government Spending Financed by Tax Increases

Suppose that government spending rises by $100 billion and that this expenditure is financed by a tax increase of $100 billion. Such a "balanced-budget" change in fiscal policy will cause equilibrium real GDP to rise. This is because government spending increases aggregate expenditures directly, but higher taxes lower aggregate expenditures indirectly through consumption spending. For instance, if taxes increase $100, consumers will not cut their spending by $100, but by some fraction, say 9/10, of the increase. If consumers spend 90 percent of a change in their disposable income, then a tax increase of $100 would lower consumption by $90. So the net effect of raising government spending and taxes by the same amount is an increase in aggregate demand, illustrated in Figure 2 as the shift from AD to AD_1. However, it may be incorrect to assume that the only thing that changes is aggregate demand. An increase in taxes may also affect aggregate supply.

Aggregate supply measures the output that producers offer for sale at different levels of prices. When taxes go up, workers have less incentive to work because their after-tax income is lower. The cost of taking a day off or extending a vacation for a few extra days is less than it is when taxes are lower and after-tax income is higher. When taxes go up, then, output can fall, causing the aggregate supply curve to shift to the left. Such supply-side effects of taxes have been emphasized by the so-called supply-side economists.

Figure 2 shows the possible effects of an increase in government spending financed by taxes. The economy is initially in equilibrium at point A, with prices at P_1 and real GDP at Y_1. The increase in government spending shifts the aggregate demand curve from AD to AD_1. If this was the only change, the economy would be in equilibrium at point B. But if the increase in taxes reduces output, the aggregate supply curve moves back from AS to AS_1, and output does not expand all the way to Y_p. The decrease in aggregate supply creates a new equilibrium at point C. Here real GDP is at Y_2 (less than Y_p) and the price level is P_3 (higher than P_2).

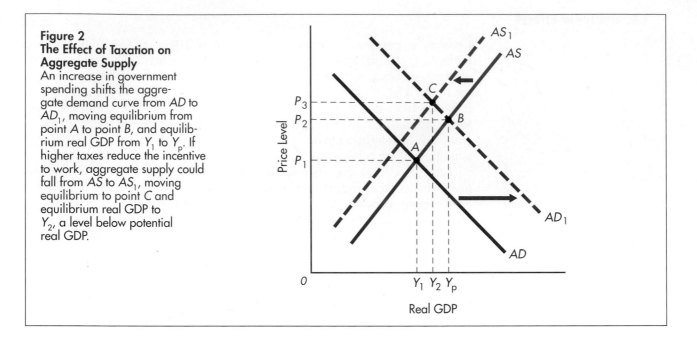

Figure 2
The Effect of Taxation on Aggregate Supply
An increase in government spending shifts the aggregate demand curve from AD to AD_1, moving equilibrium from point A to point B, and equilibrium real GDP from Y_1 to Y_p. If higher taxes reduce the incentive to work, aggregate supply could fall from AS to AS_1, moving equilibrium to point C and equilibrium real GDP to Y_2, a level below potential real GDP.

The standard analysis of government spending and taxation assumes that aggregate supply is not affected by the change in fiscal policy, leading us to expect a greater change in real GDP than may actually occur. If tax changes do affect aggregate supply, the expansionary effects of government spending financed by tax increases are moderated. The actual magnitude of the effect is the subject of debate among economists. Most argue that the evidence in the United States indicates that tax increases have a fairly small effect on aggregate supply.

1.d. Government Spending Financed by Borrowing

The standard multiplier analysis of government spending does not differentiate among the different methods of financing that spending. Yet you just saw how taxation can offset at least part of the expansionary effect of higher government spending. Borrowing to finance government spending can also limit the increase in aggregate demand.

A government borrows funds by selling bonds to the public. These bonds represent debt that must be repaid at a future date. Debt is, in a way, a kind of substitute for current taxes. Instead of increasing current taxes to finance higher spending, the government borrows the savings of households and businesses. Of course the debt will mature and have to be repaid. This means that taxes will have to be higher in the future in order to provide the government with the funds to pay off the debt.

Current government borrowing, then, implies higher future taxes. This can limit the expansionary effect of increased government spending. If households and businesses take higher future taxes into account, they tend to save more today so that they will be able to pay those taxes in the future. And as saving today increases, consumption today falls.

1.e. Crowding Out

■ **crowding out:**
a drop in consumption or investment spending caused by government spending

Expansionary fiscal policy can crowd out private-sector spending; that is, an increase in government spending can reduce consumption and investment. **Crowding out** is usually discussed in the context of government spending financed by borrowing rather than by taxing. Though we have just seen how future taxes can cause consumption to fall today, investment can also be affected. Increases in government borrowing drive up interest rates. As interest rates go up, investment falls. This sort of indirect crowding out works

Many government expenditures are unrelated to current economic conditions. For instance, the provision of national defense, a legal system, and police and fire protection are all cases where government expenditures would not typically fluctuate with the business cycle. This Canadian mountie serving in Banff National Park in Alberta is employed through booms and recessions in the Canadian economy. Although macroeconomists focus typically on the discretionary elements of fiscal policy that may be altered to combat business cycles, the nondiscretionary elements account for the bulk of governments' budgets.

through the bond market. The U.S. government borrows by selling Treasury bonds or bills. Because the government is not a profit-making institution, it does not have to earn a profitable return from the money it raises by selling bonds. A corporation does, however. When interest rates rise, fewer corporations offer new bonds to raise investment funds because the cost of repaying the bond debt may exceed the rate of return on the investment.

Crowding out is important in principle, but economists have never demonstrated conclusively that its effects can substantially alter spending in the private sector. Still, you should be aware of the possibility to understand the potential shortcomings of changes in government spending and taxation.

RECAP

1. Fiscal policy refers to government spending and taxation.
2. By increasing spending or cutting taxes, a government can close the GDP gap.
3. If government spending and taxes increase by the same amount, equilibrium real GDP rises.
4. If a tax increase affects aggregate supply, then a balanced-budget change in fiscal policy will have a smaller expansionary effect on equilibrium real GDP than otherwise.
5. Current government borrowing reduces current spending in the private sector if people increase current saving in order to pay future tax liabilities.
6. Increased government borrowing can crowd private borrowers out of the bond market so that investment falls.

2. FISCAL POLICY IN THE UNITED STATES

Our discussion of fiscal policy assumes that policy is made at the federal level. In the modern economy this is a reasonable assumption. This was not the case before the 1930s, however. Before the Depression, the federal government limited its activities largely to national defense and foreign policy, and left other areas of government policy to the individual states. With the growth of the importance of the federal government in fiscal policy has come a growth in the role of the federal budget process.

2.a. The Budget Process

Fiscal policy in the United States is the product of a complex process that involves both the executive and legislative branches of government (Figure 3). The fiscal year for the U.S. government begins October 1 of one year and ends September 30 of the next. The budget process begins each spring, when the president directs the federal agencies to prepare their budgets for the fiscal year that starts almost eighteen months later. The agencies submit their budget requests to the Office of Management and Budget (OMB) by early September. The OMB reviews and modifies each agency's request and consolidates all of the proposals into a budget that the president presents to Congress in January.

Once Congress receives the president's budget, the Congressional Budget Office (CBO) studies it and committees modify it before funds are appropriated. The budget is evaluated in Budget Committee hearings in both the House of Representatives and the Senate. In addition, the CBO reports to Congress on the validity of the economic assumptions made in the president's budget. A budget resolution is passed by April 15 that sets out major expenditures and estimated revenues. (Revenues are estimated because future tax payments can never be known exactly.) The resolution is followed by *reconciliation*, a process in which each committee of Congress must coordinate relevant tax and spending decisions. Once the reconciliation process is completed, funds are appropriated. The process is supposed to end before Congress recesses for the summer, at the end of June. When talking about the federal budget, the monetary amounts of various categories of expenditures are so huge that they are often difficult to comprehend. But if one were to divide up the annual budget by the number of individual taxpayers, you'd

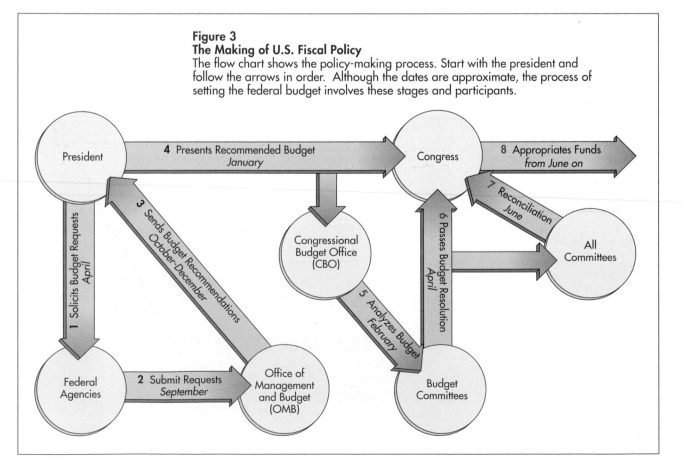

Figure 3
The Making of U.S. Fiscal Policy
The flow chart shows the policy-making process. Start with the president and follow the arrows in order. Although the dates are approximate, the process of setting the federal budget involves these stages and participants.

come up with an average individual statement that might make more sense, as shown in the Economic Insight "The Taxpayer's Federal Government Credit Card Statement."

The federal budget is determined as much by politics as economics. Politicians respond to different groups of voters by supporting different government programs regardless of the needed fiscal policy. It is the political response to constituents that tends to drive up federal budget deficits (the difference between government expenditures and tax revenues), not the need for expansionary fiscal policy. As a result, deficits have become commonplace.

2.b. The Historical Record

The U.S. government has grown dramatically since the early part of the century. Figure 4 shows federal revenues and expenditures over time. Figure 5 places the growth of government in perspective by plotting U.S. government spending as a percentage of gross domestic product over time. Before the Great Depression, federal spending was approximately 3 percent of the GDP; by the end of the Depression, it had risen to almost 10 percent. The ratio of spending to GDP reached its peak during World War II, when federal spending hit 45 percent of the GDP. After the war, the ratio fell dramatically and then slowly increased to a little more than 20 percent today.

Fiscal policy has two components: discretionary fiscal policy and automatic stabilizers. **Discretionary fiscal policy** refers to changes in government spending and taxation aimed at achieving a policy goal. **Automatic stabilizers** are elements of fiscal policy that automatically change in value as national income changes. Figures 4 and 5 suggest that government spending is dominated by growth over time. But there is no indication here of discretionary changes in fiscal policy, changes in government spending and taxation aimed at meeting specific policy goals. Perhaps a better way to evaluate the fiscal policy record is in terms of the budget deficit. Government expenditures can rise, but the effect on aggregate demand could be offset by a simultaneous increase in taxes, so that there is no expansionary effect on the equilibrium level of national income. By looking at the deficit, we see the combined spending and tax policy results that are missing if only government expenditures are considered.

■ **discretionary fiscal policy:** changes in government spending and taxation aimed at achieving a policy goal

■ **automatic stabilizer:** an element of fiscal policy that changes automatically as income changes

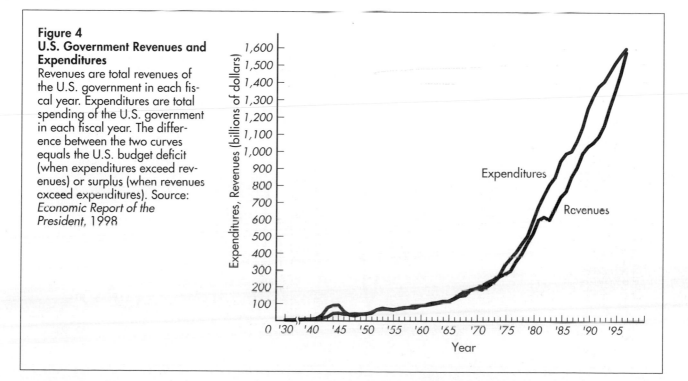

Figure 4
U.S. Government Revenues and Expenditures
Revenues are total revenues of the U.S. government in each fiscal year. Expenditures are total spending of the U.S. government in each fiscal year. The difference between the two curves equals the U.S. budget deficit (when expenditures exceed revenues) or surplus (when revenues exceed expenditures). Source: *Economic Report of the President, 1998*

Figure 5
U.S. Government Expenditures as a Percentage of Gross Domestic Product

U.S. federal government spending as a percentage of the GDP reached a high of 45 percent in 1943 and 1944. Discounting wartime spending and cutbacks after the war, you can see the upward trend in U.S. government spending, which has constituted a larger and larger share of the GDP over time.

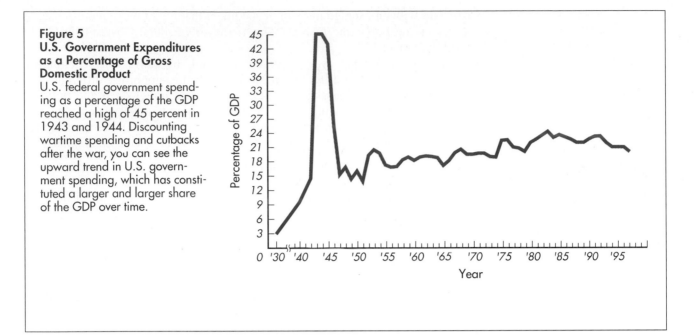

Figure 6 illustrates the pattern of the U.S. federal deficit and the deficit as a percentage of GDP over time. Part (a) shows that the United States ran close to a balanced budget for much of the 1950s and 1960s. There were large deficits associated with financing World War II, and then large deficits resulting from fiscal policy decisions in the 1970s, 1980s, and 1990s. Figure 6(b) shows that the deficit as a percentage of GDP was much larger during World War II than in recent years.

The deficit increase in the mid-1970s was a product of a recession that cut the growth of tax revenues. Historically, aside from wartime, budget deficits increase the most during recessions. When real GDP falls, tax revenues go down and government spending on unemployment and welfare benefits goes

Figure 6
The U.S. Deficit

As part (a) shows, since 1940 the U.S. government has rarely shown a surplus. For much of the 1950s and 1960s, the United States was close to a balanced budget. Part (b) shows the federal deficit as a percentage of GDP. The deficits during the 1950s and 1960s generally were small. The early 1980s were a time of rapid growth in the federal budget deficit, and this is reflected in the growth of the deficit as a percentage of GDP.

(a) Federal Surplus (+) or Deficit (–)

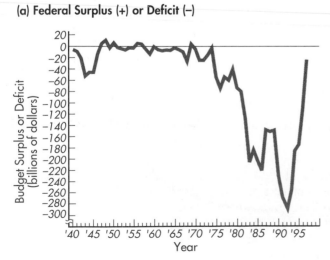

(b) Federal Deficit as a Percent of GDP (absolute value of deficit)

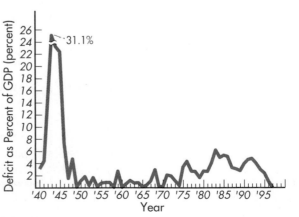

The Taxpayer's Federal Government Credit Card Statement

Suppose the U.S. government's expenditures and revenues were accounted for annually to each individual income tax payer like a credit card statement. For 1997, the statement would look like the following.

Statement for 1997 budget year		
Previous balance (your average taxpayer share of the beginning-of-year national debt)		**$45,170.01**
New purchases during the year (your average taxpayer share)		
Social security	$3,217.09	
National defense	2,327.81	
Income security	2,083.70	
Medicare	1,691.37	
Commerce and housing credit	−78.47	
Health	1,115.95	
Education, training, and employment	444.64	
Veterans' benefits and services	348.74	
Transportation	340.02	
Natural resources and environment	200.52	
Science, space, and technology	148.21	
International affairs	130.78	
Agriculture	87.18	
Administration of justice	183.09	
General government	113.34	
Community and regional development	113.34	
Energy	17.43	
Payments received—Thank you (your average taxpayer share)		
Individual income taxes		$5,867.48
Corporate income taxes		1,534.44
Social security taxes		4,673.06
Other		1,054.43
Finance charge (your average taxpayer share of net interest on the national debt)	**$2,153.44**	
New balance due (your average taxpayer share of the end of-year national debt)		**$46,678.78**

up. These are examples of automatic stabilizers in action. As income falls, taxes fall and personal benefit payments rise to partially offset the effect of the drop in income. The rapid growth of the deficit in the 1980s involved more than the recessions in 1980 and 1982, however. The economy grew rapidly after the 1982 recession ended, but so did the fiscal deficit. The increase in the deficit was the product of a rapid increase in government spending to fund new programs and enlarge existing programs while taxes were held constant. The reduction in the deficit in the late 1990s was the result of strong economic growth generating surprisingly large tax revenue gains combined with only moderate government spending increases.

2.c. Deficits and the National Debt

The recent increase in the federal deficit has led many observers to question whether a deficit can harm the economy. Figure 6 shows how the fiscal deficit has changed over time. One major implication of a large deficit is the resulting increase in the national debt, the total stock of government bonds outstanding. Table 1 lists data on the debt of the United States. The total debt more than doubled between 1980 and 1986. Column 3 shows debt as a percentage of GDP. In recent years, the debt has been rising as a percent of GDP. During World War II, the debt was greater than the GDP for five years. Despite the talk of "unprecedented" federal deficits in recent years, clearly the ratio of the debt to GDP was by no means unprecedented.

We have not yet answered the question of whether deficits are bad. To do so, we have to consider their potential effects.

2.c.1. Deficits, Interest Rates, and Investment Because government deficits mean government borrowing and debt, many economists argue that deficits raise interest rates. Increased government borrowing raises interest rates, which in turn can depress investment. (Remember that as interest rates rise, the rate of return on investment drops, along with the incentive to invest.) What happens when government borrowing crowds out private investment? Lower investment means fewer capital goods in the future. So deficits lower the level of output in the economy both today and in the future. In this sense, deficits are potentially bad.

2.c.2. Deficits and International Trade If government deficits raise real interest rates (the nominal interest rate minus the expected inflation rate), they also may have an effect on international trade. A higher real return on U.S. securities makes those securities more attractive to foreign investors. As the foreign demand for U.S. securities increases, so does the demand for U.S. dollars in exchange for Japanese yen, British pounds, and other foreign currencies. As the demand for dollars increases, the dollar *appreciates* in value on the foreign exchange market. This means that the dollar becomes more expensive to foreigners while foreign currency becomes cheaper to U.S. residents. This kind of change in the exchange rate encourages U.S. residents to buy more foreign goods, and foreign residents to buy fewer U.S. goods. Ultimately, then, as deficits and government debt increase, U.S. net exports fall. Many economists believe that the growing fiscal deficits of the 1980s were responsible for the record decline in U.S. net exports during that period.

The U.S. federal budget deficit rose from $73.8 billion in 1980 to $212.3 billion in 1985. During this time, the dollar appreciated in value from 1.95 German marks per dollar to 3.32 marks per dollar and from 203 Japanese yen per dollar to 260 yen per dollar. These changes in the dollar exchange rate caused U.S. goods to rise in price to foreign buyers. For instance, a $1,000 IBM personal computer would sell for 1,950 German marks at the exchange rate of 1.95 marks per dollar. But at the rate of 3.32 marks per dollar, the $1,000 computer would sell for 3,320 marks. Furthermore, foreign currencies became cheaper to U.S. residents, making foreign goods cheaper in dollars. In 1980, one German mark sold for $.51. In 1985, one mark sold for $.30. At these prices, a Volkswagen wheel that sells for 100 marks would have changed in dollar price from $51 to $30 as the exchange rate changed. The combination of the dollar price of U.S. imports falling and the foreign currency price of U.S. exports rising caused U.S. net exports to fall dramatically at the same time that the fiscal deficit rose dramatically. Such foreign trade effects are another potentially bad effect of deficits.

2.c.3. Interest Payments on the National Debt

The national debt is the stock of government bonds outstanding. It is the product of past and current budget deficits. As the size of the debt increases, the interest that must be paid on the debt tends to rise. Column 4 of Table 1 lists the amount of interest paid on the debt; column 5 lists the interest as a percentage of government expenditures. The numbers in both columns have risen steadily over time and only recently started to level off.

The steady increase in the interest cost of the national debt is an aspect of fiscal deficits that worries some people. However, to the extent that U.S. citizens hold government bonds, we owe the debt to ourselves. The tax liability of funding the interest payments is offset by the interest income bondholders earn. In this case there is no net change in national wealth when the national debt changes.

Of course, we do not owe the national debt just to ourselves. The United States is the world's largest national financial market, and many U.S. securities, including government bonds, are held by foreign residents. In the late 1990s, foreign holdings of the U.S. national debt amounted to about 30 percent of the outstanding debt. Because the tax liability for paying the interest on the debt falls on U.S. taxpayers, the greater the payments made to foreigners, the lower the wealth of U.S. residents, other things being equal.

Other things are not equal, however. To understand the real impact of foreign holdings on the economy, we have to evaluate what the economy would have been like if the debt had not been sold to foreign investors. If the foreign savings placed in U.S. bonds allowed the United States to increase investment and its productive capacity beyond what would have been possible in the absence of foreign lending, then the country could very well be better off for selling government bonds to foreigners. The presence of foreign funds may

TABLE 1
Debt of the U.S. Government (dollar amounts in billions)

(1) Year	(2) Total Debt	(3) Debt/GDP (percent)	(4) Net Interest	(5) Interest/Government Spending (percent)
1958	$ 279.7	63	$ 5.6	6.8
1960	290.5	57	6.9	7.5
1962	302.9	55	6.9	6.5
1964	316.1	50	8.2	6.9
1966	328.5	44	9.4	7.0
1968	368.7	43	11.1	6.2
1970	380.9	39	14.4	7.4
1972	435.9	38	15.5	6.7
1974	483.9	34	21.4	8.0
1976	629.0	37	26.7	7.3
1978	776.6	36	35.4	7.9
1980	909.1	34	52.5	9.1
1982	1,137.3	36	85.0	11.6
1984	1,564.7	42	111.1	13.2
1986	2,120.6	50	136.0	13.7
1988	2,601.3	54	151.8	14.3
1990	3,206.6	59	184.2	14.7
1992	4,002.1	68	199.4	14.4
1994	4,643.7	70	203.0	13.9
1996	5,181.9	69	241.1	15.5

keep interest rates lower than they would otherwise be, preventing the substantial crowding out associated with an increase in the national debt.

So while deficits are potentially bad due to the crowding out of investment, larger trade deficits with the rest of the world, and greater interest costs of the debt, we cannot generally say that all deficits are bad. It depends on what benefit the deficit provides. If the deficit spending allowed for greater productivity than would have occurred otherwise, the benefits may outweigh the costs.

2.d. Automatic Stabilizers

We have largely been talking about discretionary fiscal policy, the changes in government spending and taxing that policymakers make consciously. *Automatic stabilizers* are the elements of fiscal policy that change automatically as income changes. Automatic stabilizers partially offset changes in income: as income falls, automatic stabilizers increase spending; as income rises, automatic stabilizers decrease spending. Any program that responds to fluctuations in the business cycle in a way that moderates the effect of those fluctuations is an automatic stabilizer. Examples are progressive income taxes and transfer payments.

In our examples of tax changes, we have been using *lump-sum taxes*—taxes that are a flat dollar amount regardless of income. However, income taxes are determined as a percentage of income. In the United States, the federal income tax is a **progressive tax**: as income rises, so does the rate of taxation. A person with a very low income pays no income tax, while a person with a high income can pay more than a third of that income in taxes. Countries use different rates of taxation on income. Taxes can be *regressive* (the tax rate falls as income rises) or *proportional* (the tax rate is constant as income rises). But most countries, including the United States, use a progressive tax, the percentage of income paid as taxes rising with taxable income.

■ **progressive tax:**
a tax whose rate rises as income rises

Progressive income taxes act as an automatic stabilizer. As income falls, so does the average tax rate. Suppose a household earning $60,000 must pay 30 percent of its income ($18,000) in taxes, leaving 70 percent of its income ($42,000) for spending. If that household's income drops to $40,000 and the tax rate falls to 25 percent, the household has 75 percent of its income ($30,000) available for spending. But if the tax rate is 30 percent at all levels of income, the household earning $40,000 would have only 70 percent of its income ($28,000) to spend. By allowing a greater percentage of earned income to be spent, progressive taxes help offset the effect of lower income on spending.

Recall that a transfer payment is a payment to one person that is funded by taxing others. Food stamps, welfare benefits, and unemployment benefits are all government transfer payments: current taxpayers provide the funds to pay those who qualify for the programs. Transfer payments that use income to establish eligibility act as automatic stabilizers. In a recession, as income falls, more people qualify for food stamps or welfare benefits, raising the level of transfer payments.

Unemployment insurance is also an automatic stabilizer. As unemployment rises, more workers receive unemployment benefits. Unemployment benefits tend to rise in a recession and fall during an expansion. This counter-cyclical pattern of benefit payments offsets the effect of business cycle fluctuations on consumption.

RECAP

1. Fiscal policy in the United States is a product of the budget process.
2. Federal spending in the United States has grown rapidly over time, from just 3 percent of the GDP before the Great Depression to approximately 24 percent of the GDP in the early 1990s.

3. Government budget deficits can hurt the economy through their effect on interest rates and private investment, net exports, and the tax burden on current and future taxpayers.

4. Automatic stabilizers are government programs that are already in place and that respond automatically to fluctuations in the business cycle, moderating the effect of those fluctuations.

3. FISCAL POLICY IN DIFFERENT COUNTRIES

A country's fiscal policy reflects its philosophy toward government spending and taxation. In this section we present comparative data that demonstrate the variety of fiscal policies in the world.

3.a. Government Spending

Our discussion to this point has centered on U.S. fiscal policy. But fiscal policy and the role of government in the economy can be very different across countries. Government has played an increasingly larger role in the major industrial countries over time. Table 2 shows how government spending has gone up as a percentage of output in five industrial nations. In every case, government spending accounted for a larger percentage of output in 1994 than it did 100 years earlier. For instance, in 1880, government spending was only 10 percent of the GNP in the United Kingdom. By 1929 it had risen to 24 percent; and by 1994 to 40 percent.

Historically in industrial countries, the growth of government spending has been matched by growth in revenues. But in the 1960s, government spending began to grow faster than revenues, creating increasingly larger debtor nations.

Developing countries have not shown the uniform growth in government spending found in industrial countries. In fact, in some developing countries (for instance, Chile, the Dominican Republic, and Peru), government spending was a smaller percentage of GDP in 1994 than it was 20 years earlier. And we find a greater variation in the role of government in developing countries.

One important difference between the typical developed country and the typical developing country is that government plays a larger role in investment spending in the developing country. One reason for this difference is that state-owned enterprises account for a larger percentage of economic activity in developing countries than they do in developed countries. Also, developing countries usually rely more on government than the private sector to build their infrastructure—schools, roads, hospitals—than do developed countries.

TABLE 2
Share of Government Spending in GNP in Selected Industrial Countries, 1880, 1929, and 1994 (percent)

Year	France	Germany	Sweden	United Kingdom	United States
1880	15	10*	6	10	8
1929	19	31	8	24	10
1994	45	32	50	40	22

*1881

Source: Data come from *World Development Report* various issues by The World Bank.

How a government spends its money is a function of its income. Here we find differences not only between industrial and developing countries but also among developing countries. Figure 7 divides developing countries into low-income (the poorest) and middle-income (not as poor) groups. It clearly illustrates the relative importance of social welfare spending in industrial and developing countries. Although standards of living are lowest in the poorest countries, these countries do not have the resources to spend on social services (education, health, housing, social security, welfare). The industrial countries, on average, spend 58 percent of their budgets on social programs. Middle-income developing countries spend 39 percent of their budgets on social programs. Low-income countries spend only 24 percent of their budgets on these programs.

The labor forces in industrial countries are much better educated than those in developing countries. Figure 8 shows why. The figure measures the cost of educating a student for a year as a percentage of per capita GDP. On average it costs 49 percent of per capita GDP to educate a college student in an industrial country. It costs 370 percent of per capita GDP to provide a year of college education in the average developing country. In the poorest region of the world, sub-Saharan Africa, a year of college costs 800 percent of per capita GDP. Governments in the poorest countries simply cannot afford to provide a comprehensive system of higher education.

3.b. Taxation

There are two different types of taxes: *direct taxes* (on individuals and firms) and *indirect taxes* (on goods and services). Figure 9 compares the importance of different sources of central government tax revenue across industrial and developing countries. The most obvious difference is that personal income taxes are much more important in industrial countries than in developing countries. Why? Because personal taxes are hard to collect in agricultural nations, where a large percentage of household production is for personal

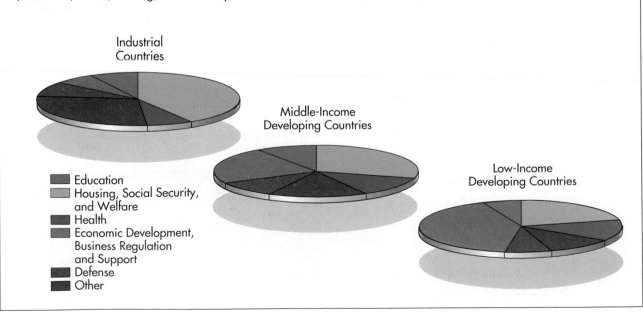

Figure 7
Central Government Spending by Functional Category
The charts show the pattern of government spending in industrial countries, middle-income developing countries, and low-income developing countries. Social programs (education, health, housing, social security, and welfare) account for 58 percent of federal government expenditures in industrial countries, but only 39 percent in middle-income countries and 24 percent in low-income countries. Source: Data are from World Bank, *World Development Report 1994* (Washington, D.C., 1994).

Part III / The National and Global Economies

Figure 8
Cost per Student of Public Education as a Percentage of GDP per Capita in Three Country Groups
Industrial countries have much better educated populations than do poor countries. One reason is the higher cost of education in poor countries in terms of percentage of per capita GDP. A year of college education for one student costs an average of 49 percent of per capita GDP in industrial countries; it costs 370 percent on average in developing countries. In the poorest region in the world, sub-Saharan Africa, one year of higher education costs 800 percent of per capita GDP. Source: From *World Development Report 1988* by The World Bank. Copyright © 1988 by the International Bank for Reconstruction and Development/The World Bank. Reprinted by permission of Oxford University Press, Inc.

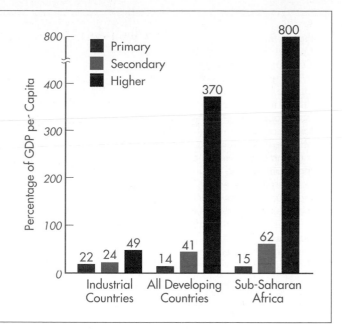

consumption. Taxes on businesses are easier to collect, and thus are more important in developing countries.

That industrial countries are better able to afford social programs is reflected in the great disparity in social security taxes between industrial countries and developing countries. With so many workers living near the subsistence level in the poorest countries, their governments simply cannot tax workers for retirement and health security programs.

Figure 9 also shows that taxes on international trade are very important in developing countries. Because goods arriving or leaving a country must pass through customs inspection, export and import taxes are relatively easy to collect compared to income taxes. In general, developing countries depend more heavily on indirect taxes on goods and services than do developed countries.

Figure 9 lists "goods and services" taxes. Of these, 65 percent are **value-added (VAT) taxes** for industrial countries, while 61 percent of developing country commodity taxes come from value-added taxes. A value-added tax is an indirect tax imposed on each sale at each stage of production. Each seller from the first stage of production on collects the VAT from the buyer, and then deducts any VATs it has paid in buying its inputs. The difference is remitted to the government. From time to time, Congress has debated the merits of a VAT in the United States, but has never approved this kind of tax.

■ **value-added tax (VAT):**
a general sales tax collected at each stage of production

RECAP

1. Over time, government spending has become more important in industrial countries.

2. Governments in developing countries typically play a larger role in investment spending in their economies than do the governments of developed countries.

3. Developing countries depend more on indirect taxes on goods and services as a source of revenue than on direct taxes on individuals and businesses.

4. Value-added taxes are general sales taxes that are collected at every stage of production.

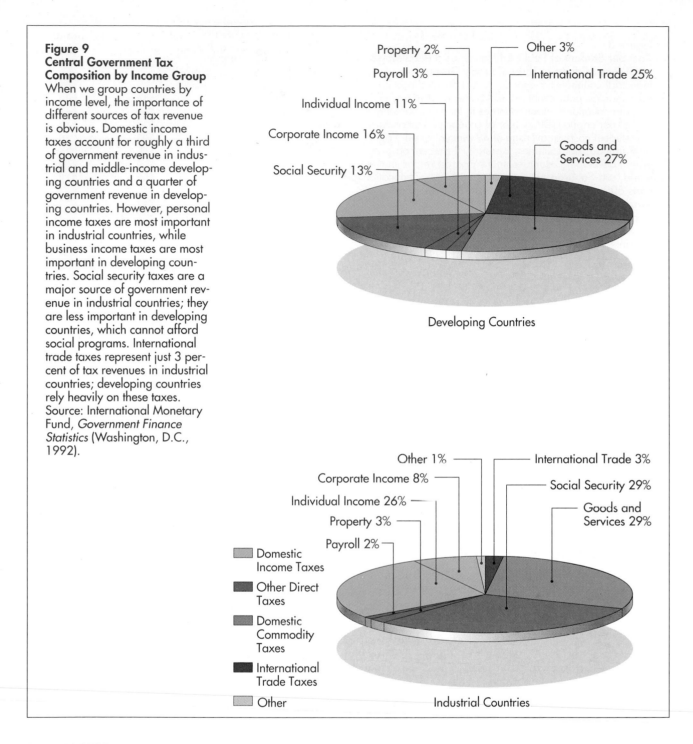

Figure 9
Central Government Tax Composition by Income Group
When we group countries by income level, the importance of different sources of tax revenue is obvious. Domestic income taxes account for roughly a third of government revenue in industrial and middle-income developing countries and a quarter of government revenue in developing countries. However, personal income taxes are most important in industrial countries, while business income taxes are most important in developing countries. Social security taxes are a major source of government revenue in industrial countries; they are less important in developing countries, which cannot afford social programs. International trade taxes represent just 3 percent of tax revenues in industrial countries; developing countries rely heavily on these taxes.
Source: International Monetary Fund, *Government Finance Statistics* (Washington, D.C., 1992).

Property 2%
Payroll 3%
Individual Income 11%
Corporate Income 16%
Social Security 13%
Other 3%
International Trade 25%
Goods and Services 27%

Developing Countries

Other 1%
Corporate Income 8%
Individual Income 26%
Property 3%
Payroll 2%
International Trade 3%
Social Security 29%
Goods and Services 29%

Domestic Income Taxes
Other Direct Taxes
Domestic Commodity Taxes
International Trade Taxes
Other

Industrial Countries

SUMMARY

How can fiscal policy eliminate a GDP gap?

1. A GDP gap can be closed by increasing government spending or by cutting taxes.

2. Government spending affects aggregate expenditures directly; taxes affect aggregate expenditures indirectly, through their effect on consumption.

3. Aggregate expenditures must rise to bring equilibrium real GDP up to potential real GDP—to eliminate the GDP gap.

4. An increase in government spending matched by an increase in taxes raises equilibrium spending and real GDP.

5. If the public expects to pay higher taxes as a result of government borrowing, then the expansionary effects of government deficits may be reduced.

6. Government borrowing can crowd out private spending by raising interest rates and reducing investments.

7. Fiscal policy in the United States is a product of the budget process.

8. Federal government spending in the United States has increased from just 3 percent of the GDP before the Great Depression to a little more than 20 percent of the GDP today.

9. Fiscal policy has two components: discretionary fiscal policy and automatic stabilizers.

10. Budget deficits, through their effects on interest rates, international trade, and the national debt, can reduce investment, output, net exports, and national wealth.

11. Progressive taxes and transfer payments are automatic stabilizers, elements of fiscal policy that change automatically as national income changes.

12. Industrial countries spend a much larger percentage of their government budget for social programs than do developing countries.

13. Industrial countries depend more on direct taxes and less on indirect taxes than do developing countries.

KEY TERMS

crowding out
discretionary fiscal policy
automatic stabilizer

progressive tax
value-added tax (VAT)

EXERCISES

1. What is the role of aggregate demand in eliminating the GDP gap? How does the slope of the AS curve affect the fiscal policy actions necessary to eliminate the GDP gap?

2. Briefly describe the process of setting the federal budget in the United States. What is the time lag between the start of the process and the point at which the money is actually spent?

3. In what ways are government deficits harmful to the economy?

4. Define and give three examples of automatic stabilizers.

5. Briefly describe the major differences between fiscal policy in industrial countries and that in developing countries.

6. Why will real GDP tend to rise when government spending and taxes rise by the same amount?

7. How can a larger government fiscal deficit cause a larger international trade deficit?

8. Why do government budget deficits grow during recessions?

9. Taxes can be progressive, regressive, or proportional. Define each, and briefly offer an argument for why income taxes are usually progressive.

INTERNET EXERCISE

In this chapter, we discussed how different governments raise revenue. To see how the U.S. government raises its revenue, go to the Boyes/Melvin *Fundamentals of Economics* Web site at **http://www.hmco.com/college/** and click on the Internet Exercise link for Chapter 13. Now answer the questions that appear on the Boyes/Melvin Web site.

14

Money and Banking

---

1. What is money?

2. How is the U.S. money supply defined?

3. How do countries pay for international transactions?

4. Why are banks considered intermediaries?

5. How does international banking differ from domestic banking?

6. How do banks create money?

U p to this point, we have been talking about aggregate expenditures, aggregate demand and supply, and fiscal policy without explicitly discussing money. Yet money is used by every sector of the economy in all nations and plays a crucial role in every economy. In this chapter we discuss what money is, how the quantity of money is determined, and the role of banks in determining this quantity. In the next chapter, we examine the role of money in the aggregate demand and supply model.

As you will see in the next two chapters, the quantity of money has a major impact on interest rates, inflation, and the amount of spending in the economy. Money is, then, important for macroeconomic policy making, and government officials use both monetary and fiscal policy to influence the equilibrium level of real GDP and prices.

Banks and the banking system also play key roles, both at home and abroad, in the determination of the amount of money in circulation and the movement of money between nations. After we define money and its functions, we look at the banking system. We begin with banking in the United States, and then discuss international banking. Someone once joked that banks follow the rule of 3-6-3. They borrow at 3 percent interest, lend at 6 percent interest, and close at 3 P.M. If those days ever existed, clearly they do not today. The banking industry in the United States and the rest of the world has undergone tremendous change in recent years. New technology and government deregulation are allowing banks to respond to changing economic conditions in ways that were unthinkable only a few years ago, and these changes have had dramatic effects on the economy. ■

1. WHAT IS MONEY?

■ **money:**
anything that is generally acceptable to sellers in exchange for goods and services

Money is anything that is generally acceptable to sellers in exchange for goods and services. The cash in your wallet can be used to buy groceries or a movie ticket. You simply present your cash to the cashier, who readily accepts it. If you want to use your car to buy groceries or a movie ticket, the exchange is more complicated. You would probably have to sell the car before you could use it to buy other goods and services. Cars are seldom exchanged directly for goods and services (except for other cars). Because cars are not a generally acceptable means of paying for other goods and services, we don't consider them to be money.

■ **liquid asset:**
an asset that can easily be exchanged for goods and services

Money is the most liquid asset. A **liquid asset** is an asset that can easily be exchanged for goods and services. Cash is a liquid asset; a car is not. How liquid must an asset be before we consider it money? To answer this question, we must first consider the functions of money.

1.a. Functions of Money

Money serves four basic functions: it is a *medium of exchange*, a *unit of account*, a *store of value*, and a *standard of deferred payment*. Not all monies serve all of these functions equally well, as will be apparent in the following discussion. But to be money, an item must perform enough of these functions to induce people to use it.

1.a.1. Medium of Exchange Money is a medium of exchange; it is used in exchange for goods and services. Sellers willingly accept money in payment for the products and services they produce. Without money, we would have to resort to *barter*, the direct exchange of goods and services for other goods and services.

For a barter system to work, there must be a *double coincidence of wants.* Suppose Bill is a carpenter and Jane is a plumber. In a monetary economy, when Bill needs plumbing repairs in his home, he simply pays Jane for the repairs using money. Because everyone wants money, money is an acceptable means of payment. In a barter economy, Bill must offer his services as a carpenter in exchange for Jane's work. If Jane does not want any carpentry work done, Bill and Jane cannot enter into a mutually beneficial transaction. Bill has to find a person who can do what he wants and also wants what he can do—there must be a double coincidence of wants.

The example of Bill and Jane illustrates the fact that barter is a lot less efficient than using money. This means that the cost of a transaction in a barter economy is higher than the cost of a transaction in a monetary economy. The use of money as a medium of exchange lowers transaction costs.

The people of Yap Island highly value and thus accept as their medium of exchange giant stones. But in most cultures, money must be portable in order to be an effective medium of exchange—a property the stone money of Yap Island clearly lacks. Another important property of money is *divisibility*. Money must be measurable in both small units (for low-value goods and services) and large units (for high-value goods and services). Yap stone money is not divisible, so it is not a good medium of exchange for the majority of goods bought and sold.

1.a.2. Unit of Account   Money is a unit of account; we price goods and services in terms of money. This common unit of measurement allows us to compare relative values easily. If whole-wheat bread sells for a dollar a loaf and white bread sells for 50 cents, we know that whole-wheat bread is twice as expensive as white bread.

Using money as a unit of account is efficient. It reduces the costs of gathering information on what things are worth. The use of money as a unit of account lowers information costs relative to barter. In a barter economy, people constantly have to evaluate the worth of the goods and services being offered. When money prices are placed on goods and services, their relative value is obvious.

1.a.3. Store of Value   Money functions as a store of value or purchasing power. If you are paid today, you do not have to hurry out to spend your money. It will still have value next week or next month. Some monies retain their value better than others. In colonial New England, fish and furs both served as money. But because fish does not store as well as furs, its usefulness as a store of value was limited. An important property of a money is its *durability,* its ability to retain its value over time.

Inflation plays a major role in determining the effectiveness of a money as a store of value. The higher the rate of inflation, the faster the purchasing power of money falls. In high-inflation countries, workers spend their pay as fast as possible because the purchasing power of their money is falling rapidly. It makes no sense to hold on to a money that is quickly losing value. In countries where the domestic money does not serve as a good store of value, it ceases to fulfill this function of money and people begin to use something else as money, like the currency of another nation. For instance, U.S. dollars have long been a favorite store of value in Latin American countries that have experienced high inflation. This phenomenon—**currency substitution**—has been documented in Argentina, Bolivia, Mexico, and other countries during times of high inflation.

■ **currency substitution:** the use of foreign money as a substitute for domestic money when the domestic economy has a high rate of inflation

1.a.4. Standard of Deferred Payment   Finally, money is a standard of deferred payment. Debt obligations are written in terms of money values. If you have a credit card bill that is due in 90 days, the value you owe is stated in monetary units—for example, dollars in the United States and yen in

Japan. We use money values to state amounts of debt and use money to pay our debts.

We should make a distinction here between money and credit. Money is what we use to pay for goods and services. **Credit** is available savings that are lent to borrowers to spend. If you use your Visa or MasterCard to buy a shirt, you are not buying the shirt with your money. You are taking out a loan from the bank that issued the credit card in order to buy the shirt. Credit and money are different. Money is an *asset,* something you own. Credit is *debt,* something you owe.

■ **credit:**
available savings that are lent to borrowers to spend

1.b. The U.S. Money Supply

The quantity of money available for spending is an important determinant of many key macroeconomic variables, since changes in the money supply affect interest rates, inflation, and other indicators of economic health. When economists measure the money supply, they measure spendable assets. Identifying those assets, however, can be difficult. Although it would seem that *all* bank deposits are money, some bank deposits are held for spending while others are held for saving. In defining the money supply, then, economists must differentiate among assets on the basis of their liquidity and the likelihood of their being used for spending.

The problem of distinguishing among assets has produced several definitions of the money supply: M1, M2, and M3. Economists and policymakers use all three definitions to evaluate the availability of funds for spending. Although economists have tried to identify a single measure that best influences the business cycle and changes in interest rates and inflation, research indicates that different definitions work better to explain changes in macroeconomic variables at different times.

1.b.1. M1 Money Supply The narrowest and most liquid measure of the money supply is the **M1 money supply**, the financial assets that are immediately available for spending. This definition emphasizes the use of money as a medium of exchange. The M1 money supply consists of currency, travelers' checks, demand deposits, and other checkable deposits. Demand and other checkable deposits are **transactions accounts**; they can be used to make direct payments to a third party.

■ **M1 money supply:**
financial assets that are the most liquid

■ **transactions account:**
a checking account at a bank or other financial institution that can be drawn on to make payments

Currency Currency includes coins and paper money in circulation (in the hands of the public). In 1998, currency represented 39 percent of the M1 money supply. A common misconception about currency today is that it is backed by gold or silver. This is not true. There is nothing backing the U.S. dollar except the confidence of the public. This kind of monetary system is called a *fiduciary monetary system*. Fiduciary comes from the Latin *fiducia,* which means "trust." Our monetary system is based on trust. As long as we believe that our money is an acceptable form of payment for goods and services, the system works. It is not necessary for money to be backed by any precious object. As long as people believe that a money has value, it will serve as money.

The United States has not always operated under a fiduciary monetary system. At one time the U.S. government issued gold and silver coins and paper money that could be exchanged for silver. In 1967, Congress authorized the U.S. Treasury to stop redeeming "silver certificate" paper money for silver. Coins with an intrinsic value are known as *commodity money;* they have value as a commodity in addition to their face value. The problem with commodity money is that as the value of the commodity increases, the money stops being circulated. People hoard coins when their commodity value exceeds their face value. For example, no one would take an old $20 gold piece to the grocery store to buy $20 worth of groceries because the gold is worth much more than $20 today.

Travelers' Checks Outstanding U.S. dollar–denominated travelers' checks issued by nonbank institutions are counted as part of the M1 money supply. There are several nonbank issuers, among them American Express and Cook's. (Travelers' checks issued by banks are included in demand deposits. When a bank issues its own travelers' checks, it deposits the amount paid by the purchaser in a special account that is used to redeem the checks. Because this amount is counted as part of demand deposits, it is not counted again as part of outstanding travelers' checks.) Travelers' checks accounted for less than 1 percent of the M1 money supply in 1998.

Demand Deposits Demand deposits are checking account deposits at a commercial bank. These deposits pay no interest. They are called *demand deposits* because the bank must pay the amount of the check immediately on the demand of the depositor. Demand deposits accounted for 37 percent of the M1 money supply in 1998.

Other Checkable Deposits Until the 1980s, demand deposits were the only kind of checking account. Today there are many different kinds of checking accounts, known as *other checkable deposits (OCDs)*. OCDs are accounts at financial institutions that pay interest and give the depositor check-writing privileges. Among the OCDs included in the M1 money supply are the following:

Negotiable orders of withdrawal (NOW) accounts These are interest-bearing checking accounts offered by savings and loan institutions.

Automatic transfer system (ATS) accounts These are accounts at commercial banks that combine an interest-bearing savings account with a non-interest-bearing checking account. The depositor keeps a small balance in the checking account; anytime the checking account balance is overdrawn, funds automatically are transferred from the savings account.

Credit union share draft accounts Credit unions offer their members interest-bearing checking accounts called *share drafts*.

Demand deposits at mutual savings banks Mutual savings banks are nonprofit savings and loan organizations. Any profits after operating expenses have been paid may be distributed to depositors.

1.b.2. M2 Money Supply The components of the M1 money supply are the most liquid assets, the assets most likely to be used for transactions. M2 is a broader definition of the money supply that includes assets in somewhat less liquid forms. The M2 money supply includes the M1 money supply plus:

- **Savings deposits** Savings deposits are accounts at banks and savings and loan associations that earn interest but offer check-writing privileges.

- **Small-denomination time deposits** These deposits are often called *certificates of deposit*. Funds in these accounts must be deposited for a specified period of time. (*Small* means less than $100,000.)

- **Retail money market mutual fund balances** These money market mutual funds combine the deposits of many individuals and invest them in government Treasury bills and other short-term securities. Many money market mutual funds grant check-writing privileges but limit the size and number of checks.

1.b.3. M3 Money Supply The M3 money supply equals the M2 money supply plus:

- **Large-denomination time deposits** These are deposits of $100,000 or more made for a specified period of time.

- **Repurchase agreements (RPs)** A repurchase agreement is an agreement between a bank and a customer under which the customer buys U.S. government securities from the bank one day and then sells them back to the bank later at a price that includes the interest earned. Overnight RPs are used by firms that have excess cash one day that may be needed the next.

- **Eurodollar deposits** These are deposits denominated in dollars but held outside the U.S. domestic bank industry.

- **Institution-only money market fund balances** These money market mutual funds do not include the balances of individuals.

These additional assets are less liquid than those found in the M1 or M2 money supply. Figure 1 summarizes the three definitions of the money supply.

1.c. Global Money

So far we have discussed the money supply in a domestic context. Just as the United States uses dollars as its domestic money, every nation has its own monetary unit of account. Japan has the yen, Mexico the peso, Canada the Canadian dollar, and so on. Since each nation uses a different money, how do countries pay for transactions that involve residents of other countries? As you saw in Chapter 10, the foreign exchange market links national monies together, so that transactions can be made across national borders. If Sears in the United States buys a home entertainment system from Sony in Japan, Sears can exchange dollars for yen in order to pay Sony in yen. The exchange rate between the dollar and yen determines how many dollars are needed to purchase the required number of yen. For instance, if Sony wants 1,000,000 yen for the component and the exchange rate is ¥100 = $1, Sears needs $10,000 (1,000,000/100) to buy the yen.

Sales contracts between developed countries usually are written (invoiced) in the national currency of the exporter. To complete the transaction, the importer buys the exporter's currency on the foreign exchange market. Trade between developing and developed nations typically is invoiced in the currency of the developed country, whether the developed country is the exporter or importer, because the currency of the developed country is usually more stable and more widely traded on the foreign exchange market than the currency of the developing country. As a result, the currencies of the major developed countries tend to dominate the international medium-of-exchange and unit-of-account functions of money.

1.c.1. International Reserve Currencies Governments hold monies as a temporary store of value until money is needed to settle international debts. At one time gold was the primary **international reserve asset**, an asset used to settle debts between governments. Although gold still serves as an international reserve asset, its role is unimportant relative to that of currencies. Today national currencies function as international reserves. The currencies that are held for this purpose are called **international reserve currencies**.

Table 1 shows the importance of the major international reserve currencies over time. In the mid-1970s, the U.S. dollar comprised almost 80 percent of

■ **international reserve asset:** an asset used to settle debts between governments

■ **international reserve currency:** a currency held by a government to settle international debts

TABLE 1
International Reserve Currencies (Percentage Shares of National Currencies in Total Official Holdings of Foreign Exchange)

Year	U.S. Dollar	Pound Sterling	Deutsche Mark	French Franc	Japanese Yen	Swiss Franc	Netherlands Guilder	ECUs	Unspecified Currencies
1976	78.8	1.0	8.7	1.5	1.9	2.1	0.8	—	5.2
1996	58.9	3.4	13.6	1.6	6.0	0.7	0.3	5.9	9.5

Source: Data from International Monetary Fund, *Annual Report,* http://www.imf.org/external/pubs/ft/ar/97/pdf/file12.pdf

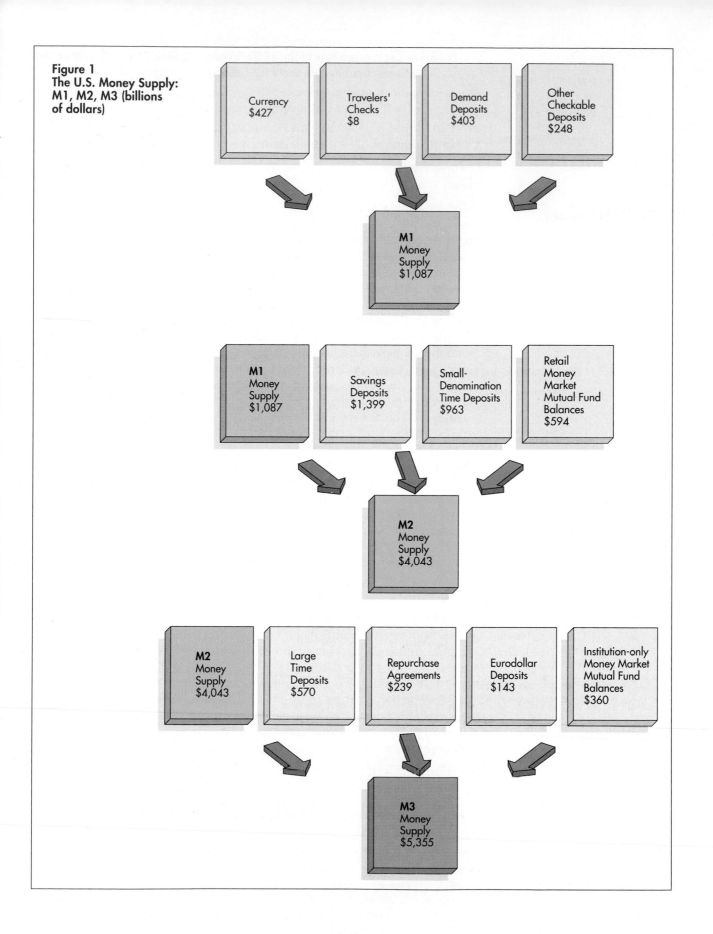

Figure 1
The U.S. Money Supply: M1, M2, M3 (billions of dollars)

Currency $427

Travelers' Checks $8

Demand Deposits $403

Other Checkable Deposits $248

M1 Money Supply $1,087

M1 Money Supply $1,087

Savings Deposits $1,399

Small-Denomination Time Deposits $963

Retail Money Market Mutual Fund Balances $594

M2 Money Supply $4,043

M2 Money Supply $4,043

Large Time Deposits $570

Repurchase Agreements $239

Eurodollar Deposits $143

Institution-only Money Market Mutual Fund Balances $360

M3 Money Supply $5,355

international reserve holdings. By 1990 its share had fallen to less than 50 percent, but the share has risen again recently.

1.c.2. Composite Currencies The industrial nations of western Europe introduced a new unit of currency, the **European currency unit (ECU)**, in March 1979. These nations use ECUs to settle debts between them. The ECU is a **composite currency**; its value is an average of the values of several different national currencies. The European Monetary System, an organization made up of the participating nations, determines the amount of each currency that is used to make up the ECU and regularly publishes its value.

The ECU is not an actual money but is an accounting entry transferred between two parties. However, there will soon be an actual money, *the euro,* that will replace the ECU and will circulate throughout the member countries as a European money. Ultimately, each country will eliminate its national money and adopt the euro as its money.

Another composite currency used in international financial transactions is the **special drawing right (SDR)**. The value of the SDR is an average of the values of the currencies of the five major industrial countries: the U.S. dollar, the French franc, the German mark, the Japanese yen, and the U.K. pound. This currency was created in 1970 by the International Monetary Fund, an international organization that oversees the monetary relationships among countries. SDRs, like ECUs, are an international reserve asset; they are used to settle international debts by transferring governments' accounts held at the International Monetary Fund.

■ **European currency unit (ECU):**
a unit of account used by western European nations as their official reserve asset

■ **composite currency:**
an artificial unit of account that is an average of the values of several national currencies

■ **special drawing right (SDR):**
a composite currency whose value is the average of the value of the U.S. dollar, the French franc, the German mark, the Japanese yen, and the U.K. pound

RECAP

1. Money is the most liquid asset.
2. Money serves as a medium of exchange, a unit of account, a store of value, and a standard of deferred payment.
3. The use of money lowers transaction and information costs relative to barter.
4. To be used as money, an asset should be portable, divisible, and durable.
5. The M1 money supply is the most liquid definition of money and equals the sum of currency, travelers' checks, demand deposits, and other checkable deposits.
6. The M2 money supply equals the sum of the M1 money supply, savings and small-denomination time deposits, and retail money market mutual fund balances.
7. The M3 money supply equals the sum of the M2 money supply, large time deposits, repurchase agreements, Eurodollar deposits, and institution-only money market mutual fund balances.
8. International reserve currencies are held by governments to settle international debts.
9. ECUs and SDRs are composite currencies; their value is an average of the values of several national currencies.

2. BANKING

Commercial banks are financial institutions that offer deposits on which checks can be written. In the United States and most other countries, commercial banks are privately owned. *Thrift institutions* are financial institutions that historically offered just savings accounts, not checking accounts. Savings and loan associations, credit unions, and mutual savings banks are all thrift institutions. Prior to 1980, the differences between commercial banks and thrift institutions were much greater than they are today. For example, only commercial banks could offer checking accounts, and those accounts earned no interest. The law also regulated maximum interest rates. In 1980 Congress passed the Depository Institutions Deregulation and Monetary Control Act, in part to stimulate competition among financial institutions. Now thrift institutions and even brokerage houses offer many of the same services as commercial banks.

2.a. Financial Intermediaries

Both commercial banks and thrift institutions are *financial intermediaries,* middlemen between savers and borrowers. Banks accept deposits from individuals and firms, then use those deposits to make loans to individuals and firms. The borrowers are likely to be different individuals or firms from the depositors, although it is not uncommon for a household or business to be both a depositor and a borrower at the same institution. Of course, depositors and borrowers have very different interests. For instance, depositors typically prefer short-term deposits; they don't want to tie their money up for a long time. Borrowers, on the other hand, usually want more time for repayment. Banks typically package short-term deposits into longer-term loans. To function as intermediaries, banks must serve the interests of both depositors and borrowers.

A bank is willing to serve as an intermediary because it hopes to earn a profit from this activity. It pays a lower interest rate on deposits than it charges on loans; the difference is a source of profit for the bank. Islamic banks are prohibited by holy law from charging interest on loans; thus they use a different system for making a profit (see the Economic Insight "Islamic Banking").

2.b. U.S. Banking

2.b.1. Current Structure Banking in the United States went through many changes in the 1980s. The Depository Institutions Deregulation and Monetary Control Act narrowed the distinction between commercial banks and thrift institutions. The act also narrowed the distinctions among commercial banks. If you add together all the pieces of the pie chart in Figure 2, you see that there were 66,767 banking offices operating in the United States in 1996. Roughly half of these offices were operated by *national banks,* banks chartered by the federal government; the other half, by *state banks,* banks chartered under state laws. Before the deregulation act was passed, the regulations placed on national banks were more stringent than the regulations placed on

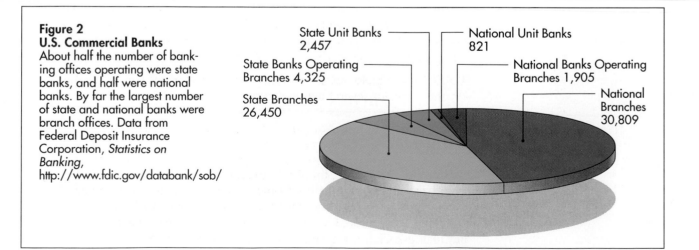

Figure 2
U.S. Commercial Banks
About half the number of banking offices operating were state banks, and half were national banks. By far the largest number of state and national banks were branch offices. Data from Federal Deposit Insurance Corporation, *Statistics on Banking,* http://www.fdic.gov/databank/sob/

State Unit Banks 2,457

State Banks Operating Branches 4,325

State Branches 26,450

National Unit Banks 821

National Banks Operating Branches 1,905

National Branches 30,809

Islamic Banking

According to the Muslim holy book, the Koran, Islamic law prohibits interest charges on loans. Banks that operate under Islamic law still act as intermediaries between borrowers and lenders. However, they do not charge interest on loans or pay interest on deposits. Instead they take a predetermined percentage of the borrowing firm's profits until the loan is repaid, then share those profits with depositors.

Since the mid-1970s, over a hundred Islamic banks have opened, most in Arab nations. Deposits in these banks have grown rapidly. In fact, in some banks deposits have grown faster than good loan opportunities, forcing the banks to refuse new deposits until their loan portfolio could grow to match available deposits. One bank in Bahrain claimed that over 60 percent of deposits during its first two years in operation were made by people who had never made a bank deposit before.

In addition to profit-sharing deposits, Islamic banks typically offer checking accounts, travelers' checks, and trade-related services on a fee basis. The return on profit-sharing deposits has fluctuated with regional economic conditions. In the late 1970s and early 1980s, when oil prices were high, returns were higher than they were in the mid-1980s, when oil prices were depressed.

Because the growth of deposits has usually exceeded the growth of local investment opportunities, Islamic banks have been lending money to traditional banks, to fund investments that satisfy the moral and commercial needs of both, such as lending to private firms. These funds cannot be used to invest in interest-bearing securities or in firms that deal in alcohol, pork, gambling, or arms. The growth of mutually profitable investment opportunities suggests that Islamic banks are meeting both the dictates of Muslim depositors and the profitability requirements of modern banking.

state banks. The deregulation act made the regulations affecting state and national banks more equal.

Another change that has taken place in the U.S. bank market is the growth of interstate banking. Historically, banks were allowed to operate in just one state. In some states, banks could operate in only one location. This is known as *unit banking*. Today there are still many unit banks, but these are typically small community banks. Figure 2 shows that less than half of all state banks (2,457) and national banks (821) operated as unit banks; the rest operated 26,450 state branch offices and 30,809 national branch offices.

Over time, legal barriers have been reduced so that today almost all states permit entry to banks located out of state. In the future, banking is likely to be done on a national rather than a local scale. The growth of automated teller machines (ATMs) is a big step in this direction. ATM networks give bank customers access to services over a much wider geographic area than any single bank's branches cover. These international networks allow a bank customer from Dallas to withdraw cash in Seattle, Zurich, or almost anywhere in the world. Today more than one-fourth of ATM transactions occur at banks that are not the customer's own bank.

2.b.2. Bank Failures   Banking in the United States has had a colorful history of booms and panics. Banking is like any other business. Banks that are poorly managed can fail; banks that are properly managed tend to prosper. Regional economic conditions are also very important. In the mid-1980s, hundreds of banks in states with large oil industries, like Texas and Oklahoma, and farming states, like Kansas and Nebraska, could not collect many of their loans due to falling oil and agricultural prices. Those states that are heavily dependent on the oil industry and farming had significantly more banks fail than did other states. The problem was not so much bad management as it was a matter of unexpectedly bad business conditions. The lesson here is simple: commercial banks, like other profit-making enterprises, are not exempt from failure.

At one time a bank panic could close a bank. A bank panic occurs when depositors, fearing a bank's closing, rush to withdraw their funds. Banks keep only a fraction of their deposits on reserve, so bank panics often result in bank closings as depositors try to withdraw more money than the banks have on a given day. In the United States today, this is no longer true. The **Federal Deposit Insurance Corporation (FDIC)** was created in 1933. The FDIC is a federal agency that insures bank deposits in commercial banks so that depositors do not lose their deposits when a bank fails. Figure 3 shows the number of failed banks and the number without deposit insurance. In the 1930s, many of the banks that failed were not insured by the FDIC. In this environment, it made sense for depositors to worry about losing their money. In the 1980s, the number of bank failures increased dramatically, but none of the failed banks were uninsured. Deposits in those banks were protected by the federal government. Even though large banks have failed in recent times, the depositors have not lost their deposits.

■ **Federal Deposit Insurance Corporation (FDIC):** a federal agency that insures deposits in commercial banks

2.c. International Banking

Large banks today are truly transnational enterprises. International banks, like domestic banks, act as financial intermediaries, but they operate in a different legal environment. The laws regulating domestic banking in each nation are typically very restrictive, yet many nations allow international banking to operate largely unregulated. Because they are not hampered by regulations, international banks typically can offer depositors and borrowers better terms than could be negotiated at a domestic bank.

2.c.1. Eurocurrency Market Because of the competitive interest rates offered on loans and deposits, there is a large market for deposits and loans at international banks. For instance, a bank in London, Tokyo, or the Bahamas may accept deposits and make loans denominated in U.S. dollars. The international deposit and loan market often is called the **Eurocurrency market**, or **offshore banking**. In the Eurocurrency market, the currency used in a banking transaction generally is not the domestic currency of the country in which the bank is located. (The prefix *Euro* is misleading here. Although the market originated in Europe, today the market is global and operates with different foreign currencies; it is in no way limited to European currencies or European banks.)

■ **Eurocurrency market (offshore banking):** the market for deposits and loans generally denominated in a currency other than the currency of the country in which the transaction occurs

In those countries that allow offshore banking, we find two sets of banking rules: restrictive regulations for banking in the domestic market and little or no regulation of offshore-banking activities. Domestic banks are required to hold reserves against deposits and to carry deposit insurance; and they often face government-mandated credit or interest rate restrictions. The

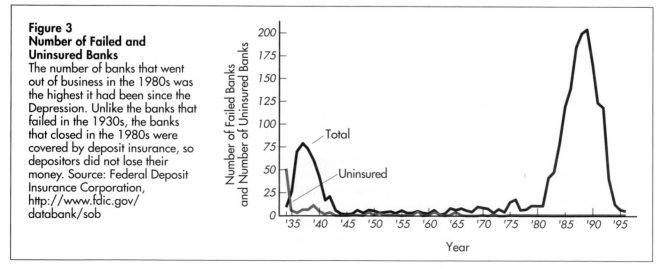

Figure 3
Number of Failed and Uninsured Banks
The number of banks that went out of business in the 1980s was the highest it had been since the Depression. Unlike the banks that failed in the 1930s, the banks that closed in the 1980s were covered by deposit insurance, so depositors did not lose their money. Source: Federal Deposit Insurance Corporation, http://www.fdic.gov/databank/sob

Eurocurrency market operates with few or no costly restrictions, and international banks generally pay lower taxes than domestic banks. Because offshore banks operate with lower costs, they are able to offer better terms to their customers than domestic banks.

The Eurocurrency market exists for all of the major international currencies, but the value of activity in Eurodollars dwarfs the rest. Eurodollars account for about 60 percent of deposit and loan activity in the Eurocurrency market. This emphasizes the important role the U.S. dollar plays in global finance. Even deposits and loans that do not involve a U.S. lender or borrower often are denominated in U.S. dollars.

2.c.2. International Banking Facilities

The term *offshore banking* is somewhat misleading in the United States today. Prior to December 1981, U.S. banks were forced to process international deposits and loans through their offshore branches. Many of the branches in places like the Cayman Islands and the Bahamas were little more than "shells," small offices with a telephone. Yet these branches allowed U.S. banks to avoid the reserve requirements and interest rate regulations that restricted domestic banking activities.

■ **international banking facility (IBF):**
a division of a U.S. bank that is allowed to receive deposits from and make loans to nonresidents of the United States without the restrictions that apply to domestic U.S. banks

In December 1981, the Federal Reserve Board legalized **international banking facilities (IBFs)**, allowing domestic banks to take part in international banking on U.S. soil. IBFs are not a physical entity; they are a bookkeeping system set up in existing bank offices to record international banking transactions. IBFs can receive deposits from and make loans to nonresidents of the United States or other IBFs. These deposits and loans must be kept separate from other transactions because IBFs are not subject to the reserve requirements, interest rate regulations, or FDIC deposit insurance premiums that apply to domestic U.S. banking.

The goal of the IBF plan was to allow banking offices in the United States to compete with offshore banks without having to use offshore banking offices. The location of IBFs reflects the location of banking activity in general. It is not surprising that 47 percent of IBFs are located in New York State, the financial center of the country. New York also receives over 75 percent of IBF deposits.

RECAP

1. The Depository Institutions Deregulation and Monetary Control Act (1980) eliminated many of the differences between commercial banks and thrift institutions.

2. Banks are financial intermediaries.

3. The deregulation act also eliminated many of the differences between national and state banks.

4. Since the FDIC began insuring bank deposits in commercial banks, bank panics are no longer a threat to the banking system.

5. The international deposit and loan market is called the Eurocurrency market, or offshore banking.

6. With the legalization in 1981 of international banking facilities, the Federal Reserve allowed international banking activities on U.S. soil.

3. BANKS AND THE MONEY SUPPLY

■ **fractional reserve banking system:**
a system in which banks keep less than 100 percent of the deposits available for withdrawal

Banks create money by lending money. They take deposits, then lend a portion of those deposits in order to earn interest income. The portion of deposits that banks keep on hand is a *reserve* to meet the demand for withdrawals. In a **fractional reserve banking system**, banks keep less than 100 percent of their deposits on reserve. If all banks hold 10 percent of their deposits as a reserve, for example, then 90 percent of their deposits are available for loans. When they loan these deposits, money is created.

3.a. Deposits and Loans

Figure 4 shows a simple balance sheet for First National Bank. A *balance sheet* is a financial statement that records a firm's assets (what the firm owns) and liabilities (what the firm owes). The bank has cash assets ($100,000) and loan assets ($900,000). The deposits placed in the bank ($1,000,000) are a liability (they are an asset of the depositors).[1] Total assets always equal total liabilities on a balance sheet.

Banks keep a percentage of their deposits on reserve. In the United States the reserve requirement is set by the Federal Reserve Board (which will be discussed in detail in the next chapter). Banks can keep more than the minimum reserve if they choose. Let's assume that the reserve requirement is set at 10 percent and that banks always hold actual reserves equal to 10 percent of deposits. With deposits of $1,000,000, the bank must keep $100,000 (.10 × $1,000,000) in cash reserves held in its vault. This $100,000 is the bank's **required reserves**, as the Federal Reserve requires the banks to keep 10 percent of deposits on reserve. This is exactly what First National Bank has on hand in Figure 4. Any cash held in excess of $100,000 would represent **excess reserves**. Excess reserves can be loaned by the bank. A bank is *loaned up* when it has zero excess reserves. Because its total reserves equal its required reserves, First National Bank has no excess reserves and is loaned up.

■ **required reserves:**
the cash reserves (a percentage of deposits) a bank must keep on hand

■ **excess reserves:**
the cash reserves beyond those required, which can be loaned

$$\text{excess reserves} = \text{total reserves} - \text{required reserves}$$
$$= \$100,000 - \$100,000$$
$$= 0$$

The bank cannot make any new loans.

What happens if the bank receives a new deposit of $100,000? Figure 5 shows the bank's balance sheet right after the deposit is made. Its cash reserves are now $200,000, its deposits $1,100,000. With the additional deposit, the bank's total reserves equal $200,000. Its required reserves are $110,000 (.10 × $1,100,000). So its excess reserves are $90,000 ($200,000 − $110,000). Since a bank can lend its excess reserves, First National Bank can loan an additional $90,000.

Suppose the bank lends someone $90,000 by depositing $90,000 in the borrower's First National account. At the time the loan is made, the money supply increases by the amount of the loan, $90,000. By making the loan, the bank has increased the money supply. But this is not the end of the story. The

---

[1] In our simplified balance sheet, we assume there is no net worth, or owner's equity. Net worth is the value of the owner's claim on the firm (the owner's equity) and is found as the difference between the value of assets and nonequity liabilities.

Figure 4
First National Bank Balance Sheet, Initial Position
The bank has cash totaling $100,000 and loans totaling $900,000, for total assets of $1,000,000. Deposits of $1,000,000 make up its total liabilities. With a reserve requirement of 10 percent, the bank must hold required reserves of 10 percent of its deposits, or $100,000. Because the bank is holding cash of $100,000, its total reserves equal its required reserves. Because it has no excess reserves, the bank cannot make new loans.

First National Bank

Assets		Liabilities	
Cash	$100,000	Deposits	$1,000,000
Loans	900,000		
Total	$1,000,000	Total	$1,000,000

Total reserves = $100,000
Required reserves = 0.1 ($1,000,000) = $100,000
Excess reserves = 0

Part III / The National and Global Economies

Figure 5
First National Bank Balance Sheet After $100,000 Deposit
A $100,000 deposit increases the bank's cash reserves to $200,000 and deposits to $1,100,000. The bank must hold 10 percent of deposits, $110,000, on reserve. The difference between total reserves ($200,000) and required reserves ($110,000) is excess reserves ($90,000). The bank now has $90,000 available for lending.

First National Bank

Assets		Liabilities	
Cash	$200,000	Deposits	$1,100,000
Loans	900,000		
Total	$1,100,000	Total	$1,100,000

Total reserves = $200,000
Required reserves = 0.1 ($1,100,000) = $110,000
Excess reserves = $90,000

borrower spends the $90,000, and it winds up being deposited in the Second National Bank.

Figure 6 shows the balance sheets of both banks after the loan is made and the money is spent and deposited at Second National Bank. First National Bank now has loans of $990,000 and no excess reserves (the required reserves of $110,000 equal total reserves). So First National Bank can make no more loans until a new deposit is made. Second National Bank has a new deposit of $90,000 (to simplify the analysis, we assume that this is the first transaction at Second National Bank). Its required reserves are 10 percent of $90,000, or $9,000. With total reserves of $90,000, Second National Bank has excess reserves of $81,000. It can make loans up to $81,000.

Notice what has happened to the banks' deposits as a result of the initial $100,000 deposit in First National Bank. Deposits at First National Bank have increased by $100,000. Second National Bank has a new deposit of $90,000, and the loans it makes will increase the money supply even more. Table 2 shows how the initial deposit of $100,000 is multiplied through the banking system. Each time a new loan is made, the money is spent and redeposited in the banking system. But each bank keeps 10 percent of the deposit on reserve, lending only 90 percent. So the amount of money loaned decreases by 10 percent each time it goes through another bank. If we carried

Figure 6
Balance Sheets After a $90,000 Loan Made by First National Bank Is Spent and Deposited at Second National Bank
Once First National Bank makes the $90,000 loan, its cash reserves fall to $110,000 and its loans increase to $990,000. At this point the bank's total reserves ($110,000) equal its required reserves (10 percent of deposits). Because it has no excess reserves, the bank cannot make new loans.

Second National Bank receives a deposit of $90,000. It must hold 10 percent, or $9,000, on reserve. Its excess reserves equal total reserves ($90,000) minus required reserves ($9,000), or $81,000. Second National Bank can make a maximum loan of $81,000.

First National Bank

Assets		Liabilities	
Cash	$110,000	Deposits	$1,100,000
Loans	990,000		
Total	$1,100,000	Total	$1,100,000

Total reserves = $110,000
Required reserves = 0.1 ($1,100,000) = $110,000
Excess reserves = 0

Second National Bank

Assets		Liabilities	
Cash	$90,000	Deposits	$90,000
Total	$90,000	Total	$90,000

Total reserves = $90,000
Required reserves = 0.1 ($90,000) = $9,000
Excess reserves = $81,000

the calculations out, you would see that the total increase in deposits associated with the initial $100,000 deposit is $1,000,000. Required reserves would increase by $100,000, and new loans would increase by $900,000.

3.b. Deposit Expansion Multiplier

■ **deposit expansion multiplier:**
the reciprocal of the reserve requirement

Rather than calculate the excess reserves at each bank, as we did in Table 2, we can use a simple formula to find the maximum increase in deposits given a new deposit. The **deposit expansion multiplier** equals the reciprocal of the reserve requirement:

$$\text{deposit expansion multiplier} = \frac{1}{\text{reserve requirement}}$$

In our example, the reserve requirement is 10 percent, or .10. So the deposit expansion multiplier equals 1/.10, or 10. An initial increase in deposits of $100,000 expands deposits in the banking system by 10 times $100,000, or $1,000,000. The maximum increase in the money supply is found by multiplying the deposit expansion multiplier by the amount of the new deposit. With no new deposits, the banking system can increase the money supply only by the multiplier times excess reserves:

$$\text{deposit expansion multiplier} \times \text{excess reserves}$$
$$= \text{maximum increase in money supply}$$

The deposit expansion multiplier indicates the *maximum* possible change in total deposits when a new deposit is made. For the effect to be that large, all excess reserves must be loaned out and all of the money that is deposited must stay in the banking system.

If banks hold more reserves than the minimum required, they lend a smaller fraction of any new deposits, which reduces the effect of the deposit expansion multiplier. For instance, if the reserve requirement is 10 percent, we know that the deposit expansion multiplier is 10. If a bank chooses to hold 20 percent of its deposits on reserve, the deposit expansion multiplier equals 5 (1/.20).

If money (currency and coin) is withdrawn from the banking system and kept as cash, deposits and bank reserves are smaller and less money exists to loan out. This *currency drain*—removal of money—reduces the deposit expansion multiplier. The greater the currency drain, the smaller the multiplier. There is always some currency drain as people carry currency to pay for day-to-day transactions. However, during historical periods of bank panic where people lost confidence in banks, large currency withdrawals contributed to declines in money supply.

TABLE 2
The Effect on Bank Deposits of an Initial Bank Deposit of $100,000

Bank	New Deposit	Required Reserves	Excess Reserves (new loans)
First National	$ 100,000	$ 10,000	$ 90,000
Second National	90,000	9,000	81,000
Third National	81,000	8,100	72,900
Fourth National	72,900	7,290	65,610
Fifth National	65,610	6,561	59,049
Sixth National	59,049	5,905	53,144
⋮	⋮	⋮	⋮
Total	$1,000,000	$100,000	$900,000

Remember that the deposit expansion multiplier measures the *maximum* expansion of the money supply by the banking system. Any single bank can lend only its excess reserves, but the whole banking system can expand the money supply by a multiple of the initial excess reserves. Thus the banking system as a whole can increase the money supply by the deposit expansion multiplier times the excess reserves of the system. The initial bank is limited to its initial loan; the banking system generates loan after loan based on that initial loan. A new deposit can increase the money supply by the deposit expansion multiplier times the new deposit.

In the next chapter we discuss how changes in the reserve requirement affect the money supply and the economy. This area of policy making is controlled by the Federal Reserve.

RECAP

1. The fractional reserve banking system allows banks to expand the money supply by making loans.

2. Banks must keep a fraction of their deposits on reserve; their excess reserves are available for lending.

3. The deposit expansion multiplier measures the maximum increase in the money supply given a new deposit; it is the reciprocal of the reserve requirement.

4. A single bank increases the money supply by lending its excess reserves.

5. The banking system can increase the money supply by the deposit expansion multiplier times the excess reserves in the banking system.

SUMMARY

◼◼ What is money?

1. Money is anything that is generally acceptable to sellers in exchange for goods and services.

2. Money serves as a medium of exchange, a unit of account, a store of value, and a standard of deferred payment.

3. Money, because it is more efficient than barter, lowers transaction costs.

4. Money should be portable, divisible, and durable.

◼◼ How is the U.S. money supply defined?

5. There are three definitions of money based on its liquidity.

6. The M1 money supply equals the sum of currency plus travelers' checks plus demand deposits plus other checkable deposits.

7. The M2 money supply equals the sum of the M1 money supply plus savings and small denomination time deposits, and retail money market mutual fund balances.

8. The M3 money supply equals the M2 money supply plus large time deposits, repurchase agreements, Eurodollar deposits, and institution-only money market mutual fund balances.

◼◼ How do countries pay for international transactions?

9. Using the foreign exchange market, governments (along with individuals and firms) are able to convert national currencies to pay for trade.

10. The U.S. dollar is the world's major international reserve currency.

11. The European currency unit (ECU) is a composite currency whose value is an average of the values of several western European currencies.

◼◼ Why are banks considered intermediaries?

12. Banks serve as middlemen between savers and borrowers.

13. Domestic banking in most nations is strictly
regulated; international banking is not.

14. The Eurocurrency market is the international
deposit and loan market.

15. International banking facilities (IBFs) allow
U.S. domestic banks to carry on international
banking activities on U.S. soil.

How do banks create money?

16. Banks can make loans up to the amount of
their excess reserves, their total reserves
minus their required reserves.

17. The deposit expansion multiplier is the reciprocal of the reserve requirement.

18. A single bank expands the money supply by
lending its excess reserves.

19. The banking system can increase the money
supply by the deposit expansion multiplier
times the excess reserves in the system.

KEY TERMS

money

liquid asset

currency substitution

credit

M1 money supply

transactions account

international reserve asset

international reserve currency

European currency unit (ECU)

composite currency

special drawing right (SDR)

Federal Deposit Insurance Corporation (FDIC)

Eurocurrency market (offshore banking)

international banking facility (IBF)

fractional reserve banking system

required reserves

excess reserves

deposit expansion multiplier

EXERCISES

1. Describe the four functions of money using the
U.S. dollar to provide an example of how dollars serve each function.

2. Discuss how the following would serve the
functions of money.

   a. Gold
   b. Yap stone money
   c. Cigarettes
   d. Diamonds

3. What is a financial intermediary? Give an
example of how your bank or credit union
serves as a financial intermediary between you
and the rest of the economy.

4. First Bank has cash reserves of $200,000,
loans of $800,000, and deposits of $1,000,000.

   a. Prepare a balance sheet for the bank.
   b. If the bank maintains a reserve requirement of 12 percent, what is the largest
   loan it can make?

   c. What is the maximum amount the money
   supply can be increased as a result of First
   Bank's new loan?

5. Yesterday bank A had no excess reserves.
Today it received a new deposit of $5,000.

   a. If the bank maintains a reserve requirement of 2 percent, what is the maximum
   loan bank A can make?
   b. What is the maximum amount the money
   supply can be increased as a result of bank
   A's new loan?

6. The deposit expansion multiplier measures the
maximum possible expansion of the money
supply in the banking system. What factors
could cause the actual expansion of the money
supply to differ from that given by the deposit
expansion multiplier?

7. What is liquidity? Rank the following assets in
order of their liquidity: $10 bill, personal
check for $20, savings account with $400 in it,
stereo, car, house, travelers' check.

Use the following table on the components of money in a hypothetical economy to answer questions 8–10.

Money Component	Amount
Travelers' checks	$ 100
Currency	2,000
Small-denomination time deposits	3,500
Repurchase agreements	2,000
Demand deposits	5,000
Other checkable deposits	9,000
U.S. Treasury bonds	25,000
Large-denomination time deposits	8,000
Retail money market mutual funds	7,500

8. What is the value of M1 in the above table?
9. What is the value of M2 in the above table?
10. What is the value of M3 in the above table?

 INTERNET EXERCISE

In this chapter, we learned that banks, like all other businesses, sometimes fail due to bad management or unexpectedly bad performance of certain key industries where a bank has committed many loans. To see the recent experience of failed banks in the United States, go to the Boyes/Melvin *Fundamentals of Economics* Web site at **http://www.hmco.com/college/** and click on the Internet Exercise link for Chapter 14. Now answer the questions that appear on the Boyes/Melvin Web site.

15

Monetary Policy

FUNDAMENTAL QUESTIONS

1. What does the Federal Reserve do?

2. How is monetary policy set?

3. What are the tools of monetary policy?

4. What role do central banks play in the foreign exchange market?

5. What are the determinants of the demand for money?

6. How does monetary policy affect the equilibrium level of real GDP?

In the previous chapter, we saw how banks "create" money by making loans. However, that money must get into the system to begin with. Most of us never think about how money enters the economy. All we worry about is having money available when we need it. But there is a government body that controls the U.S. money supply, and in this chapter we will learn about this agency—the Federal Reserve System and the Board of Governors that oversees monetary policy.

The amount of money available for spending by individuals or businesses affects prices, interest rates, foreign exchange rates, and the level of income in the economy. Thus, having control of the money supply gives the Federal Reserve powerful influence over these important economic variables. As we learned in Chapter 13, fiscal policy, or the control of government spending and taxes, is one of two ways by which government can change the equilibrium level of real GDP. Monetary policy as carried out by the Federal Reserve is the other mechanism through which attempts are made to manage the economy. In this chapter we will also explore the tools of monetary policy and see how changes in the money supply affect the equilibrium level of real GDP. ■

1. THE FEDERAL RESERVE SYSTEM

The Federal Reserve is the central bank of the United States. A *central bank* performs several functions: accepting deposits from and making loans to commercial banks, acting as a banker for the federal government, and controlling the money supply. We discuss these functions in greater detail below, but first we look at the structure of the Federal Reserve System, or the Fed.

1.a. Structure of the Fed

Congress created the Federal Reserve System in 1913, with the Federal Reserve Act. Bank panics and failures had convinced lawmakers that the United States needed an agency to control the money supply and make loans to commercial banks when those banks found themselves without sufficient reserves. Because Americans tended to distrust large banking interests, Congress called for a decentralized central bank. The Federal Reserve System divides the nation into twelve districts, each with its own Federal Reserve bank (Figure 1).

1.a.1. Board of Governors Although Congress created a decentralized system so that each district bank would represent the special interests of its own region, in practice the Fed is much more centralized than its creators intended. Monetary policy is largely set by the Board of Governors in Washington, D.C. This board is made up of seven members, who are appointed by the president and confirmed by the Senate.

The most visible and powerful member of the board is the chairperson. In fact the chairperson of the Board of Governors has been called *the second most powerful person in the United States*. This individual serves as a leader and spokesperson for the board, and typically exercises more authority in determining the course of monetary policy than do the other governors.

The chairperson is appointed by the president to a four-year term. In recent years most chairs have been reappointed to an additional term (Table 1). The governors serve fourteen-year terms, the terms staggered so that every two years a new position comes up for appointment. This system allows continuity in the policy-making process and is intended to place the board above politics. Congress created the Fed as an independent agency: monetary policy is supposed to be formulated independent of Congress and the president. Of

Figure 1
The Federal Reserve System

The Federal Reserve System divides the country into twelve districts. Each district has its own Federal Reserve bank, headquarters for Fed operations in that district.

For example, the First District bank is in Boston; the Twelfth is in San Francisco. There are also branch banks in Los Angeles, Miami, and other cities. Source: *Federal Reserve Bulletin* (Washington, D.C.).

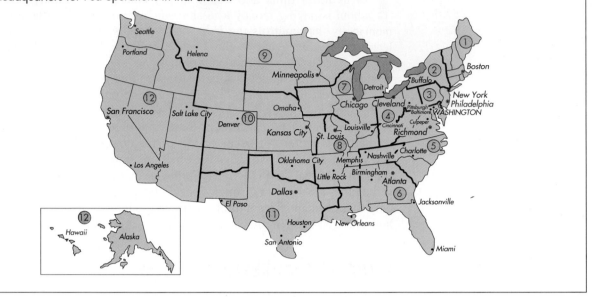

course, this is impossible in practice because the president appoints and the Senate approves the members of the board. But because the governors serve fourteen-year terms, they outlast the president who appointed them.

1.a.2. District Banks Each of the Fed's twelve district banks is formally directed by a nine-person board of directors. Three directors represent commercial banks in the district, and three represent nonbanking business interests. These six individuals are elected by the Federal Reserve System member banks in the district. The three remaining directors are appointed by the Fed's Board of Governors. District bank directors are not involved in the day-to-day operations of the district banks, but they meet regularly to oversee bank operations. They also choose the president of the bank. The president, who is in charge of operations, participates in monetary policy making with the Board of Governors in Washington, D.C.

■ **Federal Open Market Committee (FOMC):** the official policy-making body of the Federal Reserve System

1.a.3. The Federal Open Market Committee The **Federal Open Market Committee (FOMC)** is the official policy-making body of the Federal Reserve System. The committee is made up of the seven members of the Board of Governors plus five of the twelve district bank presidents. All of the district bank presidents, except for the president of the Federal Reserve Bank

TABLE 1
Recent Chairmen of the Federal Reserve Board

Name	Age at Appointment	Term Began	Term Ended	Years of Tenure
William McChesney Martin	44	4/2/51	1/31/70	18.8
Arthur Burns	65	1/31/70	2/1/78	8.0
G. William Miller	52	3/8/78	8/6/79	1.4
Paul Volcker	51	8/6/79	8/5/87	8.0
Alan Greenspan	61	8/11/87		

What's on a Dollar Bill?

The figure shows both sides of a dollar bill. We've numbered several elements for identification.

1. Currency is issued by the Federal Reserve System. The top of a dollar bill used to say "SILVER CERTIFICATE" where it now says "FEDERAL RESERVE NOTE." Silver certificates could be exchanged for silver dollars or silver bullion at the U.S. Treasury until 1967, when Congress authorized the Treasury to stop redeeming silver certificates.

2. Every dollar bill indicates which Federal Reserve bank issued it. The stamp with the *F* in the middle reads "FEDERAL RESERVE BANK OF ATLANTA GEORGIA." *F* is the sixth letter of the alphabet, and the Atlanta Fed is headquarters for the sixth Federal Reserve District. Also the serial number begins with an *F*. Finally, there is a number 6 in each corner, again indicating that the bill was issued by the Sixth District bank.

3. The dollar is the legal money of the United States. Debts and tax obligations can be legally discharged with dollars.

4. *D231* is the number of the

engraving plate used to print this dollar bill.

5. *D2*, which stands for row D, column 2, is the position on the sheet where this dollar was printed. Money is printed in large sheets, which are then cut to make individual bills.

6. There are several interesting features in the great seal.

ANNUIT COEPTIS means "He has favored our undertakings." The eye represents an all-seeing deity. The pyramid stands for strength. NOVUS ORDO SECLORUM means a "new order of the ages." The Roman numerals at the bottom of the pyramid equal 1776.

of New York, take turns serving on the FOMC. Because the New York Fed actually carries out monetary policy, that bank's president is always on the committee. In section 2 we talk more about the FOMC's role and the tactics it uses.

1.b. Functions of the Fed

The Federal Reserve System offers banking services to the banking community and the U.S. Treasury, and supervises the nation's banking system. The Fed also regulates the U.S. money supply.

1.b.1. Banking Services and Supervision The Fed provides several basic services to the banking community: it supplies currency to banks, holds their reserves, and clears checks. The Fed supplies U.S. currency (Federal Reserve notes) to the banking community through its twelve district banks. (See the

Economic Insight "What's on a Dollar Bill?") Commercial banks in each district also hold reserves in the form of deposits at their district bank. In addition, the Fed makes loans to banks. In this sense, the Fed is a *banker's bank*. And the Fed clears checks, transferring funds to the banks where checks are deposited from the banks on which the checks are drawn.

The Fed also supervises the nation's banks, ensuring that they operate in a sound and prudent manner. And it acts as the banker for the U.S. government, selling U.S. government securities for the U.S. Treasury.

1.b.2. Controlling the Money Supply All of the functions the Federal Reserve carries out are important, but none is more important than managing the nation's money supply. Before 1913, when the Fed was created, the money supply did not change to meet fluctuations in the demand for money. These fluctuations can stem from changes in income or seasonal patterns of demand. For example, every year during the Christmas season, the demand for currency rises because people carry more money to buy gifts. During the holiday season, the Fed increases the supply of currency to meet the demand for cash withdrawals from banks. After the holiday season, the demand for currency drops and the public deposits currency in banks, which then return the currency to the Fed.

The Fed controls the money supply to achieve the policy goals set by the FOMC. It does this largely through its ability to influence bank reserves and the money-creating power of commercial banks that we talked about in Chapter 14.

RECAP

1. As the central bank of the United States, the Federal Reserve accepts deposits from and makes loans to commercial banks, acts as a banker for the federal government, and controls the money supply.

2. The Federal Reserve System is made up of twelve district banks and the Board of Governors in Washington, D.C.

3. The most visible and powerful member of the Board of Governors is the chairperson.

4. The governors are appointed by the president and confirmed by the Senate to serve fourteen-year terms.

5. Monetary policy is made by the Federal Open Market Committee, whose members include the seven governors and five district bank presidents.

6. The Fed provides currency, holds reserves, clears checks, and supervises commercial banks.

7. The most important function the Fed performs is controlling the U.S. money supply.

2. IMPLEMENTING MONETARY POLICY

Changes in the amount of money in an economy affect the inflation rate, the interest rate, and the equilibrium level of national income. Throughout history, monetary policy has made currencies worthless and toppled governments. This is why controlling the money supply is so important.

2.a. Policy Goals

The ultimate goal of monetary policy is much like that of fiscal policy: economic growth with stable prices. *Economic growth* means greater output; *stable prices* mean a low, steady rate of inflation.

The chairman of the Federal Reserve Board of Governors is sometimes referred to as the second most powerful person in the United States. At the time this book was written, Alan Greenspan was the Fed chairman. His leadership of the Fed has important implications for money and credit conditions in the United States.

2.a.1. Intermediate Targets

The Fed does not control gross domestic product or the price level directly. Instead it controls the money supply, which in turn affects GDP and the level of prices. The money supply, or the growth of the money supply, is an **intermediate target**, an objective that helps the Fed achieve its ultimate policy objective—economic growth with stable prices.

■ **intermediate target:**
an objective used to achieve some ultimate policy goal

Using the growth of the money supply as an intermediate target assumes there is a fairly stable relationship between changes in money and changes in income and prices. The bases for this assumption are the equation of exchange and the quantity theory of money. The **equation of exchange** is a definition that relates the quantity of money to nominal GDP:

■ **equation of exchange:**
an equation that relates the quantity of money to nominal GDP

$$MV = PQ$$

where

$$M = \text{the quantity of money}$$
$$V = \text{the velocity of money}$$
$$P = \text{the price level}$$
$$Q = \text{the quantity of output, like real income or real GDP}$$

This equation is true by definition: money times the velocity of money will always be equal to nominal GDP.

In Chapter 14 we said there are several definitions of the money supply: M1, M2, and M3. The **velocity of money** is the average number of times each dollar is spent on final goods and services in a year. If P is the price level and Q is real GDP (the quantity of goods and services produced in the economy), then PQ equals nominal GDP. If

■ **velocity of money:**
the average number of times each dollar is spent on final goods and services in a year

$$MV = PQ$$

then

$$V = \frac{PQ}{M}$$

Suppose the price level is 2 and real GDP is $500; PQ, or nominal GDP, is $1,000. If the money supply is $200, then velocity is 5 ($1,000/$200). A velocity of 5 means that each dollar must be spent an average of 5 times during the year if a money supply of $200 is going to support the purchase of $1,000 worth of new goods and services.

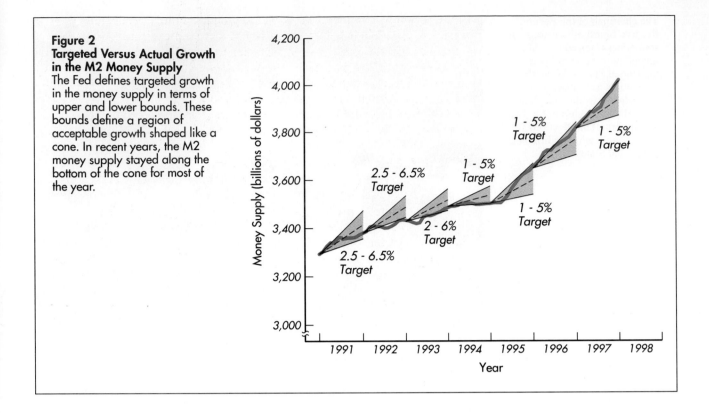

Figure 2
Targeted Versus Actual Growth in the M2 Money Supply
The Fed defines targeted growth in the money supply in terms of upper and lower bounds. These bounds define a region of acceptable growth shaped like a cone. In recent years, the M2 money supply stayed along the bottom of the cone for most of the year.

■ **quantity theory of money:**
with constant velocity, changes in the quantity of money change nominal GDP

The **quantity theory of money** uses the equation of exchange to relate changes in the money supply to changes in prices and output. If the money supply (M) increases and velocity (V) is constant, then nominal GDP (PQ) must increase. If the economy is operating at maximum capacity (producing at the maximum level of Q), an increase in M causes an increase in P. And if there is substantial unemployment so that Q can increase, the increase in M may mean a higher price level (P) as well as higher real GDP (Q).

The Fed attempts to set money growth targets that are consistent with rising output and low inflation. In terms of the quantity theory of money, the Fed wants to increase M at a rate that supports steadily rising Q with slow and steady increases in P. The assumption that there is a reasonably stable relationship among M, P, and Q is what motivates the Fed to use money supply growth rates as an intermediate target to achieve its ultimate goal—higher Q with slow increases in P.

The FOMC defines upper and lower bounds to describe its intermediate targets—the range in which it wants the money supply to grow. Figure 2 shows the ranges and the actual growth of the M2 money supply for recent years. In 1991 and 1992, the targeted growth of the M2 money supply was between 2.5 and 6.5 percent; then it dropped to 2 to 6 percent in 1993 and to 1 to 5 percent in 1994. The upper and lower lines at these growth rates create a cone that represents the region of growth targeted by the Fed. The upper part of the cone is the highest growth rate of 5 percent and the lower part of the cone is the lowest growth rate of 1 percent. The heavy line plots the actual path of the M2 money supply in each year. If the M2 money supply grew at a rate of 5 percent over the year 1994, the heavy line would be up at the top of the cone. If it grew at 1 percent, the heavy line would be at the bottom of the cone—as it was. By specifying a range of growth rather than a single rate of growth, the Fed gives itself more room to maneuver in dealing with unexpected events that might make managing the money supply difficult.

From the late 1950s to the mid-1970s, the velocity of the M1 money supply grew at a steady pace, from 3.5 in 1959 to 5.5 in 1975. Knowing that V was growing at a steady pace, the Fed was able to set a target growth rate for the

M1 money supply, confident that it would produce a fairly predictable growth in nominal GDP. But when velocity is not constant, there can be problems using money growth rates as an intermediate target. This is exactly what happened in the late 1970s and early 1980s. Although the M2 and M3 velocities continued to indicate a stable pattern of growth, M1 velocity behaved erratically. With the breakdown of the relationship between the M1 money supply and GDP, the Fed shifted its emphasis from the M1 money supply, concentrating instead on achieving targeted growth in the M2 and M3 money supplies.

Economists are still debating the reason for the fluctuations in the velocity of the M1 money supply. Some argue that new deposits and innovations in banking led to fluctuations in the money held in traditional demand deposits as bank customers switched to different types of financial assets. These changes would affect the M1 supply because its definition is so narrow. They would not affect the M2 and M3 supplies because their broader definitions include many of the new types of financial products available to the public.

In addition to targeting money growth, the Fed monitors other key variables that are used to indicate the future course of the economy. These include commodity prices, interest rates, and foreign exchange rates. The Fed may not set formal targets for all of them, but considers them in setting policy.

2.b. Operating Procedures

■ **FOMC directive:**
instructions issued by the FOMC to the Federal Reserve Bank of New York to implement monetary policy

The FOMC sets monetary targets and then implements them through the Federal Reserve Bank of New York. The mechanism for translating policy into action is an **FOMC directive**. Each directive outlines the conduct of monetary policy over the six- to eight-week period until the FOMC meets again to adjust monetary targets and specify policy tools.

2.b.1. Tools of Monetary Policy The Fed controls the money supply by changing bank reserves. There are three tools the Fed can use to change reserves: the *reserve requirement,* the *discount rate,* and *open market operations.* In the last chapter, you saw that banks can expand the money supply by a multiple of their excess reserves—the deposit expansion multiplier, the reciprocal of the reserve requirement.

Reserve Requirement The Fed requires banks to hold a fraction of their deposits on reserve. This fraction is the reserve requirement. *Transaction deposits* are checking accounts and other deposits that can be used to pay third parties. Large banks hold a greater percentage of deposits in reserve than do small banks (the reserve requirement increases from 3 to 10 percent for deposits in excess of $54 million).

Remember from Chapter 14 that required reserves are the dollar amount of reserves that a bank must hold to meet its reserve requirement. There are two ways in which required reserves may be held: vault cash at the bank or a deposit in the Fed. The sum of a bank's *vault cash* (coin and currency in the

■ **legal reserves:**
the cash a bank holds in its vault plus its deposit in the Fed

bank's vault) and deposit in the Fed is called its **legal reserves**. When legal reserves equal required reserves, the bank has no excess reserves and can make no new loans. When legal reserves exceed required reserves, the bank has excess reserves available for lending.

As bank excess reserves change, the lending and money-creating potential of the banking system changes. One way the Fed can alter excess reserves is by changing the reserve requirement. If it lowers the reserve requirement, a portion of what was previously required reserves becomes excess reserves, which can be used to make loans and expand the money supply. A lower reserve requirement also increases the deposit expansion multiplier. By raising the reserve requirement, the Fed reduces the money-creating potential of the banking system and tends to reduce the money supply. A higher reserve requirement also lowers the deposit expansion multiplier.

TABLE 2
The Effect of a Change in the Reserve Requirement

Balance Sheet of First National Bank

Assets		Liabilities	
Vault cash	$ 100,000	Deposits	$1,000,000
Deposit in Fed	200,000		
Loans	700,000		
Total	$1,000,000	Total	$1,000,000

Legal reserves (LR) equal vault cash plus the deposit in the Fed, or $300,000:

$LR = \$100,000 + \$200,000$
$\quad = \$300,000$

Excess reserves (ER) equal legal reserves minus required reserves (RR):

$ER = LR - RR$

Required reserves equal the reserve requirement (r) times deposits (D):

$RR = rD$

If the reserve requirement is 10 percent:

$RR = (.10)(\$1,000,000)$
$\quad = \$100,000$
$ER = \$300,000 - \$100,000$
$\quad = \$200,000$

First National Bank can make a maximum loan of $200,000.
The banking system can expand the money supply by the deposit expansion multiplier ($1/r$) times the excess reserves of the bank, or $2,000,000:

$(1/.10)(\$200,000) = 10(\$200,000)$
$\qquad\qquad\qquad = \$2,000,000$

If the reserve requirement is 20 percent:

$RR = (.20)(\$1,000,000)$
$\quad = \$200,000$
$ER = \$300,000 - \$200,000$
$\quad = \$100,000$

First National Bank can make a maximum loan of $100,000.
The banking system can expand the money supply by the deposit expansion multiplier ($1/r$) times the excess reserves of the bank or $500,000:

$(1/.20)(\$100,000) = 5(\$100,000)$
$\qquad\qquad\qquad = \$500,000$

Consider the example in Table 2. If First National Bank's balance sheet shows vault cash of $100,000 and a deposit in the Fed of $200,000, the bank has legal reserves of $300,000. The amount of money that the bank can lend is determined by its excess reserves. Excess reserves (ER) equal legal reserves (LR) minus required reserves (RR):

$$ER = LR - RR$$

If the reserve requirement (r) is 10 percent (.10), the bank must keep 10 percent of its deposits (D) as required reserves:

$$RR = rD$$
$$= .10\ (\$1,000,000)$$
$$= \$100,000$$

In this case, the bank has excess reserves of $200,000 ($300,000 − $100,000). The bank can make a maximum loan of $200,000. The banking system can expand the money supply by the deposit expansion multiplier ($1/r$) times the excess reserves of the bank, or $2,000,000 ($1/.10 \times \$200,000$).

If the reserve requirement goes up to 20 percent (.20), required reserves are 20 percent of $1,000,000, or $200,000. Excess reserves are now $100,000, which is the maximum loan the bank can make. The banking system can expand the money supply by $500,000:

$$\frac{1}{.20}(\$100,000) = 5\,(\$100,000)$$

$$= \$500,000$$

By raising the reserve requirement, the Fed can reduce the money-creating potential of the banking system and the money supply. And by lowering the reserve requirement, the Fed can increase the money-creating potential of the banking system and the money supply.

Discount Rate If a bank needs more reserves in order to make new loans, it typically borrows from other banks in the federal funds market. The market is called the *federal funds market* because the funds are being loaned from one commercial bank's excess reserves on deposit with the Federal Reserve to another commercial bank's deposit account at the Fed. For instance, if the First National Bank has excess reserves of $1 million, it can lend the excess to the Second National Bank. When a bank borrows in the federal funds market, it pays a rate of interest called the **federal funds rate**.

At times, however, banks borrow directly from the Fed, although the Fed restricts access to such funds. The **discount rate** is the rate of interest the Fed charges banks. (In other countries, the rate of interest the central bank charges commercial banks is often called the *bank rate*.) Another way the Fed controls the level of bank reserves and the money supply is by changing the discount rate.

When the Fed raises the discount rate, it raises the cost of borrowing reserves, reducing the amount of reserves borrowed. Lower levels of reserves limit bank lending and the expansion of the money supply. When the Fed lowers the discount rate, it lowers the cost of borrowing reserves, increasing the amount of borrowing. As bank reserves increase, so do loans and the money supply.

The discount rate is relatively stable. Although other interest rates can fluctuate daily, the discount rate usually remains fixed for months at a time. Since the late 1970s, the most the rate has been changed in a year has been seven times.

Open Market Operations The major tool of monetary policy is the Fed's **open market operations**, the buying and selling of U.S. government bonds. Suppose the FOMC wants to increase bank reserves to stimulate the growth of money. The committee issues a directive to the bond-trading desk at the Federal Reserve Bank of New York to buy bonds. The bonds are purchased from private bond dealers. The dealers are paid with checks drawn on the Federal Reserve, which then are deposited in the dealers' accounts at commercial banks. What happens? As bank deposits and reserves increase, banks are able to make new loans, which in turn expand the money supply through the deposit expansion multiplier process.

If the Fed wants to decrease the money supply, it sells bonds. Private bond dealers pay for the bonds with checks drawn on commercial banks. Commercial bank deposits and reserves drop, and the money supply decreases through the deposit expansion multiplier process.

Its open market operations allow the Fed to control the money supply. To increase the money supply, the Fed buys U.S. government bonds. To decrease the money supply, it sells U.S. government bonds. The effect of selling these bonds, however, varies according to whether or not there are excess reserves in the banking system. If there are excess reserves, the money supply does not

---

■ federal funds rate:
the interest rate a bank charges when it lends excess reserves to another bank

■ discount rate:
the interest rate the Fed charges commercial banks when they borrow from it

■ open market operations:
the buying and selling of government bonds by the Fed to control bank reserves and the money supply

TABLE 3
The Effect of an Open Market Operation

Balance Sheet of First National Bank

Assets		Liabilities	
Vault cash	$ 100,000	Deposits	$1,000,000
Deposit in Fed	200,000		
Loans	700,000		
Total	$1,000,000	Total	$1,000,000

Initially legal reserves (*LR*) equal vault cash plus the deposit in the Fed, or $300,000:

$LR = \$100,000 + \$200,000$
$\quad = \$300,000$

If the reserve requirement (*r*) is 20 percent (.20), required reserves (*RR*) equal $200,000:

$.20(\$1,000,000) = \$200,000$

Excess reserves (*ER*), then, equal $100,000 ($300,000 − $200,000). The bank can make a maximum loan of $100,000. The banking system can expand the money supply by the deposit expansion multiplier (1/*r*) times the excess reserves of the bank,
or $500,000:

$(1/.20)(\$100,000) = 5(\$100,000)$
$\qquad\qquad\qquad = \$500,000$

Open market purchase:

The Fed purchases $100,000 worth of bonds from a dealer, who deposits the $100,000 in an account at First National. At this point the bank has legal reserves of $400,000, required reserves of $220,000, and excess reserves of $180,000. It can make a maximum loan of $180,000, which can expand the money supply by $900,000 [(1/.20)($180,000)].

Open market sale:

The Fed sells $100,000 worth of bonds to a dealer, who pays with a check drawn on an account at First National. At this point, the bank has legal reserves of $200,000, required reserves of $180,000 (its deposits now equal $900,000), and excess reserves of $20,000. It can make a maximum loan of $20,000, which can expand the money supply by $100,000 [(1/.20)($20,000)].

necessarily decrease when the Fed sells bonds. The open market sale may simply reduce the level of excess reserves, reducing the rate at which the money supply increases.

Table 3 shows how open market operations change bank reserves and illustrates the money-creating power of the banking system. First National Bank's initial balance sheet shows excess reserves of $100,000 with a 20 percent reserve requirement. Therefore the bank can make a maximum loan of $100,000. Based on the bank's reserve position, the banking system can increase the money supply by a maximum of $500,000.

If the Fed purchases $100,000 worth of bonds from a private dealer, who deposits the $100,000 in an account at First National Bank, the excess reserves of First National Bank increase to $180,000. These reserves can generate a maximum increase in the money supply of $900,000. The open market purchase increases the excess reserves of the banking system, stimulating the growth of money and, eventually, nominal GDP.

What happens when an open market sale takes place? If the Fed sells $100,000 worth of bonds to a private bond dealer, the dealer pays for the bonds using a check drawn on First National Bank. First National's deposits

Figure 3
Monetary Policy: Tools, Targets, and Goals
The Fed primarily uses open market operations to implement monetary policy. The decision to buy or sell bonds is based on a short-run operating target, like the level of reserves held by commercial banks. The short-run operating target is set to achieve an intermediate target, a certain level of money supply. The intermediate target is set to achieve the ultimate goal, a certain level of gross domestic product.

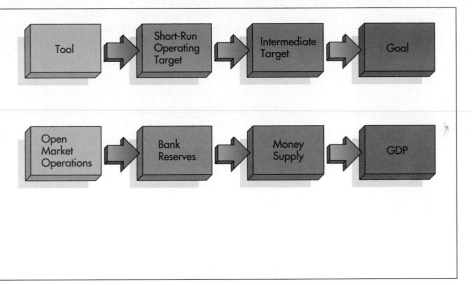

drop from $1,000,000 to $900,000, and its legal reserves drop from $300,000 to $200,000. With excess reserves of $20,000, the banking system can increase the money supply by only $100,000. The open market sale reduces the money-creating potential of the banking system from $500,000 initially to $100,000.

2.b.2. FOMC Directives When it sets monetary policy, the FOMC begins with its *ultimate goal*: economic growth at stable prices. It defines that goal in terms of GDP. Then it works backwards to identify its *intermediate target*, the rate at which the money supply must grow to achieve the wanted growth in GDP. Then it must decide how to achieve its intermediate target. In Figure 3, as is usually the case in real life, the Fed uses open market operations. But to know whether it should buy or sell bonds, the FOMC must have some indication of whether the money supply is growing too fast or too slow. The committee relies on a *short-run operating target* for this information. The short-run target indicates how the money supply should change. Both the quantity of excess reserves in the banking system and the federal funds rate can serve as short-run operating targets.

The FOMC carries out its policies through directives to the bond-trading desk at the Federal Reserve Bank of New York. The directives specify a short-run operating target that the trading desk must use in its day-to-day operations. When the FOMC first began setting intermediate monetary targets in 1970, it attempted to prescribe very specific target ranges for the federal funds interest rate. The committee chose the federal funds rate as the short-run target because it believed the rate was the best indicator of the status of reserves. Because the federal funds rate is the interest rate one bank charges another when the second bank borrows reserves from the first, the federal funds rate rises when there are few excess reserves and falls when the banking system has a large amount of excess reserves. The Fed believed that if the federal funds rate rose above the FOMC's target, it would indicate that there were not enough reserves in the banking system, that the money supply was not growing fast enough. The bond-trading desk would then purchase bonds from bond dealers.

In the 1970s, the federal funds rate target worked well to stabilize interest rates. However, the money supply fluctuated a great deal more than the FOMC wanted. For example, when people were spending at a rapid pace and so borrowing increasing amounts of money, the banking system's reserves fell and the federal funds rate rose. The rising rate signaled the trading desk to purchase bonds and increase reserves. These reserves were immediately lent, and the money supply grew more quickly. As long as the federal funds rate continued to go up, new reserves were being pumped into the banking system and the money supply grew faster and faster. Conversely, when people were not spending and excess reserves accumulated, the trading desk sold bonds, the money supply fell and continued to fall as long as the federal funds rate was below the target range. By the fall of 1979, the FOMC had decided that it needed a better indicator of money supply growth for its short-run operating target. The committee chose bank reserves.

The nature of the Fed's policy regarding reserve targeting has changed over time. In addition, the Fed takes other factors into account. For example, FOMC directives still cite a desired level for the federal funds rate, but the range is much broader than it was in the days of targeting interest rates. The directives also cite real GDP growth, the rate of inflation, and the foreign exchange value of the dollar, factors that could affect the FOMC-targeted bank reserves.

2.c. Foreign Exchange Market Intervention

In the mid-1980s, conditions in the foreign exchange market took on a high priority in FOMC directives, which continues to this day. There was concern that the value of the dollar in relation to other currencies was contributing to a large U.S. international trade deficit. Furthermore, the governments of the major industrial countries decided to work together to maintain more stable exchange rates. This meant that the Federal Reserve and the central banks of the other developed countries had to devote more attention to maintaining exchange rates within a certain target band of values, much as the federal funds rate had been targeted in the 1970s.

■ **foreign exchange market intervention:**
the buying and selling of foreign exchange by a central bank to move exchange rates up or down to a targeted level

2.c.1. Mechanics of Intervention **Foreign exchange market intervention** is the buying and selling of foreign exchange by a central bank in order to move exchange rates up or down. We can use a simple supply and demand diagram to illustrate the role of intervention. Figure 4 shows the U.S. dollar–Japanese yen exchange market. The demand curve is the demand for dollars produced by the demand for U.S. goods and financial assets. The supply curve is the supply of dollars generated by U.S. residents' demand for the products and financial assets of other countries. Here, the supply of dollars to the dollar-yen market comes from the U.S. demand to buy Japanese products.

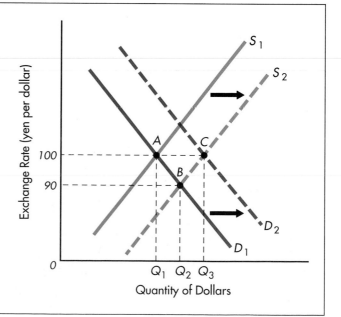

Figure 4
The Dollar-Yen Foreign Exchange Market
The demand is the demand for dollars arising out of the Japanese demand for U.S. goods and services. The supply is the supply of dollars arising out of the U.S. demand for Japanese goods and services. Initially, the equilibrium exchange rate is at the intersection of the demand curve (D_1) and the supply curve (S_1), where the exchange rate is ¥100 = $1. An increase in the U.S. demand for Japanese goods increases S_1 to S_2 and pushes the equilibrium exchange rate down to point B, where ¥90 = $1. If the Fed's target exchange rate is ¥100 = $1, the Fed must intervene, buying dollars in the foreign exchange market. This increases demand to D_2 and raises the equilibrium exchange rate to point C, where ¥100 = $1.

The initial equilibrium exchange rate is at point A, where the demand curve (D_1) and the supply curve (S_1) intersect. At point A, the exchange rate is ¥100 = $1, and Q_1 dollars are exchanged for yen. Suppose that over time, U.S. residents buy more from Japan than Japanese residents buy from the United States. As the supply of dollars increases in relation to the demand for dollars, equilibrium shifts to point B. At point B, Q_2 dollars are exchanged at a rate of ¥90 = $1. The dollar has *depreciated* against the yen, or, conversely, the yen has *appreciated* against the dollar.

When the dollar depreciates, U.S. goods are cheaper to Japanese buyers (it takes fewer yen to buy each dollar). The depreciated dollar stimulates U.S. exports to Japan. It also raises the price of Japanese goods to U.S. buyers, reducing U.S. imports from Japan. Rather than allow exchange rates to change, with the subsequent changes in trade, central banks often seek to maintain fixed exchange rates because of international agreements or desired trade in goods or financial assets.

Suppose the Fed sets a target range for the dollar at a minimum exchange rate of ¥100 = $1. If the exchange rate falls below the minimum, the Fed must intervene in the foreign exchange market to increase the value of the dollar. In Figure 4, you can see that the only way to increase the dollar's value is to increase the demand for dollars. The Fed intervenes in the foreign exchange market by buying dollars in exchange for yen. It uses its holdings of Japanese yen to purchase $Q_3 - Q_1$ dollars, shifting the demand curve to D_2. Now equilibrium is at point C, where Q_3 dollars are exchanged at the rate of ¥100 = $1.

The kind of intervention shown in Figure 4 is only temporary because the Fed has a limited supply of yen. Under another intervention plan, the Bank of Japan would support the ¥100 = $1 exchange rate by using yen to buy dollars. The Bank of Japan could carry on this kind of policy indefinitely because it has the power to create yen. A third alternative is *coordinated intervention,* in which both the Fed and the Bank of Japan sell yen in exchange for dollars to support the minimum yen-dollar exchange rate.

2.c.2. Effects of Intervention Intervention can be used to shift the demand and supply for currency and thereby change the exchange rate. Foreign exchange market intervention also has effects on the money supply. If the Federal Reserve wanted to increase the dollar price of the French franc, it would create dollars to purchase francs. Thus when foreign exchange market intervention involves the use of domestic currency to buy foreign currency, it increases the domestic money supply. The expansionary effect of this intervention can be offset by a domestic open market operation, in a process called **sterilization**. If the Fed creates dollars to buy French francs, for example, it increases the money supply, as we have just seen. To reduce the money supply, the Fed can direct an open market bond sale. The bond sale sterilizes the effect of the intervention on the domestic money supply.

■ **sterilization:**
the use of domestic open market operations to offset the effects of a foreign exchange market intervention on the domestic money supply

RECAP

1. The ultimate goal of monetary policy is economic growth with stable prices.
2. The Fed controls GDP indirectly, through its control of the money supply.
3. The equation of exchange ($MV - PQ$) relates the quantity of money to nominal GDP.
4. The quantity theory of money states that with constant velocity, changes in the quantity of money change nominal GDP.

5. Every six to eight weeks, the Federal Open Market Committee issues a directive to the Federal Reserve Bank of New York that defines the FOMC's monetary targets and policy tools.

6. The Fed controls the nation's money supply by changing bank excess reserves.

7. The tools of monetary policy are reserve requirements, the discount rate, and open market operations.

8. The money supply tends to increase (decrease) as the reserve requirement falls (rises), the discount rate falls (rises), and the Fed buys (sells) bonds.

9. Each FOMC directive defines its short-run operating target in terms of bank reserves and the federal funds rate, while also considering the growth of real GDP, the rate of inflation, and the foreign exchange rate of the dollar.

10. Foreign exchange market intervention is the buying and selling of foreign exchange by a central bank to achieve a targeted exchange rate.

11. Sterilization is the use of domestic open market operations to offset the money supply effects of foreign exchange market intervention.

3. MONETARY POLICY AND EQUILIBRIUM INCOME

To see how changes in the money supply affect the equilibrium level of real GDP, we incorporate monetary policy into the aggregate demand and supply model. The first step in understanding monetary policy is understanding the demand for money. If you know what determines money demand, you can see how monetary policy is used to shift aggregate demand and change the equilibrium level of real GDP.

3.a. Money Demand

Why do you hold money? What does it do for you? What determines how much money you will hold? These questions are addressed in this section. Wanting to hold more money is not the same as wanting more income. You can decide to carry more cash or keep more dollars in your checking account even though your income has not changed. The quantity of dollars you want to hold is your demand for money. By summing the quantity of money demanded by each individual, we can find the money demand for the entire economy. Once we understand what determines money demand, we can put that demand together with the money supply and examine how money influences the interest rate and the equilibrium level of income.

In Chapter 14 we discussed the functions of money, that is, what money is used for. People use money as a unit of account, a medium of exchange, a store of value, and a standard of deferred payment. These last functions help explain the demand for money.

■ **transactions demand for money:**
the demand to hold money to buy goods and services

People use money for transactions, to buy goods and services. The **transactions demand for money** is a demand to hold money in order to spend it on goods and services. Holding money in your pocket or checking account is a demand for money. Spending money is not demanding it; by spending it you are getting rid of it.

If your boss paid you the same instant that you wanted to buy something, the timing of your receipts and expenditures would match perfectly. You would not have to hold money for transactions. But because receipts typically occur much less often than expenditures, money is necessary to cover transactions between paychecks.

■ precautionary demand for money:
the demand for money to cover unplanned transactions or emergencies

■ speculative demand for money:
the demand for money created by uncertainty about the value of other assets

People also hold money to take care of emergencies. The **precautionary demand for money** exists because emergencies happen. People never know when an unexpected expense will crop up or when actual expenditures will exceed planned expenditures. So they hold money as a precaution.

Finally, there is a **speculative demand for money**, a demand created by uncertainty about the value of other assets. This demand exists because money is the most liquid store of value. If you want to buy a stock, but you believe the price is going to fall in the next few days, you hold the money until you are ready to buy the stock.

The speculative demand for money is not necessarily tied to a particular use of funds. People hold money because they expect the price of any asset to fall. Holding money is less risky than buying the asset today if the price of the asset seems likely to fall. For example, suppose you buy and sell fine art. The price of art fluctuates over time. You try to buy when prices are low and sell when prices are high. If you expect prices to fall in the short term, you hold money rather than art until the prices do fall. Then you use money to buy art for resale when the prices go up again.

3.a.1. The Money Demand Function If you understand why people hold money, you can understand what changes the amount of money they hold. As you've just seen, people hold money in order to: (1) carry out transactions (transactions demand), (2) be prepared for emergencies (precautionary demand), and (3) speculate on purchases of various assets (speculative demand). The interest rate and nominal income (income measured in current dollars) influence how much money people hold in order to carry out these three activities.

The Interest Rate There is an inverse relationship between the interest rate and the quantity of money demanded (see Figure 5). The interest rate is the *opportunity cost* of holding money. If you bury a thousand dollar bills in your backyard, that currency is earning no interest—you are forgoing the interest. At a low interest rate, the cost of forgone interest is small. At a higher interest rate, however, the cost of holding wealth in the form of money means giving up more interest. The higher the rate of interest, the greater the interest forgone by holding money, so the less money held. The costs of holding money limit the amount of money held.

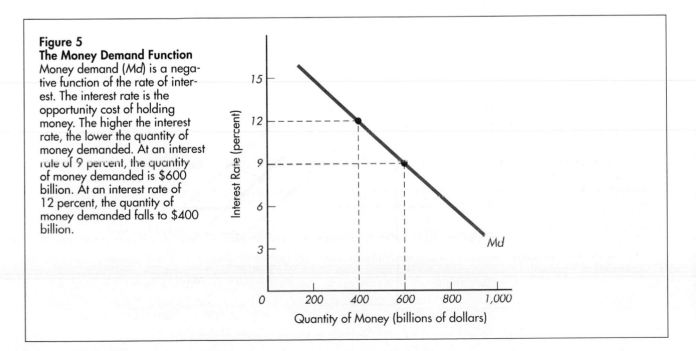

Figure 5
The Money Demand Function
Money demand (*Md*) is a negative function of the rate of interest. The interest rate is the opportunity cost of holding money. The higher the interest rate, the lower the quantity of money demanded. At an interest rate of 9 percent, the quantity of money demanded is $600 billion. At an interest rate of 12 percent, the quantity of money demanded falls to $400 billion.

Some components of the money supply pay interest to the depositor. Here the opportunity cost of holding money is the difference between the interest rate on a bond or some other nonmonetary asset and the interest rate on money. If a bond pays 9 percent interest a year and a bank deposit pays 5 percent, the opportunity cost of holding the deposit is 4 percent.

Figure 5 shows a money demand function where the demand for money depends on the interest rate. The downward slope of the money demand curve (*Md*) shows the inverse relation between the interest rate and the quantity of money demanded. For instance, at an interest rate of 12 percent, the quantity of money demanded is $400 billion. If the interest rate falls to 9 percent, the quantity of money demanded increases to $600 billion.

Nominal Income The demand for money also depends on nominal income. Money demand varies directly with nominal income because as income increases, more transactions are carried out and more money is required for those transactions.

The greater nominal income, the greater the demand for money. This is true whether the increase in nominal income is a product of a higher price level or an increase in real income. Both generate a greater dollar volume of transactions. If the prices of all goods increase, then more money must be used to purchase goods and services. And as real income increases, more goods and services are being produced and sold and living standards rise, which means more money is being demanded to execute the higher level of transactions.

A change in nominal income changes the demand for money at any given interest rate. Figure 6 shows the effect of changes in nominal income on the money demand curve. If income rises from Y_0 to Y_1, money demand increases from *Md* to Md_1. If income falls from Y_0 to Y_2, money demand falls from *Md* to Md_2. When the money demand function shifts from *Md* to Md_1, the quantity of money demanded at an interest rate of 9 percent increases from $600 billion to $800 billion. When the money demand function shifts from *Md* to Md_2, the quantity of money demanded at 9 percent interest falls from $600 billion to $400 billion.

3.a.2. The Money Supply Function The Federal Reserve is responsible for setting the money supply. The fact that the Fed can choose the money supply means that the money supply function is independent of the current interest rate and income. Figure 7 illustrates the money supply function (*Ms*). In the figure, the money supply is $600 billion at all interest rate levels. If the Fed

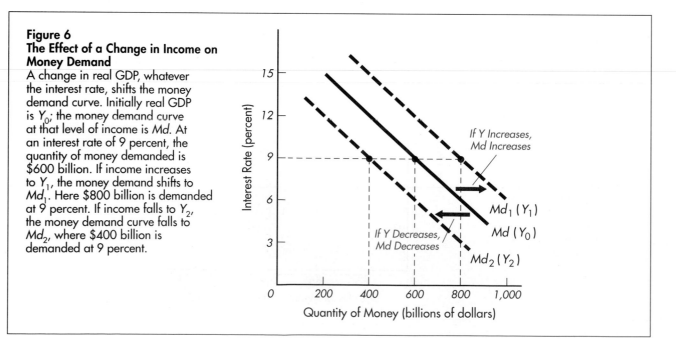

**Figure 6
The Effect of a Change in Income on Money Demand**
A change in real GDP, whatever the interest rate, shifts the money demand curve. Initially real GDP is Y_0; the money demand curve at that level of income is *Md*. At an interest rate of 9 percent, the quantity of money demanded is $600 billion. If income increases to Y_1, the money demand shifts to Md_1. Here $800 billion is demanded at 9 percent. If income falls to Y_2, the money demand curve falls to Md_2, where $400 billion is demanded at 9 percent.

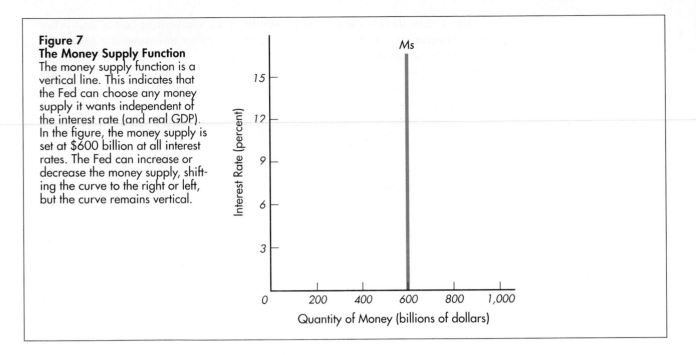

Figure 7
The Money Supply Function
The money supply function is a vertical line. This indicates that the Fed can choose any money supply it wants independent of the interest rate (and real GDP). In the figure, the money supply is set at $600 billion at all interest rates. The Fed can increase or decrease the money supply, shifting the curve to the right or left, but the curve remains vertical.

increases the money supply, the vertical money supply function shifts to the right. If the Fed decreases the money supply, the function shifts to the left.

3.a.3. Equilibrium in the Money Market To find the equilibrium interest rate and quantity of money, we have to combine the money demand and money supply functions in one diagram. Figure 8 graphs equilibrium in the money market. Equilibrium, point *e*, is at the intersection of the money demand and money supply functions. In the figure the equilibrium interest rate is 9 percent and the quantity of money is $600 billion.

What forces work to ensure that the economy tends toward the equilibrium rate of interest? Let's look at Figure 8 again to understand what happens if the interest rate is not at equilibrium. If the interest rate falls below 9 percent, there will be an excess demand for money. People will want more money than the Fed is supplying. But because the supply of money does not change, the demand for more money just forces the interest rate to rise. How? Suppose

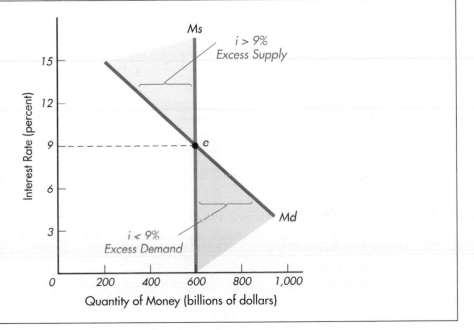

Figure 8
Equilibrium in the Money Market
Equilibrium is at point *e*, where the money demand and money supply curves intersect. At equilibrium, the interest rate is 9 percent and the money supply is $600 billion. An interest rate above 9 percent would create an excess supply of money because the quantity of money demanded falls as the interest rate rises. An interest rate below 9 percent would create an excess demand for money because the quantity of money demanded rises as the interest rate falls.

people try to increase their money holdings by converting bonds and other nonmonetary assets into money. As bonds and other nonmonetary assets are sold for money, the interest rate goes up.

To understand the connection between the rate of interest and buying and selling bonds, you must realize that the current interest rate (yield) on a bond is determined by the bond price:

$$\text{current interest rate} = \frac{\text{annual interest payment}}{\text{bond price}}$$

The numerator, the annual interest payment, is fixed for the life of the bond. The denominator, the bond price, fluctuates with supply and demand. As the bond price changes, the interest rate changes.

Suppose a bond pays $100 a year in interest and sells for $1,000. The interest rate is 10 percent ($100/$1,000). If the supply of bonds increases because people want to convert bonds to money, the price of bonds falls. Suppose the price drops to $800. At that price the interest rate equals 12.5 percent ($100/$800). This is the mechanism by which an excess demand for money changes the interest rate. As the interest rate goes up, the excess demand for money disappears.

Just the opposite occurs at interest rates above equilibrium. In Figure 8, any rate of interest above 9 percent creates an excess supply of money. Now people are holding more of their wealth in the form of money than they would like. What happens? They want to convert some of their money balances into nonmonetary assets, like bonds. As the demand for bonds rises, bond prices increase. And as bond prices go up, interest rates fall. This drop in interest rates restores equilibrium in the money market.

3.b. Money and Equilibrium Income

Now we are ready to relate monetary policy to the equilibrium level of real GDP. We use Figure 9 to show how a change in the money supply affects real GDP. In part (a), as the money supply increases from Ms_1 to Ms_2, the equilibrium rate of interest falls from i_1 to i_2.

Remember that investment (business spending on capital goods) declines as the rate of interest increases. The interest rate is the cost of borrowed funds. As the interest rate rises, the return on investment falls and with it the level of investment. As the interest rate falls, the return on investment rises and with it

Figure 9
Monetary Policy and Equilibrium Income
The three diagrams show the sequence of events by which a change in the money supply affects the equilibrium level of Real GDP. In part (a), the money supply increases, lowering the equilibrium interest rate. In part (b), the lower interest rate pushes the equilibrium level of investment up. In part (c), the increase in investment increases aggregate demand and equilibrium Real GDP.

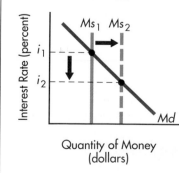

(a) Money Supply Increases and Interest Rate Falls

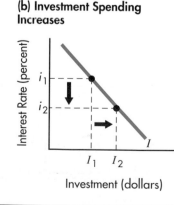

(b) Investment Spending Increases

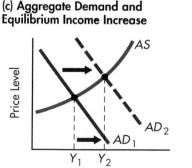

(c) Aggregate Demand and Equilibrium Income Increase

the level of investment. In part (a) of Figure 9, the interest rate falls. In part (b) of the figure you can see the effect of the lower interest rate on investment spending. As the interest rate falls from i_1 to i_2, investment increases from I_1 to I_2.

Figure 9(c) is the aggregate demand and supply equilibrium diagram. When investment spending increases, aggregate expenditures are higher at every price level, so the aggregate demand curve shifts to the right, from AD_1 to AD_2. The increase in aggregate demand increases equilibrium income from Y_1 to Y_2.

How does monetary policy affect equilibrium income? As the money supply increases, the equilibrium interest rate falls. As the interest rate falls, the equilibrium level of investment rises. Increased investment increases aggregate demand and equilibrium income. A decrease in the money supply works in reverse: as the interest rate rises, investment falls; as investment falls, aggregate demand and equilibrium income go down.

The mechanism we have just described is an oversimplification because the only element of aggregate expenditures that changes in this model is investment. But an excess demand for or supply of money involves more than simply selling or buying bonds. An excess supply of money probably would be reflected in increased consumption as well. If households are holding more money than they want to hold, they buy not only bonds but also goods and services so that consumption increases. If they are holding less money than they want to hold, they will sell bonds and consume less. So the effect of monetary policy on aggregate demand is a product of a change in both investment and consumption.

RECAP

1. The transactions demand for money is a demand to hold money to buy goods and services.

2. The precautionary demand for money exists because all expenditures cannot be planned.

3. The speculative demand for money is created by uncertainty about the value of other assets.

4. There is an inverse relationship between the interest rate and the quantity of money demanded.

5. The greater nominal income, the greater the demand for money.

6. Because the Federal Reserve sets the money supply, the money supply function is independent of the interest rate and nominal income.

7. The current yield on a bond equals the annual interest payment divided by the price of the bond.

8. An increase in the money supply lowers the interest rate, which raises the level of investment, which in turn increases aggregate demand and equilibrium income. A decrease in the money supply works in reverse.

SUMMARY

▬ What does the Federal Reserve do?

1. The Federal Reserve is the central bank of the United States.

2. The Federal Reserve System is operated by twelve district banks and a Board of Governors in Washington, D.C.

3. The Fed services and supervises the banking system, acts as the banker of the U.S. Treasury, and controls the money supply.

▬ How is monetary policy set?

4. The Fed controls nominal GDP indirectly by

controlling the quantity of money in the nation's economy.

5. The Fed uses the growth of the money supply as an intermediate target to help it achieve its ultimate goal—economic growth with stable prices.

▬▬ What are the tools of monetary policy?

6. The three tools of monetary policy are the reserve requirement, the discount rate, and open market operations.

7. The Fed buys bonds to increase the money supply and sells bonds to decrease the money supply.

8. The Federal Open Market Committee (FOMC) issues directives to the Federal Reserve Bank of New York outlining the conduct of monetary policy.

▬▬ What role do central banks play in the foreign exchange market?

9. Central banks intervene in the foreign exchange market when it is necessary to maintain a targeted exchange rate.

▬▬ What are the determinants of the demand for money?

10. The demand for money stems from the need to buy goods and services, to prepare for emergencies, and to retain a store of value.

11. There is an inverse relationship between the quantity of money demanded and the interest rate.

12. The greater nominal income, the greater the demand for money.

13. Because the Fed sets the money supply, the money supply function is independent of the interest rate and real GDP.

▬▬ How does monetary policy affect the equilibrium level of real GDP?

14. By altering the money supply, the Fed changes the interest rate and the level of investment, shifting aggregate demand and the equilibrium level of real GDP.

KEY TERMS

Federal Open Market Committee (FOMC)

intermediate target

equation of exchange

velocity of money

quantity theory of money

FOMC directive

legal reserves

federal funds rate

discount rate

open market operations

foreign exchange market intervention

sterilization

transactions demand for money

precautionary demand for money

speculative demand for money

EXERCISES

1. The Federal Reserve System divides the nation into twelve districts.
   a. List the twelve cities where the district banks are located.
   b. Which Federal Reserve district do you live in?

2. Briefly describe the functions the Fed performs for the banking community. In what sense is the Fed a banker's bank?

3. Draw a graph showing equilibrium in the money market. Carefully label all curves and axes and explain why the curves have the slopes they do.

4. Using the graph you prepared for exercise 3, illustrate and explain what happens when the Fed decreases the money supply.

5. When the Fed decreases the money supply, the equilibrium level of income changes. Illustrate and explain how.

6. Describe the quantity theory of money, defining each variable. Explain how changes in the money supply can affect real GDP and the price level. Under what circumstances could an increase in the money supply have *no* effect on nominal GDP?

7. There are several tools the Fed uses to implement monetary policy.

   a. Briefly describe these tools.

   b. Explain how the Fed would use each tool in order to increase the money supply.

8. First Bank has total deposits of $2,000,000 and legal reserves of $220,000.

   a. If the reserve requirement is 10 percent, what is the maximum loan that First Bank can make, and what is the maximum increase in the money supply based on First Bank's reserve position?

   b. If the reserve requirement is changed to 5 percent, how much can First Bank lend, and how much can the money supply be expanded?

9. Suppose you are a member of the FOMC and the U.S. economy is entering a recession. Write a directive to the New York Fed about the conduct of monetary policy over the next two months. Your directive should address targets for the rate of growth of the M2 and M3 money supplies, the federal funds rate, the rate of inflation, and the foreign exchange value of the dollar versus the Japanese yen and German mark. You may refer to the *Federal Reserve Bulletin* for examples, since this publication reports FOMC directives.

10. Suppose the Fed has a target range for the yen-dollar exchange rate. How would it keep the exchange rate within the target range if free market forces push the exchange rate out of the range? Use a graph to help explain your answer.

11. Why do you demand money? What determines how much money you keep in your pocket, purse, or bank accounts?

12. What is the current yield on a bond? Why do interest rates change when bond prices change?

13. If the Fed increases the money supply, what will happen to each of the following (other things being equal)?

    a. Interest rates

    b. Money demand

    c. Investment spending

    d. Aggregate demand

    e. The equilibrium level of national income

14. Suppose the banking system has vault cash of $1,000, deposits at the Fed of $2,000, and demand deposits of $10,000.

    a. If the reserve requirement is 20 percent, what is the maximum potential increase in the money supply given the banks' reserve position?

    b. If the Fed now purchases $500 worth of government bonds from private bond dealers, what are excess reserves of the banking system? (Assume that the bond dealers deposit the $500 in demand deposits.) How much can the banking system increase the money supply given the new reserve position?

■ INTERNET EXERCISE

In this chapter, we learned that the FOMC meetings produce a directive as a guideline for the course of monetary policy over the near future. To see what current FOMC policy is, look at the most recent directive found by going to the Boyes/Melvin *Fundamentals of Economics* Web site at **http://www.hmco.com/college/** and clicking on the Internet Exercise link for Chapter 15. Now answer the questions that appear on the Boyes/Melvin Web site.

16

Macroeconomic Policy, Business Cycles, and Growth

FUNDAMENTAL QUESTIONS

1. Is there a tradeoff between inflation and the unemployment rate?

2. How does the tradeoff between inflation and the unemployment rate vary from the short to the long run?

3. What is the relationship between unexpected inflation and the unemployment rate?

4. How are macroeconomic expectations formed?

5. Are business cycles related to political elections?

6. How do real shocks to the economy affect business cycles?

7. How is inflationary monetary policy related to government fiscal policy?

8. How are economic growth rates determined?

9. What is productivity?

Macroeconomics is a dynamic discipline. Monetary and fiscal policies change over time. And so does our understanding of those policies. Economists debate the nature of business cycles and economic growth, and what, if anything, government can do about them. Some economists argue that policies that lower the unemployment rate tend to raise the rate of inflation. Others insist that only unexpected inflation can influence real GDP and employment. If the latter economists are right, does government always have to surprise the public in order to improve economic conditions?

Some economists claim that politicians manipulate the business cycle to increase their chances of reelection. If they are right, we should expect economic growth just before national elections. But what happens after the elections? What are the long-term effects of political business cycles? Because of these issues, the material in this chapter should be considered somewhat controversial. ∎

1. THE PHILLIPS CURVE

In 1958 a New Zealand economist, A. W. Phillips, published a study of the relationship between the unemployment rate and the rate of change in wages in England. He found that over the period from 1826 to 1957 there had been an inverse relationship between the unemployment rate and the rate of change in wages: the unemployment rate fell in years when there were relatively large increases in wages and rose in years when wages increased relatively little. Phillip's study started other economists searching for similar relationships in other countries. In those studies, it became common to substitute the rate of inflation for the rate of change in wages.

Early studies in the United States found an inverse relationship between inflation and the unemployment rate. The graph that illustrates this relationship is called a **Phillips curve**. Figure 1 shows a Phillips curve for the United States in the 1960s. Over this period, lower inflation rates were associated with higher unemployment rates, as shown by the downward-sloping curve.

The slope of the curve in Figure 1 depicts an inverse relationship between the rate of inflation and the unemployment rate: As the inflation rate falls, the unemployment rate rises. In 1969 the inflation rate was relatively high, at 5.5

∎ **Phillips curve:**
a graph that illustrates the relationship between inflation and the unemployment rate

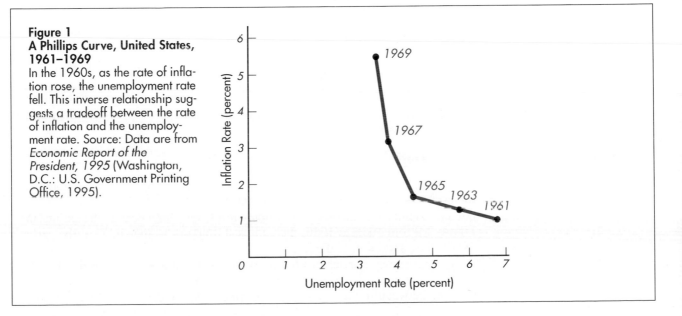

Figure 1
A Phillips Curve, United States, 1961–1969
In the 1960s, as the rate of inflation rose, the unemployment rate fell. This inverse relationship suggests a tradeoff between the rate of inflation and the unemployment rate. Source: Data are from *Economic Report of the President, 1995* (Washington, D.C.: U.S. Government Printing Office, 1995).

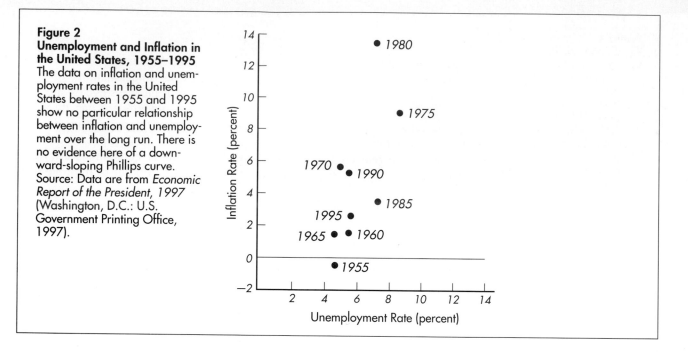

Figure 2
Unemployment and Inflation in the United States, 1955–1995
The data on inflation and unemployment rates in the United States between 1955 and 1995 show no particular relationship between inflation and unemployment over the long run. There is no evidence here of a downward-sloping Phillips curve.
Source: Data are from *Economic Report of the President, 1997* (Washington, D.C.: U.S. Government Printing Office, 1997).

percent, while the unemployment rate was relatively low, at 3.5 percent. In 1967 an inflation rate of 3.1 percent was consistent with an unemployment rate of 3.8 percent; and in 1961, 1 percent inflation occurred with 6.7 percent unemployment.

The downward-sloping Phillips curve seems to indicate a tradeoff between unemployment and inflation. A country could have a lower unemployment rate by accepting higher inflation, or a lower rate of inflation by accepting higher unemployment. Certainly this was the case in the United States in the 1960s. But is the curve depicted in Figure 1 representative of the tradeoff over long periods of time?

1.a. An Inflation-Unemployment Tradeoff?

Figure 2 shows unemployment and inflation rates in the United States for several years from 1955 to 1995. The points in the figure do not lie along a downward-sloping curve like the one shown in Figure 1. For example, in 1955 the unemployment rate was 4.4 percent and the inflation rate was −.4 percent. In 1960 the unemployment rate was 5.5 percent and the inflation rate was 1.7 percent. Both unemployment and inflation rates had increased since 1955. Moving through time, you can see that the inflation rate tended to increase along with the unemployment rate through the 1960s and 1970s. By 1980, the unemployment rate was 7.1 percent and the inflation rate was 13.5 percent.

The scattered points in Figure 2 show no evidence of a tradeoff between unemployment and inflation. A downward-sloping Phillips curve does not seem to exist over the long term.

1.b. Short-Run Versus Long-Run Tradeoffs

Most economists believe that the downward-sloping Phillips curve and the tradeoff it implies between inflation and unemployment are short-term phenomena. Think of a series of Phillips curves, one for each of the points in Figure 2. From 1955 to 1980, the curves shifted out to the right. In the early 1980s, they shifted in to the left.

Figure 3 shows a series of Phillips curves that could account for the data in Figure 2. At any point in time, a downward-sloping Phillips curve indicates a tradeoff between inflation and unemployment. Many economists believe that

Figure 3
The Shifting Phillips Curve
We can reconcile the long-run data on unemployment and inflation with the downward-sloping Phillips curve by using a series of Phillips curves. (In effect, we treat the long run as a series of short-run curves.) The Phillips curve for the early 1960s shows 5 percent unemployment and 2 percent inflation. Over time, the short-run curve shifted out to the right. The early 1970s curve shows 5 percent unemployment and 6 percent inflation. And the short-run curve for the late 1970s shows 5 percent unemployment and 10 percent inflation. In the early 1980s, the short-run Phillips curve began to shift down toward the origin. By the late 1980s, 5 percent unemployment was consistent with 4 percent inflation.

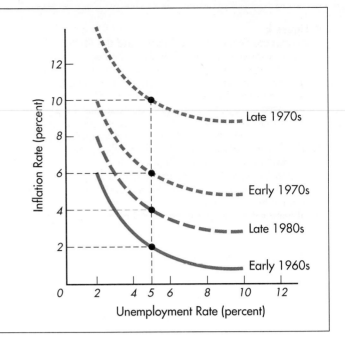

this kind of tradeoff is just a short-term phenomenon. Over time, the Phillips curve shifts so that the short-run tradeoff between inflation and unemployment disappears in the long run.

On the early 1960s curve in Figure 3, 5 percent unemployment is consistent with 2 percent inflation. By the early 1970s, the curve had shifted up. Here 5 percent unemployment is associated with 6 percent inflation. On the late 1970s curve, 5 percent unemployment is consistent with 10 percent inflation. For more than two decades, the tradeoff between inflation and unemployment worsened as the Phillips curves shifted up, so that higher and higher inflation rates were associated with any given level of unemployment. Then in the 1980s, the tradeoff seemed to improve as the Phillips curve shifted down. On the late 1980s curve, 5 percent unemployment is consistent with 4 percent inflation.

The Phillips curves in Figure 3 represent changes that took place over time in the United States. We cannot be sure of the actual shape of a Phillips curve at any time, but an outward shift of the curve in the 1960s and 1970s and an inward shift during the 1980s are consistent with the data. Later in this chapter we describe how changing government policy and the public's expectations about that policy may have shifted aggregate demand and aggregate supply and produced these shifts in the Phillips curves.

1.b.1. In the Short Run Figure 4 uses aggregate demand and supply analysis to explain the Phillips curve. Initially the economy is operating at point 1 in both diagrams. In part (a), the aggregate demand curve (AD_1) and aggregate supply curve (AS_1) intersect at price level P_1 and real GDP level Y_p, the level of potential real GDP. Remember that potential real GDP is the level of income and output generated at the natural rate of unemployment, the unemployment rate that exists in the absence of cyclical unemployment. In part (b), point 1 lies on Phillips curve I, where the inflation rate is 3 percent and the unemployment rate is 5 percent. We assume that the 5 percent unemployment rate at the level of potential real GDP is the natural rate of unemployment (U_n).

What happens when aggregate demand goes up from AD_1 to AD_2? A new equilibrium is established along the short-run aggregate supply curve (AS_1) at point 2. Here the price level (P_2) is higher, as is the level of real GDP (Y_2). In part (b), the increase in price and income is reflected in the movement along

Figure 4

Aggregate Demand and Supply and the Phillips Curve

The movement from point 1 to point 2 to point 3 traces the adjustment of the economy to an increase in aggregate demand. Point 1 is initial equilibrium in both diagrams. At this point potential real GDP is Y_p and the price level is P_1 in the aggregate demand and supply diagram, and the inflation rate is 3 percent with an unemployment rate of 5 percent (the natural rate) along short-run curve 1 in the Phillips curve diagram.

If the aggregate demand curve shifts from AD_1 to AD_2, equilibrium real GDP goes up to Y_2 and the price level rises to P_2 in the aggregate demand and supply diagram. The increase in aggregate demand pushes the inflation rate up to 6 percent and the unemployment rate

down to 3 percent along Phillips curve I. The movement from point 1 to point 2 along the curve indicates a trade-off between inflation and the unemployment rate.

Over time the AS curve shifts in response to rising production costs at the higher rate of inflation. Along AS_2, equilibrium is at point 3, where real GDP falls back to Y_p and the price level rises to P_3. As we move from point 2 to point 3 in part (b), we shift to short-run Phillips curve II. Here the inflation rate remains high (at 6 percent), while the unemployment rate goes back up to 5 percent, the rate consistent with production at Y_p. In the long run, then, there is no tradeoff between inflation and unemployment. The vertical long-run aggregate supply curve at the potential level of real GDP is associated with the vertical long-run Phillips curve at the natural rate of unemployment.

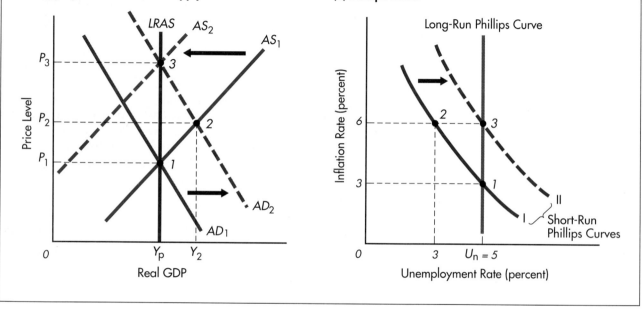

(a) Aggregate Demand and Supply

(b) Phillips Curve

Phillips curve I to point 2. At point 2, the inflation rate is 6 percent and the unemployment rate is 3 percent. The increase in expenditures raises the inflation rate and lowers the unemployment rate (because national output has surpassed potential output).

Notice that there appears to be a tradeoff between inflation and unemployment on Phillips curve I. The increase in spending increases output and stimulates employment, so that the unemployment rate falls. And the higher spending pushes the rate of inflation up. But this tradeoff is only temporary. Point 2 in both diagrams is only a short-run equilibrium.

1.b.2. In the Long Run

As we discussed in Chapter 12, the short-run aggregate supply curve shifts over time as production costs rise in response to higher prices. Once the aggregate supply curve shifts to AS_2, long-run equilibrium occurs at point 3, where AS_2 intersects AD_2. Here, the price level is P_3 and real GDP returns to its potential level, Y_p.

The shift in aggregate supply lowers real GDP. As income falls, the unemployment rate goes up. The decrease in aggregate supply is reflected in the movement from point 2 on Phillips curve I to point 3 on Phillips curve II. As real GDP returns to its potential level (Y_p), unemployment returns to the natural rate (U_n), 5 percent. In the long run, as the economy adjusts to an increase in aggregate demand and expectations adjust to the new inflation rate, there is a period in which real GDP falls and the price level rises.

Over time there is no relationship between the price level and the level of real GDP. You can see this in the aggregate demand and supply diagram. Points 1 and 3 both lie along the long-run aggregate supply curve (*LRAS*) at potential real GDP. The *LRAS* curve has its analogue in the long-run Phillips curve, a vertical line at the natural rate of unemployment. Points 1 and 3 both lie along this curve.

RECAP

1. The Phillips curve shows an inverse relationship between inflation and unemployment.
2. The downward slope of the Phillips curve indicates a tradeoff between inflation and unemployment.
3. Over the long run that tradeoff disappears.
4. The long-run Phillips curve is a vertical line at the natural rate of unemployment, analogous to the long-run aggregate supply curve at potential real GDP.

2. THE ROLE OF EXPECTATIONS

The data and analysis in the previous section indicate that there is no long-run tradeoff between inflation and unemployment. But they do not explain the movement of the Phillips curve in the 1960s, 1970s, and 1980s. To understand why the short-run curve shifts, you must understand the role that unexpected inflation plays in the economy.

2.a. Expected Versus Unexpected Inflation

Figure 5 shows two short-run Phillips curves like those in Figure 4. Each curve is drawn for a particular expected rate of inflation. Curve I shows the tradeoff between inflation and unemployment when the inflation rate is expected to be 3 percent. If the actual rate of inflation (measured along the vertical axis) is 3 percent, the economy is operating at point 1, with an unemployment rate of 5 percent (the natural rate). If the inflation rate unexpectedly increases to 6 percent, the economy moves from point 1 to point 2 along

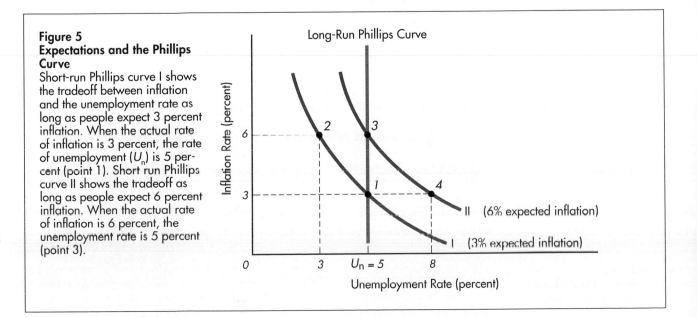

Figure 5
Expectations and the Phillips Curve
Short-run Phillips curve I shows the tradeoff between inflation and the unemployment rate as long as people expect 3 percent inflation. When the actual rate of inflation is 3 percent, the rate of unemployment (U_n) is 5 percent (point 1). Short run Phillips curve II shows the tradeoff as long as people expect 6 percent inflation. When the actual rate of inflation is 6 percent, the unemployment rate is 5 percent (point 3).

Phillips curve I. Obviously, unexpected inflation can affect the unemployment rate. There are three factors at work here: wage expectations, inventory fluctuations, and wage contracts.

2.a.1. Wage Expectations and Unemployment

■ **reservation wage:**
the minimum wage a worker is willing to accept

Unemployed workers who are looking for a job choose a **reservation wage**, the minimum wage they are willing to accept. They continue to look for work until they receive an offer that equals or exceeds their reservation wage.

Wages are not the only factor that workers take into consideration before accepting a job offer. A firm that offers good working conditions and fringe benefits can pay a lower wage than a firm that does not offer these advantages. But other things being equal, workers choose higher wages over lower wages. We simplify our analysis here by assuming that the only variable that affects the unemployed worker who is looking for a job is the reservation wage.

The link between unexpected inflation and the unemployment rate stems from the fact that wage offers are surprisingly high when the rate of inflation is surprisingly high. An unexpected increase in inflation means that prices are higher than anticipated, as are nominal income and wages. If aggregate demand increases unexpectedly, then, prices, output, employment, and wages go up. Unemployed workers with a constant reservation wage find it easier to obtain a satisfactory wage offer during a period when wages are rising faster than the workers expected. This means that more unemployed workers find jobs, and they find those jobs quicker than they do in a period when the rate of inflation is expected. So the unemployment rate falls during a period of unexpectedly high inflation (Figure 6).

In Figure 5, an expected increase in inflation moves us from point 1 on curve I to point 3 on curve II. When increased inflation is expected, the reservation wage reflects the higher rate of inflation and there is no tradeoff between inflation and the unemployment rate. Instead the economy moves along the long-run Phillips curve, with unemployment at its natural rate. The clockwise movement from point 1 to point 2 to point 3 is the pattern that follows an unexpected increase in aggregate demand.

What if the inflation rate is lower than expected? Here we find a reservation wage that reflects higher expected inflation. This means that those people who are looking for jobs are going to have a difficult time finding acceptable wage offers, the number of unemployed workers is going to increase, and the unemployment rate is going to rise. This sequence is shown in Figure 5, as the economy moves from point 3 to point 4. When the actual inflation rate is 6 percent and the expected inflation rate is also 6 percent, the economy is operating at the natural rate of unemployment. When the inflation rate falls to 3 percent but workers still expect 6 percent inflation, the unemployment rate

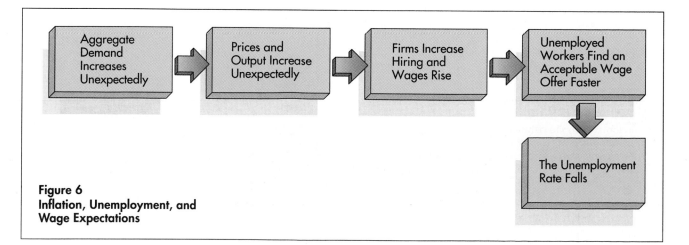

Figure 6
Inflation, Unemployment, and Wage Expectations

rises (at point 4 along curve II). Eventually, if the inflation rate remains at 3 percent, workers adjust their expectations to the lower rate and the economy moves to point 1 on curve I. The short-run effect of unexpected *disinflation* is rising unemployment. Over time the short-run increase in the unemployment rate is eliminated.

As long as the actual rate of inflation equals the expected rate, the economy remains at the natural rate of unemployment. The tradeoff between inflation and the unemployment rate comes from unexpected inflation.

2.a.2. Inventory Fluctuations and Unemployment Businesses hold inventories based on what they expect their sales to be. When aggregate demand is greater than expected, inventories fall below targeted levels. To restore inventories to the levels wanted, production is increased. Increased production leads to increased employment. If aggregate demand is lower than expected, inventories rise above targeted levels. To reduce inventories, production is cut back and workers are laid off from their jobs until sales have lowered unwanted inventories. Once production increases, employment rises again.

Inventory, production, and employment all play a part in the Phillips curve analysis (Figure 7). Expected sales and inventory levels are based on an expected level of aggregate demand. If aggregate demand is greater than expected, inventories fall and prices rise on the remaining goods in stock. With the unexpected increase in inflation, the unemployment rate falls as businesses hire more workers to increase output to offset falling inventories. This sequence represents movement along a short-run Phillips curve because there is a tradeoff between inflation and the unemployment rate. We find the same tradeoff if aggregate demand is lower than expected. Here inventories increase and prices are lower than anticipated. With the unexpected decrease in inflation, the unemployment rate goes up as workers are laid off to reduce output until inventory levels fall.

2.a.3. Wage Contracts and Unemployment Another factor that explains the short-run tradeoff between inflation and unemployment is labor contracts that fix wages for an extended period of time. When an existing contract expires, management must renegotiate with labor. A firm facing lower demand for its products may negotiate lower wages in order to keep as many workers employed as before. If the demand for a firm's products falls while a wage contract is in force, the firm must maintain wages, which means it is going to have to lay off workers.

In the national economy, wage contracts are staggered; they expire at different times. Each year only 30 to 40 percent of all contracts expire across the entire economy. As economic conditions change, firms with expiring wage contracts can adjust *wages* to those conditions; firms with existing contracts must adjust *employment* to those conditions.

How do long-term wage contracts tie in with the Phillips curve analysis? The expected rate of inflation is based on expected aggregate demand and reflected in the wage that is agreed on in the contract. When the actual rate of

Figure 7
Inflation, Unemployment, and Inventories

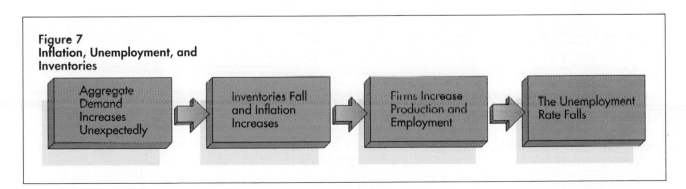

inflation equals the expected rate, businesses retain the same number of workers they had planned on when they signed the contract. For the economy overall, when actual and expected inflation rates are the same, the economy is operating at the natural rate of unemployment. That is, businesses are not hiring new workers because of an unexpected increase in aggregate demand, and they are not laying off workers because of an unexpected decrease in aggregate demand.

When aggregate demand is higher than expected, those firms with unexpired wage contracts hire more workers at the fixed wage, reducing unemployment (Figure 8). Those firms with expiring contracts have to offer higher wages in order to maintain the existing level of employment at the new demand condition. When aggregate demand is lower than expected, those firms with unexpired contracts have to lay off workers because they cannot lower the wage, while those firms with expiring contracts negotiate lower wages in order to keep their workers.

If wages were always flexible, unexpected changes in aggregate demand might be reflected largely in *wage* rather than *employment* adjustments. Wage contracts force businesses to adjust employment when aggregate demand changes unexpectedly.

2.b. Forming Expectations

Expectations play a key role in explaining the short-run Phillips curve, the tradeoff between inflation and the unemployment rate. How are these expectations formed?

2.b.1. Adaptive Expectations
Expectations can be formed solely on the basis of experience. **Adaptive expectations** are expectations that are determined by what has happened in the recent past.

■ **adaptive expectation:** an expectation formed on the basis of information collected in the past

People learn from their experiences. For example, suppose the inflation rate has been 3 percent for the past few years. Based on past experience, then, people expect the inflation rate in the future to remain at 3 percent. If the Federal Reserve increases the growth of the money supply to a rate that produces 6 percent inflation, the public will be surprised by the higher rate of inflation. This unexpected inflation creates a short-run tradeoff between inflation and the unemployment rate along a short-run Phillips curve. Over time, if the inflation rate remains at 6 percent, the public will learn that the 3 percent rate is too low and will adapt its expectations to the actual, higher inflation rate. Once public expectations have adapted to the new rate of inflation, the economy returns to the natural rate of unemployment along the long-run Phillips curve.

2.b.2. Rational Expectations
Many economists believe that adaptive expectations are too narrow. If people look only at past information, they are ignoring

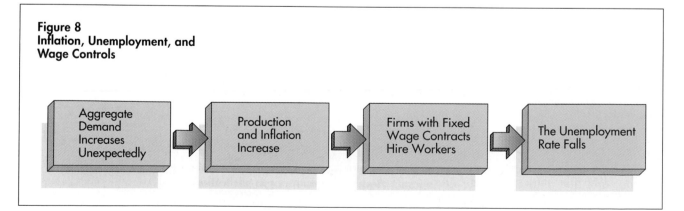

Figure 8
Inflation, Unemployment, and Wage Controls

Aggregate Demand Increases Unexpectedly → Production and Inflation Increase → Firms with Fixed Wage Contracts Hire Workers → The Unemployment Rate Falls

■ **rational expectation:**
an expectation that is formed using all available relevant information

what could be important information in the current period. **Rational expectations** are based on all available relevant information.

We are not saying that people have to know everything in order to form expectations. Rational expectations require only that people consider the information they believe to be relevant. This information includes their past experience along with what is currently happening and what they expect to happen in the future. For instance, in forming expectations about inflation, people consider rates in the recent past, current policy, and anticipated shifts in aggregate demand and supply that could affect the future rate of inflation.

If the inflation rate has been 3 percent over the past few years, adaptive expectations suggest that the future inflation rate will be 3 percent. No other information is considered. Rational expectations are based on more than the historical rate. Suppose the Fed announces a new policy that everyone believes will increase inflation in the future. With rational expectations the effect of this announcement will be considered. Here, when the actual rate of inflation turns out to be more than 3 percent, there is no short-run tradeoff between inflation and the unemployment rate. The economy moves directly along the long-run Phillips curve to the higher inflation rate, while unemployment remains at the natural rate.

If we believe that people have rational expectations, we do not expect them to make the same mistakes over and over. We expect them to learn and react quickly to new information.

RECAP

1. Wage expectations, inventory fluctuations, and wage contracts help explain the short-run tradeoff between inflation and the unemployment rate.

2. The reservation wage is the minimum wage a worker is willing to accept.

3. Because wage expectations reflect expected inflation, when the inflation rate is surprisingly high, unemployed workers find jobs faster and the unemployment rate falls.

4. Unexpected increases in aggregate demand lower inventories and raise prices. To increase output (to replenish shrinking inventories), businesses hire more workers, which reduces the unemployment rate.

5. When aggregate demand is higher than expected, those businesses with wage contracts hire more workers at the fixed wage, lowering unemployment.

6. If wages were always flexible, unexpected changes in aggregate demand would be reflected in wage adjustments rather than employment adjustments.

7. Adaptive expectations are formed on the basis of information about the past.

8. Rational expectations are formed using all available relevant information.

3. SOURCES OF BUSINESS CYCLES

In Chapter 13 we examined the effect of fiscal policy on the equilibrium level of real GDP. Changes in government spending and taxes can expand or contract the economy. In Chapter 15 we described how monetary policy affects the equilibrium level of real GDP. Changes in the money supply also produce booms and recessions. Besides the policy-induced sources of business cycles covered in earlier chapters, there are other sources of economic fluctuations that economists have studied. One is the election campaign of incumbent politicians, and when a business cycle results from this action it is called a *political business cycle*. Macroeconomic policy may be used to promote the reelection of incumbent politicians. We also examine another source of business cycles that is not related to discretionary policy actions, the *real business cycle*.

3.a. The Political Business Cycle

If a short-run tradeoff exists between inflation and unemployment, an incumbent administration could stimulate the economy just before an election to lower the unemployment rate, making voters happy and increasing the probability of reelection. Of course, after the election, the long-run adjustment to the expansionary policy would lead to higher inflation and move unemployment back to the natural rate.

Figure 9 illustrates the pattern. Before the election, the economy is initially at point 1 in parts (a) and (b). The incumbent administration stimulates the economy by increasing government spending or increasing the growth of the money supply. Aggregate demand shifts from AD_1 to AD_2 in part (a). In the short run, the increase in aggregate demand is unexpected, so the economy moves along the initial aggregate supply curve (AS_1) to point 2. This movement is reflected in part (b) of the figure, in the movement from point 1 to point 2 along short-run Phillips curve I. The pre-election expansionary policy increases real GDP and lowers the unemployment rate. Once the public adjusts its expectations to the higher inflation rate, the economy experiences a recession. Real GDP falls back to its potential level (Y_p) and the unemployment rate goes back up to the natural rate (U_n), as shown by the movement from point 2 to point 3 in both parts of the figure.

An unexpected increase in government spending or money growth temporarily stimulates the economy. If an election comes during the period of expansion, higher incomes and lower unemployment may increase support for the incumbent administration. The long-run adjustment back to potential real GDP and the natural rate of unemployment comes after the election.

Economists do not agree on whether a political business cycle exists in the United States. But they do agree that an effort to exploit the short-run tradeoff between inflation and the unemployment rate would shift the short-run Phillips curve out as shown in part (b) of Figure 9.

3.b. Real Business Cycles

■ **shock:**
an unexpected change in a variable

In recent years economists have paid increasing attention to real **shocks**—unexpected changes—in the economy as a source of business cycles. Many believe that it is not only fiscal or monetary policy that triggers expansion or contraction in the economy, but technological change, change in tastes, labor strikes, weather, or other real changes. A real business cycle is one that is generated by a change in one of those real variables.

Interest in the real business cycle was stimulated by the oil price shocks in the early 1970s and the important role they played in triggering the recession of 1973–1975. At that time, many economists were focusing on the role of unexpected changes in monetary policy in generating business cycles. They argued that these kinds of policy changes (changes in a nominal variable, the money supply) were responsible for the shifts in aggregate demand that led to expansions and contractions. When OPEC raised oil prices, it caused major shifts in aggregate supply. Higher oil prices in 1973 and 1974, and in 1979 and 1980, reduced aggregate supply, pushing the equilibrium level of real GDP down. Lower oil prices in 1986 raised aggregate supply and equilibrium real GDP.

An economywide real shock, like a substantial change in the price of oil, can affect output and employment across all sectors of the economy. Even an

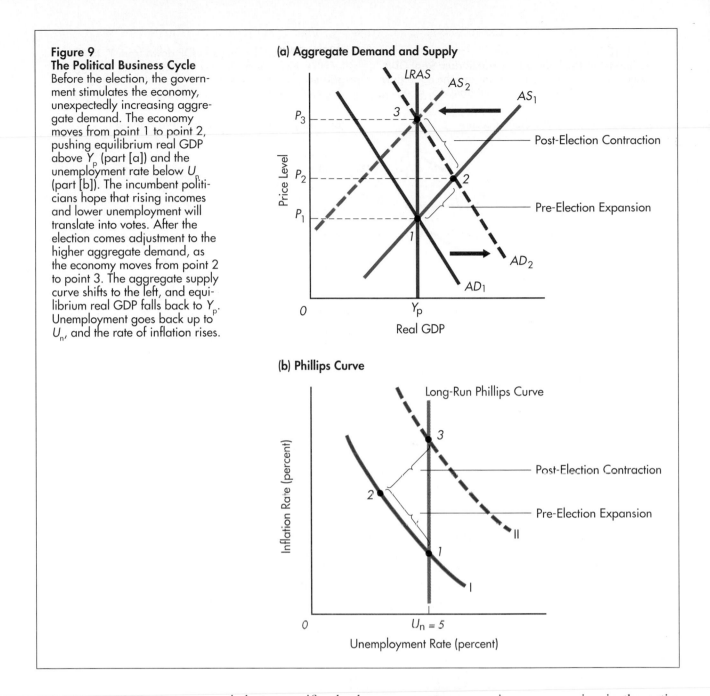

Figure 9
The Political Business Cycle
Before the election, the government stimulates the economy, unexpectedly increasing aggregate demand. The economy moves from point 1 to point 2, pushing equilibrium real GDP above Y_p (part [a]) and the unemployment rate below U_n (part [b]). The incumbent politicians hope that rising incomes and lower unemployment will translate into votes. After the election comes adjustment to the higher aggregate demand, as the economy moves from point 2 to point 3. The aggregate supply curve shifts to the left, and equilibrium real GDP falls back to Y_p. Unemployment goes back up to U_n, and the rate of inflation rises.

(a) Aggregate Demand and Supply

(b) Phillips Curve

industry-specific shock can generate a recession or expansion in the entire economy if the industry produces a product used by a substantial number of other industries. For example, a labor strike in the steel industry would have major recessionary implications for the economy as a whole. If the output of steel fell, the price of steel would be bid up by all the industries that use steel as an input. This would shift the short-run aggregate supply curve to the left, as shown in part (a) of Figure 10, and would move equilibrium real GDP from Y_1 down to Y_2.

Real shocks can also have expansionary effects on the economy. Suppose that the weather is particularly good one year and that harvests are surprisingly large. What happens? The price of food, cotton, and other agricultural output tends to fall, and the short-run aggregate supply curve shifts to the right, as shown in Figure 10(b), raising equilibrium real GDP from Y_1 to Y_2.

Real business cycles explain why national output can expand or contract in the absence of a discretionary macroeconomic policy that would shift aggregate demand. To fully understand business cycles, we must consider both pol-

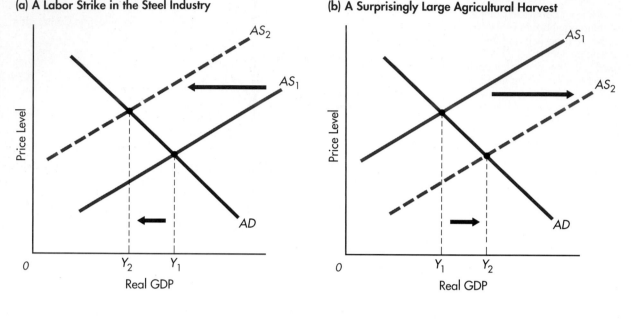

Figure 10
The Impact of Real Shocks on Equilibrium Real GDP
A labor strike in a key industry can shift the aggregate supply curve to the left, like the shift from AS_1 to AS_2.

This pushes equilibrium real GDP down from Y_1 to Y_2.
 If good weather leads to a banner harvest, the aggregate supply curve shifts to the right, like the shift from AS_1 to AS_2, raising equilibrium real GDP from Y_1 to Y_2.

(a) A Labor Strike in the Steel Industry

(b) A Surprisingly Large Agricultural Harvest

icy-induced changes in real GDP, as covered in Chapters 13 and 15, and real shocks that occur independent of government actions.

RECAP

1. The political business cycle is a short-term expansion stimulated by an administration before an election to earn votes. After the election comes the long-term adjustment (rising unemployment and inflation).
2. A real business cycle is an expansion and contraction caused by a change in tastes or technology, strikes, weather, or other real factors.

4. THE LINK BETWEEN MONETARY AND FISCAL POLICIES

In earlier chapters we have described how monetary and fiscal policies determine the equilibrium level of prices and national income. In our discussions we have talked about monetary policy and fiscal policy individually. Here we consider the relationship between them.

In some countries, monetary and fiscal policies are carried out by a single central authority. Even in the United States, where the Federal Reserve was created as an independent agency, monetary policy and fiscal policy are always related. The actions of the central bank have an impact on the proper role for fiscal policy, and the actions of fiscal policymakers have an impact on the proper role for monetary policy.

For example, suppose the central bank follows a monetary policy that raises interest rates. That policy raises the interest cost of new government debt, in the process increasing government expenditures. On the other hand, a fiscal policy that generates large fiscal deficits could contribute to higher interest rates. If the central bank has targeted an interest rate that lies below

Those who were around in the 1970s can remember the long lines and shortages at gas stations and the rapid increase in the price of oil that resulted from the oil embargo imposed by the Organization of Petroleum Exporting Countries. There was another effect of the oil price shock—the aggregate supply curve in the United States and other oil-importing nations shifted to the left, lowering the equilibrium level of real GDP while raising the price level. Such "real" sources of business cycles can explain why national output can rise or fall in the absence of any discretionary government macroeconomic policy.

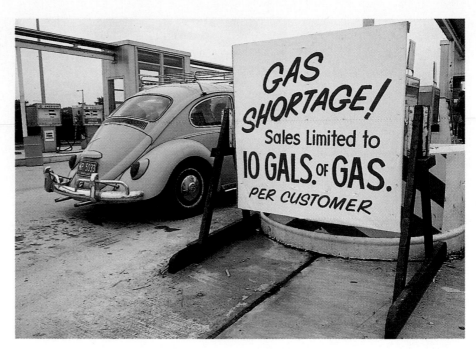

the current rate, the central bank could be drawn into an expansionary monetary policy. This interdependence between monetary and fiscal policy is important to policymakers as well as to business people and others who seek to understand current economic developments.

The *government budget constraint* clarifies the relationship between monetary and fiscal policies:

$$G = T + B + \Delta M$$

where

$$G = \text{government spending}$$

$$T = \text{tax revenue}$$

$$B = \text{government borrowing}$$

$$\Delta M = \text{the change in the money supply}[1]$$

The government budget constraint always holds because there are only three ways for the government to finance its spending: by taxing, by borrowing, and by creating money.

We can rewrite the government budget constraint with the change in M on the left-hand side of the equation:

$$\Delta M = (G - T) - B$$

In this form you can see that the change in government-issued money equals the government fiscal deficit $(G - T)$ minus borrowing. This equation is always true. A government that has the ability to borrow at reasonable costs will not have the incentive to create rapid money growth and the consequent inflation that results in order to finance its budget deficit.

In the United States and other industrial nations, monetary and fiscal policies are conducted by separate, independent agencies. Fiscal authorities (Congress and the president in the U.S.) cannot impose monetary policy on the central bank. But in typical developing countries, monetary and fiscal

---

[1]The M in the government budget constraint is government-issued money (usually called *base money,* or *high-powered money*). It is easiest to think of this kind of money as currency, although in practice base money includes more than currency.

Some aspects of the macroeconomy are beyond the control of the government. This photo depicts the damage done in Kobe, Japan, following an earthquake. Natural disasters, such as earthquakes or bad weather, sometimes play a role in determining the price level and national output in the short run. A major earthquake will lower national output and raise the price level. However, such effects should be important only in the short run as other determinants of the equilibrium price level and real GDP will dominate the forces of nature in normal times.

policies are controlled by a central political authority. Here monetary policy is often an extension of fiscal policy. Fiscal policy can impose an inflationary burden on monetary policy. If a country is running a large fiscal deficit, and much of this deficit cannot be financed by government borrowing, monetary authorities must create money to finance the deficit.

RECAP

1. The government budget constraint ($G = T + B + \Delta M$) defines the relationship between fiscal and monetary policies.
2. The implications of fiscal policy for the growth of the money supply can be seen by rewriting the government budget constraint this way: $\Delta M = (G - T) - B$.

5. ECONOMIC GROWTH

Although much of macroeconomics is aimed at understanding business cycles—recurring periods of prosperity and recession—the fact is that over the long run, most economies do grow wealthier. The long-run trend of real GDP in the United States and most other countries is positive. Yet the rate at which real GDP grows is very different across countries. In this section we examine the determinants of economic growth, to understand what accounts for the different rates of growth across countries.

5.a. The Determinants of Growth

The long-run aggregate supply curve is a vertical line at the potential level of real GDP (Y_{pl}). As the economy grows, the potential output of the economy rises. Figure 11 shows the increase in potential output as a rightward shift in the long-run aggregate supply curve. The higher the rate of growth, the farther the aggregate supply curve moves to the right. To illustrate several years' growth, we would show several curves shifting to the right.

To find the determinants of economic growth, we must turn to the determinants of aggregate supply. In Chapter 12, we identified three determinants of aggregate supply: resource prices, technology, and expectations. Changes in

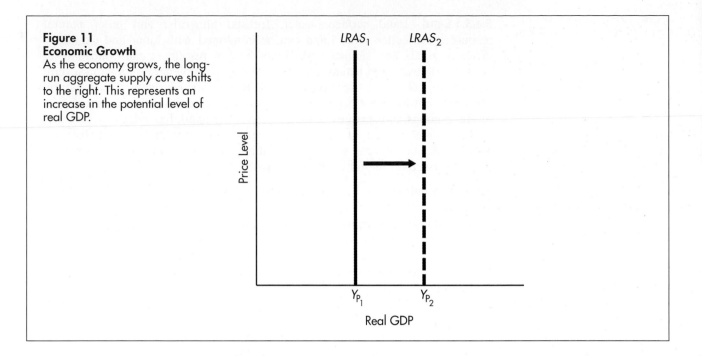

Figure 11
Economic Growth
As the economy grows, the long-run aggregate supply curve shifts to the right. This represents an increase in the potential level of real GDP.

expectations can shift the aggregate supply curve, but changing expectations are not a basis for long-run growth in the sense of continuous rightward movements in aggregate supply. The long-run growth of the economy rests on growth in productive resources (labor, capital, and land) and technological advances.

5.a.1. Labor Economic growth depends on the size and quality of the labor force. The size of the labor force is a function of the size of the working age population (sixteen and older in the United States) and the percentage of that population in the labor force. The labor force typically grows more rapidly in developing countries than in industrial countries because birthrates are higher in developing countries. The World Bank forecasts that between 1992 and 2000, the population will grow at an average annual rate of 1.6 percent in developing countries and .5 percent in industrial countries.

Based solely on growth in the labor force, it seems that developing countries are growing faster than industrial countries. But the size of the labor force is not all that matters; changes in productivity can compensate for lower growth in the labor force, as we discuss in section 5.b.

5.a.2. Capital Labor is combined with capital to produce goods and services. A rapidly growing labor force by itself is no guarantee of economic growth. Workers need machines, tools, and factories to work. If a country has lots of workers but few machines, then the typical worker cannot be very productive. Capital is a critical resource in growing economies.

The ability of a country to invest in capital goods is tied to its ability to save. A lack of current saving can be offset by borrowing, but the availability of borrowing is limited by the prospects for future saving. Debt incurred today must be repaid by not consuming all output in the future. If lenders believe that a nation is going to consume all of its output in the future, they do not make loans today.

The lower the standard of living in a country, the harder it is to forgo current consumption in order to save. It is difficult for a population living at or near subsistence level to do without current consumption. This in large part explains the low level of saving in the poorest countries.

5.a.3. Land Land surface, water, forests, minerals, and other natural resources are called *land*. Land can be combined with labor and capital to produce goods and services. Abundant natural resources can contribute to economic growth, but natural resources alone do not generate growth. Several developing countries, like Argentina and Brazil, are relatively rich in natural resources but have not been very successful in exploiting these resources to produce goods and services. Japan, on the other hand, has relatively few natural resources but has shown dramatic economic growth in recent decades. The experience of Japan makes it clear that abundant natural resources are not a necessary condition for economic growth.

■ **technology:**
ways of combining resources to produce output

5.a.4. Technology A key determinant of economic growth is **technology**, ways of combining resources to produce goods and services. New management techniques, scientific discoveries, and other innovations improve technology. Technological advances allow the production of more output from a given amount of resources. This means that technological progress accelerates economic growth for any given rate of growth in the labor force and the capital stock.

Technological change depends on the scientific community. The more educated a population, the greater its potential for technological advances. Industrial countries have better-educated populations than do developing countries. Education gives industrial countries a substantial advantage over developing countries in creating and implementing innovations. In addition, the richest industrial countries traditionally have spent 2 to 3 percent of their GNP on research and development, an investment developing countries cannot afford. The greater the funding for research and development, the greater the likelihood of technological advances.

Impeded by low levels of education and limited funds for research and development, the developing countries lag behind the industrial countries in developing and implementing new technology. Typically these countries follow the lead of the industrial world, adopting new technology developed in that world once it is affordable and feasible, given their capital and labor resources. In the next chapter we discuss the role of foreign aid, including technological assistance, in promoting economic growth in developing countries.

5.b. Productivity

■ **total factor productivity (TFP):**
the ratio of the economy's output to its stock of labor and capital

One way to assess the contribution a resource makes to output is its productivity. *Productivity* is the ratio of output produced to the amount of input. We could measure the productivity of a single resource—say labor or capital—or the overall productivity of all resources. **Total factor productivity (TFP)** is the term economists use to describe the overall productivity of an economy. It is the ratio of the economy's output to its stock of labor and capital.

5.b.1. Productivity and Economic Growth Economic growth depends on both the growth of resources and technological progress. Advances in technology allow resources to be more productive. If the quantity of resources is growing and each resource is more productive, then output grows even faster than the quantity of resources. Economic growth, then, is the sum of the growth rate of total factor productivity and the growth rate of resources:

economic growth = growth rate of *TFP* + growth rate of resources

The amount that output grows because the labor force is growing depends on how much labor contributes to the production of output. Similarly, the amount that output grows because capital is growing depends on how much capital contributes to the production of output. To relate the growth of labor and capital to the growth of output (we assume no change in natural resources), then, the growth of labor and the growth of capital must be multiplied by their relative contributions to the production of output. The most straightforward way to measure those contributions is to use the share of real GDP received by each resource. For instance, in the United States, labor receives about 70 percent (.70) of real GDP and capital receives about 30 percent (.30). So we can determine the growth of output by using this formula:

$$\%\Delta Y = \%\Delta TFP + .70(\%\Delta L) + .30(\%\Delta K)$$

where

$$\%\Delta = \text{percentage change in}$$
$$Y = \text{real GDP}$$
$$TFP = \text{total factor productivity}$$
$$L = \text{size of the labor force}$$
$$K = \text{capital stock}$$

The equation shows how economic growth depends on changes in productivity ($\%\Delta TFP$) as well as changes in resources ($\%\Delta L$ and $\%\Delta K$). Even if labor (L) and capital stock (K) are constant, technological innovation would generate economic growth through changes in total factor productivity (TFP).

For example, suppose TFP is growing at a rate of 2 percent a year. Then, even with labor and capital stock held constant, the economy grows at a rate of 2 percent a year. If labor and capital stock also grow at a rate of 2 percent a year, output grows by the sum of the growth rates of all three components (TFP, .70 times labor growth, and .30 times the capital stock growth), or 4 percent.

How do we account for differences in growth rates across countries? Because almost all countries have experienced growth in the labor force, percentage increases in labor forces have generally supported economic growth. But growth in the capital stock has been steadier in the industrial countries than in the developing countries, so differences in capital growth rates may explain some of the differences in economic growth across countries. Yet differences in resource growth rates alone cannot explain the major differences we find across countries. In recent years, those differences seem to be related to productivity.

RECAP

1. Economic growth raises the potential level of real GDP, shifting the long-run aggregate supply curve to the right.
2. The long-run growth of the economy is a product of growth in labor, capital, and natural resources, and advances in technology.
3. Technology is the way that resources are combined to produce output.
4. Hampered by low levels of education and limited financial resources, developing countries lag behind the industrial nations in developing and implementing new technology.
5. Productivity is the ratio of output produced to the amount of input.
6. Total factor productivity is equal to a nation's real GDP (output) divided by its stock of labor and capital.
7. Economic growth is the sum of the growth of total factor productivity and the growth rate of resources (labor and capital).

SUMMARY

▬▬ Is there a tradeoff between inflation and the unemployment rate?

1. The Phillips curve shows the relationship between inflation and the unemployment rate.

▬▬ How does the tradeoff between inflation and the unemployment rate vary from the short to the long run?

2. In the long run, there is no tradeoff between inflation and the unemployment rate.

3. The long-run Phillips curve is a vertical line at the natural rate of unemployment.

▬▬ What is the relationship between unexpected inflation and the unemployment rate?

4. Unexpected inflation can affect the unemployment rate through wage expectations, inventory fluctuations, and wage contracts.

▬▬ How are macroeconomic expectations formed?

5. Adaptive expectations are formed on the basis of past experience; rational expectations are formed on the basis of all available relevant information.

▬▬ Are business cycles related to political elections?

6. A political business cycle is created by politicians who want to improve their chances of reelection by stimulating the economy just before an election.

▬▬ How do real shocks to the economy affect business cycles?

7. Real business cycles are a product of unexpected change in technology, weather, or some other real variable.

▬▬ How is inflationary monetary policy related to government fiscal policy?

8. The government budget constraint defines the relationship between monetary and fiscal policies.

9. When government-issued money is used to finance fiscal deficits, inflationary monetary policy can be a product of fiscal policy.

▬▬ How are economic growth rates determined?

10. The growth of the economy is tied to the growth of productive resources and technological advances.

11. Because their populations tend to grow more rapidly, developing countries typically experience faster growth in the labor force than do industrial countries.

12. The inability to save limits the growth of capital stock in developing countries.

13. Abundant natural resources are not necessary for rapid economic growth.

14. Technology defines the ways in which resources can be combined to produce goods and services.

▬▬ What is productivity?

15. Productivity is the ratio of output produced to the amount of input.

16. Total factor productivity is the overall productivity of an economy.

17. The percentage change in real GDP equals the percentage change in total factor productivity plus the percentage changes in labor and capital multiplied by the share of GDP taken by labor and capital.

KEY TERMS

Phillips curve
reservation wage
adaptive expectation
rational expectation

shock
technology
total factor productivity (TFP)

EXERCISES

1. What is the difference between the short-run Phillips curve and the long-run Phillips curve? Use an aggregate supply and demand diagram to explain why there is a difference between them.

2. Give two reasons why there may be a short-run tradeoff between unexpected inflation and the unemployment rate.

3. Economists have identified two kinds of macroeconomic expectations.
   a. Define them.
   b. What are the implications for macroeconomic policy of these two forms of expectations?

4. Write down the government budget constraint and explain how it can be used to understand the relationship between fiscal and monetary policies.

5. Suppose tax revenues equal $100 billion, government spending equals $130 billion, and the government borrows $25 billion. How much do you expect the money supply to increase given the government budget constraint?

6. If the government budget deficit equals $220 billion and the money supply increases by $100 billion, how much must the government borrow?

7. Discuss how each of the following sources of real business cycles would affect the economy.
   a. Farmers go on strike for six months.
   b. Oil prices fall substantially.
   c. Particularly favorable weather increases agricultural output nationwide.

8. Using an aggregate demand and aggregate supply diagram, illustrate and explain how a political business cycle is created.

9. Suppose labor's share of GDP is 70 percent and capital's is 30 percent, real GDP is growing at a rate of 4 percent a year, the labor force is growing at 2 percent, and the capital stock is growing at 3 percent. What is the growth rate of total factor productivity?

10. Suppose labor's share of GDP is 70 percent and capital's is 30 percent, total factor productivity is growing at an annual rate of 2 percent, the labor force is growing at a rate of 1 percent, and the capital stock is growing at a rate of 3 percent. What is the annual growth rate of real GDP?

11. Is the following statement true or false? Explain your answer. "Abundant natural resources are a necessary condition for economic growth."

12. What is the growth rate for an economy where there is no growth of resources but *TFP* grows at a rate of 1 percent per year?

13. What is the growth rate for an economy where *TFP* is constant, labor grows at a rate of 1 percent per year, capital grows at a rate of 2 percent per year, and labor's share of output equals 60 percent, while capital's share equals 40 percent?

14. What is the growth rate for an economy where *TFP* grows at a rate of 3 percent per year, the size of the labor force is unchanged, the capital stock grows at a rate of 2 percent per year, and labor and capital each account for 50 percent of output?

▢ INTERNET EXERCISE

In this chapter, we discussed business cycles and economic growth. One way that countries can potentially improve economic performance in both areas is through international policy coordination so that countries work together to achieve common goals. One organization that aids the process of policy coordination is the Organization for Economic Cooperation and Development (OECD). To learn more about the OECD and its activities, go to the Boyes/Melvin *Fundamentals of Economics* Web site at **http://www.hmco.com/college/** and click on the Internet Exercise link for Chapter 16. Now answer the questions that appear on the Boyes/Melvin Web site.

17

Issues in International Trade and Finance

FUNDAMENTAL QUESTIONS

1. What determines the goods a nation will export?

2. What are the sources of comparative advantage?

3. Why do countries restrict international trade?

4. How do countries restrict the entry of foreign goods and promote the export of domestic goods?

5. What kinds of exchange-rate arrangements exist today?

The world is a global marketplace and all nations are interdependent. An understanding of international trade and finance is critical to understanding the modern economy. While earlier chapters have frequently considered international implications of various topics, in this chapter we delve more deeply into the global economic linkages.

Besides studying the determinants of international trade and how and why nations restrict such trade, we also will learn about the variety of exchange rate regimes that exist in the world today. Some countries allow the value of their currency to "float" with the free market forces of supply and demand while other countries choose to "fix" the value of their currency at some constant value against another currency. Still other countries choose some sort of hybrid exchange rate system. Since exchange rates are the prices that link the currencies of the world, we better understand the interrelationships among countries when we understand the current exchange rate environment. ■

1. AN OVERVIEW OF WORLD TRADE

Recall from Chapter 1 that trade occurs because it makes people better off. International trade occurs because it makes people better off than they would be if they could consume only domestically produced products. Who trades with whom, and what sorts of goods are traded? The underlying reasons for trade are found in comparative advantage.

1.a. Comparative Advantage

In Chapter 1, you learned that *comparative advantage* is the ability to produce a good or service at a lower opportunity cost than someone else. This is true for countries as well as individuals. Comparative advantage is found by comparing the relative costs of production in each country. We measure the cost of producing a particular good in two countries in terms of opportunity costs—what other goods must be given up in order to produce more of the good in question.

Table 1 presents a hypothetical example of two countries, the United States and India, that both produce two goods, wheat and cloth. The table lists the hours of labor required to produce 1 unit of each good. This example assumes that labor productivity differences alone determine comparative advantage. In the United States, 1 unit of wheat requires 3 hours of labor, and 1 unit of cloth requires 6 hours of labor. In India, 1 unit of wheat requires 6 hours of labor, and 1 unit of cloth requires 8 hours of labor.

The United States has an **absolute advantage**—a lower resource cost—in producing both wheat and cloth. Absolute advantage is determined by comparing the absolute cost in different countries of producing each good. Since it requires fewer hours of labor to produce either good in the United States

■ absolute advantage:
an advantage derived from one country having a lower absolute input cost of producing a particular good than another country

TABLE 1
An Example of Comparative Advantage

Labor Hours Required to Produce One Unit Each of Two Goods		
	U.S.	**India**
1 unit of wheat	3	6
1 unit of cloth	6	8

Comparative advantage is based on what a country can do relatively better than other countries. This photo shows a woman in Sri Lanka picking tea leaves. Sri Lanka is one of the few countries that export a significant amount of tea. Due to favorable growing conditions (a natural resource), these countries have a comparative advantage in tea production.

than in India, the United States is the more efficient producer of both goods in terms of the domestic labor hours required.

It might seem that since the United States is the more efficient producer of both goods, there would be no need for trade with India. But absolute advantage is not the critical consideration. What matters in determining the benefits of international trade is comparative advantage. To find the comparative advantage—the lower opportunity cost—we must compare the opportunity cost of producing each good in each country.

The opportunity cost of producing wheat is what must be given up in cloth using the same resources, or number of labor hours. Look again at Table 1 to see the labor hours required for the production of wheat and cloth in the two countries. If the 3 labor hours it takes to produce wheat in the United States are devoted to cloth production, only 1/2 unit of cloth will result, since 6 labor hours are required to produce a full unit of cloth. The opportunity cost of producing wheat equals 3/6, or 1/2 unit of cloth:

$$\frac{\text{No. of labor hours to produce 1 unit of wheat}}{\text{No. of labor hours to produce 1 unit of cloth}} = \begin{array}{l}\text{opportunity cost of} \\ \text{producing 1 unit of wheat} \\ \text{(in terms of cloth given up)}\end{array}$$

$$3/6 = 1/2$$

Applying the same thinking to India, we find that devoting 6 hours of wheat production to the production of cloth yields 6/8, or 3/4 unit of cloth. The opportunity cost of producing 1 unit of wheat in India is 3/4 unit of cloth.

A comparison of the domestic opportunity costs in each country will reveal which one has the comparative advantage in producing each good. The U.S. opportunity cost of producing 1 unit of wheat is 1/2 unit of cloth; the Indian opportunity cost is 3/4 unit of cloth. Because the United States has a lower domestic opportunity cost, it has the comparative advantage in wheat production and will export wheat. Since wheat production costs are lower in the United States, India is better off trading for wheat rather than trying to produce it domestically.

The comparative advantage in cloth is found the same way. A unit of cloth requires 6 hours of labor in the United States. Since a unit of wheat requires 3 hours of labor, producing 1 more unit of cloth costs 2 units of wheat:

$$\frac{\text{No. of labor hours to produce 1 unit of cloth}}{\text{No. of labor hours to produce 1 unit of wheat}} = \begin{array}{l}\text{opportunity cost of}\\ \text{producing 1 unit of cloth}\\ \text{(in terms of wheat given up)}\end{array}$$

$$6/3 = 2$$

In India, 1 unit of cloth requires 8 hours of labor. Since 1 unit of wheat requires 6 hours of labor, shifting 8 hours of labor from wheat production to cloth production means an opportunity cost of 8/6, or 1 1/3 units of wheat for 1 unit of cloth. Comparing the U.S. opportunity cost of 2 units of wheat with the Indian opportunity cost of 1 1/3 units, we see that India has the comparative advantage in cloth production and will therefore export cloth. In this case, the United States is better off trading for cloth than producing it since India's costs of production are lower.

In international trade, as in other areas of economic decision-making, it is opportunity cost that matters—and opportunity costs are reflected in comparative advantage. Absolute advantage is irrelevant, because knowing the absolute number of labor hours required to produce a good does not tell us if we can benefit from trade. We benefit from trade if we are able to obtain a good from a foreign country by giving up less than we would have to give up to obtain the good at home. Because only opportunity cost can allow us to make such comparisons, international trade proceeds on the basis of comparative advantage.

1.b. Sources of Comparative Advantage

We know that countries specialize and trade in accordance with comparative advantage, but what gives a country a comparative advantage? Economists have suggested several theories of the source of comparative advantage. Let us review these theories.

1.b.1. Productivity Differences

The example of comparative advantage showed the United States to have a comparative advantage in wheat production and India to have a comparative advantage in cloth production. Comparative advantage was determined by differences in the labor hours required to produce each good. In this example, differences in the *productivity* of labor accounted for comparative advantage.

For over two hundred years, economists have argued that productivity differences account for comparative advantage. In fact, this theory of comparative advantage is often called the *Ricardian model*, after David Ricardo, a nineteenth-century English economist who explained and analyzed the idea of productivity-based comparative advantage. Variation in the productivity of labor can explain many observed trade patterns in the world.

Although we know that labor productivity differs across countries—and that this can help explain why countries produce the goods they do—there are factors other than labor productivity that determine comparative advantage. Furthermore, even if labor productivity were all that mattered, we would still want to know why some countries have more productive workers than others. The standard interpretation of the Ricardian model is that technological differences between countries account for differences in labor productivity. The countries with the most advanced technology would have a comparative advantage with regard to those goods that can be produced most efficiently with modern technology.

1.b.2. Factor Abundance

Goods differ in terms of the resources, or factors of production, required for their production. Countries differ in terms of the abundance of different factors of production: land, labor, and capital. It seems self-evident that countries would have an advantage in producing those goods that use relatively large amounts of their most abundant factor of production.

Certainly countries with a relatively large amount of farmland would have a comparative advantage in agriculture, and countries with a relatively large amount of capital would tend to specialize in the production of manufactured goods.

In many cases, factor abundance has served well as an explanation of observed trade patterns. However, there remain cases in which comparative advantage seems to run counter to the predictions of the factor-abundance theory. In response, economists have suggested other explanations for comparative advantage.

1.b.3. Other Theories of Comparative Advantage
New theories of comparative advantage have typically come about in an effort to explain the trade pattern in some narrow category of products. They are not intended to serve as general explanations of comparative advantage, as do factor abundance and productivity. These supplementary theories emphasize human skills, product cycles, and preferences.

Human Skills This approach emphasizes differences across countries in the availability of skilled and unskilled labor. The basic idea is that countries with a relatively abundant stock of highly skilled labor will have a comparative advantage in producing goods that require relatively large amounts of skilled labor. This theory is similar to the factor-abundance theory, except that here the analysis rests on two segments (skilled and unskilled) of the labor factor.

The human-skills argument is consistent with the observation that most U.S. exports are produced in high-wage (skilled-labor) industries, and most U.S. imports are products produced in relatively low-wage industries. Since the United States has a well-educated labor force, relative to many other countries, we would expect the United States to have a comparative advantage in industries requiring a large amount of skilled labor. Developing countries would be expected to have a comparative advantage in industries requiring a relatively large amount of unskilled labor.

Product Life Cycles This theory explains how comparative advantage in a specific good can shift over time from one country to another. This occurs because goods experience a *product life cycle*. At the outset, development and testing are required to conceptualize and design the product. For this reason, the early production will be undertaken by an innovative firm. Over time, however, a successful product tends to become standardized, in the sense that many manufacturers can produce it. The mature product may be produced by firms that do little or no research and development, specializing instead in copying successful products invented and developed by others.

The product-life-cycle theory is related to international comparative advantage in that a new product will be first produced and exported by the nation in which it was invented. As the product is exported elsewhere and foreign firms become familiar with it, the technology is copied in other countries by foreign firms seeking to produce a competing version. As the product matures, comparative advantage shifts away from the country of origin if other countries have lower manufacturing costs using the now-standardized technology.

The history of color television production shows how comparative advantage can shift over the product life cycle. Color television was invented in the United States, and U.S. firms initially produced and exported color TVs. Over time, as the technology of color television manufacturing became well known, countries like Japan and Taiwan came to dominate the business. Firms in these countries had a comparative advantage over U.S. firms in the manufacture of color televisions. Once the technology is widely available, countries with lower production costs, due to lower wages, can compete effectively against the higher-wage nation that developed the technology.

Preferences The theories of comparative advantage we have looked at so far have all been based on supply factors. It may be, though, that the demand side of the market can explain some of the patterns observed in international trade. Seldom are different producers' goods exactly identical. Consumers may prefer the goods of one firm to those of another firm. Domestic firms usually produce goods to satisfy domestic consumers. But since different consumers have different preferences, some consumers will prefer goods produced by foreign firms. International trade allows consumers to expand their consumption opportunities.

Consumers who live in countries with similar levels of development can be expected to have similar consumption patterns. The consumption patterns of consumers in countries at much different levels of development are much less similar. This would suggest that firms in industrial countries will find a larger market for their goods in other industrial countries than in developing countries.

■ **intraindustry trade:** simultaneous import and export of goods in the same industry by a particular country

Another feature of international trade that may be explained by consumer preference is **intraindustry trade**, a circumstance in which a country both exports and imports goods in the same industry. The fact that the United States exports Budweiser beer and imports Heineken beer is not surprising when preferences are taken into account. Supply-side theories of comparative advantage rarely provide an explanation of intraindustry trade, since they would expect each country to export only those goods produced in industries in which a comparative advantage exists. Yet the real world is characterized by a great deal of intraindustry trade.

We have discussed several potential sources of comparative advantage: labor productivity, factor abundance, human skills, product cycles, and preferences. Each of these theories, summarized in Figure 1, has proven useful in understanding certain trade patterns. Each has also been shown to have limitations as a general theory applicable to all cases. Once again we are reminded that the world is a very complicated place. Theories are simpler than reality. Nevertheless, they help us to understand how comparative advantage arises.

RECAP

1. Comparative advantage can arise because of differences in labor productivity.

2. Countries differ in their resource endowments, and a given country may enjoy a comparative advantage in products that intensively use its most abundant factor of production.

3. Industrial countries may have a comparative advantage in products requiring a large amount of skilled labor. Developing countries may have a comparative advantage in products requiring a large amount of unskilled labor.

4. Comparative advantage in a new good initially resides in the country that invented the good. Over time, other nations learn the technology and may gain a comparative advantage in producing the good.

5. In some industries, consumer preferences for differentiated goods may explain international trade flows, including intraindustry trade.

2. INTERNATIONAL TRADE RESTRICTIONS

International trade is rarely determined solely by comparative advantage and the free market forces of supply and demand. Governments often find that

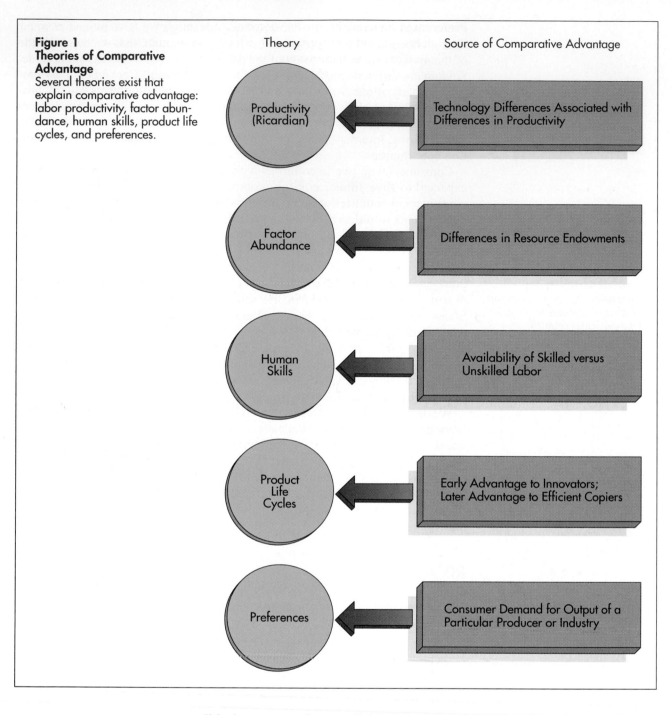

Figure 1
Theories of Comparative Advantage
Several theories exist that explain comparative advantage: labor productivity, factor abundance, human skills, product life cycles, and preferences.

Theory | Source of Comparative Advantage

Productivity (Ricardian) ← Technology Differences Associated with Differences in Productivity

Factor Abundance ← Differences in Resource Endowments

Human Skills ← Availability of Skilled versus Unskilled Labor

Product Life Cycles ← Early Advantage to Innovators; Later Advantage to Efficient Copiers

Preferences ← Consumer Demand for Output of a Particular Producer or Industry

political pressures favor policies that at least partially offset the prevailing comparative advantages. Government policy aimed at influencing international trade flows is called **commercial policy**. This section first examines the arguments in support of commercial policy and then discusses the various tools of commercial policy employed by governments.

■ **commercial policy:**
government policy that influences international trade flows

2.a. Arguments for Protection

Governments restrict foreign trade to protect domestic producers from foreign competition. In some cases the protection may be justified; in most cases it harms consumers. Of the arguments used to promote such protection, only a few are valid. We will look first at arguments widely considered to have little or no merit, and then at those that may sometimes be valid.

International trade on the basis of comparative advantage maximizes world output and allows consumers access to better-quality products at lower prices than would be available in the domestic market alone. If trade is restricted, consumers pay higher prices for lower-quality goods, and world output declines. Protection from foreign competition imposes costs on the domestic economy as well as on foreign producers. When production does not proceed on the basis of comparative advantage, resources are not expended on their most efficient uses. Whenever government restrictions alter the pattern of trade, we should expect someone to benefit and someone else to suffer. Generally speaking, protection from foreign competition benefits domestic producers at the expense of domestic consumers.

2.a.1. Creation of Domestic Jobs

If foreign goods are kept out of the domestic economy, it is often argued, jobs will be created at home. This argument holds that domestic firms will produce the goods that otherwise would have been produced abroad, thus employing domestic workers instead of foreign workers. The weakness of this argument is that only the protected industry would benefit in terms of employment. Since domestic consumers will pay higher prices to buy the output of the protected industry, they will have less to spend on other goods and services, which could cause employment in other industries to drop. If other countries retaliate by restricting entry of U.S. exports, the output of U.S. firms that produce for export will fall as well. Typically, restrictions to "save domestic jobs" simply redistribute jobs by creating employment in the protected industry and reducing employment elsewhere.

2.a.2. Creation of a "Level Playing Field"

Special interest groups sometimes claim that other nations that export successfully to the home market have unfair advantages over domestic producers. Fairness, however, is often in the eye of the beholder. People who call for creating a "level playing field" believe that the domestic government should take steps to offset the perceived advantage of the foreign firm. They often claim that foreign firms have an unfair advantage because foreign workers are willing to work for very low wages. "Fair trade, not free trade" is the cry that this claim generates. But advocates of fair trade are really claiming that production in accordance with comparative advantage is unfair. This is clearly wrong. A country with relatively low wages is typically a country with an abundance of low-skilled labor. Such a country will have a comparative advantage in products that use low-skilled labor most intensively. To create a "level playing field" by imposing restrictions that eliminate the comparative advantage of foreign firms will make domestic consumers worse off and undermine the basis for specialization and economic efficiency.

Some calls for "fair trade" are based on the notion of reciprocity. If a country imposes import restrictions on goods from a country that does not have similar restrictions, reciprocal tariffs and quotas may be called for in the latter country in order to stimulate a reduction of trade restrictions in the former country. For instance, it has been claimed that U.S. construction firms are discriminated against in Japan, because no U.S. firm has had a major construction project in Japan since the 1960s. Yet Japanese construction firms do billions of dollars' worth of business in the United States each year. Advocates of fair trade could argue that U.S. restrictions should be imposed on Japanese construction firms.

One danger of calls for fairness based on reciprocity is that calls for fair trade may be invoked in cases where, in fact, foreign restrictions on U.S. imports do not exist. For instance, suppose the U.S. auto industry wanted to restrict the entry of imported autos to help stimulate sales of domestically produced cars. One strategy might be to point out that U.S. auto sales abroad had fallen and to claim that this was due to unfair treatment of U.S. auto exports in other countries. Of course, there are many other possible reasons why foreign sales of U.S. autos might have fallen. But blaming foreign trade restrictions might win political support for restricting imports of foreign cars into the United States.

2.a.3. Government Revenue Creation Tariffs on trade generate government revenue. Industrial countries, which find income taxes easy to collect, rarely justify tariffs on the basis of the revenue they generate for government spending. But many developing countries find income taxes difficult to levy and collect, while tariffs are easy to collect. Customs agents can be positioned at ports of entry to examine all goods that enter and leave the country. The observability of trade flows makes tariffs a popular tax in developing countries, whose revenue requirements may provide a valid justification for their existence. Table 2 shows that tariffs account for a relatively large fraction of government revenue in many developing countries, and only a small fraction in industrial countries.

2.a.4. National Defense It has long been argued that industries crucial to the national defense, like shipbuilding, should be protected from foreign competition. Even though the United States does not have a comparative advantage in shipbuilding, a domestic shipbuilding industry is necessary since foreign-made ships may not be available during war. This is a valid argument as long as the protected industry is genuinely critical to the national defense. In some industries, like copper or other basic metals, it might make more sense to import the crucial products during peacetime and store them for use in the event of war; these products do not require domestic production to be useful. Care must be taken to ensure that the national-defense argument is not used to protect industries other than those truly crucial to the nation's defense.

2.a.5. Infant Industries Nations are often inclined to protect new industries on the basis that the protection will give those industries adequate time to develop. New industries need time to establish themselves and to become efficient enough that their costs are no higher than those of their foreign rivals. An alternative to protecting young and/or critical domestic industries with tariffs and quotas is to subsidize them. Subsidies allow such firms to charge lower prices and to compete with more efficient foreign producers, while permitting consumers to pay the world price rather than the higher prices associated with tariffs or quotas on foreign goods.

Protecting an infant industry from foreign competition may make sense, but only until the industry matures. Once the industry achieves sufficient size, protection should be withdrawn, and the industry should be made to compete with its foreign counterparts. Unfortunately, such protection is rarely withdrawn, because the larger and more successful the industry becomes, the

TABLE 2
Tariffs as a Percentage of Total Government Revenue

Country	Tariffs as Percentage of Government Revenue
United Kingdom	0.1%
Japan	1.2
United States	1.5
Costa Rica	16.1
Ghana	31.2
Dominican Republic	44.2
Lesotho	55.1

Source: Data are from World Bank, *World Development Report*, 1997.

more political power it wields. In fact, if an infant industry truly has a good chance to become competitive and produce profitably once it is well established, it is not at all clear that government should even offer protection to reduce short-run losses. New firms typically incur losses, but they are only temporary if the firm is successful.

2.a.6. Strategic Trade Policy
There is another view of international trade that regards as misleading the description of comparative advantage presented earlier. According to this outlook, called **strategic trade policy**, international trade largely involves firms that pursue economies of scale—that is, firms that achieve lower costs per unit of production the more they produce. In contrast to the constant opportunity costs illustrated in the example of wheat and cloth, opportunity costs in some industries may fall with the level of output. Such **increasing-returns-to-scale industries** will tend to concentrate production in the hands of a few very large firms, rather than many competitive firms. Proponents of strategic trade policy contend that government can use tariffs or subsidies to allow domestic firms with decreasing costs an advantage over their foreign rivals.

A monopoly exists when there is only one producer in an industry, and no close substitutes for the product exist. If the average costs of production decline with increases in output, then the larger a firm is, the lower its per unit costs will be. One large producer will be more efficient than many small ones. A simple example of a natural-monopoly industry will indicate how strategic trade policy can make a country better off. Suppose that the production of buses is an industry characterized by increasing returns to scale and that there are only two firms capable of producing buses: Mercedes-Benz in Germany and General Motors in the United States. If both firms produce buses, their costs will be so high that both will experience losses. If only one of the two produces buses, however, it will be able to sell buses at home and abroad, creating a level of output that allows the firm to earn a profit.

Assume further that a monopoly producer will earn $100 million and that if both firms produce, they will each lose $5 million. Obviously, a firm that doesn't produce earns nothing. Which firm will produce? Because of the decreasing-cost nature of the industry, the firm that is the first to produce will realize lower costs and be able to preclude the other firm from entering the market. But strategic trade policy can alter the market in favor of the domestic firm.

Suppose Mercedes-Benz is the world's only producer of buses. General Motors does not produce them. The U.S. government could offer General Motors an $8 million subsidy to produce buses. General Motors would then enter the bus market, since the $8 million subsidy would more than offset the $5 million loss it would suffer by entering the market. Mercedes-Benz would sustain losses of $5 million once General Motors entered. Ultimately, Mercedes-Benz would stop producing buses to avoid the loss, and General Motors would have the entire market and earn $100 million plus the subsidy.

Strategic trade policy is aimed at offsetting the increasing-returns-to-scale advantage enjoyed by foreign producers and at stimulating production in domestic industries capable of realizing decreasing costs. One practical problem for government is the need to understand the technology of different industries and to forecast accurately the subsidy needed to induce domestic firms to produce new products. A second problem is the likelihood of retaliation by the foreign government. If the U.S. government subsidizes General Motors in its attack on the bus market, the German government is likely to subsidize Mercedes-Benz rather than lose the entire bus market to a U.S. producer. As a result, taxpayers in both nations will be subsidizing two firms, each producing too few buses to earn a profit.

> ■ **strategic trade policy:**
> the use of trade restrictions or subsidies to allow domestic firms with decreasing costs to gain a greater share of the world market

> ■ **increasing-returns-to-scale industry:**
> an industry in which the costs of producing a unit of output fall as more output is produced

2.b. Tools of Policy

Commercial policy makes use of several tools, including tariffs, quotas, subsidies, and nontariff barriers like health and safety regulations that restrict the entry of foreign products. Since 1945, barriers to trade have been reduced. Much of the progress toward free trade may be linked to the *General Agreement on Tariffs and Trade*, or *GATT*, that began in 1947. In 1995, the World Trade Organization (WTO) was formed to incorporate the agreements under GATT into a formal permanent international organization that oversees world trade. The WTO has three objectives: help global trade flow as freely as possible, achieve reductions in trade restrictions gradually through negotiation, and provide an impartial means of settling disputes. Nevertheless, restrictions on trade still exist and this section will review the most commonly used restrictions.

■ **tariff:**
a tax on imports or exports

2.b.1. Tariffs   A **tariff** is a tax on imports or exports. Every country imposes tariffs on at least some imports. Some countries also impose tariffs on selected exports as a means of raising government revenue. Brazil, for instance, taxes coffee exports. The United States does not employ export tariffs, which are forbidden by the U.S. Constitution.

Tariffs are frequently imposed in order to protect domestic producers from foreign competition. The dangers of imposing tariffs are well illustrated in the Economic Insight "Smoot-Hawley Tariff." The effect of a tariff is illustrated in Figure 2, which shows the domestic market for oranges. Without international trade, the domestic equilibrium price, P_d, and quantity demanded, Q_d, are determined by the intersection of the domestic demand and supply curves. If the world price of oranges, P_w, is lower than the domestic equilibrium price, this country will import oranges. The quantity imported will be the difference between the quantity Q_1 produced domestically at a price of P_w and the quantity Q_2 demanded domestically at the world price of oranges.

When the world price of the traded good is lower than the domestic equilibrium price without international trade, free trade causes domestic production to fall and domestic consumption to rise. The domestic shortage at the world price is met by imports. Domestic consumers are better off, since they can buy more at a lower price. But domestic producers are worse off, since they now sell fewer oranges and receive a lower price.

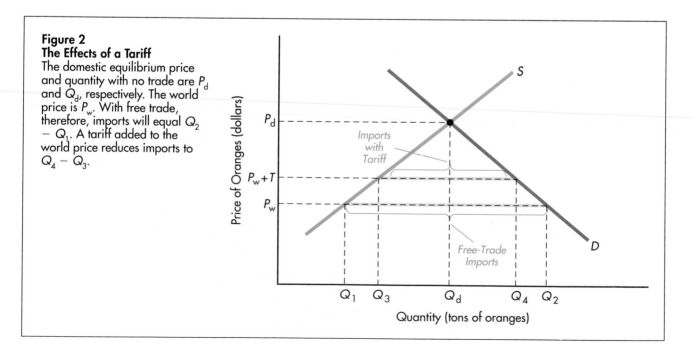

Figure 2
The Effects of a Tariff
The domestic equilibrium price and quantity with no trade are P_d and Q_d, respectively. The world price is P_w. With free trade, therefore, imports will equal $Q_2 - Q_1$. A tariff added to the world price reduces imports to $Q_4 - Q_3$.

Smoot-Hawley Tariff

Many economists believe that the Great Depression of the 1930s was at least partly due to the Smoot-Hawley Tariff Act, signed into law by President Herbert Hoover in 1930. Hoover had promised that, if elected, he would raise tariffs on agricultural products to raise U.S. farm income. Congress began work on the tariff increases in 1928. Congressman Willis Hawley and Senator Reed Smoot conducted the hearings.

In testimony before Congress, manufacturers and other special interest groups also sought protection from foreign competition. The resulting bill increased tariffs on over twelve thousand products. Tariffs reached their highest levels ever, about 60 percent of average import values. Only twice before in

U.S. history had tariffs approached the levels of the Smoot-Hawley era.

Before President Hoover signed the bill, thirty-eight foreign governments made formal protests, warning that they would retaliate with high tariffs on U.S. products. A petition signed by 1,028 economists warned of the harmful effects of the bill. Nevertheless, Hoover signed the bill into law.

World trade collapsed as other countries raised their tariffs in response. Between 1930 and 1931, U.S. imports fell 29 percent, but U.S. exports fell 33 percent. By 1933, world trade was about one-third of the 1929 level. As the level of trade fell, so did income and prices. In 1934, in an effort to correct the mistakes of Smoot-Hawley,

Congress passed the Reciprocal Trade Agreements Act, which allowed the president to lower U.S. tariffs in return for reductions in foreign tariffs on U.S. goods. This act ushered in the modern era of relatively low tariffs. In the United States today, tariffs are about 5 percent of the average value of imports.

Many economists believe the collapse of world trade and the Depression to be linked by a decrease in real income caused by abandoning production based on comparative advantage. Few economists argue that the Great Depression was caused solely by the Smoot-Hawley tariff, but the experience serves as a lesson to those who support higher tariffs to protect domestic producers.

Suppose a tariff of T (the dollar value of the tariff) is imposed on orange imports. The price paid by consumers is now $P_w + T$, rather than P_w. At this higher price, domestic producers will produce Q_3 and domestic consumers will purchase Q_4. The tariff has the effect of increasing domestic production and reducing domestic consumption, relative to the free trade equilibrium. Imports fall accordingly, from $Q_2 - Q_1$ to $Q_4 - Q_3$.

Domestic producers are better off, since the tariff has increased their sales of oranges and raised the price they receive. Domestic consumers pay higher prices for fewer oranges than they would with free trade, but they are still better off than they would be without trade. If the tariff had raised the price paid by consumers to P_d, there would be no trade, and the domestic equilibrium quantity, Q_d, would prevail.

The government earns revenue from imports of oranges. If each ton of oranges generates tariff revenue of T, the total tariff revenue to the government is found by multiplying the tariff by the quantity of oranges imported. In Figure 2, this amount is $T \times (Q_4 - Q_3)$. As the tariff changes, so does the quantity of imports and the government revenue.

2.b.2. Quotas Quotas are limits on the quantity or value of goods imported and exported. A **quantity quota** restricts the physical amount of a good. For instance, through 1994 the United States allowed only 2.5 million tons of sugar to be imported. Even though the United States is not a competitive sugar producer compared to other nations like the Dominican Republic or Cuba, the quota allowed U.S. firms to produce about 6 percent of the world's sugar output. A **value quota** restricts the monetary value of a good that may be traded. Instead of a physical quota on sugar, the United States could have limited the dollar value of sugar imports.

■ **quantity quota:**
a limit on the amount of a good that may be imported

■ **value quota:**
a limit on the monetary value of a good that may be imported

Figure 3
The Effects of a Quota
The domestic equilibrium price with no international trade is P_d. At this price, 250 tons of oranges would be produced and consumed at home. With free trade, the price is P_w and 300 tons will be imported. An import quota of 100 tons will cause the price to be P_q, where the domestic shortage equals the 100 tons allowed by the quota.

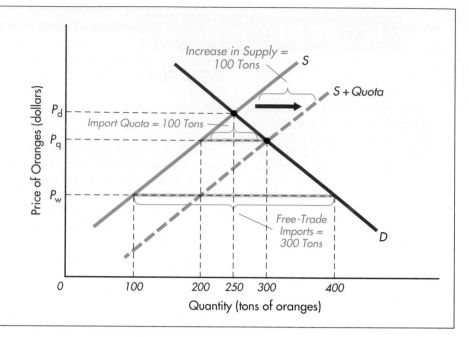

Quotas are used to protect domestic producers from foreign competition. By restricting the amount of a good that may be imported, they increase its price and allow domestic producers to sell more at a higher price than they would with free trade. Figure 3 illustrates the effect of a quota on the domestic orange market. The domestic equilibrium supply and demand curves determine the equilibrium price and quantity without trade to be P_d and 250 tons, respectively. The world price of oranges is P_w. Since P_w lies below P_d, this country will import oranges. The quantity of imports is equal to the amount of the domestic shortage at P_w. The quantity demanded at P_w is 400 tons, and the quantity supplied domestically is 100 tons, so imports will equal 300 tons of oranges. With free trade, domestic producers sell 100 tons at a price of P_w.

But suppose domestic orange growers convince the government to restrict orange imports. The government then imposes a quota of 100 tons on imported oranges. The effect of the quota on consumers is to shift the supply curve to the right by the amount of the quota, 100 tons. Since the quota is less than the quantity of imports with free trade, the quantity of imports will equal the quota. The domestic equilibrium price with the quota occurs at the point where the domestic shortage equals the quota. At price P_q, the domestic quantity demanded (300 tons) is 100 tons more than the domestic quantity supplied (200 tons).

Quotas benefit domestic producers in the same way that tariffs do. Domestic producers receive a higher price (P_q instead of P_w) for a greater quantity (200 instead of 100) than they do under free trade. The effect on domestic consumers is also similar to that of a tariff: they pay a higher price for a smaller quantity than they would with free trade. A tariff generates government tax revenue; quotas do not (unless the government auctioned off the right to import under the quota). Furthermore, a tariff only raises the price of the product in the domestic market. Foreign producers receive the world price, P_w. With a quota, both domestic and foreign producers receive the higher price, P_q, for the goods sold in the domestic market. So foreign producers are hurt by the reduction in the quantity of imports permitted, but they do receive a higher price for the amount they sell.

In some cases, countries negotiate *voluntary export restraints* rather than imposing quotas. A voluntary export restraint limits the quantity of goods

Part III / The National and Global Economies

shipped from the exporting country to an importing country, so such restraints have the same practical effect as a quota. For instance, since 1981 the United States has negotiated voluntary export restraints on Japanese auto exports to the United States. In 1992, the agreement allowed 1.65 million autos ranging from 480,000 Toyotas to 30,000 Suzukis. The Japanese Automobile Manufacturers Association monitors the exports for the Japanese government.

2.b.3. Other Barriers to Trade   Tariffs and quotas are not the only barriers to the free flow of goods across international borders. There are three additional sources of restrictions on free trade: subsidies, government procurement, and health and safety standards. Though often enacted for reasons other than protection from foreign competition, a careful analysis reveals their import-reducing effect.

Before discussing these three types of barriers, let us note the cultural or institutional barriers to trade that also exist in many countries. Such barriers may exist independently of any conscious government policy. For instance, Japan has frequently been criticized by U.S. officials for informal business practices that discriminate against foreigners. Under the Japanese distribution system, goods typically pass through several layers of middlemen before appearing in a retail store. A foreign firm faces the difficult task of gaining entry to this system to supply goods to the retailer. Furthermore, a foreigner cannot easily open a retail store. Japanese law requires a new retail firm to receive permission from other retailers in the area in order to open a business. A firm that lacks contacts and knowledge of the system cannot penetrate the Japanese market.

In the fall of 1989, the U.S. toy firm Toys "R" Us announced its intent to open several large discount toy stores in Japan. However, local toy stores in each area objected to having a Toys "R" Us store nearby. The U.S. government has argued that the laws favoring existing firms are an important factor in keeping Japan closed to foreign firms that would like to enter the Japanese market. Eventually, Toys "R" Us opened stores in Japan.

■ **subsidies:**
payments made by government to domestic firms to encourage exports

Subsidies   Subsidies are payments by a government to an exporter. Subsidies are paid to stimulate exports by allowing the exporter to charge a lower price. The amount of a subsidy is determined by the international price of a product relative to the domestic price in the absence of trade. Domestic consumers are harmed by subsidies in that their taxes finance the subsidies. Also, since the subsidy diverts resources from the domestic market toward export production, the increase in the supply of export goods could be associated with a decrease in the supply of domestic goods, causing domestic prices to rise.

Subsidies may take forms other than direct cash payments. These include tax reductions, low-interest loans, low-cost insurance, government-sponsored research funding, and other devices. The U.S. government subsidizes export activity through the U.S. Export-Import Bank, which provides loans and insurance to help U.S. exporters sell their goods to foreign buyers. Subsidies are more commonplace in Europe than in Japan or the United States.

Government Procurement   Governments are often required by law to buy only from local producers. In the United States, a "buy American" act passed in 1933 required U.S. government agencies to buy U.S. goods and services unless the domestic price was more than 12 percent above the foreign price. This kind of policy allows domestic firms to charge the government a higher price for their products than they charge consumers; the taxpayers bear the burden. The United States is by no means alone in the use of such policies. Many other nations also use such policies to create larger markets for domestic goods.

Health and Safety Standards   Government serves as a guardian of the public health and welfare by requiring that products offered to the public be safe and fulfill the use for which they are intended. Government standards for products sold in the domestic marketplace can have the effect (intentional or not) of protecting domestic producers from foreign competition. These effects should be considered in evaluating the full impact of such standards.

The government of Japan once threatened to prohibit foreign-made snow skis from entering the country for reasons of safety. Only Japanese-made skis were determined to be suitable for Japanese snow. Several western European nations announced that U.S. beef would not be allowed into Europe because hormones approved by the U.S. government are fed to U.S. beef cattle. In the late 1960s, France required tractors sold there to have a maximum speed of 17 miles per hour; in Germany, the permissible speed was 13 mph, and in the Netherlands it was 10 mph. Tractors produced in one country had to be modified to meet the requirements of the other countries. Such modifications raise the price of goods and discourage international trade.

Product standards may not eliminate foreign competition, but standards different from those of the rest of the world do provide an element of protection to domestic firms.

RECAP

1. Government restrictions on foreign trade are usually aimed at protecting domestic producers from foreign competition.

2. Import restrictions may save domestic jobs, but the costs to consumers may be greater than the benefits to those who retain their jobs.

3. Advocates of "fair trade," or the creation of a "level playing field," call for import restrictions as a means of lowering foreign restrictions on markets for domestic exports.

4. The national-defense argument in favor of trade restrictions is that protection from foreign competition is necessary to ensure that certain key defense-related industries continue to produce.

5. The infant-industries argument in favor of trade restriction is to allow a new industry a period of time in which to become competitive with its foreign counterparts.

6. Strategic trade policy is intended to provide domestic increasing-returns-to-scale industries an advantage over their foreign competitors.

7. A tariff is a tax on imports or exports. Tariffs protect domestic firms by raising the prices of foreign goods.

8. Tariffs are an important source of revenue in many developing countries.

9. Quotas are government-imposed limits on the quantity or value of an imported good. Quotas protect domestic firms by restricting the entry of foreign products to a level less than the quantity demanded.

10. Subsidies are payments by the government to domestic producers. Subsidies lower the price of domestic goods.

11. Governments are often required by law to buy only domestic products.

12. Health and safety standards can also be used to protect domestic firms.

3. EXCHANGE RATE SYSTEMS AND PRACTICES

The world today consists of some countries with fixed exchange rates, whose governments keep the exchange rates between two or more currencies constant over time; other countries with floating exchange rates, which shift on a

The IMF and the World Bank

The International Monetary Fund (IMF) and the World Bank were both created at the Bretton Woods conference in 1944. The IMF oversees the international monetary system, promoting stable exchange rates and macroeconomic policies. The World Bank promotes the economic development of the poor nations. Both organizations are owned and directed by their 181 member countries.

The IMF provides loans to nations having trouble repaying their foreign debts. Before the IMF lends any money, however, the borrower must agree to certain conditions. IMF *conditionality* usually requires that the country meet targets for key macroeconomic variables like money-supply growth, inflation, tax collections, and subsidies. The conditions attached to IMF loans are aimed at promoting stable economic growth.

The World Bank assists developing countries by providing long-term financing for development projects and programs. The Bank also provides expertise in many areas in which poor nations lack expert knowledge: agriculture, medicine, construction, and education, as well as economics. The IMF primarily employs economists to carry out its mission.

The diversity of World Bank activities results in the employment of about 6,500 people. The IMF has a staff of approximately 1,700. Both organizations post employees around the world, but most work at the headquarters in Washington, D.C.

World Bank funds are largely acquired by borrowing on the international bond market. The IMF receives its funding from member-country subscription fees, called *quotas*. A member's quota determines its voting power in setting IMF policies. The United States, whose quota accounts for the largest fraction of the total, has the most votes.

---

daily basis according to the forces of supply and demand; and still others whose exchange-rate systems lie somewhere in between. Table 3, which lists the exchange rate arrangements of over 180 countries, illustrates the diversity of exchange-rate arrangements currently in effect. We will focus here on the differences between fixed and floating exchange rates. All of the other exchange-rate arrangements listed in Table 3 are special versions of these two general exchange-rate systems.

■ managed floating exchange rates:
the system whereby central banks intervene in the floating foreign exchange market to influence exchange rates

As Table 3 shows, some countries maintain **managed floating exchange rates**. Although Table 3 lists countries like Japan and the United States as "independently floating," in fact their central banks, such as the Federal Reserve in the United States and the Bank of Japan in Japan, intervene from time to time in the foreign exchange market. Since exchange-rate variations can alter the prices of goods traded internationally, governments often attempt to push exchange rates to values consistent with some target value of international trade or investment. For example, on April 5, 1995, the U.S. Treasury and the Federal Reserve were concerned that the dollar had fallen in value too much, and investors were becoming concerned about the future stability of the currency. As a result, the Fed bought over $1 billion in exchange for German marks and Japanese yen. This intervention in the foreign exchange market caused the dollar to rise temporarily in value more than private-market pressures would have done.

Some countries, like Antigua, Barbuda, and Benin, maintain a fixed value (or peg) relative to a single currency, such as the dollar or French franc. Fixed exchange rates are often called *pegged* exchange rates. Other countries, like Bangladesh, peg to a composite of currencies by setting the value of their currency at the average value of several foreign currencies.

Some currencies are pegged to the *SDR*, as you learned in Chapter 14. The SDR, which stands for special drawing right, is an artificial unit of account. Its value is determined by combining the values of the U.S. dollar, German mark, Japanese yen, French franc, and British pound. A country that pegs to

TABLE 3
Exchange-Rate Arrangements[1]

		Currency Pegged to		
U.S. Dollar	**French Franc**	**Other Currency**	**SDR**	**Other Composite[2]**
Angola	Benin	Bhutan (Indian	Libya	Bangladesh
Antigua and	Burkina Faso	rupee)	Myanmar	Botswana
Barbuda	Cameroon	Bosnia and Herzegovina		Burundi
Argentina	C. African Rep.	(deutsche mark)		Cape Verde
Bahamas, The	Chad	Brunei Darussalam		Cyprus
Barbados	Comoros	(Singapore dollar)		Fiji
Belize	Congo, Rep. of	Bulgaria		Iceland
Djibouti	Côte d'Ivoire	(deutsche mark)		Jordan
Dominica	Equatorial	Estonia		Kuwait
Grenada	Guinea	(deutsche		Malta
Iraq	Gabon	mark)		Morocco
Liberia	Guinea-Bissau	Kiribati		Samoa
Lithuania	Mali	(Australian		Seychelles
Marshall Islands	Niger	dollar)		Slovak
Micronesia, Fed.	Senegal	Lesotho (South		Republic
States of	Togo	African rand)		Solomon
Nigeria		Namibia (South		Islands
Oman		African rand)		Tonga
Panama		Nepal (Indian rupee)		Vanuatu
St. Kitts and Nevis		San Marino		
St. Lucia		(Italian lira)		
St. Vincent and		Swaziland (South		
the Grenadines		African rand)		
Syrian Arab Rep.				

[1]For members with dual or multiple exchange markets, the arrangement shown is that in the major market.

[2]Comprises currencies which are pegged to various "baskets" of currencies of the members' own choice, as distinct from the SDR basket.

the SDR determines its currency's value in terms of an average of the five currencies that make up the SDR.

The column entitled "Cooperative Arrangements" in Table 3 lists the countries that belong to the **European Monetary System**, or **EMS**. These countries maintain fixed exchange rates against each other but allow their currencies to float jointly against the rest of the world. In other words, the values of currencies in the EMS all shift together relative to currencies outside the EMS.

At the time this text was written, most of the EMS countries were planning to introduce a common money, the *euro,* on January 1, 1999. The individual national monies will circulate jointly with the euro for a few years, after which the national monies will disappear and the euro will become the common money used for each of the countries.

Table 4 lists the end-of-year exchange rates for several currencies versus the U.S. dollar from the 1950s to the 1990s. For most of the currencies, there was little movement in the 1950s and 1960s, the era of the Bretton Woods agreement. In the early 1970s, exchange rates began to fluctuate. More recently, there has been considerable change in the foreign exchange value of a dollar, as Table 4 illustrates.

■ **European Monetary System (EMS):**
an organization composed of western European nations that maintain fixed exchange rates among themselves and floating exchange rates with the rest of the world

TABLE 3
Exchange-Rate Arrangements (cont.)

Flexibility Limited
in Terms of a Single Currency
or Group of Currencies

Single Currency[3]	Cooperative Arrangements[4]
Bahrain	Austria
Qatar	Belgium
Saudi	Denmark
Arabia	Finland
United	France
Arab	Germany
Emirates	Ireland
	Italy
	Luxembourg
	Netherlands
	Portugal
	Spain

More Flexible

Other Managed Floating		Independently Floating			
Algeria	Latvia	Afghanistan,	Guinea	Moldova	South Africa
Belarus	Macedonia	Islamic	Guyana	Mongolia	Sweden
Brazil	Malaysia	State of	Haiti	Mozambique	Switzerland
Cambodia	Maldives	Albania	India	New Zealand	Tajikistan
Chile	Mauritius	Armenia	Indonesia	Papua New	Tanzania
China, P.R.	Nicaragua	Australia	Jamaica	Guinea	Trinidad and
Colombia	Norway	Azerbaijan	Japan	Paraguay	Tobago
Costa Rica	Pakistan	Bolivia	Kazakhstan	Peru	Uganda
Croatia	Poland	Canada	Kenya	Philippines	United
Czech Republic	Russia	Congo, Dem. Rep.	Lebanon	Romania	Kingdom
Dominican	Singapore	Ethiopia	Madagascar	Rwanda	United States
Republic	Slovenia	Gambia, The	Malawi	Sao Tome and	Yemen
Ecuador	Sri Lanka	Ghana	Mauritania	Principe	Zaire
Egypt	Sudan	Guatemala	Mexico	Sierra Leone	Zambia
El Salvador	Suriname			Somalia	Zimbabwe
Eritrea	Thailand				
Georgia	Tunisia				
Greece	Turkmenistan				
Honduras	Turkey				
Hungary	Ukraine				
Iran	Uruguay				
Israel	Uzbekistan				
Korea	Venezuela				
Kyrgyz Rep.	Vietnam				
Lao, P.D.					
Rep. of					

[3]Exchange rates of all currencies have shown limited flexibility in terms of the U.S. dollar.

[4]Refers to the cooperative arrangement maintained under the European Monetary System.

Source: International Monetary Fund, *International Financial Statistics,* Washington, D.C., January 1998.

TABLE 4
Exchange Rates of Selected Countries (currency units per U.S. dollar)

Year	Canadian Dollar	Japanese Yen	French Franc	German Mark	Italian Lira	British Pound
1950	1.06	361	3.50	4.20	625	.36
1955	1.00	361	3.50	4.22	625	.36
1960	1.00	358	4.90	4.17	621	.36
1965	1.08	361	4.90	4.01	625	.36
1970	1.01	358	5.52	3.65	623	.42
1975	1.02	305	4.49	2.62	684	.50
1980	1.19	203	4.52	1.96	931	.42
1985	1.40	201	7.56	2.46	1,679	.69
1990	1.16	134	5.13	1.49	1,130	.52
1995	1.36	103	4.90	1.43	1,584	.65
1997	1.43	130	5.95	1.78	1,744	.60

Source: End-of-year exchange rates from International Monetary Fund, *International Financial Statistics,* Washington, D.C. Reprinted by permission.

RECAP

1. Fixed exchange rates are maintained by government intervention in the foreign exchange market; governments or central banks buy and sell currencies to keep the equilibrium exchange rate steady.

2. Some countries choose floating exchange rates; others peg their currencies to a single currency or a composite.

3. The European Monetary System maintains fixed exchange rates among several western European currencies, which then float jointly against the rest of the world. A new common money, the euro, will circulate in many of these countries and ultimately will displace the existing national monies.

SUMMARY

▰ What determines the goods a nation will export?

1. Comparative advantage is based on the opportunity costs of production.

▰ What are the sources of comparative advantage?

2. The productivity-differences and factor-abundance theories of comparative advantage are general theories that seek to explain patterns of international trade.

3. Other theories of comparative advantage aimed at explaining trade in particular kinds of goods focus on human skills, product life cycles, and consumer preferences.

▰ Why do countries restrict international trade?

4. Commercial policy is government policy that influences the direction and volume of international trade.

5. Protecting domestic producers from foreign competition usually imposes costs on domestic consumers.

6. Rationales for commercial policy include saving domestic jobs, creating a fair-trade relationship with other countries, raising tariff revenue, ensuring a domestic supply of key defense goods, allowing new industries a chance to become internationally competitive, and giving domestic industries with increasing returns to scale an advantage over foreign competitors.

How do countries restrict the entry of foreign goods and promote the export of domestic goods?

7. Tariffs protect domestic industry by increasing the price of foreign goods.

8. Quotas protect domestic industry by limiting the quantity of foreign goods allowed into the country.

9. Subsidies allow relatively inefficient domestic producers to compete with foreign firms.

10. Government procurement practices and health and safety regulations can protect domestic industry from foreign competition.

What kinds of exchange-rate arrangements exist today?

11. Today some countries have fixed exchange rates, others have floating exchange rates, and still others have managed floats or other types of systems.

KEY TERMS

absolute advantage

intraindustry trade

commercial policy

strategic trade policy

increasing-returns-to-scale industry

tariff

quantity quota

value quota

subsidies

managed floating exchange rates

European Monetary System (EMS)

EXERCISES

1. Why must voluntary trade between two countries be mutually beneficial?

Use the following table to answer questions 2–5.

Labor Hours Required to Produce One Unit of Each Good

	Canada	Japan
Beef	2	4
Computers	6	5

2. Which country has the absolute advantage in beef production?

3. Which country has the absolute advantage in computer production?

4. Which country has the comparative advantage in beef production?

5. Which country has the comparative advantage in computer production?

6. How would each of the following theories of comparative advantage explain the fact that the United States exports computers?

   a. Productivity differences

   b. Factor abundance

   c. Human skills

   d. Product life cycle

   e. Preferences

7. Which of the theories of comparative advantage could explain why the United States exports computers to Japan at the same time that it imports computers from Japan? Explain.

8. What are the potential benefits and costs of a commercial policy designed to pursue each of the following goals?

   a. Save domestic jobs

   b. Create a level playing field

   c. Increase government revenue

   d. Provide a strong national defense

   e. Protect an infant industry

   f. Stimulate exports of an industry with increasing returns to scale

9. For each of the goals listed in question 8, discuss what the appropriate commercial policy is likely to be (in terms of tariffs, quotas, subsidies, etc.).

10. Tariffs and quotas both raise the price of foreign goods to domestic consumers. What is

the difference between the effects of a tariff and the effects of a quota on the following?

a. The domestic government

b. Foreign producers

c. Domestic producers

11. Draw a graph of the U.S. automobile market in which the domestic equilibrium price without trade is P_d and the equilibrium quantity is Q_d. Use this graph to illustrate and explain the effects of a tariff if the United States were an auto importer with free trade. Then use the graph to illustrate and explain the effects of a quota.

12. How would the effects of international trade on the domestic orange market change if the world price of oranges were above the domestic equilibrium price? Draw a graph to help explain your answer.

13. Suppose the world price of kiwi fruit is $20 per case and the U.S. equilibrium price with no international trade is $35 per case. If the U.S. government had previously banned the import of kiwi fruit but then imposed a tariff of $5 per case and allowed kiwi imports, what would happen to the equilibrium price and quantity of kiwi fruit consumed in the United States?

14. What kinds of exchange rate arrangements do the countries of the world use? What is the most popular exchange rate arrangement for the major industrial countries?

🖳 INTERNET EXERCISE

In this chapter, we introduced the World Trade Organization (WTO) as an organization overseeing the global trading system with a goal of promoting free trade. To learn more about the WTO, go to the Boyes/Melvin *Fundamentals of Economics* Web site at **http://www.hmco.com/college/** and click on the Internet Exercise link for Chapter 17. Now answer the questions that appear on the Boyes/Melvin Web site.

Photo Credits

Page xiv: Jeff Greenberg/The Image Works; page 7: Robert Freck/Odyssey/Chicago; page 9: Cameramann/The Image Works; page 24: Enrique Marti/Impact Visuals; page 49: © Andy Freeberg; page 53: Jim Harrison/Stock Boston; page 57: Ferdinando Scianna/Magnum Photos; page 60: Scott J. Witte/The Picture Cube; page 66: David R. Frazier/Photo Library; page 78: James Schnepf/Gamma Liaison; page 83: Bob Crandall/Stock Boston; page 97: P. Werner/The Image Works; page 112: Lisa Quinones/Black Star; page 121: Jonathan Nourok/Tony Stone Images; page 137: Jerry Howard/ Positive Images; page 142: J. Nordell/The Image Works; page 188: Margaret Bourke White/Life Magazine © Time Warner; page 191: Giles Mingasson/Gamma Liaison; page 221: David R. Frazier/Photo Library; page 233: © Suzanne and Nick Geary/Tony Stone Images; page 267: © Patrick Aventurier/Gamma Liaison; page 269: Bettmann Newsphoto; page 308: Jean-Leo Dugast/Sygma.

Index

Output, measures of, 163–170

Partnership, defined, 103
Payments, transfer, 156
Peak load pricing, 104–105
Perfectly elastic, defined, 67
Perfectly inelastic, defined, 68
Personal income, 169
    disposable, 169
Peseta, as currency, 12
Peso, as currency, 12
Phillips curve, 287–291
PI. *See* Personal income
Policy
    fiscal, 154
    monetary, 154
Political business cycle, 296, 297
Positive economic profit, 81
Positive externality, 124
Positive quadrant, graphs, 16 (fig.)
Potential real gross domestic product, 192
Pound, as currency, 12
Poverty, 135
    discrimination and, 135–138, 136 (table)
PPI. *See* Producer price index
Precautionary demand for money, 281
Price ceiling, 55–56
Price changes, relative, *versus* absolute, 196
Price discrimination, 69–70, 103–104
Price elasticity
    of demand, 67–68
    demand curve, 67–68
    determinants of, 70–71
    revenue, 68–70
Price floor, 56–58, 57 (fig.)
Price index, 171–174
    gross domestic product, 173 (fig.)
    types of, 173–174
Price leadership, 108–109
Price-level effects
    aggregate demand, 214–215
    aggregate quantity supplied, 218, 219
Price strategies, 103–106
    bundling, 105
    discount coupons, 105
    peak load pricing, 104–105
    price discrimination, 103–104
    rebates, 105–106
Private property rights, 124–125
Private sector, 150, 157–159
Producer price index, 173
Producer surplus, 93–94
Product differentiation reputation, 95–96
Production possibilities, 8 (table)
    graph curve, 17, 18 (fig.)

Productivity, 302–303
    economic growth and, 302–303
Profit
    economic, 80–82
    maximizing, 74–89
    social responsibility and, 82
Progressive tax, 240
Public sector, 157–159

Quadrant, positive, of graph, 16 (fig.)
Quantity quota, 317
Quota, 317–319
    effects of, 318 (fig.)

Rand, as currency, 12
Rational expectations, 294–295
Reading graphs, 16–20
Real gross domestic product, 171
Real interest rate, 198
Rebates, 105–106
Recession, 185
Record of unemployment, 193–196, 194–195 (table)
Regulation, 114. *See also* Government
    of firms, 113–115
    social, 114
Relative price changes, *versus* absolute, 196
Renewable natural resources, 121
Rent controls, 56 (fig.)
    market intervention, 51–58
Required reserves, 258
Responsibility, social, profits and, 82
Restrictions, on international trade, 311–320
Revenue, 63–65
    total, 63
Rial, as currency, 12
Riyal, as currency, 12
Ruble, as currency, 12
Rupee, as currency, 12
Russia, currency, 12

Safety standards, 319–320
Saudi Arabia, currency, 12
Scale
    diseconomies of, 98
    economies of, 97–98
Scarcity, 4, 5, 24 (fig.)
Schilling, as currency, 12
Schooling, opportunity cost, 6–7
SDR. *See* Special drawing right
Sectors
    linking, 157–159
    private, 150, 157–159
    public, 157–159

Unskilled labor, 51 (fig.)

Value added, defined, 165
Value-added tax, 243
Value quota, 317
Variable costs, 85
VAT. *See* Value-added tax
Venezuela, currency, 12

Wage, minimum, 132–133
    unemployment among teens, 134
Wage differential, compensating, 50, 50 (fig.)
War on drugs, 128–129
Wealth effect, 212
    aggregate demand curve and, 212
World Bank, 321
World trade, overview of, 307–311

Yen, as currency, 12
Yuan, as currency, 12

Zero economic profit, 81